God the Spirit

God the Spirit

Michael Welker

Translated by
John F. Hoffmeyer

Fortress Press   Minneapolis

For Jürgen Moltmann

GOD THE SPIRIT

First English-language edition published 1994. Translated from the German, *Gottes Geist: Theologie des Heiligen Geistes,* © 1992 Neukirchener Verlag, Neukirchen-Vluyn. English translation by John F. Hoffmeyer copyright © 1994 Augsburg Fortress. All rights reserved. Except for brief quotations in critical articles or reviews, no part of this book may be reproduced in any manner without prior written permission from the publisher. Write to: Permissions, Augsburg Fortress, 426 S. Fifth St., Box 1209, Minneapolis, MN 55440.

Scripture quotations, unless translated by the author, are adapted from the New Revised Standard Version of the Bible, copyright © 1989 by the Division of Christian Education of the National Council of the Churches of Christ in the United States of America. Used by permission.

Cover design: Carol Evans-Smith

Library of Congress Cataloging-in-Publication Data

Welker, Michael.
   [Gottes Geist. English]
   God the spirit / by Michael Welker; translated by John F. Hoffmeyer. — 1st English-language ed.
     p.   cm.
   Translation of: Gottes Geist.
   Includes bibliographical references and indexes.
   ISBN 0-8006-2766-0 (alk. paper)
   1. Holy Spirit. I. Title.
BT121.2.W4413   1994
231'.3—dc20   94-10029

Manufactured in the U.S.A.   AF 1-2766
98   97   96   95   94   1   2   3   4   5   6   7   8   9   10

Contents

Preface

In my view, the most important contribution of the present book on "God the Spirit" is that it provides help in coming to a new perception of God and of God's power. By stimulating readers to experience and to understand God and God's power in new ways, the book serves as a guide past the mistaken paths of totalistic metaphysics, merely speculative trinitarianism, abstract mysticism, and irrationalism undertaken by conventional understandings of the Holy Spirit. It likewise serves as a guide past empty formulas and mere silence—be it meaningful or meaningless. The Holy Spirit is neither an intellectual construct nor a numinous entity.

My original intention was to begin my lengthier publications on the most important themes of Christian theology with a volume on "God's Law and God's Gospel." Yet the contents and problems, the actual substance that was to be treated in working on that topic directed my attention, questions, and research over and over again to "God the Spirit." Finally, what was theologically correct also came to make sense on a practical level: to give the Holy Spirit precedence over law and gospel.

In positive terms, the book seeks first to articulate the broad spectrum of experiences of God's Spirit, searches and quests for the Spirit, and skepticism toward the Spirit that define the contemporary world. From this vantage point the book will introduce its readers into the contexts of the diverse testimonies to God's Spirit that we find in the various biblical traditions. An interwoven fabric of testimonies and accounts of God and of God's powerful action among human beings is made clear in a new way. The condition in which these testimonies in general find themselves in academic and popular theologies can be compared to a mosaic that is partly covered with rubble and partly broken in pieces. If the mosaic is to present pictures again, it must first be laid bare and pieced together again. Or the condition of the biblical testimonies can be compared to a network of paths that must be redis-covered and resurveyed if it is again to afford access to desired destina-tions and views of the countryside.

We encounter the attested experiences of God's Spirit firmly em-bedded in various life experiences, particularly in experiences of life that is threatened and endangered, but also of life that has been deliv-ered and liberated. A people is threatened with annihilation. A politi-cal system collapses or is abruptly reshaped. The moral network of a community is rent asunder. The sun sets on a historical world. People receive a new identity. A dispersed people is led together again. People who are strange or even hostile to each other open God's reality for each other. A disintegrated world grows together. Inasmuch as we in-vestigate more closely the testimonies of such varied experiences and seek to grasp their complex interconnections, we are referred from a number of different perspectives to the rich *reality and vitality of the Holy Spirit*. We have to reckon with a complex pattern of intercon-nected testimonies that at first glance seem impossible to bring into agreement, let alone to harmonize and to systematize. A type of thought that is not sensitive to differences, that would like to jump immediately to "the whole" and to the way in which the Spirit presents a whole, will continue as in the past: stuck in the realm of the numi-nous, in the conjuration of merely mystical experience, and in global moral appeals. Only by drawing on their differences do the biblical tes-timonies mutually illuminate, strengthen, and clarify each other. It is precisely in this way that they can teach us to discover and to experi-ence God's Spirit in our times and our cultures as well.

The procedure chosen here is, to be sure, not yet common in sys-tematic theology. If one is seeking an academic label for this procedure, one could call it a "realistic theology."

A realistic theology is a theology that is related to various struc-tural patterns of experience and that cultivates a sensitivity to the dif-ferences of those various patterns. It is precisely in this diverse and complex relation to God's reality and to creaturely reality as intended by God that realistic theology seeks to performs its task. We try to squeeze God's reality into simple systematizations and forms of experi-ence. As finite and limited human beings, we necessarily make this re-ductionist attempt. A realistic theology makes clear that God's reality is much richer than the forms into which we attempt to make it fit. A realistic theology makes clear that our experiences, our worldviews, our moral systems, and our value structures must be enlightened and changed in order to correspond to creaturely reality. A realistic theology also makes clear the way in which this must transpire.

Many theologies grounded in human experiences and forms of experience need to take as their points of departure both actual demonstrations of God's power within creation and people's search for God in the realm of that which is creaturely. This is true whether the orientation of such theologies be empirical, pietistic, moral, epistemological-philosophical, or otherwise. A realistic theology mediates this need of theologies grounded in human experience with the concern of classical, Reformation, and dialectical theologies "from above" to take God's divinity seriously and not to obstruct enjoyment of the fullness and glory of God.

Authoritarian theologies of one-upmanship have sought to grasp and expound God and God's revelation in numerous abstract formulas: God always comes "from above," God always "precedes," God is the "all-determining" reality. The theology of the Holy Spirit will challenge us to replace these formulas or to render them superfluous. It will teach us to concentrate in a new way on seeing God's reality make its appearance in tension-filled interconnections of different realms of experience that are not necessarily compatible with each other.

We live in many such interconnections of different realms of experience. Preeminent examples of such realms of experience are the moral market, the mass media market, the political market, and the public opinions market. Both in themselves and in their interconnections with each other, these realms of experience are charged with tension, confusing, and impossible to survey from any one vantage point. This book is an attempt to avoid succumbing to the pressure of these markets and being sucked in by them in the effort to know God's reality. On the basis of those testimonies to God's Spirit that have been and will continue to be the primary determinants of the life and thought of Israel and of Christian churches, this book has the goal of acquiring clarity concerning those traits that are characteristic and unavoidable for the appearance of God's reality and God's power in the midst of the structural patterns of human life.

In principle it would also be possible to characterize this theology
of the Holy Spirit not as "realistic theology," but as "biblical theology"
or as "postmodern theology." Unless I am mistaken, this book could
even be regarded as the first comprehensive "biblical theology of the
Holy Spirit." But the designation "biblical theology" does not at
present make sufficiently clear the systematic and constructive concern that is directed not only to past experiences and expectations
of God, but to present and future ones as well. Why not "postmodern
theology"? As a matter of fact, this book does gain new insight into
primarily "premodern" experiences by cautiously employing "postmodern," relativistic forms of thought that have been developing for
over fifty years, particularly in North America. But the expression
"postmodern" is currently too faddish, too bandied about in the mass
commercial press, and above all too formal to be able adequately to
summarize essential concerns of this book. "Realistic theology" is thus
the preferable label, remembering that the "realism" shows itself and
verifies itself precisely by simultaneously doing two things. On the one
hand, it links a number of domains and forms of experience that are in
part mutually compatible, and in part can be directly reconciled only
with great difficulty, if at all. On the other hand, it remains sensitive
to the differences of these realms and forms of experience.

Many readers may be sighing, "Those were the days, when every
theology afoot had only 'two sides' (above and below, God and 'the'
human person, the ego and the whole, experience or transcendence)
or even just one system of reference (reality in the singular, 'the' modern subject, religious experience in the singular)." To that nostalgia
one should calmly respond, "Those were also the days in which evidently no forms of thought and experience could be found that enabled
clear insight into the testimonies to the Spirit of God. Those were the
days in which demonstrations of God's power and reality that happened by the Spirit of God received only distorted and misleading theological exposition and recognition, if they received any at all."

Parts and early versions of chapters of this book were presented for
discussion in lectures in Tübingen, Princeton, Münster, and Heidelberg. I am grateful to my students for their questions and their constructive critique, as well as for their enthusiasm, which stimulated the
search for theological understanding. I especially thank my wife, Ul-
rike Welker, who critically read the first draft and the final versions of

the chapters of this book, and who proposed countless improvements. I should also acknowledge at this point my debt to Patrick D. Miller, Old Testament scholar at Princeton Theological Seminary, for one of the key insights of this theology of the Holy Spirit. Finally, I owe great thanks to my co-workers in Münster and Heidelberg, especially Sigrid Brandt, Michael Abstiens, Evamaria Bohle, Petra Jurick, Ellen Kiener, Rahel Maria Liu, and Markus Michel. They have helped me in diverse ways with the acquisition of literature, the technical preparation of the manuscript, and setting up the index. In addition they provided many suggestions about points of detail.

Heidelberg   —*Michael Welker*

Abbreviations

ATD	Das Alte Testament Deutsch
BEvT	Beiträge zur evangelischen Theologie
BKAT	Biblischer Kommentar: Altes Testament
BWANT	Beiträge zur Wissenschaft vom Alten und Neuen Testament
CD	K. Barth, *Church Dogmatics*, ed. G. W. Bromiley and T. F. Torrance (Edinburgh: T. and T. Clark, 1936–1962).
ChrTo	*Christianity Today*
EK	*Evangelische Kommentare*
EKKNT	Evangelisch-katholischer Kommentar zum Neuen Testament
EvT	*Evangelische Theologie*
Inst.	J. Calvin, *Calvin: Institutes of the Christian Religion*, ed. J. T. McNeill, trans. F. L. Battles, The Library of Christian Classics 20–21 (Philadelphia: Westminster, 1960).
JBL	*Journal of Biblical Literature*
JBT	*Jahrbuch für Biblische Theologie*
LW	*Luther's Works*
LXX	Septuagint
MySal	J. Feiner and M. Löhrer, eds., *Mysterium Salutis: Grundriss heilsgeschichtlicher Dogmatik*, 3d ed. (Einsiedeln: Benziger, 1965–1981).
NovT	*Novum Testamentum*

NTD   Das Neue Testament Deutsch
OTL   Old Testament Library
PG   J.-P. Migne, ed., *Patrologiae cursus completus:
            Series graeca*
PL   J.-P. Migne, ed., *Patrologiae cursus completus:
            Series latina*
QD   Quaestiones Disputatae
RevExp   *Review and Expositor*
RGG   *Die Religion in Geschichte und Gegenwart:
            Handwörterbuch für Theologie und Religionswissenschaft,*
            3d ed.
SANT   Studien zum Alten und Neuen Testament
SNTSMS   Society for New Testament Studies Monograph Series
THAT   *Theologisches Handwörterbuch zum Alten Testament*
ThSt[B]   *Theologische Studiën,* ed. K. Barth
TLZ   *Theologische Literaturzeitung*
TRE   *Theologische Realenzyklopädie*
WA   M. Luther, *Werke,* Kritische Gesamtausgabe ("Weimar"
            edition)
WMANT   Wissenschaftliche Monographien zum Alten und Neuen
            Testament
ZAW   *Zeitschrift für die alttestamentliche Wissenschaft*
ZTK   *Zeitschrift für Theologie und Kirche*

CHAPTER 1

God the Spirit—A Problem of Experience in Today's World?

Without question, in our day people have experienced God's Spirit and continue to do so. Or are, for example, 300 million people—the current estimated size of the Charismatic Movement—in error? No one can exclude that possibility a priori. But if the members of the largest religious movement in history are not in error, is the so-called secular world, for whom the Spirit of God is to a large extent a phantom, blind? Has this world, by means of its forms of experience, its language, and its construction of "reality" in the singular, obstructed the functioning of its capacity to perceive God's Spirit? Has this world immunized itself against the power with which God is present among human beings and acts on them? This possibility as well cannot simply be excluded. But is it meaningful to attempt to change the secular world's habitual forms of experience in the direction of a greater openness to experience of the Spirit, if we do not know with certainty that we can trust the experiences of persons who appeal to the Spirit of God?

Those who today want to overcome such uncertainties and doubts and to go beyond their own forms of experience and the religious experiences of our day cannot expect any easy answer. To set out on the path to a new intimacy with the reality of the Spirit, one must expose oneself to numerous different perceptions of, and attestations to, the Spirit. And one must expose oneself to helplessness and skepticism with regard to such attestations.

A view that does not arbitrarily block out these difficulties must note at the outset that the secular common sense of the West has great difficulty in gaining even a distant perception of anything approaching God's Spirit. While this everyday understanding presumably only "sees ghosts" in the doctrine of the Holy Spirit, members of the

1

Charismatic Movement are not the only ones who take seriously God's
Spirit as a reality that unquestionably can be and is experienced. Many
people in many lands can attribute the powerful spread of theologies of
liberation in our world only to the action of God's Spirit. In societies
that are dominated by individual, national, economic, and cultural
forms of egotism, how could theologies of liberation develop into one of
the most important forms of theology and piety? In massively patriarchal churches, how could feminist theologies make so much headway
in barely two decades? How could this happen if not through God's
Spirit, who, according to prophetic promise and Pentecostal confirmation, enables men and women, male and female slaves, old and young,
local residents and people from other lands, intimates and strangers, to
open God's reality with each other and for each other? How could this
happen if a Spirit were not at work who—in accord with the prospect
held out by the messianic promises of the Spirit—wills to make universal righteousness, mercy, and knowledge of God a reality?

In what follows I propose to take up the different types of perspectives on God's Spirit held by the contemporary world. We will be able to
hear interconnections, differences, and incompatibilities of the many
voices engaged in a questioning search for God's Spirit, and of the expectations placed on the Spirit. We will also be able to hear the similarly polyphonic negation of God's Spirit.

From this complex beginning I will turn to the very diverse testimonies to the Spirit of God found in the biblical traditions. These testimonies make use of a realism that remains to be discovered anew.
Their realistic approach will help clarify the disparate contemporary
experiences of God's Spirit and the doubts about God's Spirit. This
should clear the way for experiencing the Holy Spirit in the future, for
expecting the Spirit of God, for talking about the Spirit, for invoking
this power of God, and for concurring in its action.

1.1: God the Spirit and the modern consciousness of the distance of God

The Spirit of God makes God's power knowable. The Spirit reveals the
power of God in and on human beings and in and on their fellow creatures. The Spirit reveals this power through them and for them. The

Spirit makes it possible to know the *creative power of God*, which brings the diversity of all that is creaturely into rich, fruitful, life-sustaining, fortifying, and protective relations. The Spirit of God reveals the *power of God's mercy*, which God extends particularly to the weak, the neglected, the excluded, and the infirm. The Spirit enables God's glory to be known through creatures and for creatures precisely inasmuch as what is weak becomes strengthened, what is excluded is reintegrated, and what is infirm is enabled to stand erect and healthy. The Spirit also makes it possible to know *God's conflict* with the mighty and autocratic among the creatures of this world. The Spirit shows that human beings cannot bear abundance, vitality, richness, freedom, and the divine vocation to reflect God's glory. Instead, we persistently work against that. The Spirit of God makes clear that God, full of love, grapples with the machinations and powers that seek to counteract the divine creativity and mercy. God does not let human beings and other creatures out of their vocation to reflect God's glory for each other.[1]

Experiences of God's Spirit are thus not merely private experiences, nor are they limited to conventicles or to other isolated groups. God does not make Godself knowable to "me" alone. God does not act merely "among us" here and now. Totally regardless of whether I or we are able or willing to experience it, God acts on people near and far in our time, but also in times both before and after us. This acting on other persons can happen through us, independently of whether we perceive it or not. Consciously or unconsciously, we are taken into God's service. Conversely, God exercises an influence on us through other people.

God's acting on human beings through human beings, on creatures through creatures, is not always easy to recognize.[2] It is often

---

1. This is shown especially by §§3.1, 4.5, 5.2ff., and 6.1ff.
2. To be sure, J. G. Hamann spoke eloquently in saying: "Speak, that I may see you!—This wish was fulfilled by creation, which is a speaking [on God's part] to what is created through what is created" (*Sämtliche Werke* 2, ed. J. Nadler [Vienna: Herder, 1950], 198). Yet Psalm 19, with which Hamann supports his claim, says not only that the heavens are praising God's glory, that the firmament announces God's handiwork, that one day tells it to another and one night makes it known to another; the Psalm also calls attention to the problem of the *clarity* and *comprehensibility* of God's speech "to what is created through what is created." The Psalm adds that this message, which goes out into the whole world, occurs with "no speech, nor are there

difficult to distinguish the reciprocal relations defined by God's Spirit from other relations between people and between creatures. A whole culture, a whole age can to a large extent lose this capacity to distinguish, lose the capacity to perceive the divine action, the action of the Spirit. The God who is near is then difficult to grasp. Piety retreats into the private sphere and then hardly makes sense to an outsider. Theologies flee into increasingly bald and sterile abstractions. There remains nothing to conjure other than "experience in itself" or simply "experience with experience." The arid assurance that every theology is practical, indeed "eminently practical," the assertion that faith makes people "capable of acting," and similarly empty formulas are supposed to hide the embarrassment that it is impossible to talk convincingly about God and God's action.

But why is the attempt to do so unsuccessful, if God's Spirit is present, is effective, and can be experienced in the world? God's Spirit, the Holy Spirit, is not only a power by which God once upon a time intervened in past worlds and made Godself knowable. God's Spirit, the Holy Spirit, is also the power and the force by which God intervenes in constantly new ways in the present world and makes Godself knowable to people living in the present and in the future. Yet this is understood only in parts of the contemporary world, only within certain spheres of contemporary humanity. In other parts of the world a theology of the Holy Spirit must reckon with the prejudice that every attempt to recognize and to make God's presence knowable is nothing more than an empty promise. The Holy Spirit counts for nothing more than an intellectual construct, a product of fantasy. Why?

"The modern world has lost God and is seeking him." This is the judgment passed by the mathematician, natural scientist, and philosopher Alfred North Whitehead.[3] Many people of our day would subscribe to his judgment. Others would even claim that the world has

---

words; their voice is not heard." On Hamann and the theology of creation that followed his lead, see O. Bayer, "Schöpfung als 'Rede an die Kreatur durch die Kreatur': Die Frage nach dem Schlüssel zum Buch der Natur und Geschichte," *EvT* 40 (1980): 316ff.; O. Bayer, *Schöpfung als Anrede: Zu einer Hermeneutik der Schöpfung* (Tübingen: Mohr, 1986).

3. A. N. Whitehead, *Religion in the Making* (New York: Macmillan, 1926), 74.

given up seeking God. Or they would regard the search for God as an enterprise doomed to failure: There never was a God.[4]

A theology of the Holy Spirit even provokes claims that God is distant or dead or does not exist at all. How can a world lose God if indeed a power of God is at work that intervenes in this world? How can a world land in the situation of seeking God in vain, if God makes Godself knowable in this world—not only privately, but publicly as well? If it is characteristic of God, by the Spirit, to intervene in this world and to make Godself knowable, is then the modern public experience that God is absent not a proof that there is no God at all? If a theology of the Holy Spirit disputes that God is a past, lost, distant, inaccessible God who cannot be experienced, and if a theology of the Holy Spirit emphasizes that God acts mightily, that God is present and can be experienced, such a theology will serve as an intensified provocation to laments over God's distance from this world.

It might still be possible to swallow a "creator God" sometime "in the beginning" and "on high." It might still be possible to swallow a Christ who marks the transition into the Common Era. It might still be possible to swallow a God as part of a story about what happened "once upon a time." But in the face of the widespread experience that God is distant, it is too much to ask people to accept the claim that in God's Spirit God is near them, that in the Spirit God is present among them and acts on them. Theology can quote as zealously and as often as it wishes Karl Barth's remark that the Holy Spirit is the most intimate friend of common sense.[5] Unfortunately, this is a far cry from making common sense a friend of the Holy Spirit!

---

4. In his description of "How the 'True World' Finally Became a Fable," Friedrich Nietzsche has strikingly depicted the step-by-step distancing of Western culture not only from belief in God, but also from philosophical metaphysics and from all forms of morality (*Twilight of the Idols*, in *The Portable Nietzsche*, ed. and trans. W. Kaufmann [New York: Penguin Books, 1976], 485–86).

5. K. Barth, *CD* 4/4, 28: "There is no more intimate friend of common sense than the Holy Spirit" [translation altered]; E. Jüngel, "Zur Lehre vom heiligen Geist," in U. Luz and H. Weder, eds., *Die Mitte des Neuen Testaments: Einheit und Vielfalt neutestamentlicher Theologie: Festschrift für Eduard Schweizer zum siebzigsten Geburtstag* (Göttingen: Vandenhoeck, 1983), 97ff., 100: "The belief 'that by my own reason or strength I cannot believe in Jesus Christ, my Lord, or come to him' . . . demonstrates that the Holy Spirit is the best friend of common sense."

Today in many cultures common sense simply has difficulty recip-
rocating the friendship of the Holy Spirit, whether because common
sense cannot even perceive that friendship or because common sense
receives little help in its occasional attempts to make friends with the
Holy Spirit. In this way the suspicion is solidified that the Holy Spirit
is a phantom, a ghost. But common sense knows, especially since the
Enlightenment, that there are no such things as ghosts.

The suspicion of so-called common sense that the Holy Spirit is a
phantom is strengthened by theologies and religious attitudes that
emphasize the abstract transcendence and otherworldliness, the naked
supernaturalness, or the mysterious and numinous character of the
Holy Spirit. These theologies point to an unclaimed territory, so to
speak, that common sense has left open. They do so with the shallow
assertion that something is at work in what is transcendent, otherworldly, supernatural, mysterious, and numinous, where common sense
can perceive (or assumes) only emptiness, illusion, and deceit.

By contrast, the many biblical testimonies to the action of God's
Spirit—testimonies that are determinative for faith—talk about this
Spirit having entered into diverse realities of human life. They report
that the Spirit has "descended" like rainfall on human beings or has
been "poured out" upon them. They report that in concrete situations
of distress and affliction, the Spirit has intervened in realities of human life, bringing vitality and renewal. And they report how the Spirit
has done so. They do not sidestep the thorny question of how the
Spirit of God and the Spirit's action were experienced and can be experienced. They face head-on the challenges that the action, the complex reality, and the experience of the Spirit present to the realities of
our everyday lives and to our ways of experience. And they do not skirt
the problems involved in the fact that the action of the Spirit is uncontrollable and often seemingly insignificant, and even remains intermit-
tently distant.

The theology of the Holy Spirit that lies before you has the conscious aim of confronting the tensions and conflicts between the attestations that in the Spirit God is acting and can be experienced,
and the assertions of secular common sense that God is distant and
powerless. The two positions can not be torn apart into a spiritless
"here and now" and a "beyond" that is inaccessible to rationality and
experience. It is a real question whether such obscure and empty

words as "the transcendent," "the supernatural," "the otherworldly," and "the numinous" ought to be used at all in the doctrine of the Holy Spirit. If they should be, then *that in which* the Holy Spirit's "transcendence" and "supernaturalness" consists must become clear in relation to the Spirit's intervention in the present. It must be made clear *what* about this force and power is and remains "otherworldly" and "mysterious."

The theology of the Holy Spirit that lies before you consciously enters the charged field established by the poles of, on the one hand, the experience of God's proximity and, on the other hand, the consciousness of God's distance. By doing so, this theology sets itself the task of making clear the reason why certain ways of comprehending reality, certain forms of so-called common sense, acquire only with difficulty a capacity to perceive the action of God's Spirit. This theology sets itself the task of making clear that certain constructions of reality and certain forms of experience practically make themselves immune to experiences of the Spirit. But it also confronts the problem of why contemporary worldwide religious movements, which in no way share the secular consciousness of God's distance and which explicitly appeal to experiences of the Spirit's might, have so far not had persuasive and contagious repercussions on many secular regions of the world.

1.2: God the Spirit and the worldwide Charismatic Movement

That the Spirit of God is effective among human beings today is asserted and attested in a religious movement that is expanding worldwide. This movement is composed of several intra- and extra-ecclesial currents. Adherents of the so-called Charismatic Movement or Charismatic Renewal have a number of things in common. They appeal to the powerful experience of the reality and presence of God in the Spirit. They report intense and joyful community experiences, particularly in worship, preaching, and praise of God. They open themselves to the plurality and individuality of the gifts of the Spirit and strive to overcome hierarchical community structures and denominational isolation. Many people who stand outside this development—whether connected with a church or of a secular orientation—find these experiences strikingly lacking in clarity and determinacy. Evidently these experiences are not easy for everyone to follow. What is the reason for this?

The Charismatic Movement is considered to be the fastest-growing religious movement of our time. It is the largest religious movement in history, period. At the end of the 1980s its membership was estimated at over 300 million people in 230 countries. According to an estimate made in 1988, the movement is growing at a yearly rate of 19 million members.[6] Although the figures given in different estimates diverge widely,[7] there is hardly an account that does not

---

6. The figures given are from D. B. Barrett, chief editor of the respected *World Christian Encyclopedia: A Comparative Survey of Churches and Religions in the Modern World A.D. 1900–2000* (Oxford: Oxford Univ. Press, 1982). The data for 1988 are located in his article "The Twentieth-Century Pentecostal/Charismatic Renewal in the Holy Spirit, with Its Goal of World Evangelization," in North American Renewal Service Committee, ed., A.D. 2000 *Together* 2, no. 5 (1988): 1ff. See also W. J. Hollenweger, *Handbuch der Pfinstbewegung* (New Haven: Atlas Board of Microtexts, 1965–1967); W. J. Hollenweger, *Enthusiastisches Christentum: Die Pfingstbewegung in Geschichte und Gegenwart* (Wuppertal: Brockhaus, 1969); C. E. Jones, *A Guide to the Study of the Pentecostal Movement*, 2 vols. (Metuchen, N.J.: Scarecrow, 1983); W. E. Mills, *Charismatic Religion in Modern Research: A Bibliography* (Macon, Ga.: Mercer Univ. Press, 1985); J. A. Jongeneel, ed., *Experiences of the Spirit: Conference on Pentecostal and Charismatic Research in Europe at Utrecht University 1989* (Frankfurt am Main: Peter Lang, 1991).

7. Barrett estimates the adherents of the classical Pentecostal movement alone at 78 million for 1975, 104 million for 1980, 149 million for 1985, and 176 million for 1988 ("Twentieth-Century Pentecostal/Charismatic Renewal," 2–3). By contrast, on the basis of an estimate made in the mid-1970s, A. Bittlinger speaks of 30 million to 40 million (*Charismatische Erneuerung—eine Chance für die Gemeinde?* ed. Koordinierungsausschuss für Charismatische Gemeindeerneuerung in der Evangelischen Kirche [Metzingen: 1979], 4). Barrett initially set the figures in the *World Christian Encyclopedia* at a lower level, but their upward revision was recommended by, for example, P. A. Pomerville, "Pentecostalism and Mission: Distortion or Correction? The Pentecostal Contribution to Contemporary Mission Theology," Ph.D. diss., Fuller Theological Seminary, 1982, 58ff. See also Pomerville's depiction of the difficulties in securing reliable figures and in adequately grasping essential characteristics when developments are changing so quickly. For example, at the end of the 1970s Bittlinger particularly highlights "the independent African churches, whose members today number some 8 million" (*Charismatische Erneuerung—Chance?* 4). A decade later Barrett is particularly impressed by the Chinese "'House church' Pentecostals," whom he estimates have some 40 million adherents.

emphasize the breathtaking success of this movement, which in a quarter of a century has spread over the whole earth and "in one form or another has found entry into all denominations and churches, both state and independent."[8] For most of the adherents of the Charismatic Movement, their successful development is a direct proof that the Holy Spirit can be experienced and that in the Spirit God is present and acting in our contemporary world.

This attitude is shared even where differentiations and differences inside the movement are emphasized and negative aspects of the success story are highlighted.[9] Throughout the literature three or four currents are distinguished that either designate themselves as "charismatic" or are so named by outsiders:

1. The so-called *classical Pentecostal movement* grows out of Methodism and a number of Baptist churches in Topeka, Kansas, in 1901.[10] At first usually reproved and isolated by the mother churches, the movement expands with enormous speed, especially in Latin America and Africa. Different developments quickly arise, including both independent churches and sects.

2. In 1960 a second charismatic awakening, the *"Charismatic Renewal,"* begins in the U.S.A. It begins first among Anglicans

---

8. H. Kägi, *Der Heilige Geist in charismatischer Erfahrung und theologischer Reflexion* (Zurich: Theologischer Verlag Zurich, 1989), 3.

9. According to Barrett, "Twentieth-Century Pentecostal/Charismatic Renewal," with the great success of the movement has come the phenomenon of enormous numbers of people turning away from the Charismatic Movement. He calls attention to the "growing dilemma" that many charismatics in the non-Pentecostal mainline Protestant and Catholic churches become inactive or leave the church entirely after two or three years. For 1988 he estimates that there were already 80 million "postcharismatics" (ibid., 3), as he puts it in his study—a study that is not exactly free from the imperialistic compulsion to take everybody into one overarching structure. The four million "radio/television charismatics" whom he takes into account could also be reckoned among the negative aspects of the movement—and of its evaluation (ibid., 1–2).

10. See D. W. Dayton's informative discussion in "Theological Roots of Pentecostalism," *Pneuma: The Journal of the Society for Pentecostal Studies* 2 (1980): 3ff.

and Episcopalians, then in other churches of the Reformation.[11] In 1967 the Charismatic Renewal reaches the Catholic
church and spreads there like wildfire.[12] About 1971 the movement takes hold of the Greek Orthodox Church as well.[13]

3. Parallel to this movement arises so-called *Neo-Pentecostalism*.
Like the Charismatic Renewal, Neo-Pentecostalism wishes to
remain within the existing churches. In opposition to the
Charismatic Renewal, it accepts the theology of the classical
Pentecostal movement, including its fundamentalist understanding of the Bible and its Baptist understanding of baptism.
Above all it insists not only on "baptism in the Spirit" but also,
closely connected with this baptism, on *speaking in tongues*. It
treats speaking in tongues as an initiation into faith or as a cul-
minating point on the path of faith after conversion and sanctification.[14] Other characteristics of Neo-Pentecostalism are an
individual experience of faith and an interest in spectacular
experiences that supposedly underscore religious vitality.

---

11. For a treatment of the theological reactions of the mainline churches, see
J. R. Williams, "The Upsurge of Pentecostalism: Some Presbyterian/Reformed Com-
ment," *Reformed World* 31 (1971): 339ff.; also the "attempted integration" by J. Hes-
selink, "The Charismatic Movement and the Reformed Tradition," *Reformed Review*
(Philadelphia) 28 (1975): 174ff.; C. Lindberg, *The Third Reformation? Charismatic
Movements and the Lutheran Tradition* (Macon, Ga.: Mercer Univ. Press, 1983).

12. Bittlinger illustrates this by means of the attendance figures at the annual
conferences of the Catholic Charismatic Renewal in the United States, which takes
place at Notre Dame from 1967 through 1974 before being regionalized in 1975. In
1967, 70 people gather. In 1968, 150; 1969, 500; 1970, 1500; 1971, 5000; 1972,
12,000; 1973, 23,000; 1974, 37,000 (*Charismatische Erneuerung—Chance?* 5). Here,
as well, attempts at theological integration quickly result. See, e.g., E. O'Connor,
"The Hidden Roots of the Charismatic Renewal in the Catholic Church," in
V. Synan, ed., *Aspects of Pentecostal-Charismatic Origins* (South Plainfield, N.J.:
Bridge, 1975), 169ff. A thorough overall exposition is to be found in R. Laurentin,
Catholic Pentecostalism (London: Darton, Longman and Todd, 1977).

13. Cf. J. R. Williams, "A Profile of the Charismatic Movement," *ChrTo* 19
(1975): 9ff. But see also the critical and defensive examination by J. W. Morris,
"The Charismatic Movement: An Orthodox Evaluation," *Greek Orthodox Theological Review* 28 (1983): 103ff.

14. See A. I. C. Heron, *The Holy Spirit* (Philadelphia: Westminster, 1983),
132ff. See also §§5.1 and 5.5 of this book.

4. Finally, recent literature mentions, with some uncertainty, *"Third-wavers."* This term is supposed to designate so-called evangelicals or other Christians who since the 1980s have been developing a piety centered on the Holy Spirit and on experiences of the Spirit, without being directly connected to the Pentecostal movement or the Charismatic Movement.[15]

The success of the Charismatic Movement is striking. Yet equally striking is the fact that the reasons for its success are not easily communicated to outsiders.[16] Conversations with its members and the copious literature on the distinctive contours and the theology of the Charismatic Movement at the very least make common sense suspicious by virtue of the indeterminacy of their statements. More likely they scare common sense away. Obviously the forms of expression and of exposition are lacking that could communicate the defining impressions and underlying experiences to the outside, to another spectrum of forms of thought, experience, and life. The clearest and most helpful descriptions of the distinctive contours of the Charismatic Movement[17] name the following elements as characteristic:

1. Members of the Charismatic Movement emphasize that they have experienced with new power the *reality and presence of God*. One particular component of this experience is recognition of the vitality and contemporary meaning of the biblical

---

15. See Barrett, "Twentieth-Century Pentecostal/Charismatic Renewal," 19; C. P. Wagner, *The Third Wave of the Holy Spirit: Encountering the Power of Signs and Wonders Today* (Ann Arbor, Mich.: Servant, 1988).

16. This is reflected to an equal extent in the depiction of what is positive and of what is problematic in the Charismatic Renewal. Thus, e.g., see Y. Congar, *I Believe in the Holy Spirit*, vol. 2, *"He Is Lord and Giver of Life,"* trans D. Smith (New York: Seabury, 1983), esp. 145–212; or Schütz, *Einführung in die Pneumatologie* (Darmstadt: Wissenschaftliche Buchgesellschaft, 1985), 274ff.

17. With regard to the following discussion, cf. esp. Williams, "Profile of the Charismatic Movement," 9ff.; as well as A. Bittlinger, "Die charismatische Erneuerung der Kirchen: Aufbruch urchristlicher Geisterfahrung," in C. Heitmann and H. Mühlen, eds., *Erfahrung und Theologie des Heiligen Geistes* (Hamburg: Agentur des Rauhen Hauses; Munich: Kösel, 1974), 19ff.

world.[18] Another component is development of the capacity—
often experienced for the first time—to pray, to enjoy prayer,
and to talk about God in a new way with joy and power.

2. Members of the Charismatic Movement emphasize that they
   have come to a *new awareness of community* and to new community experiences. In this regard members often emphasize the
   connection between enjoyment of the community and *communal proclamation and glorification of God.* [19]

3. Members of the Charismatic Movement emphasize that among
   themselves the abundance and diversity of the *gifts of the Spirit*
   (1 Cor. 12:8-10; Rom. 12:6-8; 1 Pet. 4:10-11) are taken seriously. They also insist that the gifts and endowments of individual human beings are thereby discovered and valued. They say
   that this leads to dismantling the separation of persons within
   the community into professionals who play the lead roles and
   laity who have only minor parts.[20]

4. Members of the Charismatic Movement emphasize that for
   them the relativizing and removing of confessional boundaries,
   and an attendant *opening to an ecumenical Christianity*, have become an important sign of the power of the Spirit's action.[21]

5. Finally, members of the Charismatic Movement emphasize the
   experience termed "baptism in the Holy Spirit"[22]—an experience that is evidently difficult even for them to describe. This
   baptism can be followed by *speaking in tongues*. For members of

---

18. Cf. T. F. Zimmerman, "Priorities and Beliefs of Pentecostals," *ChrTo* 25
(1981): 1109–1110.

19. Cf. Williams, "Profile of the Charismatic Movement," 10; H. Mühlen, "Die
Geisterfahrung als Erneuerung der Kirche," in O. A. Dilschneider, ed., *Theologie des
Geistes* (Gütersloh: Mohn, 1980), 69ff., 72ff.

20. Cf. Bittlinger, *Charismatische Erneuerung—Chance?* 6–7, 14ff.; Mühlen,
"Geisterfahrung," 83ff.

21. Cf. W. J. Hollenweger, "Charisma und Ökumene: Der Beitrag der Pfingstbewegung zur weltweiten Kirche," in *Rondom het Woord* 12 (1970): 300ff.; G. Gass-
mann and H. Meyer, eds., *Neue transkonfessionelle Bewegungen: Dokumente aus der
evangelikalen, aktionszentrierten und der charismatischen Bewegung*, Ökumenische
Dokumentation 3 (1976).

22. See §5.1.

Pentecostal churches and for Neo-Pentecostals, the succession is inevitable. Speaking in tongues is regarded above all as the acquisition of a new form of prayer language, a new way to express oneself in prayer, to give utterance to spiritual power, and to praise God.[23]

If we juxtapose these experiences of charismatics to secularized common sense's experiences of God's distance in the modern world, we can formulate the following initial reservations regarding the movements of the Charismatic Renewal:

Certainly it is comprehensible to long for powers of the Spirit, for demonstrations that faith is powerful, has its own special qualities, and generates enthusiasm. Certainly one can only share the need for a rich, diverse community that takes individuals seriously and grows in the exchange of the individual gifts of the Spirit. Certainly we ought to work against forms of piety that one-sidedly emphasize cognitive and rational functions. But why are the experiences of the Spirit and of the Spirit's power so difficult to communicate to others who wish to understand them? Why are they so difficult to translate into many contexts of European and North American life? Don't practices such as speaking in tongues tend to repel people rather than to attract them— at any rate people of the Western world in the twentieth century? Don't these practices form new hierarchies in the community, especially the hierarchy of those gifted with interpretation and speech in contrast to the others? If this assessment is on the mark, are these endowments and manners of behavior really to be regarded as powers of faith and of the Spirit?

By contrast, because of their destructive forces, the dominant, mostly imperialistic forms for structuring experience, especially in Western cultures, are the object of increasing reproach from the ranks of the Charismatic Renewal. This reproach calls attention to the fixation on forms of technical-scientific rationality and to the ways in which they compel conformity in the Western world. To these the Charismatic Renewal opposes a shared sensibility for the miraculous

---

23. Appealing to, say, Rom. 8:26-27; Eph. 6:18; Jude 20; as well as to 1 Cor. 14:1ff. For greater detail see §5.5.

and the inexplicable and a liberation of "emotional intelligence."[24] On the one side is a spirit of the age, a *Zeitgeist* that destroys sustaining and sheltering environments, both natural and cultural.[25] On the other side is the strengthening of the "subjective sphere of experience" and of the "subjective competence to judge," as well as the connection with traditions that set in opposition to the specific achievements of the technical-scientific world a source of powerful alternatives for changing forms of life. Experience stands against experience!

On the secular side this same difference is of course "read" differently: Certainly it is correct that the dominant cultures of the Western world have maneuvered themselves into diverse disastrous processes that, once engaged, exercise their own ineluctable dynamic. Certainly it is correct that these cultures are marked by rationalities whose destructive potentials are becoming more and more readily recognizable. It is also an accurate assessment that these cultures hardly manifest forces for the renewal of their ethos, forces for the renewal of their forms of communication and understanding that would be able to meet the challenge of those self-destructive processes. But this does not validate the claims of an escapist version of religious cultural critique whose positive initiatives and whose alternatives cannot be clearly communicated to others. Specifically, this does not mean that such escapism can lay claim to the delivering and saving powers of God's Holy Spirit—provided that such a thing even exists.

If we free ourselves from this alternative and consider it from the outside, the following questions become unavoidable with regard to the Charismatic Movement.[26] Is the Spirit to which it appeals the Spirit of *truth?* Is the retreat to subjective feelings, and to a certainty that even within the church of Christ can only be communicated to a limited extent, appropriate to this Spirit? If we have to do with the Spirit of *truth,* then in any case it is inadequate to point to the *success* of the movement that appeals to this Spirit, even when that success is spectacular. Must not the liberating power of truth show itself in the fact that the insights of faith wrought by the Spirit could be carried over to

---

24. With regard to the following discussion, cf. H. Kirchner et al., eds., *Charismatische Erneuerung und Kirche* (Neukirchen-Vluyn: Neukirchener, 1984), esp. 108–14.

25. See §1.5.

26. With regard to secular consciousness, see esp. §§1.4 and 1.5.

faith within secularized cultures and postures of consciousness? Must not the liberating power of truth make recognizable in a way that is also accessible to this latter faith the dominant cultures' ruling powers of self-endangerment and self-destruction? Must not the liberating power of truth contribute to "driving out" these powers?

Within the Charismatic Movement the interest in the Holy Spirit seems frequently to concentrate on the unusual, *sensational* action of the Spirit. This may be a reaction against the enlightened skepticism of the average Western mentality, against the rationality, homogeneity, predictability, and foreseeability of the ways in which that average Western mentality goes through life. Perhaps only the subjectivity, irrationality, exotic character, and implausibility attributed to religious life by the Enlightenment are emphasized and obstinately accepted. Perhaps that is the reason for highlighting the interest in the charisms of speaking in tongues and of faith healing— an interest that on the one hand has a strong public effect, but on the other hand is regarded with suspicion by publics both inside and outside the church. Perhaps that is precisely why unique, peculiar, or spectacular personal experiences, which are inaccessible to outsiders and which contradict the rationalities that the culture has drummed into its members, are regarded as "experiences of the Spirit" and made the focus of attention.

Without a doubt the biblical traditions also talk about charisms and particular experiences that come across to us today as spectacular and implausible. Without a doubt the biblical traditions connect some of these experiences with the action of the Spirit. Yet in no way do the biblical traditions regard an anomalous action of the Spirit as the best path to the experience and knowledge of God's Spirit. Instead of busying itself with unusual, sensational actions of the Spirit, a theology of the Holy Spirit ought to work toward an understanding of experiences of the Spirit that are open to sober and realistic perception. Only from that vantage point should a theology of the Holy Spirit then continue with circumspect questioning aimed at a greater understanding of the spectacular action of the Spirit. This approach is not meant to exclude the possibility that in the end the speaking in tongues wrought by the Spirit will perhaps appear less complex and astounding than, for example, the fact that the Holy Spirit brings righteousness, joy, and peace.

1.3: God the Spirit and the spread of liberation and feminist theologies

According to the messianic promises, God establishes justice, mercy, and knowledge of God through a "Chosen One" on whom rests the Spirit of God, as well as through the "pouring out" of the Spirit. There is no righteousness without mercy, without integration of the weak, without liberation of the oppressed, without those who have been forced to the margins of society participating in the processes of economic, judicial, social, and cultural life. For the revelation and execution of this divine purpose, women and men, old and young, slaves both male and female, people from "here" and people from other lands, adherents of "our" religion and those who come from other religious traditions are taken into God's service.

Liberation and feminist theologies of our day proceed de facto from these premises. The diversity of movements corresponds to the fullness of the Spirit who, according to the promises, neither brings nor wills to bring deliverance through only one group and for only one group, from only *one* perspective and in the framework of only *one* program or *one* plan for the world. It is in the various movements' orientation toward righteousness and freedom in the force field of justice, mercy, and knowledge of God that they receive their differentiated unanimity and the power that results from mutual strengthening.[27]

Within the space of two decades, liberation and feminist theologies[28] have, in the phrase of Leonardo and Clodovis Boff, "already made [their] presence felt worldwide."[29] This means not only that they

---

27. See esp. §§3.1, 3.3, 3.4, 4.1, and 5.3.

28. Concerning the structural analogy between, on the one hand, the various forms of liberation theology and, on the other hand, feminist theology, which likewise has acquired a great deal of internal differentiation, see E. Moltmann-Wendel, *A Land Flowing with Milk and Honey: Perspectives on Feminist Theology*, trans. J. Bowden (New York: Crossroad, 1986), 63ff.; A. E. Carr, *Transforming Grace: Christian Tradition and Women's Experience* (San Francisco: Harper & Row, 1988), 148ff.

29. L. Boff and C. Boff, *Introducing Liberation Theology*, trans. P. Burns (Maryknoll, N.Y.: Orbis, 1989), 78. The internal differentiation within Latin American liberation theology is documented by R. Gibellini, ed., *Frontiers of Theology in Latin America* (Maryknoll, N.Y.: Orbis, 1979); K. Rahner et al., eds., *Befreiende Theologie: Der Beitrag Lateinamerikas zur Theologie der Gegenwart* (Stuttgart: Kohlhammer, 1977).

belong among the most significant forms of theology existing today, but that every credible act of asking about God and talking about God must confront the challenges and impetuses of these theologies. The thought and feeling characteristic of liberation and feminist theologies have begun to infuse all forms of theological thought and feeling. This is due not only to the fact that these theologies have great moral, political, and humanitarian rights on their side. Nor is it due, as conservative critics opine, to a temporary political and moral mood that sustains and enhances the success of these theologies. Liberation and feminist theologies take up central concerns of the biblical legal traditions and of God's will as expressed in these traditions. In addition, those theologies stand in the power of the promise of the Spirit of righteousness.[30] Thus they will continue to infuse and to change all forms of theology and piety and to exercise a transforming and renewing influence on the secular world.

To characterize the new departure effected by liberation and feminist theologies, people have spoken of a "paradigm shift" in religious life and piety, in theology and the church.[31] Interpretations of this development have been offered from the perspectives of morality, politics, intellectual history, and cultural criticism. Thus it has been claimed that the sharpening of social conflicts observable throughout the world in our day, the desolation and destruction of natural and cultural environments, or the crises of orientation in the transition from modern to postmodern culture underlie this change of religious life and piety. Yet all these interpretations remain outside the concrete new discovery of God's word. How has this word again intervened in human life? How has this word again really laid claim on people?

As we see today, underlying this change in the Christian world was, along with impetus given by the Exodus event, primarily the motive

---

30. See, besides chap. 2, H. Mühlen, "Der gegenwärtige Aufbruch der Geister-fahrung und die Unterscheidung der Geister," in W. Kasper, ed., *Gegenwart des Geistes: Aspekte der Pneumatologie*, QD 85 (Freiburg: Herder, 1979), esp. 41ff.; E. Schüssler Fiorenza, *In Memory of Her: A Feminist Reconstruction of Christian Origins* (New York: Crossroad, 1983), 160–204; G. Gutiérrez, *We Drink from Our Own Wells: The Spiritual Journey of a People*, trans. M. J. O'Connell (Maryknoll, N.Y.: Orbis, 1984); J. Comblin, *The Holy Spirit and Liberation*, trans. P. Burns (Maryknoll, N.Y.: Orbis, 1989), esp. 7–13 and the unfortunately very abstract statements on 20–23.

31. H. Küng and D. Tracy, eds., *Paradigm Change in Theology: A Symposium for the Future*, trans. M. Kohl (New York: Crossroad, 1989).

power of provisions of biblical *law*. At issue are provisions concerning *mercy* as well as provisions concerning the interconnection between justice and mercy. At issue are also promises of the action of the Spirit that envision a fulfillment of this law, which aims at the universal realization of justice and mercy.

The provisions of the law concerning mercy are found—along with stipulations regulating justice and cultic life—in all bodies of law in the Old Testament.[32] Through the mediation of the messianic promises, they continue to have a powerful effect in the New Testament.[33] The mercy laws and the promises of the Spirit look forward to God's particular partiality for those in a community who are weak, oppressed, and in distress. They overcome the merely moral or even sentimental moral attitudes that turn mercy over to kindhearted individuals and to situations that elicit kindhearted action.[34] The mercy laws cultivate among people the binding expectation of a continual focus on the weak and oppressed. They cultivate the expectation that those who are privileged will withdraw their own claims—even to the point of forgoing their legal rights—for the benefit of those who are weak and in distress. They cultivate the logical consequence of this: namely, the struggle for liberation from the systematic constraints of oppression and of being oppressed.[35]

32. Cf. M. Welker, "Erwartungssicherheit und Freiheit: Zur Neuformulierung der Lehre von Gesetz und Evangelium I," *EK* 18 (1985): 680ff.; M. Welker, "Erbarmen und soziale Identität: Zur Neuformulierung der Lehre von Gesetz und Evangelium II," *EK* 19 (1986): 39ff.; M. Welker, "Security of Expectations: Reformulating the Theology of Law and Gospel," trans. J. Hoffmeyer, *Journal of Religion* 66 (1986): 237ff.

33. See M. Welker, "Gesetz und Geist," *JBT* 4, ed. O. Hofius and P. Stuhlmacher (1989): 215ff. With regard to the following discussion, cf. esp. §§3.1 and 5.3.

34. The process of theological reeducation is readily observable with regard to the doctrine of God in J. Moltmann's reworking of an article on God the "motherly Father," which first appeared in *God as Father*, ed. J.-B. Metz, E. Schillebeeckx, and M. Lefébure, *Concilium* 143, no. 3 (1981): 51–56. In 1981 the height of the motherly Father's giving is seen in the romantic "unending pain of love." By contrast, the 1991 version speaks of the "power of mercy" ("The Motherly Father and the Power of His Mercy," in *History and the Triune God: Contributions to Trinitarian Theology*, trans. J. Bowden [London: SCM Press, 1991], 19–25, esp. 23–25).

35. L. Boff and C. Boff foster sensitivity to the various levels of mercy by differentiating between a "'Band-Aid' approach," "reformism," and systemic change (*Introducing Liberation Theology*, 4ff. and 25ff.).

The impetuses that go forth from the mercy laws and from the messianic promises that pick up on the mercy laws have left a deep mark on piety and theology worldwide. In terms of theological content, they form the deep structure of the theology of liberation.[36] This is true whether the biblical traditions mark the individual currents of liberation theology in a way that is conscious, detailed, and direct,[37] or whether they do so through the mediation of dogmatic reflection.[38] Mercy laws and the promise of the Spirit also form the material

---

36. This is not contradicted by the fact that a Neomarxism marked by Left Hegelianism, and a theological appropriation of that Neomarxism (one can hardly overestimate the impetus provided by J. Moltmann, *Theology of Hope: On the Ground and the Implications of a Christian Eschatology*, trans. J. W. Leitch [London: SCM Press, 1967]), were important midwives in the birth of liberation theology. The development from Hegel to Marx, the goal of which was that philosophical theory might become "practical," was defined by thinkers who were fundamentally influenced by the Judeo-Christian legacy (Hegel, Feuerbach), and especially by messianism (Bruno Bauer, Moses Hess). This messianism prevails against all attempts to secularize it by means of morality, grassroots politics, or politics in the narrow, "professional" sense. It explains the characteristic vacillation of Left Hegelianism and Neomarxism between critique of religion and passionate interest in it. See, e.g., E. Bloch, *Atheism in Christianity: The Religion of the Exodus and the Kingdom*, trans. J. T. Swann (New York: Herder and Herder, 1972); J. Moltmann, *Im Gespräch mit Ernst Bloch: Eine theologische Wegbegleitung* (Munich: Kaiser, 1976), esp. 13ff., 43ff. D. Henrich convincingly sketches the stages of philosophical, moral, and political orientation of the early Marx—stages that Marx left behind, but that Neomarxism brought to life again in relation to orthodox Marxism ("Karl Marx als Schüler Hegels," in *Hegel im Kontext* [Frankfurt am Main: Suhrkamp, 1971], 187ff.). This orientation of the early Marx is a force that relativizes orthodox Marxism from the perspective of its own roots, and a force that has been overlooked not only by conservative critics.

37. Cf. G. Gutiérrez, *A Theology of Liberation: History, Politics, and Salvation*, trans. C. Inda and J. Eagleson (Maryknoll, N.Y.: Orbis, 1988), esp. 83–105; G. Gutiérrez, *On Job: God-Talk and the Suffering of the Innocent* (Maryknoll, N.Y.: Orbis, 1988); J. H. Cone, *God of the Oppressed* (San Francisco: Harper & Row, 1975), esp. 62ff.; P. Trible, *God and the Rhetoric of Sexuality* (Philadelphia: Fortress, 1978); C. Mesters, *Die Botschaft des leidenden Volkes* (Neukirchen-Vluyn: Neukirchener, 1982).

38. Cf. P. C. Hodgson, *New Birth of Freedom: A Theology of Bondage and Liberation* (Philadelphia: Fortress, 1976); J. Sobrino, *The True Church and the Poor* (Maryknoll, N.Y.: Orbis, 1984); R. R. Ruether, *Sexism and God-Talk: Toward a Feminist Theology* (Boston: Beacon, 1983); F. Herzog, *God-Walk: Liberation Shaping Dogmatics* (Maryknoll, N.Y.: Orbis, 1988).

theological basis where the worlds and linguistic forms of the biblical tradition are criticized[39] as patriarchal,[40] often nationalistic, and supportive of the formation of class societies.[41]

In the mercy law and in the messianic promises that look forward to the fulfillment of that law, a new and clear path to knowledge of God's word was again opened. This fact has in part elicited and in part strengthened a new departure, an exodus that takes many forms in churches and societies. The messianic promises assign the name "Spirit of God" to the power that both promises and realizes new community for poor and rich, strong and weak, people separated and alienated by economics, politics, racism, and sexism. The publications of liberation theologies suggest that these theologies have not identified that power as their central motive force as decisively as was the case with the Charismatic Renewal Movement.[42]

Undoubtedly this is the result of several factors working together. One must not underestimate the well-founded fear of feminist and liberation theologies that either a conservative or a liberal position will, in the name of a "Spirit" defined by other traditions and structures, fit them as "parts" into an overarching "whole," at the very least marginalizing them in the process.[43] It is still difficult to perceive the

---

39. R. R. Ruether calls attention to the "biblical critical principle" of the "prophetic-messianic tradition" ("Feminist Interpretation: A Method of Correlation," in L. M. Russell, ed., *Feminist Interpretation of the Bible* [Philadelphia: Westminster, 1985], 117ff.); similarly L. M. Russell, "Authority and the Challenge of Feminist Interpretation," in ibid., 138ff.

40. Cf. Schüssler Fiorenza, *In Memory of Her*; and the discussion documented in Russell, ed., *Feminist Interpretation*.

41. A. N. Whitehead is helpful in making clear the way in which the slaveholder mentality was taken for granted in "classical" civilizations: "We differ from the ancients on the one premise on which they were all agreed. Slavery was the presupposition of political theorists then; Freedom is the presupposition of political theorists now" (*Adventures of Ideas* [New York: Free Press, 1933], 13).

42. Students who have lived in Latin American base communities, however, repeatedly report a well-defined pneumatological piety. M. Volf sketches analogies and differences between both movements with the intent of reducing the latter ("Materiality of Salvation: An Investigation in the Soteriologies of Liberation and Pentecostal Theologies," *Journal of Ecumenical Studies* 26 [1989]: 447ff.).

43. In response to the discussion carried out in the volumes edited by Küng and Tracy (see n. 31 above), see M. Welker, "Theologischer Paradigmenwechsel?," *EK* 16

invigorating forces of the specific "pluralism of the Spirit" and to distinguish them from the vitiating, disintegrative pluralisms within secular cultures.[44] It is likewise still difficult to recognize and to make
accessible on a practical level the powerful interplay of mercy, justice,
and cultic life or, alternatively, mercy, justice, and knowledge of God.
And it is difficult to recognize and to make accessible on a practical
level the culture of community expectations and forms of behavior
that issues from this interplay.[45] Unfortunately, in the face of opposition the chances of success still seem greater for those who resort to
small-minded partisan politics than for those who build on the Spirit.[46]
This could be changed by recognition of the particular power of the
Spirit in the midst of the Spirit's apparent weakness in situations
where it appears to be impossible to get an overview of how the Spirit
is working.

1.4: God the Spirit, pluralism and individualism

God's Spirit makes God's power and God's righteousness knowable
through and for women and men, slaves both female and male, old and
young, people from "here" and people from other lands, adherents of
"our" church and those outside our church who are seeking righteousness and knowledge of God. The Spirit reveals God's power by simultaneously illumining different people and groups of people, and by
enabling them to become not only recipients, but also bearers of God's
revelation. The Spirit reveals the power of God in strong, upbuilding,
pluralistic structures. This pluralism is not a disintegrative, Babel-like
pluralism, but constitutes enriching, invigorating force fields. It is not
bound up with an abstract, uniform individualism that reduces everything to an unrealistic, abstract equality, reducing everything to "the

---

(1983): 376ff. M. K. Taylor provides an excellent discussion of the "trilemma" of
postmodern theology and philosophy: namely, how to do justice to the task that
requires us simultaneously "to acknowledge tradition, to celebrate plurality, and to
resist domination" (*Remembering Esperanza: A Cultural-Political Theology for North
American Praxis* [Maryknoll, N.Y.: Orbis, 1990], 40ff.).

44. See §1.4; also §§3.3, 3.4, and 5.1.

45. These last two sentences frame the task of a "theology of law."

46. See §1.6.

ego," "the subject," the decision-maker, the consumer, or the payee.[47] The individualism of the Spirit is marked by diverse concreteness and by concrete diversity, without crumbling into the indeterminate plurality of "pure" individuality. No one is totally the same as others, and no one is unique in every respect. The Spirit of God gives rise to a multiplace force field that is sensitive to differences. In this force field, enjoyment of creaturely, invigorating differences can be cultivated while unjust, debilitating differences can be removed in love, mercy, and gentleness.[48]

People have emphasized over and over again that God's Spirit works union, unanimity, and unity among human beings,[49] indeed that the Spirit "holds together" all that is created.[50] Not only has this been emphasized repeatedly, it has been emphasized in connection with the widest possible variety of interests.[51] Less clarity and energy have been devoted to saying that the "unity of the Spirit" not only tolerates differences and differentiation, but that it maintains and cultivates differences that do not contradict justice, mercy, and knowledge of God.[52] According to the prophetic promises whose fulfillment is proclaimed on Pentecost, the Spirit gives rise to a unity that speaks to and includes not only people of the most varied languages and traditions. The Spirit gives rise to a unity in which the prophetic witness of women is no less important than that of men, that of the young is no less significant than that of the old, that of the socially disadvantaged is no less relevant than that of the privileged. The promised Spirit of God is effective in that differentiated community which is sensitive to differences, and in which the differences that

---

47. See D. Bonhoeffer's classic confrontation with modern individualism and social atomism, *The Communion of Saints: A Dogmatic Inquiry into the Sociology of the Church*, trans. R. G. Smith et al. (New York: Harper & Row, 1963), 20ff., 23ff., and passim.

48. See §§3.1ff., 5.1, 5.3, 5.4, and 6.3.

49. See, e.g., Phil. 1:27, Eph. 4:3-4, Jude 19; also esp. §§2.1, 5.1, and 6.2.

50. Wisdom of Sol. 1:7. See §3.5.

51. Congar (*"He Is Lord and Giver of Life"*) designates the Spirit as the "principle of unity" (15), which he sees as supporting the "pastoral hierarchy" (17), on the one hand, and somehow taking account of individual diversity, on the other hand; cf. esp. 15–23; 213–30.

52. Cf. §§2.2, 3.1–3.5, 4.5, 5.1–5.3.

stand in opposition to justice, mercy, and knowledge of God are being steadily reduced.

To be sure, in baptism human beings are "baptized into one body" (1 Cor. 12:13) through the Spirit. But the text immediately adds with double emphasis that "Jews or Greeks, slaves or free" have been given the one Spirit to drink (1 Cor. 12:13b), and that the unity of the body that arises consists in the interplay of a differentiated diversity that cannot be reduced to a simple unity (1 Cor. 12:14ff.).[53]

Although this differentiated diversity through the Spirit exists with reference to Christ, it is not arranged according to a hierarchical order in the relations of the members *among themselves.* Just as for a body in some situations the eyes are particularly important, in some the hands, and in still others the ears or the feet, so the unity at issue here is a flexible one that permits many hierarchical structures to exist side by side and to alternate with each other. Unity and equality—in the sense of the interplay of all members—are here bound up with polyindividual diversity and abundance.

Powerful and invigorating forms of pluralism are thus just as much to be distinguished from disintegrative and debilitating forms as are forms of individualism that enrich community from forms that destroy it. The plurality that constitutes the unity of the Spirit does not mean simply the infinite diversity of individual human beings in their respective uniqueness.[54] The promises of the Spirit of righteousness, the pouring out of the Spirit, the Pentecost account, and the statements about the gifts of the Spirit take as their starting points *typical differences* that are bound together by the Spirit: old and young, rich and poor, socially privileged and subordinated men and women of various religious, national, and cultural backgrounds.[55] To be sure, such a multitude tends toward a diversity of individuality that cannot be taken in from any one perspective. Yet at the same time this multitude is characterized by solid, undeniable commonalities and by regularities that can be revised only with great difficulty, if at all. Admittedly, talk of "the individuality" of people whose services the Spirit enlists can generate the appearance of an almost arbitrary conformity of persons

---

53. Cf. §§5.2–5.5 and 6.2.

54. Thus evidently—like many others—Congar, *"He Is Lord and Giver of Life,"* 16ff.

55. See §§3.1, 3.3, 3.4, and 5.1ff.

one to another. It can generate the appearance that it is "individuals" who are being changed. Yet what is crucial to note here is a realism that our cultures are only laboriously beginning to learn.

For instance, many of common sense's theories and postures of consciousness regard me as a free individual, infinitely capable of dialogue and correspondingly capable of undergoing change ("subject," "ego," "person," and whatever other concepts are mixed together). Yet the undeniable truth is that I am an aging, white, Protestant man shaped by the German and North American systems of education, belonging to an extremely affluent society and to a people that has achieved many cultural, intellectual, and economic successes, a people that has taken on corresponding positions of leadership and that has seriously discredited itself on a long-term basis through a history, not yet relegated to the distant past in international memory, of political demonism and culpable collective callousness and brutality. In my thought, speech, and action, I may or may not take account of all these specifications, which some people share with me fully while others share them to a large extent or in part. I may or may not take them into account, but I cannot eliminate them. Over and over again I am legitimately regarded and defined in terms of them. These are specifications that impose innumerable limits on my "free individuality." If I do not want to develop an unrealistic self-relation, I must heed these specifications. I must examine carefully the extent to which these boundaries influence and mark not only myself as a concrete individual, but also my general view and statements about "the individual," "the person," the good, the rational, the timely, indeed even what is "willed by God." I must learn to grasp the fact that due to this given framework, there are many people with whom I am capable of dialogue only with great effort, if at all. I must learn to grasp the fact that due to this given framework, there are many people for whom I am unworthy of dialogue, at least as things now stand.

In comparison with the illusion of an infinite capacity for communication and an infinite worthiness of communication,[56] the

---

56. N. Luhmann's critique of J. Habermas is helpful in coming to a recognition of this illusion. See J. Habermas and N. Luhmann, *Theorie der Gesellschaft oder Sozialtechnologie—Was leistet die Systemforschung?* (Frankfurt am Main: Suhrkamp, 1971), esp. 398ff.

"pluralism of the Spirit" is more realistic and more modest. The promises of the pouring out of the Spirit give witness to a specific sensitivity to differences. They discern typical traits of individuals that either establish or hinder "natural" commonality. By doing so they require realistic evaluations of self and other. At the same time they require the distinction between creaturely wealth, which is to be retained, and differences generated by unrighteousness, which are to be done away with. The unity of the Spirit becomes a reality not by imposing an illusory homogeneity, but by cultivating creaturely differences and by removing unrighteous differences.

This implies anything but the position that all differences should or could be reinforced, and that everything should or could continue as it has been. It is natural for us to learn. We change not only by means of conversations, but also by means of other experiences, not mediated through conversation. We automatically grow older. Our history also grows older. Positions of leadership and claims to leadership change. In addition to these natural and not undramatic changes, it accords with the promised Spirit of righteousness that wrong be steadily replaced by right; that economic, social, and cultural inequality and subordination be removed; and that the consciousness of God's distance be overcome by the knowledge of God. Yet all this cannot and should not occur apart from an awareness of difference and a sensitivity to difference. Realistic, honest, self-critical, penitent renewal, not idealistic and moral skimming over the surface, is what accords with the action of the Spirit. In our cultures it is still difficult for us to respond to the action of the Spirit in a way that is sensitive to difference. We should and must change the uncontrolled generalizations made from a specific, typical perspective. These generalizations are perhaps subjectively well-intentioned, but objectively they cause distortion. Such generalizations must be corrected by a diversity of experiences, visions, search movements, and expectations of salvation and deliverance. This diversity must be "in tune" and must be retuned in each new situation. There is no getting around the effort involved in laboring for the emergence of ever-new forms of the "unity of the Spirit," in waiting for this emergence and in praying for it.

The action of God's Spirit is pluralistic for the sake of God's righteousness, for the sake of God's mercy, and for the sake of the full testimony to God's plenitude and glory. Yet this pluralism can be replaced by a "pluralism" in name only, a dangerous phenomenon that generates illusions and masks them at the same time. This happens when the typical multitude that aims at individuality is replaced by the individualism of abstract equality or by unlimited individualism with its empty and shallow emphasis on the mere uniqueness of "the individual."

Both these abstract forms of individualism generate the false appearance of realized equality. They generate a "social atomism," a disintegrative situation of which it is impossible to get an overview. Both forms of individualism have in common that they generate the false appearance of an endless capacity for dialogue and for change. The clouds of indeterminacy swallow up tall promises about full equality and the change of individuals and "structures" at will by means of dialogue, trust, and a willingness to learn. The pluralism of the Spirit makes it possible to see through this illusion. Men do not become women and women do not become men. The young do of course become old, but the old do not become young. The oppressed who have been liberated must also live with their history of suffering. These factors, as well as racial and national background and location in a specific phase of historical development, impose considerable limits on the capacity for dialogue (not only subjectively, but especially, in diverse ways, from outside). It is necessary to pay heed to limits that are creaturely and enriching as well as to those that are unrighteous and oppressive. It is necessary to pay heed to limitations that are good and bad, salutary and isolating, liberating and demonic.

The search for a quick way out of this situation is understandable. It is understandable because this situation compels permanent self-criticism and the acceptance of finitude. It is understandable because this situation brings with it the impossibility of acquiring an overview of that which is alive. It is understandable because this situation brings with it the exertion involved in having to seek out righteousness in constantly new ways. Human beings have great difficulty tolerating this social complexity. Again and again the attempt is made to find the connecting link that is ultimately *common to all:* definitions are offered of "the" human person, "the" subject, "the" one universal history, "the" encompassing structure of intersubjectivity, "the" lifeworld, "the" conflicts, "the" requirements of morality, "the" threat to humankind. That is the beginning of either vain attempts or successful campaigns to gain wider currency for ideological patterns and structures.

By contrast, many societies today have by their conscious choice of pluralism demonstrated at least a vague sense of the action of the Spirit. Admittedly, they have frequently fostered that apparent, dissociative "pluralism" which is destroyed by individualism, which results in the dissolution of all forms, and which wields the weapons of ideology and power politics in its fight for specific portions of consciousness and definitions of reality. With a minimum of theological instinct, theologies and church leaders have, on the basis of a simplistic understanding of "unity" (e.g., monohierarchical unity), condemned pluralism as if it were a unitary phenomenon. In so doing they have demonstrated an absence of the power to distinguish between individually disintegrative pluralism and the life-enhancing, invigorating pluralism of the Spirit.[57] Theologies and churches have reacted sensitively to individualism, as the success story of "existential interpretation" makes clear. They have thrown open the door to the abstract and indeterminate "individual." In doing so they have made room for illusory political and moral postures, as well as for many of the processes of a profound societal self-endangerment and self-destruction.

---

57. The theologies of F. Schleiermacher and of D. Bonhoeffer present, each in their own way, famous exceptions. For Schleiermacher see esp. *The Christian Faith*, trans. D. M. Baillie et al., ed. H. R. Mackintosh and J. S. Stewart (Edinburgh: T. and T. Clark, 1928), §§121ff. For Bonhoeffer see, e.g., *Communion of Saints*, 55ff. and 117. Important new approaches have been developed by J. B. Cobb, *Christ in a Pluralistic Age* (Philadelphia: Westminster, 1975); and D. Tracy, *The Analogical Imagination: Christian Theology and the Culture of Pluralism* (New York: Crossroad, 1981). Both thinkers are distinguished by conscious openness to ecumenical, intercultural, and interreligious dialogues. To be sure, they both also suffer from unrealistic estimates of the subjective and objective capacity for dialogue. Cobb presupposes an only weakly defined "creative transformation" and capacity for transformation of human beings. See M. Welker, *Universalität Gottes und Relativität der Welt: Theologische Kosmologie im Dialog mit dem amerikanischen Prozessdenken nach Whitehead*, 2d ed. (Neukirchen-Vluyn: Neukirchener, 1988), 192ff. In spite of more promising directions suggested in Tracy's own work, he uses the old scheme of "God-self-world" over and over again. He works from correspondingly abstract concepts of "the conversation" and from indeterminately concretized conceptions of individual participants in this conversation. On the difficulty of grasping the interconnection between pluralism and "universal validity," see T. Rendtorff, *Vielspältiges: Protestantische Beiträge zur ethischen Kultur* (Stuttgart: Kohlhammer, 1991), e.g., 262.

1.5: God the Spirit, the self-endangerment of modern societies, and "postmodern" sensibility

God's Spirit is the power and might of God in which in constantly new ways people are rescued and led out of distress and danger, out of demonic possession, and above all out of diverse forms of self-endangerment and self-destruction.

From early on, God's Spirit has been experienced as a power that exercises deliverance by means of appearances and processes that are difficult to grasp—appearances and processes that can be termed "emergent."[58] In the midst of disintegration, the Spirit restores community in an unexpected, improbable way. The Spirit connects human beings, interweaving them in an unforeseen manner in diverse structural patterns of life. The Spirit is "poured out" on human beings in diverse structural patterns of life. The Spirit comes bringing life "from all sides." Thus the Spirit heals and revives human hearts and human societies, causing them to grow together anew. The Spirit restores and strengthens communities of creaturely solidarity. The Spirit produces communities of faith and hope among the living and the dead. These

---

58. See esp. §§2.1, 2.2, 2.4, 3.5, 4.2, 5.1, 6.2, and 6.3. The concept of emergence has already been introduced into the discussion by A. N. Whitehead, S. Alexander, and L. Morgan. Although not particularly easy to handle (see N. Luhmann, *Soziale Systeme: Grundriss einer allgemeinen Theorie* [Frankfurt am Main: Suhrkamp, 1984], 43–44, 157, 650, 658, and passim), the concept has been acquiring increasing significance. Picking up on the work of Whitehead, G. H. Mead defined emergence as "the presence of things in two or more different systems, in such a fashion that its presence in a later system changes its character in the earlier system or systems to which it belongs" (G. H. Mead, *The Philosophy of the Present*, ed. A. E. Murphy (La Salle, Ill.: Open Court, 1959], 69; cf. 10ff., 35ff., 65ff.). I characterize as "emergent" those constellations, conditions, and structures whose appearance on the scene cannot be derived from preceding constellations, conditions, and structures, although diverse elements that define both conditions persist in them. From the perspective of emergent levels of reality, "the world is seen anew," to borrow the phrase of N. Luhmann (*Soziale Systeme*, 658). The past world and the former identity of the elements involved in the process of emergence are also seen anew. And one must add that there is also nothing at all left over.

In the realm of theology, P. Tillich tried in an admittedly metaphysical pneumatology to bring to bear the substance of the phenomenon of emergence. See his talk of "the appearance of a new dimension of life" (*Systematic Theology* 3 [Chicago: Univ. of Chicago Press, 1963], 25ff.).

communities are realities, even if they sometimes surpass contemporary and finite conceptual capacities.

Modern societies are destroying their cultural environments with enormous speed and putting themselves in serious jeopardy through a process of systematic internal dissociation. Yet it is not obvious to a casual observer that they are in pressing need of the emergent action of the Spirit. With their markets and media, modern societies have developed what amount to substitute forms that seem to render superfluous any action of God's Spirit. In an environment that can produce apparently corresponding effects with supposedly readily controllable substitute forms, the Spirit and its action are easily dismissed as an illusion.

Modern societies have developed challenging forms for optimizing and accelerating the powerful spread of those societies: the functional differentiation of their dominant subsystems; mass media communication, especially that of the electronic mass media; and a narcissistic individualism that allows the individual human being to produce extreme behavioral combinations of refusal and adaptation.

Among the general sociological knowledge of our day is the recognition that modern societies are distinguished from earlier societies by the "functional differentiation" of their most important subsystems.[59] In other words, in these societies, subregions such as economy, law, religion, education, and family seek to become increasingly independent in relation to the other subsystems. They seek to do so, and must seek to do so, precisely to improve the way in which they execute their functions on behalf of "the whole" of society.[60] They increase their competence and efficiency by rendering their basic operations and their forms of understanding more precise, by limiting their extension

---

59. Thus—picking up on E. Durkheim, T. Parsons, and others—N. Luhmann, "Gesellschaft," in *Soziologische Aufklärung: Aufsätze zur Theorie sozialer Systeme* 1 (Opladen: Westdeutscher Verlag, 1971), 146ff. This insight is repeated as a sort of "sociological credo" in most of Luhmann's numerous publications.

60. See N. Luhmann, *Ecological Communication*, trans. J. Bednarz, Jr. (Chicago: Univ. of Chicago Press, 1989), 48–49: "On one hand, functional differentiation is possible only through the *rejection of redundancy*. Function systems cannot step in for, replace or even simply relieve one another. . . . Politics cannot take the place of science, nor can science the place of law—and so forth for all relations between systems. The old, multifunctional institutions and moralitites are, therefore, dissolved and replaced by a coordination of specific codes to specific systems that distinguishes modern society from all those before it."

in many respects, by loosening or even doing away with the interconnections among themselves, and above all by giving up the orientation to an overarching, hierarchical order. The society no longer has a middle, a center. It is organized and perceived polycentrically. It is obvious that the tasks that are important to the whole society do not culminate in a central task. Rather, a plurality of system-relative perceptions of "the whole," "the most important factor," and "the central factor" are operating side by side, interwoven more or less clearly and well.

It is difficult for so-called common sense and for supposedly healthy moral feeling to go beyond the external recognition of this fact to letting it orient their lives. Both of them lose the capacity to get an overview of "the whole," "society" in the singular, "reality" in the singular, "social life" in the singular, and so on. Both of them lose the capacity to communicate about such things. "As a consequence of this development the societal *interconnection* of these problems becomes too abstract and too complex to continue to be institutionalized in the form of a common consciousness that knows itself as common."[61]

Societal development uses the institution of *mass media communication* as a massive means of counteracting functional differentiation and the attendant loss of an encompassing common consciousness. With the help of mass media communication, societies maintain the fiction of "the" public sphere and of the "unity" of the public sphere. They maintain the illusion that processes in the world are under the control of common sense and of tried and true moralities.[62] Yet as a matter of fact the functionally differentiated society decomposes the unity of the public sphere into a plurality of publics that develop different guiding interests and different forms of understanding.[63] Mass

---

61. Luhmann, "Gesellschaft," 147. Concerning the consequences of differentiation for religion, see N. Luhmann, *Funktion der Religion* (Frankfurt am Main: Suhrkamp, 1977), 50ff.; N. Luhmann, *Religious Dogmatics and the Evolution of Societies,* trans. P. Beyer, Studies in Religion and Society 9 (New York: Edwin Mellen, 1984), 28ff.

62. See the chapter on "Die massenmediale Realitätsunterstellung und ihre Gefahren," in M. Welker, *Kirche ohne Kurs?: Aus Anlass der EKD-Studie "Christsein gestalten"* (Neukirchen-Vluyn: Neukirchener, 1987), 35ff.

63. D. Tracy has taken this to heart with regard to theology. By consciously distinguishing three publics (society, academy, and church), he has defined more precisely the tasks of theology (*Analogical Imagination,* 6ff.).

media communication and popular common sense form only two of many types of public spheres. This state of affairs becomes clear in common sense's painful awareness that it can no longer understand and influence economic processes, intellectual developments, displacements in family life and in morals, and many other things. Or if it can understand and influence them, it can do so only in a wholly inadequate manner. Yes, the mass media achieve the truly amazing by way of a concoction of "reality" in the singular that is palatable to the dominant common sense. Yes, the mass media give plausibility and sensual immediacy to a "world" that to a large extent is incomprehensible and remains uncomprehended. And yes, in many individual cases the reflection and control exercised by the mass media have a powerful capability to effect political changes. Yet in spite of all this, mass media communication cannot stop common sense and public moralities from becoming more and more powerless.[64]

It would be cynical to condemn this feeling of powerlessness as only the expression of insatiable curiosity and of an unsatisfied search for control and domination on the part of the "average citizen" in a world whose quantum leaps in cultural complexity make it impossible to satisfy that curiosity and that search for control and domination. It would be frivolous to despise the dream of a transparent unity of reality that could be taken in with one grand sweep of vision. It would be frivolous to despise the dream of having what is "central" and essential so near that its shape could be controlled, or at least of being able to regulate the world by means of moral appeals to "the public sphere." It would be frivolous to despise these dreams—dreams that are nourished by the three forms of religious thought that continue to predominate even to this day.[65] It would be frivolous to despise them, for the

---

64. The mass media can claim great accomplishments in giving sensual immediacy to highly complex states of affairs. The mass media can also score momentary "political" successes. But this must not lead us to overlook the still larger illusion that the mass media generate by their widespread and palpably near presence. The illusion they generate is that of a public sphere so near that it can be touched and accordingly influenced, while at the same time it is universal ("the" public sphere). The detailed treatment of mass media communication belongs in a theology of law, since the mass media are primarily secular equivalents of cultic life.

65. See §1.6.

functional differentiation that today is naively accepted or even celebrated brings with it thoroughly dangerous consequences.

The world that is defined by the functional differentiation of
modern societies—a world that is integrated in a largely fictional
manner by mass media and by conventional forms of being religious,
and one that escapes the control of common sense and of public
morality—this world is threatened in the most massive way. It is not
threatened primarily from without, but rather from within.[66] The danger to which modern societies expose themselves can be characterized
as "systematically generated and systematically intensified helplessness." It is typical of modern, functionally differentiated societies to
experience a steadily and systematically intensified helplessness in the
face of dangers unleashed by the destruction and devastation of their
environments. Not only are natural and cultural environments laid
waste with great speed and power; not only are the repercussions of
this destruction enormous for the societies involved. Modern society
has to a large extent incapacitated itself and rendered itself powerless
by means of its functional differentiation and by generating public fictions of control and of regulatory measures being taken to counteract
this functional differentiation.

On the basis of a clear vision of the character of modern society,
Niklas Luhmann has responded with great skepticism to the question:
"Can modern society respond to ecological dangers?"[67] What is the
reason for his skepticism? Not only do the dominant subsystems of
society (economy, law, religion, science,[68] politics, and so on) in all
their operations carry out important functions for the society as a
whole. Whether it be economy, law, science, politics, or another subsystem, in each of its operations it constitutes, confirms, and solidifies

---

66. Concerning the classical fixation on dangers and threats "from without"
and the corresponding blindness to self-imposed dangers, see Welker, *Kirche ohne
Kurs?* 29ff.; M. Welker, "The Self-Jeopardizing of Human Societies and Whitehead's
Conception of Peace," trans. J. Hoffmeyer, *Soundings* 70 (1987): 309ff.

67. Luhmann, *Ecological Communication*, 115–20.

68. "Science" is a notoriously poor translation of the German *Wissenschaft*,
since "science" is often used with the limited reference of the "natural sciences."
The German word gives no such preference to that particular branch of knowing, to
that particular *scientia*, but refers equally to physics and philosophy, chemistry and
art history—TRANS.

itself as a subsystem, marks out its boundaries in relation to other subsystems, and works against a simple, comprehensive continuum of perception and understanding. If a subsystem tries to get an action or reaction of the "whole society" off the ground—perhaps in a situation of imminent and considerable danger for the whole society—as a rule the subsystem generates at best a diffuse mood of alarm in the other subsystems. In Luhmann's words, it elicits not "resonance," but "noise."

Take, for example, a "movement for. . ./ against . . ." controlled by common sense and by a general morality. The desired object of that movement cannot be politically or judicially implemented. Or it is economically impractical, or cannot be institutionalized in the education system. What is possible judicially does not make sense to the general moral consciousness, or cannot be executed politically because it is economically difficult to make into a reality, and so on. The mutual hindrances and impediments are numerous. They cannot, however, simply be traced back to malice, shortsightedness, convenience, or other factors open to moral qualification and influence. Rather they are grounded in forms of perception and understanding that typify the particular subsystem at issue, while these forms themselves are inseparable from the forms in which this subsystem organizes and maintains itself.

On the basis of the perspectivally correct perception that its own function is indispensable to society as a whole, the particular subsystem in any given case will value self-preservation and self-optimization as highly as preservation of society as a whole—to the extent that it is capable of perceiving at all the problems of preserving society as a whole. It will locate the risks to itself and the continuation and optimization of its own functions on the same level as the perceived risks to the preservation of society as a whole—which at any rate are perceived only from a limited perspective. Thus in politics an electoral campaign is contested as if a decision about the survival of society as a whole were at stake. For the economy, an economic collapse is tantamount to a collapse of "everything." For education, when the quality of education is endangered the quality of life and the survival capacity of the society as a whole are at stake. And so forth.

The situation is complicated by the fact that for common sense, two real states of affairs—along with fictions such as those generated by the mass media—nourish the illusion that the interconnections of society as a whole can be regulated. These states of affairs are the *de facto collaboration* of the various subsystems and the fact that human beings are, after all, *simultaneously present* in various subsystems.[69] Yet it is important to make a distinction. The de facto collaboration of the functional realms and, beyond that, the momentary technical coordination that meets with steady success, are not the same as an effective, practical regulation of society as a whole. In the face of society's endangering itself in a massive way by means of steadily accumulating risks and increasing environmental destruction, common sense launches the appeal for basic countermeasures and a basic change of course. But the technically interwoven interaction brings about aimless, "emergent" structural changes at best. In addition to the directly desired "solution," this interaction results in countless contingent, undesired effects that may either strengthen each other or incapacitate each other. In all that, it attains the illusion of help, while the reality is one of continued helplessness in the midst of progressive self-endangerment.[70]

No less helpless is the attempt to stake one's money on the presence of "the human person," the free individual in various societal subsystems, and to expect from this alone a "rational," moral, or other countermeasure against the self-endangerment of modern societies. This approach is an illusion. It fails to see that it is not specific, typical, tangible individuals who have brought society into its forms and directions of development. Rather, individuals have been pressed from all sides toward accommodation to modern, differentiated society.[71] It

---

69. Cf. S. Brandt's exemplary analysis and critique of E. Herms, *Erfahrbare Kirche: Beiträge zur Ekklesiologie* (Tübingen: Mohr, 1990): Brandt, "Kirche als System? Zu den Theoriegrundlagen von Eilert Herms' Buch *Erfahrbare Kirche*," *EvT* 51 (1991): 296ff.

70. This has been acutely observed with regard to the sphere of public morality by C. Lasch, *The Minimal Self: Psychic Survival in Troubled Times* (New York: W. W. Norton, 1984), esp. 253ff. Lasch attempts to counteract the "pathology of purposefulness" and the "cult of technique" with a concept that tries "to restore the intermediate world of practical activity" (255–56).

71. On this point and on the mistaken psychologizing of problems configured at the level of society as a whole, an instructive work is R. Sennett, *The Fall of Public Man* (Cambridge: Cambridge Univ. Press, 1974). "It could be said that people are losing the 'will' to act socially, or that they are losing the 'desire.' These words as

is, of course, trivially correct that an infinite abundance of individuals confirms, solidifies, and continues a society. This occurs, however, in uncontrollable and opaque forms of interplay. Under the conditions of modern society, this interplay triggers not only intended and desired effects, but also countless unintended effects and disagreeable repercussions. For this interplay, to whose various conditions we are to a large extent still blind, modern society has *fashioned a type of individuality* that corresponds to itself. Some of the most acute diagnosticians of those societies that are currently dominant call this type of individuality *narcissistic.* [72]

We have already considered functional differentiation and fictions, nourished by the mass media, religion, or in other ways, that suggest it is possible to get an overview of and to control "the whole" or "the" public sphere. Adding to these the narcissistic type of individuality, we have three readily coordinated factors in the self-endangerment of modern societies.

Predicates such as "self-involvement," "selfishness," "egoism," "hedonism," and "being in love with oneself" do not even present a successful caricature of the narcissistic personality structure. The narcissistic human being is searching for himself—and with the best of intentions *cannot* find himself. The narcissistic person relates himself—seeking and fleeing—to a disintegrated, empty self. [73] The narcissistic person seeks to constitute himself in the futile search for himself—every self-definition is shallow and inadequate—and in the futile flight from himself—every dismissal of self-definitions remains incomplete and does not lead to the imagined purity and fullness of

---

pure psychological states mislead because they do not explain how a whole society could lose its will together, or change its desires. They further mislead in suggesting a therapeutic solution, to shake people out of this self-absorption—as if the environment which has eroded their social will and transformed their desires might suddenly welcome changed individuals with open arms" (ibid., 26).

72. Thus ibid.; C. Lasch, *The Culture of Narcissism* (New York: W. W. Norton, 1978); Lasch, *Minimal Self*, 18ff., 57ff., 178ff.

73. Therefore Lasch has correctly observed that "narcissism signifies a loss of selfhood, not self-assertion. It refers to a self threatened with disintegration and by a sense of inner emptiness." He thus proposes, for additional clarity, that the "culture of narcissism" also be characterized as a "culture of survivalism" (Lasch, *Minimal Self*, 57).

identity. In the process the narcissist achieves extreme combinations of conformity and the refusal to conform. Perhaps he does so by quickly changing roles. Perhaps he does so by living with sharply conflicting expectations for himself, or with expectations that are both incompatible and unalterable. Perhaps he does so by consciously accumulating risks and anxieties. Diverse conflicting and ephemeral self-definitions and the refusal to accept integration characterize the narcissistic personality. Addiction, the Faustian lurching from desire to enjoyment and the languishing for desire in enjoyment, is only a decadent and reductionist form of the characteristics that define the narcissistic human being. He comes to grief in addiction, in that he ends his eccentric path in quicksand.

The ultimate point of reference to which the narcissistic personality clings for stability is "inner feeling," and this means nothing other than the individual's own condensed and self-involved lack of a stable point of reference. Fear of death and compulsive movement, trademarks of modern consciousness,[74] become concentrated in the feeling of "the fear of closure" and in the feeling of "blankness."[75] The narcissistic person is at the same time continually searching for himself and continually fleeing from being tied to his self-definition. He relies on his naked feelings for the very reason that they always dance around him, they always dance him around in such a way that his life's eccentric trajectory is not disturbed. The narcissistic person believes that his feelings have counseled him well precisely when they suggest that he avoid "an engagement in worldly experience[s] beyond [his] control."[76] This means nothing other than that only what is compatible with the basic uncontrollability of the narcissistic self is acceptable before the court of feeling.

So it is that the narcissistic person remains trapped in instability. In this instability and in his solitary, self-willed withdrawal from the world, he can try to find in the emptiness of his own self only fleeting

---

74. See D. Henrich, "Die Grundstruktur der modernen Philosophie," in H. Ebeling, ed., *Subjektivität und Selbsterhaltung: Beiträge zur Diagnose der Moderne* (Frankfurt am Main: Suhrkamp, 1976), 97ff., 102ff.

75. Sennett, *Fall of Public Man*, 335.

76. Ibid., 334, further developing thoughts of M. Weber.

moments of self-stabilization.[77] Ephemeral self-stabilization in repulsion and in transition—it is precisely in the context of a diverse, always transitory presence in conflicting subsystems of society that unfathomable feeling can "integrate" the "true" identity that in every situation is always holding itself back, always pulling out.[78] Helpless and unstable, this person corresponds to the reality of modern differentiated society. He conforms himself to it, as he is made to fit into its form. He "leaves his mark" on it, as he is recursively marked by it in experiences of confirmation and of disappointment.

"Postmodern" ecological sensibility is a reaction to this situation of a self-endangerment governed by several factors. This sensibility is trying to grasp the emergent developments, reciprocally strengthening and reciprocally blocking each other, which come from a variety of environments. This requires some explanation. The name "postmodern" has been given to a culture and to a posture of consciousness that attempt to see through, or are able to grasp, the differentiated realities and forms of consciousness created by modern society. The expression has been connected with hopes to "find the key" to modernity, and to leave modernity behind by recognizing and changing the paradigm. Theories or intellectual positions are called "postmodern"[79] if they abandon the assumption of the "unity of reality" and of the "unity of experience." Into its place steps a different assumption, one that is sensitive to differences. This is the assumption of a "reality" or realities that consist of a plurality of structural

---

77. Theological critics of the "autonomy of the modern ego" have overestimated this achievement and, contrary to their intention, have glorified it in their critique. See, for example, F. Gogarten's most mature exposition of "modern self-consciousness" and of the self-understanding of modernity, *Die Verkündigung Jesu Christi: Grundlagen und Aufgabe* (Tübingen: Mohr, 1948), 405ff., 454ff. Cf. my analysis and critique of Gogarten and Tillich in M. Welker, *Der Vorgang Autonomie: Philosophische Beiträge zur Einsicht in theologischer Rezeption und Kritik* (Neukirchen-Vluyn: Neukirchener, 1975), 129ff., 154ff.

78. Feeling thus mediates the basic traits that E. Goffman defines as "the individual as a vehicular unit and as a participation unit" (*Relations in Public: Microstudies of the Public Order* [New York: Basic Books, 1971], 27 and passim).

79. The expression was already being used in the early 1970s in North American process theology and process philosophy: e.g., Cobb, *Christ in a Pluralistic Age*, 25ff., 244.

patterns of life and of interconnected events—structural patterns that
are partially compatible and partially incompatible with each other.[80]

For postmodern consciousness, the cheap moralism of breezy,
"totalizing" dicta (One world—or no world!) is a thing of the past.
Postmodern consciousness has also abandoned the attempt to grasp
"reality" in the singular by means of indeterminate or determinate
forms of unification (totality of meaning, universal history) or by
means of mere dichotomizations (reality is marked by the "subject-
object split"). Postmodern consciousness considers and assesses these
forms as more or less ineffectual efforts to gain orientation in a situation for which no one perspective affords an overview (a situation con-
sisting of a plurality of systems of reference that in part overlap and in
part are incompatible with each other). Postmodern consciousness is
interested not only in complex unity, but equally in the recognition
of *difference*. For it is only through recognizing differences that the
"interwoven order . . . that underlies the process of civilization"[81]—
more precisely, the interwoven orders that underlie it—can be traced.

Postmodern ecological sensibility sees all events and structural
patterns of events in a number of reciprocally strengthening or reciprocally debilitating environments. In the face of the ecological self-
endangerment of modern societies, postmodern ecological sensibility
does not simply evoke the revenge of "the" environment. This sensibility does not advise global attempts to take our orientation from
"nature" in the singular. (In view of the complexity of "nature," such
attempts can only entail dangerous reductionist approaches or experiences of futility.) Nor does it dream of a "single system of environment
combined with high human civilization."[82]

---

80. Worth reading on this score is J.-F. Lyotard, *The Postmodern Condition: A
Report on Knowledge*, trans. G. Bennington and B. Massumi (Manchester: Man-
chester Univ. Press, 1984); also H. Blumenberg, *Wirklichkeiten, in denen wir leben:
Aufsätze und eine Rede* (Stuttgart: Reclam, 1981).

81. N. Elias, *Über den Prozess der Zivilisation: Soziogenetische und psychogenetis-
che Untersuchungen*, vol. 2, *Wandlungen der Gesellschaft: Entwurf zu einer Theorie der
Zivilisation*, 6th ed. (Frankfurt am Main: Suhrkamp, 1979), 314.

82. G. Bateson, *Steps to an Ecology of Mind* (New York: Ballantine, 1972), 494,
emphasis in original omitted. For a critique of this vague holism, which many well-
intentioned people share with Bateson, see Lasch, *Minimal Self*, 252ff. and passim.
At the level of our current insight, "nature" in the singular does no more than

Postmodern ecological sensibility looks for the interwoven dangers that arise out of various environments and contexts of events. But it also looks for the resources that counteract the processes of disintegration and destruction. It attempts to perceive, conceive, and prudently influence processes of emergence.[83] A sensibility of this sort can, for example, begin with very concrete, different, yet comparable states of consciousness (for instance, solidarity or refusal of solidarity in typical cases), test the extent of their compass, seek to foster the desired stance, and prepare for analogous developments.[84]

A postmodern sensibility of this type aims at emergent change of the deep structures of personality forms, of moral communication, of educational forms, or of the acquisition of political loyalty.[85] It works toward emergent change, always with the awareness that we live in various forms of reality, structures of legitimacy, moral markets, models of reality, and primary loyalties, and that many people must try to find their way with several moralities, rationalities, and so on, and may also desire to do so.

A theology of the Holy Spirit can be developed better against this background than in the artificial light of an apparently unbroken

---

"culture" in the singular to afford specific instructions for an overall cultural reorientation, although—to avoid any misunderstanding—it certainly does send many concrete signals that require concrete, goal-oriented action and especially the avoidance of destructive practices! Due to that absence of specific instructions, the "holistic path" sooner or later leads back to uncertainty and resignation. This also holds for the consciousness (particularly lovable in many respects) that shapes North American individualism: "We must 'get involved.' " This approach fosters an attitude that admittedly renders individualism problematic by providing a momentary way out of it, but at the same time solidifies and confirms individualism by its continually renewed recourse to the "involved" subject. This is accurately shown by R. Bellah et al., *Habits of the Heart: Individualism and Commitment in American Life* (Berkeley and Los Angeles: Univ. of California Press, 1985), 142ff., esp. 163.

83. See n. 58 above.

84. Thus R. Rorty starts from the question of why some societies at the time of the Third Reich gave stronger support to their fellow human beings who were Jews, while others gave weaker support. He then uses this question to gain insights into the solidarity that can be expected and practiced in modern society (*Contingency, Irony, and Solidarity* [New York: Cambridge Univ. Press, 1989], cf. 190ff.).

85. The works of R. Sennett, C. Lasch, and R. Rorty are to be read in this way. The major works of A. N. Whitehead and N. Luhmann in particular, but also of N. Goodman, are situated on other levels, geared toward knowledge and epistemology.

reality and rationality continuum. It can be better developed against this background than in the midst of an integral moral market or of other powerful ideological devices. For against this background a theology of the Holy Spirit can more clearly call attention to the power that the "primary witnesses"[86] see at work in the very situations where human beings and societies are rent completely asunder, in their dispersion and in the act of their being brought together. These primary witnesses saw God's Spirit at work precisely in the implausible reciprocal mediation of the valid perceptions of reality of persons who were separated and alienated from each other by sexist, social, racist, nationalistic, and religious "systems of order" and "models of reality." This Spirit, this power, this dynamic, the forms of this Spirit's action await new discovery. Postmodern ecological sensibility is less of an obstacle to the recognition of the Spirit's action than are the forms of theological reflection that continue dominant. Postmodern sensibility tries to turn its attention to several environments and to the ways in which they strengthen and hinder each other. It is disposed to perceive processes of emergence and patterns of interweaving in a manner that is sensitive to difference. But the dominant forms of theological reflection have led theology and piety into a threefold Babylonian captivity.

1.6: God the Spirit, the captivity of theology and piety in three forms of thought, and realistic theology

God's Spirit opens the path to the knowledge of God's power through and for creatures. The Spirit is seen in worldwide religious movements. The Spirit universally establishes justice, mercy, and knowledge of God. The Spirit makes this a reality through women and men, female and male slaves, young and old from various cultures and traditions. The Spirit liberates and delivers from distress, possession/obsession, captivity, and disintegration. It is evidently only with great difficulty that the Spirit who does all this can be grasped in the predominant forms of theological reflection in the Western world. The Spirit cannot be grasped in theological models and forms of thought that want to

---

86. See K. Barth, *Evangelical Theology: An Introduction*, trans. G. Foley (New York: Holt, Rinehart and Winston, 1963), 3d lecture.

use *part-whole patterns* as well as uniform or unidirectional, hierarchical conceptions of unity to comprehend and to expound the rich, interdependent action of creatures seized and connected by the Spirit. Only in a fully distorted manner can the Spirit be depicted in theological models and in forms of religious thought that systematically and methodically reduce the rich and complex relation between God and human beings and their fellow creatures to an *I-Thou relation* (in which more complex relationships are always only "implied") between God and "the human person." Finally, the Spirit also cannot be comprehended in the framework of the *conception of a moral market*, in the framework of a community that attempts to govern its further development and its shaping of the world by the attribution or withdrawal of respect.

Of course, the Spirit of God also touches human beings who seek to understand and to shape themselves, each other, and their reality in such forms of thought and experience. But the Spirit removes these forms, steadily relativizes and broadens them, in order to reveal the fullness of God's glory on, through, and for human beings and their fellow creatures. This revelation goes hand in hand with the eagerness to realize a continually deeper and more careful practice of mercy, a righteousness of continually greater integrative power and sensitivity to differences, and a continually clearer knowledge of God.[87]

Christian theology and piety have let themselves be ruled by forms of thought that enjoyed temporary success and plausibility, but in the long run incapacitated Christian theology and piety and blocked their access to the wealth of their own contents and traditions, as well as blocking the access of those outside the Christian tradition. There are three forms of thought that even today rule large parts of Christian theology. Their simplicity and ready plausibility are alluring, and they possess a correspondingly *universal* effectiveness and capacity to win out over competitors.

The first form of thought is the orientation toward *old European metaphysics*, which sees the essential contribution of religion and theology in the fact that they make available and solidify *one* universal system of reference. Theology and thoughtful religious life are supposed to grasp, formulate, and reflect on "the whole" or the "unity of reality"—

---

87. See esp. the biblical traditions presented in §§3.1ff.

under obfuscatory formulas such as "universal history," "totality of meaning," and so on. In doing so, theology shows "the" interconnection, "the" unity, or "the" order in a reality of which it has become impossible to get an overview, a reality that seems to be torn apart. In the course of the twentieth century, common sense has begun to suspect that totalizing conceptions are ideological and to find them intolerable.[88] There has been a growing insight into the fact that even highly abstract totalizing conceptions are determined by interests. This, along with the simple experience that *every* "setting in life" results in its own models of totality and that these perspectival models of totality cannot be integrated according to the parts-whole pattern, has removed almost all credibility from the approach of old European metaphysics. Of course, within the parameters of this approach one can try to understand the Spirit in a "totalizing" manner as a universal force or structure that infuses all reality or surpasses and transcends all reality. In doing so one may indeed appeal to a few statements of the biblical traditions that emphasize the so-called ubiquity of God's Spirit: "The Spirit of the Lord has filled the world, and that which holds all things together knows what is said" (Wisd. of Sol. 1:7); "For your immortal Spirit is in all things" (Wisd. of Sol. 12:1).[89]

Yet this general observation that the Spirit of God infuses everything does not tell us very much. Moreover, it is an untenable position to claim that a force that infuses "everything" is as such a guarantor of "life." *How* are we to mediate these few statements about the Spirit that appear to accord with thought patterns of old European metaphysics, with the numerous passages that make *specific* statements

---

88. See the changes of orientation described in popular form by J. Naisbitt, *Megatrends: Ten New Directions Transforming Our Lives* (New York: Warner, 1984). Classical "large-scale theories" distinguish themselves by, on the one hand, leaving behind the practice of thinking in terms of one system of reference and, on the other hand, still aspiring to universal validity. The attempt to develop such theories in the framework of "natural" language encounters considerable difficulties, as is explained in my article "Hegel and Whitehead: Why Develop a Universal Theory?" trans. J. Hoffmeyer, in G. R. Lucas, Jr., ed., *Hegel and Whitehead: Contemporary Perspectives on Systematic Philosophy* (Albany: SUNY Press, 1986), 121–32.

89. Similarly Ps. 139:7. Psalm 104:29 and Job 34:14-15 are also brought forward as passages that evince a so-called "universal effectiveness" of God's Spirit. But see §§2.5 and 3.5.

about the Spirit and about the Spirit's determinate action? How are we to connect the observation that God's Spirit is *in everything* and effects *everything,* with the recognition that the Spirit is *creatively* effective? Is the "ubiquitous" spirit of old European metaphysical theories the Spirit who has come upon particular human beings in particular situations of distress, who leads to Jesus Christ, and who builds up the church as the body of Christ?

We must first understand the universality of the Spirit and of the Spirit's action from the perspectives of the *various specifications* of the Spirit and of the Spirit's action. Only thus do we reach a level on which we can really relate current cosmological, sociotheoretical, and philosophical questions and problems to the action of God's Spirit.

The orientation toward *dialogical personalism* continues to represent the second of the forms of thought currently dominant in theology and piety. This orientation attempts to comprehend all essential contents of faith, thought, and action in the *I-Thou(-love) correlation.* Theology reflects on and formulates the self-relation of the triune God, the relation of God and human beings, as well as intrahuman relations by taking the readily surveyable form of I-Thou communication and projecting it into all religious and social relations.

This model admittedly has a basis in the biblical traditions. Yet the passages are few that connect the action of *the Spirit* to a genuine situation of I-Thou communication, or even to the alternating pattern of speech and response. This paucity of passages stands in striking contrast to the way in which dialectical theology and its followers turned this constellation into an absolute paradigm.[90] In his later work Karl Barth did indeed perceive this and took some steps toward

---

90. It is worth noting in this context that both Brunner and Gogarten justifiably reproached Barth on the grounds that, without admitting it, he was also doing "natural theology" with his ingenuous assumption of a "subjecthood" of God analogous to human "subjecthood," and with his assumption of a corresponding I-Thou communication in the relation between God and "the human person." See E. Brunner, "Nature and Grace," in P. Fraenkel, trans., *Natural Theology* (London: Geoffrey Bles—Centenary, 1946), 54–55; F. Gogarten, *Gericht oder Skepsis: Eine Streitschrift gegen Karl Barth* (Jena: Diederichs, 1937), 154ff. Barth reacted with uncertainty to Brunner's reproach, saying, "Let the reader decide whether he is right. It was certainly not done purposely or consciously" (K. Barth, "No!: Answer to Emil Brunner," in *Natural Theology,* 128).—Brunner *is* right.

a reorientation, particularly in the doctrine of reconciliation. He attempted precisely with regard to the doctrine of the Holy Spirit to break loose from the dialogistic reduction and imprisonment of theological reflection. Many theologians have taken note of the remarks made by Barth shortly before his death on his relation to Friedrich Schleiermacher. In these remarks, Barth considered the idea that a theology of the Holy Spirit perhaps could bridge the chasm that he saw—we should come right out and say: the chasm that he opened up—between his own theology and Schleiermacher's.[91] Here Barth's instinct was on target. Pneumatology provides a perspective (but so do other doctrinal loci) that requires and makes it possible that the basic formal patterns of dialogistic theology be relativized and broadened, or replaced by more appropriate forms.

The third dominant form of contemporary theological thought is the orientation toward a *social moralism* that brings all experience and action under a pressure to change. It does this by giving a fundamental place to the conception of a process, regulated at both the individual and the community level, which is ruled by a system of gradation in terms of "better" and "worse." This social moralism is undergirded primarily by an *attachment to the idea of progress,* such as the hypothesis that we all (or a specific group of human beings) participate in a process that runs, for example, from bondage to freedom, insofar as everyone (or the members of the appropriate group) behave in a certain way. This pattern of thought developed great cultural influence with Immanuel Kant's work *Religion within the Limits of Reason Alone,* if not earlier.[92] In Left Hegelianism this pattern of thought was further developed in diverse ways. In our day it has developed into probably the most important of the forms of thought employed, either consciously or unconsciously, in Christian theology and piety.

---

91. Cf. K. Barth, "Epilogue," in H. Bolli, ed., *Schleiermacher-Auswahl* (Munich: Siebernstern, 1968), esp. 310–11; Barth, *CD* 4/1, 643ff.; *CD* 4/2, 614ff.; *CD* 4/3, 681ff.; *CD* 4/4, 3ff. With regard to pneumatology, the conceptual captivity of Barth's theology can be most clearly recognized in a formulation that persists throughout his theology: the Holy Spirit supposedly has to do with the "subjective side" or with the "subjective realization" of reconciliation.

92. I. Kant, *Religion within the Limits of Reason Alone,* trans. T. M. Greene and H. H. Hudson (Chicago: Open Court, 1934).

Among other reasons, this form of theological reflection has become so effective, and of all three dominant forms stands nearest to a theological pneumatology, because it allows very general and at the same time very specific statements to be made about the interconnection between God's action and human participation in that action. Thus it can encompass abstract and speculative statements not intended in a moral sense, for example, that we human beings are given a part in the movement from God to God; that in this movement we are drawn into "relationally rich differentiation from . . . God"; and that in this permanent process of becoming, both distinct from God and related to God, we are becoming "ever more human," or more precisely, "peculiarly human."[93]

Without changing this pattern of thought, one can abandon the level of abstract universality and proceed to levels of the *perception of specific conflicts*. Suppose one starts with the concern that the process of becoming peculiarly human should be concretized and distinguished from an infinite process that sails off into what is merely peculiar, or tails off into the indeterminate and the numinous. To meet this concern, the pattern of "progressive becoming" can be filled in with specific themes and correspondingly moralized. The selection of perceptions of specific conflicts can be dictated by a person and life history, by the person's social environment, by particular themes of the media, but also by whatever happen to be the predominant moral, ecological, and theological sensibilities. This form, which is uncommonly many-sided in the aspects it can assume, and which can prove its worth equally in the culture of an academic elitism and as the motive power of a neighborhood initiative—this form can be designated "social moralism."

In comparison with the other dominant forms of thought, the orientation toward social moralism has distinguished itself by its possibilities for hooking up with the theology of law, by its openness to

---

93. E. Jüngel, *God as the Mystery of the World: On the Foundation of the Theology of the Crucified One in the Dispute between Theism and Atheism*, trans. D. L. Guder (Grand Rapids: Eerdmans, 1983), 395–96. Jüngel himself of course does not intend for this process of increasing humanity to be grounded and understood in a moral sense. Rather he fits it into a dialogistic pattern (the relation between God and "the" human person).

pluralistic structures, and by other forms of conceptual superiority. Yet it shares their difficulties in showing that the righteousness, peace, and freedom to be attained in each particular case are in fact the righteousness wrought by the *Spirit of God,* the peace given by the *Holy Spirit,* and the freedom that is *in the Spirit.* To what extent is it the Holy Spirit who is at work in the imagined and initiated processes, and not a form of common sense, a form of moral sensibility, a normal measure of humanity and sympathy, or a simple feeling for right and wrong, for what engenders conflict and what prevents it, or for oppressive and liberating structures and forms of life? Or is the Holy Spirit only a way of expressing this sensibility, this humanity? Is it only an obfuscatory formula for this sensibility? Is it perhaps only an official title that is supposed to lend some emphasis to the concerns of the well-meaning and devout when the less well-meaning and devout do not take righteousness, peace, and freedom as seriously and as scrupulously?

In other words, is there a *reality of the Spirit* that makes itself knowable in the midst of processes of moral communication? Is there a recognizable reality of the Spirit that clearly mediates God's presence to us, that is capable of giving us an orientation in our difficulties of understanding and in the real conflicts of our lives? How can we gain theological access to this reality of the Spirit? What consequences does such access have for the certainty of God's presence, for our theological reflection, and for our life in the church and in the world?

Realistic theology undertakes the attempt to give a definite answer to these questions without sliding back into the other forms of thought. What is meant by the programmatic term *realistic theology*?

First, a realistic theology is a theology that consciously takes seriously the various biblical traditions with their differing "settings in life"—traditions whose experiences and expectations sometimes stand in continuity and sometimes do not, sometimes are compatible with each other and sometimes cannot be directly mediated with each other.[94] Realistic theology assumes that no human experience is in control of "God *as such,*" but rather that God mediates God's revelation in diverse human attestations to God's presence. Since these are *human*

---

94. See D. Ritschl, " 'Wahre,' 'reine' oder 'neue' biblische Theologie? Anfragen zur neueren Diskussion um 'Biblische Theologie,' " in *Konzepte: Ökumene, Medizin, Ethik: Gesammelte Aufsätze* (Munich: Kaiser, 1986), 111ff.

attestations, they are endangered by obstruction, error, and lies. Insofar as they refer to God, they can also, in diverse ways, reciprocally challenge and strengthen each other and provide an initiation into a clearer knowledge of God.

Second, a realistic theology is one that in constantly new ways examines past, present, and future experiences and expectations of God, testing them for interconnections and for differences. In this process the development of a sensitivity to differences and discontinuities is hardly less important than interest in continuities and forms of unity. The orientation toward the biblical traditions has its material foundation here insofar as they present a highly differentiated and complex interconnection of testimonies to God's presence and action—an interconnection that has been tested in a diversity of ways for authenticity, continuity, and fruitfulness of differences.

Third, a realistic theology is one that in the process of paying attention to these interconnections and differences of experiences and expectations of God, concentrating on the "primary testimonies" of the biblical traditions and the secondary testimonies in our cultures, wants to let the experienced or expected *reality* of God come forward in ever-new ways.

With regard to metaphysical "totalization," this means that a realistic theology gives up the illusion that a single system of reference could put God and God's power at our disposal. God acts neither only in those particular structural patterns of life that are "ours," nor only in abstract generalizations of those structural patterns. God does not fit into metaphysical constructs that we have designed in harmony with important characteristics of our structural patterns of life. Rather God's vitality and God's freedom are expressed in a plurality of contexts and structural patterns of life, including ones that are not automatically compatible with each other. The theology of the Holy Spirit is concerned with the criteria of the coherence and clarity of this knowledge of God.

With regard to the dialogistic approach, this means that a realistic theology gives up the illusion of being able to exhaust God's reality according to individually concretized conceptions of intimacy and to the abstractions constructed on them (I-Thou model). A realistic theology also criticizes the untenable attempt to broaden and to improve the I-Thou model by contrasting it and "dialectically" mediating it with naive conceptions of objectivity (subject-object model). The subject-object model cannot even manage a reconstruction of the extrareligious comprehension of reality, because it leaves reality and objectivity underdetermined.[95] To be sure, the I-Thou and subject-object models, simplistic on many fronts, owe their careers to the insight that theology supposedly must talk in this way about God and that this way of talking can cover the simplest experiential patterns of life as it is really lived. Yet especially in the languishing so-called mainline churches, it is high time to recognize that even the most elementary perception of the world cannot be grasped and reconstructed by means of person-to-person relations, or by contrasting such relations with those between a person and an object of perception. It is a mistake to think that all good theology must remain within the two-sided formal pattern of "God and 'the human person.' "[96]

With regard to social moralism, this means that a realistic theology gives up the illusion—in our day probably the most difficult to give up—that confuses God's reality with the constitution of a moral market, with its flexibility and binding character. A realistic theology is conscious that even the highest and most noble experiences, goals, and conceptions of value can be corrupted by human selfishness and by the

---

95. See D. Tracy's description of positivism's dream of discovering "a reality without quotation marks: a realm of pure data and facts, red spots 'out there' and sharp pains 'in here.' " Tracy goes on to comment on the shock caused by "the fact that 'fact' means not an uninterpreted 'already-out-there-now real,' but a verified possibility," and by "the acknowledgement that all data are theory-laden" (*Plurality and Ambiguity: Hermeneutics, Religion, Hope* [San Francisco: Harper & Row, 1987], 47–48). The latter point was emphasized as early as the 1920s by A. N. Whitehead. See especially *Process and Reality: An Essay in Cosmology*, ed. D. R. Griffin and D. W. Sherburne (New York: Free Press, 1978), 15–17 and passim.

96. The fact that considerable differentiations can be achieved within the framework of this pattern is demonstrated by the "material" part of I. U. Dalferth's *Existenz Gottes und christlicher Glaube: Skizzen zu einer eschatologischen Ontologie* (Munich: Kaiser, 1984), 193ff. A comparison with Dalferth's more recent work casts light on the fruitfulness and knowledge-generating capacity of the supersession of the dialogistic approach to pneumatology (ibid., 197ff.) by the assumption of a pluralistic structure. Cf. I. U. Dalferth, *Kombinatorische Theologie: Probleme theologischer Rationalität*, QD 130 (Freiburg: Herder, 1991), 125ff. See also §4.5.

corresponding perspectival distortion.[97] A realistic theology sees that even far-reaching moralities and postures of consensus find themselves powerless and unable to make connections in relation to past and future social environments. A realistic theology sees the continually threatening danger that moral markets collapse into self-righteousness, in which they either resort to dime-a-dozen appeals to an "outside audience," or disintegrate along the dividing lines of interest politics. A realistic theology knows that the desired power to reach a broader public is lost in the process.[98]

If we are to regain a sensitivity to the saving power of God's presence, as well as enjoyment of the wealth and abundance of this presence, we must renounce a reductionism hungry for theological control, which makes use of metaphysical conceptions of totality, dialogistic conceptions of intimacy, and the suggestive power of the moral market. This renunciation, though, cannot be attained by abstract demands. The forms of the Babylonian captivity of piety and of theological reflection will fall away only when the very contents that they are attempting to comprehend do away with them and renew knowledge and language in a new openness to God's reality.

---

97. Of fundamental significance in this context is G. A. Lindbeck's instructive critique of forms of theology that he calls "experiential-expressive," and his proposed alternative, which he designates as "cultural-linguistic" (*The Nature of Doctrine: Religion and Theology in a Postliberal Age* [Philadelphia: Westminster, 1984], esp. 30ff., 112ff.). The model of a realistic theology mediates between the two positions insofar as it challenges theology, first, to interrogate cultural and linguistic systematizations concerning the diversity of past structural patterns of experience that are now objectified in them. A realistic theology mediates between the two positions insofar as it challenges theology, second, to hold cultural and linguistic systematizations open and accessible to new structural patterns of experience. Without this ever-renewed dissolution and reconstruction, a theology and religious life embedded in cultural and linguistic forms loses its authenticity, its realism, and its openness to God's reality. For general observations on the danger of this indifference, see Whitehead, *Adventures of Ideas*, 156ff., 285–86.

98. B. Burnett helps make this interconnection clear from a pneumatological perspective ("The Spirit and Social Action," in M. Harper, ed., *Bishops' Move* [London: Hodder and Stoughton, 1978], esp. 45ff.).

CHAPTER 2

Early, Unclear Experiences of the Spirit's Power

The knowledge of God is not something fixed once and for all. To be sure, God remains true to Godself, but God is also alive. The knowledge of God can lose clarity, but human beings can and also ought to increase in the knowledge of God (Col. 1:10). But what is the standard that makes it possible to distinguish knowledge of God which is more clear from that which is less clear? The biblical texts have been read in such a way that precisely the Spirit of God, the power and might by which God is involved with creatures, seemed to destroy the hope for clear knowledge of God and for a clear standard for that knowledge.

Taking as a point of departure the observation that the Old Testament employs the same word for *spirit, breath,* and *wind,* the opinion has been advanced again and again that God's Spirit is a fully incomprehensible, numinous power. According to this view, the only thing we can know with certainty about God's Spirit is that we are *not* able to say *anything* definite about the Spirit. An oft-cited New Testament verse seems to fit well with this view: "The wind blows where it chooses, and you hear the sound of it, but you do not know where it comes from or where it goes. So it is with everyone who is born of the Spirit" (John 3:8).

It would have been possible to read those statements that apparently point to the incomprehensibility and indeterminacy of the Spirit in the light of those testimonies that communicate clarity. Instead, the opposite has occurred in theology. Those testimonies that are helpful and advance the knowledge of the Spirit have been placed in the shadow of those that apparently emphasize the incomprehensibility of the Spirit: concerning the Spirit of God nothing more can be said; the

Spirit is as invisible as breath and no more to be grasped than the wind.[1]

The realistic theology of the Holy Spirit presented here does not share the mood of resignation in the face of the difficulty in saying something definite about God's presence in the Spirit. This theology does not of course deny the fact that God's Spirit is not to be controlled by human beings, and that the Spirit is difficult to grasp. But this theology is interested in understanding that fact. To this end we cannot omit the observation even of the early and unclear experiences of the Spirit's power, as expressed by the biblical traditions.

The Spirit of God is seen at work in the deliverance of a community—one that hardly knows what is happening to it in the process. The Spirit of God is placed in connection with the action of a leader figure who does not really fit into any community, and in this way the Spirit connects ruptured communities across time and gives them orientation and a firm footing. In the breakdown and breakup of a political order, in the decline of a ruling family of an era, the Spirit is at work giving new order and a new orientation. Abrupt, radical changes of the whole of life's reality are occasions for the experience of God's Spirit. It is no wonder that people are stunned, that they find themselves driven about as if by the wind.

The early and unclear testimonies to the Spirit do not permit a comprehensive, clear, and unambiguous knowledge of God. They are signposts to keep the traces left behind by the Spirit from being overlooked on account of the "wind." The early and unclear experiences of the Spirit's power are indispensable signposts pointing into the clearer, more readily surveyable regions that we will consider in the subsequent chapters of this book.

---

1. Nor has this approach to the biblical attestation of the Spirit been altered by those theologies which rightly insist that precisely the doctrine of the Holy Spirit must grasp the "real presence" of the triune God in the life of the community and of its individual members (cf. P. Jacobs, *Theologie reformierter Bekenntnisschriften in Grundzügen* [Neukirchen-Vluyn: Neukirchener, 1959], 99), that in the Holy Spirit God not only comes to the human person, but is in the human person and by the power of God's own self opens the human person to God (see K. Barth, *CD* 1/1, 450 and passim). This approach has not even been altered by those theologies that are on the mark in speaking of a "realism of the Spirit" (O. Noordmans, *Das Evangelium des Geistes* [Zurich: EVZ-Verlag, 1960], 46ff.).

2.1: In deliverance out of collective distress and sin: Restoration of solidarity and of the community's capacity for action— Spirit and processes of emergence

God's Spirit was originally experienced in collective distress. Early testimonies to the action of God's Spirit report situations of danger in which no escape could be seen. They report situations of distress in which no hope remained. And they report wholly unexpected deliverance.

The following situations share similarities:

- Israel is suffering under such hard and lasting oppression and enslavement by another people that it "cries out to God."
- Superior powers are gathering for a major attack against Israel.
- Attempts to end a foreign people's war of aggression through peaceful understanding and to avoid further bloodshed go awry.
- The threat of a superior military power produces such anxiety that Israel offers to subjugate itself formally to the enemy. When this is accepted only on the condition that the right eye of every Israelite be gouged out, "all the people" weep aloud.

In all these cases the Spirit of God is experienced as the power that turns the tide—not directly, but certainly indirectly.

In contrast to the initial impression, God's Spirit is anything but a spirit of war. God's Spirit does not "come upon" heroes and those who radiate the glory of victory. The Spirit produces a new unanimity in the people of God, frees that people from the consequences of the powerlessness brought about by their own "sin," and raises up the life that has been beaten down by oppression.

In the situations described, it is not only individual persons who are threatened—an entire people is in distress. The people cannot evade the superior power, and their powers of resistance are inadequate. The force that is oppressing or threatening the people, the attacking enemy, is simply stronger. In the face of collective powerlessness and general helplessness, two possibilities remain according to human calculation. Either the people are reduced to a collection of isolated individuals by a *sauve qui peut* or "save oneself" attitude, or the people are faced with common misery, collective disgrace, and death. To the recognition of general helplessness corresponds public complaint, loud weeping, a cry to God.

The accounts tell us that in situations of this sort, God's Spirit brought deliverance. This deliverance does not happen all at once. It does not happen in an unambiguously miraculous way. The presumably first reliable testimonies to the action of God's Spirit[2] report instead an *unexpected, unforeseeable renewal of the people's unanimity and capacity for action, a renewal of the people's power of resistance in the midst of universal despair, and a resulting change of fate.* This renewal and restoration of the capacity for action and the power of resistance is traced back to a specific human being. *God's Spirit* is said to have *come upon* this person. In situations of distress, God's Spirit lays hold of or comes upon a specific human being. This person succeeds in restoring loyalty, solidarity, and the capacity for communal action among the people. Israel shakes off the yoke of oppression; Israel withstands the threat; the people defend themselves, liberate themselves, dispose of imminent danger, and escape distress:

> The Israelites did what was evil in the sight of the LORD, forgetting the LORD their God, and worshiping the Baals and the Asherahs. Therefore the anger of the LORD was kindled against Israel, and God sold them into the hand of King Cushan-rishathaim of Aram-naharaim; and the Israelites served Cushan-rishathaim eight years.

---

2. See C. Westermann, "Geist im Alten Testament," *EvT* 41 (1981): 223–25. "A solid, clearly demarcated and reliably attested use first occurs in the time of the Judges in the context of charismatic leadership" (225). Besides this article, the following works distinguish themselves by abstaining to a large extent from assuming systematic patterns that block the way to real understanding: W. H. Schmidt, "Geist / Heiliger Geist / Geistesgaben: I. Altes Testament," *TRE* 12 (1984): 170ff.; R. Albertz and C. Westermann, "*rûaḥ* / Geist," *THAT* 2 (1976): 726ff.; H. H. Schmid, "Ekstatische und charismatische Geistwirkungen im Alten Testament," in C. Heitmann and H. Mühlen, eds., *Erfahrung und Theologie des Heiligen Geistes* (Hamburg: Agentur des Rauhen Hauses; Munich: Kösel, 1974), 83ff.; G. H. Davies, "The Holy Spirit in the Old Testament," *RevExp* 63 (1966): 129ff.; G. T. Montague, *The Holy Spirit: Growth of a Biblical Tradition* (New York: Paulist Press, 1976), 3ff. Representative older expositions are those of W. R. Shoemaker, "The Use of רוּחַ in the Old Testament, and of πνευμα in the New Testament," *JBL* 23 (1904): 13ff.; P. Volz, *Der Geist Gottes und die verwandten Erscheinungen im Alten Testament und im anschliessenden Judentum* (Tübingen: Mohr, 1910).

But when the Israelites cried out to the LORD, the LORD raised up
a deliverer for the Israelites, who delivered them, Othniel son of
Kenaz, Caleb's younger brother. *The Spirit of the LORD came upon
him*, and he judged Israel; he went out to war, and the LORD gave
King Cushan-rishathaim of Aram into his hand; and his hand prevailed over Cushan-rishathaim. So the land had rest forty years.
Then Othniel son of Kenaz died. (Judg. 3:7-11[3])

Then all the Midianites and the Amalekites and the people of the
East came together, and crossing the Jordan they encamped in the
valley of Jezreel. *But the Spirit of the LORD had "clothed" Gideon;*
and he sounded the trumpet, and the Abiezrites were called out to
follow him. He sent messengers throughout all Manasseh, and they
too were called out to follow him. He also sent messengers to Asher,
Zebulun, and Naphtali, and they went up to meet them. (Judg.
6:33-35)

Once again Jephthah sent messengers to the king of the Ammonites. . . . "It is not I who have sinned against you, but you are
the one who does me wrong by making war on me. Let the LORD,
who is judge, decide today for the Israelites or for the Ammonites."
But the king of the Ammonites did not heed the message that Jephthah sent him. *Then the Spirit of the LORD came upon Jephthah,* and
he passed through Gilead and Manasseh. He passed on to Mizpah
of Gilead, and from Mizpah of Gilead he passed on to the Ammonites. . . . Jephthah judged Israel six years. Then Jephthah the
Gileadite died, and was buried in his town in Gilead. (Judg.
11:14, 27-29; 12:7)

[The people of Jabesh report to Saul that the Ammonites who are
laying siege to them are unwilling to accept their capitulation and
to conclude a treaty with them, except under one terrible condition. Each of the people of Jabesh must have their right eye gouged
out, resulting in "disgrace upon all Israel."] *And the Spirit of God
came upon Saul in power* when he heard these words, and his anger

---

3. Emphases in this and the following quotations are added by the author. On
Judg. 3:7ff., 6:33ff., 11:14ff., cf. J. A. Soggin, *Judges: A Commentary*, OTL (London:
SCM Press, 1981), esp. 45–47, 129–34, 208ff. For 1 Sam. 11:1ff., cf. H. J. Stoebe,
Das erste Buch Samuelis, Kommentar zum Alten Testament 8/1 (Gütersloh: Mohn,
1973), 223ff.

was greatly kindled. He took a yoke of oxen, and cut them in pieces and sent them throughout all the territory of Israel by messengers, saying, "Whoever does not come out after Saul and Samuel, so shall it be done to his oxen!" Then the dread of the LORD fell upon the people, and they came out as one. (1 Sam. 11:6-7)

Even a fleeting look at these accounts gives rise to the pressing question, "What do these war stories have to do with God's Spirit, and what does the Spirit of God have to do with these war stories?" The early testimonies to the action of God's Spirit may then appear as expressions of the religious glorification of a "typically male" strategy for managing conflict: hit first, ask questions later. Not only do these stories come across in part as legends, they are also dismaying and annoying—at any rate for civilizations seeking to develop in the direction of humaneness and working toward the day when all attempts to "solve" political conflicts by making war will be unnecessary and simply contemptible.

As tempting as such a reading and such a judgment may be, they are the consequence of a superficial understanding. They mislead people into being too hasty to take the early testimonies and file them away at the back of the drawer. They obstruct decisive means of access to a theology of the Holy Spirit: important insights into the power—and into the problematic—of the early action of the Spirit.

The early testimonies to the action of God's Spirit do not yet mediate any clear knowledge, let alone an exhaustive knowledge, of this Spirit. Rather they pose, more strongly than many later testimonies of the biblical traditions, the task of "discerning the spirits."[4] Yet in spite of their lack of clarity and their aptness to be misunderstood, they already provide indications that God's Spirit is precisely not a spirit of war, but delivers out of distress and helplessness as a "Spirit of righteousness and mercy." They also provide indications concerning the way in which such deliverance occurs. In addition, they make it impossible to deny that, although God's Spirit unleashes unexpected forces and produces improbable results, this Spirit acts under the conditions of what is creaturely and finite. The services of imperfect,

---

4. See particularly §2.4. This problem will be taken up again from various perspectives, esp. in §§4.2, 4.4, 5.4, and 6.1.

mortal human beings are enlisted by this Spirit, and they remain real human beings.

God's Spirit is neither a spirit of magic nor a spirit of war. This is true despite the fact that, according to the early testimonies, the Spirit's action can seem fantastic enough, and despite the fact that the Spirit is indirectly all too involved in militaristic actions. Yet nowhere is the claim made that this Spirit brings deliverance in an immediate, magical way. Nowhere is it said that the Spirit directly occasions militaristic actions. The texts do not say that the Spirit descended upon this or that human being—and the enemy fled. Nor does the enemy flee when Gideon blows his ram's horn or when Saul chops the oxen to pieces. There is no place where the Spirit of God immediately or directly causes a military conflict.

Instead the Spirit causes the people of Israel *to come out of a situation of insecurity, fear, paralysis, and mere complaint.* This happens by means of the persons upon whom the Spirit has come, and in concentration on these persons. In a situation of powerlessness, in a situation where it is to be expected that each individual person seek his or her welfare in flight, in a situation of perplexity and helplessness, the bearer of the Spirit—more precisely, God through the bearer of the Spirit—restores loyalty and a capacity for action among the people.[5] This can, but it need not, move or even inspire people "to voluntary collaboration."[6] In fact Saul—just after the Spirit has come upon him—procures loyalty and commitment by means of a massive threat: "Whoever does not come out after Saul and Samuel, so shall it be done to his oxen!" (namely, be cut to pieces). In other cases

---

5. 1 Samuel 7:3ff. and 1 Sam. 11:1ff. are closer to each other in terms of content than is clear from the question, "Is the charismatic regarded as a 'military leader' or not?" See Stoebe, *Samuelis*, 167ff; also the investigation by M. C. Lind—excellent in this as well as in other respects—*Yahweh Is a Warrior: The Theology of Warfare in Ancient Israel* (Scottdale, Pa.: Herald Press, 1980), 90ff., esp. 99–100. P. D. Miller points out important interconnections between militaristic changes of constellations of power, on the one hand, and the "hosts of heaven," on the other (*The Divine Warrior in Early Israel* [Cambridge: Harvard Univ. Press, 1973], 155ff.). These interconnections can be elucidated from the perspective of later traditions (cf. §§3.3, 3.4, and passim).

6. Westermann, "Geist im Alten Testament," 225.

, loyalty and unity seem to have been attained in a less dramatic and extortionist manner. After the Spirit has descended upon Othniel, he becomes a judge in Israel. Only afterwards, according to the story, does he go forth to battle in order to shake off oppression. When the Spirit has come upon Gideon and Jephthah, they gather people behind them.

In all the early attestations to the experience of God's Spirit, what is initially and immediately at issue is the restoration of an internal order, at least of new commitment, solidarity, and loyalty.[7] The direct result of the descent of God's Spirit is the gathering, the joining together of people who find themselves in distress. The support of their fellow persons is acquired; a new community, a new commitment is produced after the descent of the Spirit by the person upon whom the Spirit has come.

The texts make indubitably clear that God's Spirit is not simply a spirit of militaristic enthusiasm. They make plain that there is no way the conclusion can be drawn that the Spirit of God is always with Israel when it comes out "as one" to strike the foe. In no instance does the descent of the Spirit lead to anything like a spontaneous enthusiasm for battle. Saul must even use extortion, threatening his fellows, in order to compel them to go out to battle (1 Sam. 11:7). Admittedly, the tension in the early action of the Spirit becomes particularly clear precisely at this point: the solidarity that has been attained is immediately placed in the service of military conflict. Yet the distance in these texts from an identification of the action of the Spirit with the

---

7. This systematic insight is supported by the later texts of Chronicles that speak of the descent of "a Spirit" or of "the Spirit of God." 1 Chronicles 12:18 reports that "the Spirit came upon Amasai, chief of the Thirty," so that he gives a religiously deepened and grounded declaration of loyalty to David: "Peace, peace to you, and peace to the one who helps you! For your God is the one who helps you." As in the texts of Judges, the process has consequences in terms of power politics: "Then David received them, and made them officers of his troops." In 2 Chron. 15:1ff., the person upon whom the Spirit has come publicly announces exactly the experience that is reflected in the early testimonies: "The LORD is with you, when you are with the LORD" (concerning the explicit reference to the law, see §3.1). Finally, in 2 Chron. 20:14ff., the person upon whom the Spirit has come issues a successful summons to commitment, solidarity, and loyalty in a campaign without a battle (on this point as well see the clearer insights into the Spirit, §§3.1ff.).

arousal of militaristic enthusiasm is unmistakable. Even after the Spirit's descent upon Gideon and after the successful gathering of Israel, Gideon is still dubious about the success of a military action (Judg. 6:36ff.). In the corresponding situation, Jephthah is so uncertain that he seeks, by means of what later proves to be a fateful oath, to assure himself of God's help (Judg. 11:30ff.). With intentional attention to detail, Judg. 11:12 emphasizes that Israel is shying away from a military conflict, that it has done no wrong to the people who are attacking it, and that it has repeatedly sought a peaceful resolution to the conflict. In 1 Sam. 11:1ff. the people of Jabesh are even ready to subject themselves to slavery in order to avoid military conflicts.

Whatever may be the status of other biblical traditions with regard to the glorification of the use of military violence,[8] those texts that talk about the *intervention of God's Spirit* into the structural patterns of human life are looking at military conflicts that are not only unambiguously defensive, but explicitly unwanted and compelled only by great distress.

We have seen that God's Spirit cannot be regarded simply as a "spirit of war." It is equally true that God's Spirit does not produce superhumans, *Übermenschen*, religious or moral heroes, or even only those who radiate the glory of victory. The Spirit of God comes upon, falls upon, or clothes finite, mortal human beings. That is explicitly reported of Othniel, Gideon, Jephthah, and Saul. The earliest testimonies as well as all other testimonies of the biblical traditions leave no doubt that those upon whom the Spirit comes are and remain im-

---

8. See the differentiated exposition of W. Huber and H. R. Reuter, *Friedensethik* (Stuttgart: Kohlhammer, 1990), 36ff. With regard to the various assessments of God's involvement in militaristic action in general, cf. on the one hand G. von Rad, *Holy War in Ancient Israel*, trans. and ed. M. J. Dawn and J. H. Yoder (Grand Rapids: Eerdmans, 1991); Miller, *Divine Warrior*; and on the other hand R. Smend, *Jahwekrieg und Stämmebund: Erwägungen zur ältesten Geschichte Israels* (Göttingen: Vandenhoeck, 1963); M. Weippert, "'Heiliger Krieg' in Israel und Assyrien: Kritische Anmerkungen zu Gerhard von Rads Konzept des 'Heiligen Krieges im Alten Israel,'" *ZAW* 84 (1972): 460–93. See also the typology of Lind, *Yahweh Is a Warrior*, 24ff., 30–31. The overtly defensive action in the texts treated in §§2.1 and 2.2 is also seen, without a perspective on "God's Spirit," by T. R. Hobbs, *A Time for War: A Study of Warfare in the Old Testament*, Old Testament Studies 3 (Wilmington: M. Glazier, 1989), 40ff.

perfect, finite, mortal human beings. The texts mention relations of ancestry and of kinship, as well as subsequent misfortune, failure, and the death of those whom the Spirit of God clothes.[9]

Moreover, it is striking that the biblical traditions make passing comments which, if anything, work against a moral or religious lionizing of the "early charismatics."

A short note records an infraction by Othniel against custom and the spirit of the age (Josh. 15:18). Even after receiving God's revelation, Gideon remains a doubting, skeptical person (Judg. 6:13ff., 36ff.) who fears the reactions of his social environment (Judg. 6:27). This charismatic even ends up erecting an idol in his city (Judg. 8:27).[10] It is pointed out with particular emphasis that Jephthah is the issue of an anonymous prostitute and an unknown father. "Only the personified district of Gilead could qualify as his sire."[11] He is driven out of the house by the other sons of this "father" (Judg. 11:1ff.). It is repeatedly emphasized that he does not forget this humiliation, for which his social environment outside the family shares responsibility. According to the story, he remains distrustful and obsessed with power throughout the course of his life. Expelled, he "attracts friends from the dregs of society"[12] (cf. Judg. 11:3b). Even after the Spirit of God has come upon him, he is uncertain of his vocation (cf. esp. Judg. 11:9, 30). He is explicitly described as "a person living on the periphery of civilization and of Israelite faith."[13] In no way are the persons upon whom the Spirit of God comes persons of a higher order or ideal figures, nor do they become such. Not only imperfect, finite, mortal human beings, but also outsiders, doubters, distrustful types, persons obsessed with power,

---

9. Cf. for Othniel: Josh. 15:17; Judg. 1:13; 3:9, 11; 1 Chron. 4:13; for Gideon: Judg. 6:11, 27; 8:30, 32; for Jephthah: Judg. 11:1ff., 34ff.; 12:7; for Saul: 1 Sam. 9:1-2; 10:21; 13:16; 14:50-51; 18:17ff.; 31:3-4, 8; 1 Chron. 8:33; 9:39; 10:4.

10. For a closer characterization of the corresponding traits of Samson and of Saul, see §§2.2 and 2.3.

11. P. Trible, *Texts of Terror: Literary-Feminist Readings of Biblical Narratives*, Overtures to Biblical Theology 13 (Philadelphia: Fortress, 1984), 94. Trible is picking up on C. F. Burney, *The Book of Judges* (New York: Arden, 1970), 308.

12. Trible, *Texts of Terror*, 94.

13. Soggins, *Judges*, 218. Soggins adds that Jephthah "in all probability was not even an Israelite" (ibid.). This phenomenon is present in more acute form in the texts treated in §2.2.

who do not even shrink from using threats and extortion against their
fellow persons—that is how the biblical texts characterize the early
charismatics.

Here we meet no minigods, nor even enviable leader and con-
queror figures. According to the early testimonies, neither the person
upon whom the Spirit comes nor that person's fellows can treat the
action of the Spirit as cause for undivided rejoicing. The action of the
Spirit is surrounded by that which is uncanny, ambiguous, and dismaying, as well as by doubt and helplessness. It is clear from the story of
Jephthah's victory that the services of those upon whom the Spirit
comes can be enlisted in a most depressing way. The story clearly attests to how dismaying and dangerous the action of the Spirit and its
consequences can be. The story shows that the bearers of the Spirit are
not in a position to bring under control the action of God's Spirit and
its consequences.[14] It shows that the persons of that time have every
reason to fear becoming involved in the action of God's Spirit, even
when this Spirit is liberating the people from distress and oppression.

To be sure, the accounts of the descent of the Spirit on the early
charismatics say nothing about the people who fall in combat among
those whom the bearers of the Spirit lead into battle. They say nothing
about the sufferings of people on the "opposing side." But they decid-
edly do not filter out depressing, devastating consequences that the
Spirit's action has for the bearers of the Spirit and for persons in their
immediate environment. They reflect how these persons are handled
by God's Spirit. They reflect that explicit communication with God
should not be sought on this level of the knowledge of God and of the
Spirit. The most heartrending testimony to this is found in Judges 11,
where the Spirit of God comes upon Jephthah. He goes out to confront
the Ammonites. Like Gideon, this bearer of the Spirit is also lacking
in the certainty of victory:

> And Jephthah made a vow to the LORD, and said, "If you will give
> the Ammonites into my hand, then whoever [first] comes out of the
> doors of my house to meet me, when I return victorious from the
> Ammonites, shall be the LORD'S, to be offered up by me as a burnt
> offering." [Jephthah goes into battle. As in other stories of bearers

---

14. See also §2.3. For the analogous situation of Saul, cf. 1 Sam. 28:4ff.

of the Spirit, the ultimate outcome is that the enemy is "subdued before the people of Israel."]

Then Jephthah came to his home at Mizpah; and there was his daughter coming out to meet him with timbrels and with dancing. She was his only child; he had no son or daughter except her. When he saw her, he tore his clothes, and said, "Alas, my daughter! You have brought me very low; you have become the cause of great trouble to me. For I have opened my mouth to the LORD [i.e., he has promised something to God], and I cannot take back my vow." She said to him, "My father, if you have opened your mouth to the LORD, do to me according to what has gone out of your mouth, now that the LORD has given you vengeance against your enemies, the Ammonites." And she said to her father, "Let this thing be done for me: Grant me two months, so that I may go and wander on the mountains, and bewail my virginity, my companions and I." (Judg. 11:30-37)

The story of Jephthah's daughter is itself sufficient to call into question all superficial enthusiasm about the Spirit. We must of course leave open the question whether this story incipiently exhibits a typical feature that will be more clearly recognizable in later action of the Spirit: it remains for later, more perspicacious times to know whether, if one extrapolated from the Spirit's action here, one would detect a movement toward the active participation of women in the formation of tradition and ethos. Such participation becomes clear and undeniable at the latest from the promise of Joel onward.[15] But in no case are we permitted to underestimate the significance of the women's solidarity in mourning.[16] The afterword to the story says, "So there arose an

15. See §3.4. In the framework of contemporary perceptual possibilities, it is scarcely possible to give a clear answer to the question whether the story of Jephthah is already supposed to suggest the reversal whereby the bearer of the Spirit becomes possessed by an "evil spirit" (see §§2.3 and 2.4). The same holds true for the question whether the story of Jephthah is supposed to suggest a conflict between the Spirit and the law that prohibits human sacrifice (Lev. 18:21; 20:2-5; Deut. 12:31; 18:10).

16. Feminist theology has paid particular attention to the story. This is not because the story appears to provide material for the formation of stereotypes: on the one hand a brutal man, a chauvinist, who slaughters even his own daughter; on the other hand the defenseless woman who is handed over to this monstrosity. We

Israelite custom that for four days every year the daughters of Israel would go out to lament the daughter of Jephthah the Gileadite" (Judg. 11:39c-40).[17] Here the women's solidarity has unusually powerful consequences.[18] Besides the ambivalent fact that the young woman consciously participates and surrenders herself, we ought also to emphasize the emancipatory power of her friends' solidarity and of their common lament, as well as the normative power of the solemn annual commemoration. But the suppression of the effective history of this narrative, both in the biblical traditions and beyond, is among those things that make this story a rich theological lode to mine, as feminist interpretation has shown.

From this story in particular we are to draw the following emphatic warning: the structural pattern of life and experience that, according to early testimonies, is marked and defined by the action of the Spirit, is full of danger. The action of the Spirit is by no means

---

ought not doubt the despair of Jephthah, who is losing his only daughter. Trible (*Texts of Terror*, 101) has emphasized that "the narrator stresses the isolation of the child *and* the dilemma of the parent through an extraordinary accumulation of expressions: 'She was his one and only child; besides her he had neither son nor daughter'" (Judg. 11:34c). But Trible also gives an acute analysis of Jephthah's self-pity, which in the egoistic and androcentric perspective is the dominating factor (*Texts of Terror*, 101–2; cf. Judg. 11:35).

17. Trible, ibid., 105–7, esp. 106–7: The postscript of the Jephthah story "reports an extraordinary development. Whereas the female who has never known a man is typically numbered among the unremembered, in the case of the daughter of Jephthah the usual does not happen. 'Although *she* had not known a man, nevertheless *she* became a tradition in Israel.' In a dramatic way this sentence alters, though it does not eliminate, the finality of Jephthah's vow. The alteration comes through the faithfulness of the women of Israel, as the next line explains. . . . The unnamed virgin child becomes a tradition in Israel because the women with whom she chose to spend her last days have not let her pass into oblivion. . . . The narrative postscript, then, shifts the focus of the story from vow to victim, from death to life, from oblivion to remembrance."

18. See Trible's move toward a comparison with the story of Abraham's sacrifice of Isaac (ibid., 105). See also the panel in the church of St. Catharine's Monastery on Mount Sinai, which depicts the sacrifice of Jephthah's daughter and the sacrifice of Isaac as anticipations of Christ's sacrifice (K. Weitzmann, "The Jephthah Panel in the Bema of the Church of St. Catharine's Monastery on Mount Sinai," in *Studies in the Arts at Sinai* [Princeton, N.J.: Princeton Univ. Press, 1982], 341ff.).

necessarily connected with joy and good fortune for the person who
bears the Spirit and for this person's surroundings![19]

Yet the question remains: Why is this action of the Spirit, which
brings danger in its wake, necessary at all? Why have the people fallen
into these straits from which they see no way out? Why have loyalty
and the power of resistance disintegrated? Why are the people en-
thralled by the hostile superior power, paralyzed by fear? Why are the
people incapable of throwing off the yoke of oppression before the
Spirit of God intervenes?

In all instances the explanation is that *on the basis of sin*, Israel
loses its internal unity, its coherence.[20] Inasmuch as Israel forgets God
and turns to the idols of peoples of other lands, it loses its internal coherence. It loses the power to defend itself against outside aggression
and oppression. In response to a desperate will to repent, in response
to a confession of sin, or at least in response to a cry of distress to God,
God "raises up a deliverer" upon whom the Spirit comes. With respect
to this presupposition as well, almost all accounts of the Spirit's descent on the early charismatics share the same structure.

Othniel:
The Israelites did what was evil in the sight of the LORD, forgetting
the LORD their God, and worshiping the Baals and the Asherahs.
Therefore the anger of the LORD was kindled against Israel, and
God sold them. . . . But when the Israelites cried out to the
LORD, the LORD raised up a deliverer for the Israelites. . . . (Judg.
3:7-9a)

Gideon:
The Israelites did what was evil in the sight of the LORD, and the
LORD gave them into the hand of Midian seven years. The hand of
Midian prevailed over Israel. . . . For whenever the Israelites put
in seed, the Midianites and the Amalekites and the people of the

---

19. Cf. §2.2 as well as the account of the stoning of Zechariah in 2 Chron.
24:20ff. The Spirit had come upon Zechariah and he was reprimanding the people
for their sins and their transgressions of the law. See also in this context §§3.2 and
4.3.

20. R. Bohren has emphasized to me that this state of affairs is already present
on the level of the book of Judges.

East would come up against them. They would encamp against
them and destroy the produce of the land, as far as the neighborhood of Gaza, and leave no sustenance in Israel, and no sheep or ox
or donkey. For they and their livestock would come up, and they
would even bring their tents [families], as thick as locusts; neither
they nor their camels could be counted; so they wasted the land as
they came in. Thus Israel was greatly impoverished because of Midian; and the Israelites cried out to the LORD for help. (Judg. 6:1-6)

Jephthah:
The Israelites again did what was evil in the sight of the LORD, worshiping the Baals and the Astartes, the gods of Aram, the gods of
Sidon, the gods of Moab, the gods of the Ammonites, and the gods
of the Philistines. Thus they abandoned the LORD, and did not worship God. So the anger of the LORD was kindled against Israel, and
God sold them into the hand of the Philistines and into the hand
of the Ammonites, and they crushed and oppressed the Israelites
that year. For eighteen years they oppressed all the Israelites that
were beyond the Jordan in the land of the Amorites, which is in
Gilead. The Ammonites also crossed the Jordan to fight against
Judah and against Benjamin and against the house of Ephraim; so
that Israel was greatly distressed. So the Israelites cried to the
LORD, saying, "We have sinned against you, because we have abandoned our God and have worshiped the Baals." (Judg. 10:6-10, cf.
10:11-16)

Sin—apostasy—idolatry—subjugation by peoples of other lands—
distress—a cry to God: with varying degrees of stress attached to the
individual elements, these interconnected phenomena underlie the
texts that report the descent of God's Spirit. One story talks at great
length about the people's disintegrative fall into idolatry. Another
story depicts, with a sense for the depressing details, the increasing
devastation by the people's enemies as they render the people fully
powerless. With the descent of God's Spirit, this torment begins to
change. The process of oppression, of want, of weakness and anxiety,
and of decay comes to an end. A process of emergence[21] sets in, a process that in an unforeseen manner constitutes a new beginning, new

---

21. Concerning the concept, see §1.5, n. 58.

relations, a new reality—although the same persons remain concerned and affected. Regardless of this process of emergence, the early experiences of the delivering power of the Spirit are not yet clearly defined and developed. Yet they are anything but speculations about metaphysical entities. They are anything but indeterminate mystical "experiences," anything but "encounters" with a numinous and incomprehensible appearance and dynamic, or one that somehow infuses "everything."

Even the early experiences of God's Spirit are *experiences of how a new beginning is made toward restoring the community of God's people.* They are *experiences of the forgiveness of sins, of the raising up of the "crushed and oppressed,"* and of the renewal of the *forces of life.* Certainly these early experiences are unclear and in many respects questionable. Yet even they can lead one to think of the third article of the Creed, which talks about the communion of saints, about the forgiveness of sins, about the resurrection of the dead and the life everlasting. Most assuredly they are much closer in content to the third article of the Creed than to the innumerable metaphysical, speculative, individualistic, and irrational conceptions of the Spirit that theology has dreamed up in the course of the centuries.

2.2: In problematic preservation in the midst of ongoing affliction: Spirit and legendary integrative figures

Beginning with the earliest testimonies and continuing through all traditions, the Spirit of God is experienced as a power that not only brings deliverance in situations that appear to offer no way out, but also affords preservation in ongoing danger and distress. Even here the Spirit acts—albeit in a manner as yet unclear—as "comforter," as a power that lends steadfastness in affliction. The experience of being preserved in ongoing affliction is thoroughly ambiguous. Preservation in affliction means, after all, that human beings must persevere in a tormenting, intolerable situation. The Samson stories (Judges 13–16) make particularly clear the way in which divergent feelings are provoked by the action of the Spirit who affords preservation in a situation of continued distress.

These stories, which can be characterized as "sagas of the strong and clever hero,"[22] awaken memories of Hercules, Robin Hood, Paul Bunyan, or other legendary figures. It is difficult to see why the texts repeatedly emphasize that *the Spirit of God fell upon Samson*, when at first glance this Spirit seems to make possible nothing more than escape-artist stunts and tricks for conquering lions, brawling, and murdering.[23] Most of the stories reported about Samson appear unworthy of belief, not at all "spiritual." Others are simply offensive: they seem to depict Samson only as an agent provocateur, as someone who stirs up unrest. In these stories, which indeed "almost form a world of their own,"[24] the Spirit of God is supposedly at work.

The Spirit of God comes upon Samson, and with his bare hand he tears apart a roaring young lion (Judg. 14:6). One might still be able to interpret this as a particular—albeit strange—story of God preserving a human being. Yet in the next story Samson throws a drinking party (14:10ff.), poses a riddle to thirty drinking buddies, and wagers thirty shirts and thirty festal garments that his companions will not solve it. They are able to persuade Samson's wife both to entice Samson into divulging the solution to the riddle, and to betray the solution to them. When they had done so, "the Spirit of the LORD rushed on him, and he went down to Ashkelon. He killed thirty men of the town, took their spoil, and gave the festal garments to those who had explained the riddle." On another occasion (Judg. 15:9-17) Samson allows himself to be bound so that—again after "the Spirit of the LORD [has] rushed on him"—he might burst his bonds and strike down a thousand men with the bloody jawbone of an ass.

These are dismaying, tasteless, brutal stories, in which the Spirit of God seems to be involved in ruffians' squabbles, cheating contests, and escape-artist stunts. Nor is this dismaying quality ameliorated when one takes account of the fact that Samson was an informer, brawler, and arsonist *not on his own impetus*, but as he was *impelled* (Judg.

---

22. H. Gese, "Simson," *RGG* 6, 42.

23. Cf. Judg. 14:6; 14:19; 15:14. By contrast 13:25 sounds like a watered-down formulation. Concerning the composition of the traditions, see H. Gese, "Die ältere Simson-Überlieferung (Richter c. 14-15)," in *Alttestamentliche Studien* (Tübingen: Mohr, 1991), 52ff., esp. 54ff.

24. R. Smend, *Die Entstehung des Alten Testaments* (Stuttgart: Kohlhammer, 1981), 127.

13:25) by the Spirit of God. Nor is the dismaying quality ameliorated when one notes that Samson must end his life with his eyes gouged out, and that he dies by pulling down a house whose ruins bury him along with his opponents. How can the Spirit of God get involved with such a figure?

An initial key to answering that question is found in Judg. 14:4b: "At that time the Philistines had dominion over Israel." During the rule of the Philistines, Samson is chosen as a troublemaker who shall make clear the evil and deviousness of the Philistines, and at the same time show that the strong and clever Israelite can be superior to them. To be sure, he ultimately shipwrecks on the connection between the Philistine's deviousness and their real superiority in terms of power. But according to the symbolism and the promise of the Samson figure, when the Spirit of God comes upon the Israelite, when the Israelite refuses to trust the Philistines, then not only can one person take on thirty or a thousand—then all of Israel can shake off its yoke. In order to understand the message of the Samson stories and the statements present in them, we must become clearer about the political background.

Siegfried Herrmann has drawn a careful picture of how the impetuses to develop a united "people" Israel went hand in hand with a particular form of threat, to which the Samson stories are reacting:

> The attacks made on Israelite territory by hostile neighbours, which were countered by the charismatic leaders, were limited in scope and duration. These threats become a chronic danger with the arrival of the Philistines. Their settlement had preceded that of the Israelites; it was limited to the coastal plains. But the consolidation of their power, in the form of city kingships, heightened a desire to expand. . . . Thus an organized power gradually developed all along the western side of Israelite territory, beginning from the coastal plain, thrusting its advance posts eastwards into the hill-country. At that point it inevitably clashed with the Israelites. [This clash is reflected in the Samson stories, as well as in 1 Samuel 1–7.]
>
> The charismatic leadership was no longer an adequate answer to such a massive and permanent danger; it was limited to a summons issued to the tribes in a particular situation and dependent on the initiative and the direction of a man who was "called by Yahweh" and who therefore had to be waited for or found in each

particular instance. None of this was sufficient answer to the increasing pressure from the Philistines.[25]

It is impossible to depict with sufficient subtlety the difficulties
that arise in this time of ongoing repression. An offensive military
conflict with "the more powerful Philistines, who ultimately compel
the Danites to emigrate into the region of the sources of the Jordan,"[26]
is just as unacceptable an option as is drifting with the current toward
assimilation. Neither clear friend-foe constellations nor a peaceful
"mutualism" can help provide a way out of the crisis. How can Israel
live in proximity to the Philistines and under their superior power, and
yet preserve its own identity or even develop an identity of resistance?
How can Israel prevent its being—at least gradually—crushed by the
more powerful people, destroyed in terms of its own particular identity,
or compelled to accommodate itself to the point where it no longer
even recognizes itself?

In this situation the Samson stories depict the *difficult dialectic of
becoming involved and of keeping to one's own.* Samson's life and deeds
become a public expression of the preservation of identity in affliction. They become an expression of preservation until a better day
that will be more propitious for liberation. In doing so the stories
point beyond a specific, concrete public in two respects. First, they
speak to and connect several publics in the Israelite people, which are
distinguished by their varying degrees of resistance and accommodation to the Philistines. The Samson stories also depict an integrative
figure who simultaneously represents several mutually conflicting
publics. In doing all this, the stories take on legendary traits. They
integrate a heterogeneous public that stretches from "fierce resistance
fighters" to "pseudo-Philistines," and includes every version of defense against, and of accommodation to, peoples of other lands. Not
only do the stories capture a concrete expression of this spectrum (in
the year X, when hate for the Philistines was especially strong, or in
the year Y, when the tendencies to accommodation were dominant),
they also fit a variety of forms. They can adjust to a *history* of conflict

---

25. S. Herrmann, A *History of Israel in Old Testament Times*, rev. ed., trans.
J. Bowden (Philadelphia: Fortress, 1981), 131.
26. Gese, "Simson," 42.

and to corresponding processes of development. The integrative figure, who cannot be allowed to be exhausted by any specific group or in any specific time, takes on legendary traits. This figure of course has a "home" in a specific time and present, but at the same time he lies beyond concrete times and presents. He is contemporaneous with all of them and marks them in his particular way.

Samson gets involved with the Philistines. To the dismay of his parents, he falls in love with a Philistine woman (Judges 14). Naturally this does not imply that Samson is strategically planning to follow a middle road between, on the one hand, a simple course of confrontationally keeping to one's own and, on the other hand, an equally simple course of accommodation. The former course could not have been carried through in those days, while the latter could not be acceptable to Israel. Rather than strategically planning a middle road, Samson is impelled. "Do you have to marry a woman from those uncircumcised Philistines?" the parents ask (Judg. 14:3). They do not know that it is not Samson who is doing the planning, but God: "His father and mother did not know that this was from the LORD; for he was seeking a pretext to act against the Philistines" (Judg. 14:4). God thus makes use of Samson at a time when Israel lives in great affliction due to the predominance of the Philistines, an affliction that cannot be removed. Samson is impelled into subtly arranged conflicts.

A second key to understanding the Samson stories lies in the observation that they make no effort to depict Samson as a likable person, not to mention a heroic one. Again and again he provokes the Philistines by his inclinations and his cunning, by his cleverness and his strength. "Why must he get involved with a Philistine woman and her relations? He doesn't have to drink with them, lay wagers with them, pose them riddles, and get into trouble with them!" That may have been the reaction caused by these stories in a sensibility intent on propriety, clear identity, and keeping to one's own. Samson is not to be trusted. Again and again he is deceived by the Philistines in general and by his first and second wives in particular. Yet he continues to get involved with the hostile superior power.

This distrust of Samson is heightened by statements that he was a person "dedicated to God," a nazirite (cf. Judg. 13:5, 7; 16:17). As a nazirite he stands in a privileged relation to God. Yet he is continually breaking the nazirite oath in an appalling manner. Samson drinks

wine, although this is explicitly forbidden for a nazirite (Num. 6:3).
Samson touches what is dead and unclean (the dead lion and the ass's
jaw). He even eats of the honey from the body of the dead lion, although Num. 6:6 says of nazirites that "all the days that they separate
themselves to the LORD they shall not go near a corpse." Nevertheless
the texts emphasize Samson's constant relation with God through the
power in his hair, which in accord with the nazirite oath (Num. 6:5) is
not supposed to be trimmed or cut. Indeed precisely in situations in
which Samson breaks the oath, his strength makes itself evident—in
connection with the descent of the Spirit.[27]

The Samson upon whom the Spirit repeatedly comes, the Samson
who is a nazirite, is consciously depicted as an undependable, offensive
figure. Finally he loses his strength and his privileged relation to God
because he simply cannot keep his secrets to himself. The stories thus
disseminate a twofold moral: Anyone who cannot keep his or her distance from what is strange and hostile; anyone who cannot keep to his
or her own people; anyone who, in addition, not only shows his or her
God-given powers to unbelievers, but also reveals to them the secret
sources of these powers; anyone who cannot keep a holy secret, although he or she has repeatedly had bad experiences—anyone who
does such things has no right to be surprised if he or she is finally
burned by the fire with which he or she is continually playing. Stick
with your own people and with your own God, or else you will land in
trouble that will lead to your death—that is *one moral* of the Samson
stories.

> When he [Samson] awoke from his sleep, he thought, "I will go out
> as at other times, and shake myself free." But he did not know that
> the LORD had left him. So the Philistines seized him and gouged
> out his eyes. They brought him down to Gaza and bound him with
> bronze shackles; and he ground at the mill in the prison. [Samson is
> treated like an animal: an animal that must perform drudge labor
> for its enemies.] (Judg. 16:20-21)

---

27. It can remain an open question whether the naming of two sources for
Samson's strength—his uncut hair and the Spirit of God who descends on him—is
to be traced back to different traditions or whether this doubling is purposefully supposed to elicit uncertainty regarding Samson as a human being (here is a nazirite
who breaks his oath—here is more than a nazirite!).

One message of the Samson stories is: "Do not get into trouble. Do not get involved with the Philistines, who are devious and brutal. Above all do not reveal to them the secrets of your God-given powers, even if they come to you as your best friend or even as the wife who loves you!" This message, though, is only one side of the Samson stories.

The second message, the *second moral* of the stories is this: "The Philistines are strong, but Samson is stronger. The Philistines are devious, but Samson is more crafty. He even finds shrewd ways to turn their shrewd tricks against them." There is much that indicates that the texts also wish to emphasize that in all his actions, Samson remains at the level of "justifiable" reactions. Samson only reacts, while the Philistines with each of their actions aggressively escalate the level of illegality and enter into an intensified conflict.[28]

The descent of God's Spirit repeatedly marks the identity switch between the endangered, unappealing, and uncanny Samson, on the one hand, and the strong, victorious Samson, on the other hand. The descent of God's Spirit initiates the transition from the weak Samson to the strong; from the frivolous Samson, duped by the Philistines, to the cunning Samson who gets the best of the Philistines. If we take

---

28. This aspect would fit the observation that the conflicts placed in connection with the descent of the Spirit on the charismatics were consistently depicted as undesired, compelled only by the greatest distress (see §2.1). This aspect of course makes the—justifiable—assumption that Judg. 14:19a is a later interpolation. Gese has worked this out with great subtlety ("Simson-Überlieferung," 57ff.): "only Samson's actions remain pure reactions, because they never escalate beyond the current level of illegality in each particular case. The levels of illegality form a transparent four-part system constituted by the series: non-material offense— offense committed against material property—murder—war. . . . While Samson only reacts, the Philistines drive themselves [through heightened aggression] to ruin. Through Samson they come to nought" (59). On the first level Samson reacts to the wedding guests' act of cheating on the wager by leaving the wedding. On the second level he reacts to the breaking of the marriage contract (14:20: his wife was given to his friend who had been his best man) by burning the fields of grain. On the third level he reacts to the fiery death of the bride and her family (15:6: "so the Philistines came up, and burned her and her father") by executing blood vengeance on the murderers. On the fourth level the Philistine army's punitive expedition to Judah, which is supposed to force the handing over of Samson, leads only to Samson's victory over the army (15:13ff.). See also Gese's ingenious reflections in "Simson-Überlieferung," 63ff.

note of the effect that this descent of the Spirit has on the differentiated Israelite "public," we can see a truly astounding achievement of
integration. The descent of God's Spirit leads to a specific change in
the "witnesses," a specific change in the public or publics that react to
the Samson stories. The same people who just a moment before were
saying, "How can Samson carry on like that!" must now make the
transition to explicit recognition. The same people who a moment ago
were distancing themselves from him must now unite with him in solidarity. The more those with a particularly hostile disposition to the
Philistines have distanced themselves from Samson, the more vehemently they must applaud when that same Samson dishes out blows
with the ass's jaw. But those who, taking a friendly attitude toward the
Philistines, see themselves in Samson as he crosses back and forth
across the boundary, are brought in the course of the stories to an increasing distance from the Philistines. Their previously assuaged mistrust of the enemies is intensified. Samson thus cultivates the complex
unity of a public with a differentiated attitude toward him and toward
what is happening. He allows these differences to be maintained and
at the same time to be developed in the direction of a common state of
consciousness.

Samson is seen as a complex integrative figure. Not only does the
depiction of Samson in analogy to the early charismatics upon whom
the Spirit comes speak for this. The statement that Samson was the
"beginning of deliverance" or a "judge" in Israel also speaks for the
fact that this consciously ambiguous figure is supposed to become an
integrative figure in a people torn apart and subject to ongoing affliction. These expressions, which appear repeatedly, have been either ignored or noted without being understood.[29] Against the background of
the concentration on the charismatic or judge as a military liberator,[30]
this uncertainty is understandable. By contrast, if we do not let
ourselves get worked up by war and battle cries, we can *understand* why

---

29. Soggin, *Judges*, 228: "Samson appears as a judge only in a manner of speaking; it is a conventional designation. The texts, 13:5b; 15:20 and 16:31 say this, but
without very much conviction. He did not liberate Israel either from the power of
the Philistines or from that of any other oppressor; at the most he began this work."

30. Section 2.1 shows that this viewpoint represents a false abstraction. Cf. also
Soggin's judgment with regard to Jephthah (*Judges*, 219).

Samson is *repeatedly* called "judge," although he is not a general and does not pronounce judicial decisions. The title of "judge" describes in a comprehensive way the function of the "deliverance" of the people by one person. The title does not differentiate more closely the acts through which the deliverance occurs.[31] Without a doubt military conflict and the administration of justice are typical forms for resolving conflict: the former for external conflict, the latter for internal conflict. Yet the texts place in *direct* connection with the action of the Spirit not these particular forms, but the more general functions of producing and reproducing unanimity and the capacity to act.[32]

A *differentiated public and differentiated public opinion correspond to the changing identity of Samson, the one upon whom the Spirit comes.* On the one hand, public opinion says, "Keep clear of the Philistines. One should simply not get involved with them. They are sly and dangerous. They aim at escalating conflicts, and ultimately at killing you!" On the other hand, public opinion also says, "Don't worry about the Philistines! If the Spirit of God is with us, we are their betters. Their ropes are like strings; one of us can strike down a thousand of them with one bone!"

The Samson stories depict a *challenging, dialectical process of public moral formation.* This complicated, dialectical formation of identity takes place with regard to Samson as the bearer of the Spirit. With this dialectical process a remarkable public and a remarkable public morality are produced that reach beyond any current, concrete public and morality, and force a movement beyond all such publics and moralities. The Samson stories depict the formation of a morality and of a public in which those who wish to separate themselves from the Philistines, those who seek accommodation and appeasement, and all cases in between are placed on the same differentiated level.

---

31. This was already shown in 1939 by O. Grether, "Die Bezeichnung 'Richter' für die charismatischen Helden der vorstaatlichen Zeit," ZAW, n.s., 16 (1939): 110ff.

32. Cf. Soggin, *Judges,* 229. The fact that Samson's action has an effect beyond one concrete historical situation is documented by his elaborate birth announcement by an angel (Judg. 13:3ff.), as well as by the restrictive formulation, "It is he who shall *begin* to deliver Israel from the hand of the Philistines" (Judg. 13:5). See also K. F. D. Römheld, "Von den Quellen der Kraft (Jdc 13)," ZAW 103/104 (1991/1992): 28–52.

Numerous problems and questions arise with the recognition of this public that overarches and integrates differences. How are we to understand this gathering of the people behind Samson, with whom people identify in specific chronic relations of conflict, and with whom at the same time they neither can nor should identify? As the bearer of the Spirit, Samson gathers only a heterogeneous, polymorphous public behind himself,[33] in spite of the clear, comprehensible basic structure of the intended positive and negative identification with him. A public of this sort continually provokes the question of what criteria make it possible to distinguish a complex formation of unity and community from subtle disintegration and dissolution.

Whoever wants to confront the challenging problems of preserving an unavoidably ruptured identity in ongoing affliction will not indifferently dismiss as irrelevant and legendary the Samson figure and the testimonies of the Spirit's descent upon this figure.[34]

2.3: In the public transformation of powerholders and of political power structures: Spirit and breaks in the "tried and true" flow of experience

The early testimonies to the action of God's Spirit show a remarkable connection between *the empowerment and the disempowerment of those persons upon whom the Spirit comes.* On the one hand, the persons upon whom the Spirit comes grow "beyond themselves." Powers and abilities accrue to them. They attain public attention, acquire power over other people, command loyalty, and carry out astounding deeds. On the other hand, this extension of their person goes hand in hand with the experience of personal insecurity and helplessness, with the experience of being driven and handed over. Having the Spirit come upon one is not something a person can voluntarily bring about. It would be

---

33. See in more detail §2.4. With regard to the formation of polymorphous publics by the bearer of the Spirit and by the pouring out of the Spirit, see particularly §§3.1 and 3.4.

34. With regard to initial efforts at discerning the spirits, see §2.4. With regard to clearer testimonies of a more challenging creation of public loyalty, which also separate the action of the Spirit from military "solutions" to conflict and compel us to speak here of "early testimonies that are still unclear," see §§2.3 and 3.1ff.

nonsensical to say that a specific person or a specific group of people had made the decision to become bearers of the Spirit. Despite the subordination of their will, the persons upon whom the Spirit comes are not fully disempowered. Rather, their public influence is strong. The following statements would all be equally unthinkable: "This person decided to become a bearer of the Spirit"; "That person was seized by the Spirit, but no one noticed"; "That person was seized by the Spirit, but he was the only one who noticed." In no instance is the descent of the Spirit a merely private affair. In no instance does the descent of the Spirit cause only a private change in the person affected. If God's Spirit is at work, a *public* or even several publics are involved, either immediately or mediately.[35] Yet what occurs with the descent of the Spirit is not only a public perception, a merely public impression, something along the lines of a suspicion of witchcraft: "And the people ran together and cried, 'Look, this person has become another person; this person is a bearer of the Spirit!'" In the situations in question, *real, concrete change* in individual persons and *public reaction* to that change coincide. These situations can lead to a reformation of the public sphere, to a new capacity to act on the part of the people, as in the cases of Othniel, Gideon, and Jephthah, as well as in the story reported about Saul in 1 Samuel 11. They can also issue in general dismay, as in both of the following texts.

> Samuel took a vial of oil and poured it on his [Saul's] head, and kissed him; he said, "The LORD has anointed you ruler over God's people Israel. You shall reign over the people of the LORD and you will save them from the hand of their enemies all around" [Cf. LXX. Saul is thus informed that he is supposed to fulfill the tasks with which we are familiar from the early charismatics. That this is God's will, that God anointed Saul as ruler "over God's heritage," is something that Saul is supposed to know on the basis of a series of signs. Among the things prophesied to him are the following:] After that you shall come to Gibeath-elohim, at the place where the Philistine garrison is; there, as you come to the town, you will meet a band of prophets coming down from the shrine with harp, tambourine, flute, and lyre playing in front of them; they will be in a state of prophetic ecstasy. Then the Spirit of the LORD will possess

---

35. See esp. §§2.2 and 2.4.

you, and you will be in a state of prophetic ecstasy along with them and be turned into a different person. Now when these signs meet you, do whatever you see fit to do, for God is with you. (1 Sam. 10:1-7)

At first glance it is difficult to make sense of the extensively described circumstances accompanying the descent of the Spirit. Certainly, Saul is changed into another person. But why does this occur precisely in connection with an ecstatic state? Of course he is supposed to receive certainty about what he is ordained to be, but why are the other signs not adequate? Why is a sign that is evidently a cause for *dismay* to all persons involved used in connection with the descent of the Spirit? There can be no doubt that this sign is also a cause for dismay in the perspective of the biblical traditions. The account is explicit in reporting that the public is astonished, indeed that it even seems scornful:

When they were going from there to Gibeah, a band of prophets met him; and the Spirit of God possessed him, and he fell into prophetic ecstasy along with them. When all who knew him before saw how he had fallen into a state of ecstasy with the prophets, the people said to one another, "What has come over the son of Kish? Is Saul also among the prophets?" A man of the place answered, "And who is their father?" Therefore it became a proverb, "Is Saul also among the prophets?" (1 Sam. 10:10-12)

Neither Saul nor the public explicitly mentioned seems to be able really to understand the transferal of the prophetic ecstasy to him. There is no mention of Saul having a "certainty of election." The public attention that is evoked initially consists only of dismay. The change of identity of the person upon whom the Spirit comes evokes public astonishment. A few prophets come out of the blue who do not fit customary appearances and expected forms of life. And Saul, the son of Kish, a reasonable young man, lets himself be infected by them. His *own will is rendered powerless*[36] and he falls into a trance, from

---

36. Cf. A. Heschel, *The Prophets* (New York: Harper & Row, 1962), esp 346; G. Hölscher, *Die Propheten* (Leipzig: Hinrichs, 1914); H.-C. Schmitt, "Prophetie und Tradition," *ZTK* 74 (1977): 255–72, esp. 270–71.

which apparently nothing meaningful and useful follows. During the trance others can do nothing with Saul—outside of becoming aware of his trance and being astonished by him and by the change that has taken place in him.

The early charismatics—Saul included—upon whom the Spirit came reassembled a public and gave it a new order. When the Spirit comes upon Saul here, he initially evokes only public astonishment, public dismay, perhaps even scorn. Does the descent of the Spirit—sign of Saul's imminent installation as ruler and deliverer of the people—at first lead to his disempowerment instead of to an increase in power? The second story, 1 Samuel 19, seems to place the descent of the Spirit and the *withdrawal of power* in direct connection.

Three times Saul sends messengers to get David, who has fled to Samuel, and to kill him. A "Spirit of God" (1 Sam. 19:20) comes upon the messengers and they fall into prophetic ecstasy when they catch sight of the prophets around Samuel and David. At this point Saul himself goes to Ramah, where David is with Samuel and the group of prophets. While Saul was still en route,

> the Spirit of God came upon him. As he was going, he fell into a state of prophetic ecstasy until he came to Naioth in Ramah. He too stripped off his clothes, and he too fell into a state of prophetic ecstasy before Samuel. He lay naked all that day and all that night. Therefore it is said, "Is Saul also among the prophets?" (1 Sam. 19:23-24)

The action of the Spirit can authorize and empower. The uncontrollable and unexpected action of the Spirit can express itself where a person seized by the Spirit appears as master of the situation and the people march out in unity. But the action of the Spirit can also lead to the person upon whom the Spirit has come appearing to be "out of commission" and the observers being simply dismayed or terrified.

Can *coherent connections* be established between the different experiences of the descent of the Spirit? Help would seem to come from the observation that the weakness and the public powerlessness of the messianic bearer of the Spirit are highlighted many times.[37] But even

---

37. See §§3.1 and 3.2, as well as 4.1 and 4.2.

prior to that, it is helpful to remember the early charismatics' remarkable lack of certainty of victory.[38]

After the Spirit has come upon him, Gideon remains uncertain and skeptical. This is so despite the fact that people from the tribes of Israel are gathering around him, and despite the fact that objective signs are given that exclude the possibility of self-deception. Even after he receives the desired sign from God (see Judg. 6:36ff.), Gideon remains distrustful. He asks for a repetition of this sign, which then occurs. In other words, *the person upon whom God's Spirit comes remains uncertain, skeptical, and in need of assurance—at any rate in the early testimonies to the action of God's Spirit.* Although he is aware of what God intends ("In order to see whether you will deliver Israel by my hand, as you have said . . ."), although it was not by mistake or in a moment of excitement that he blew the ram's horn, although the people come from all sides and gather behind him, this charismatic would like to have a sign. After the sign has actually come, Gideon stands there as if it could still be a coincidence and asks for a repetition of the sign: "Do not let your anger burn against me, let me speak one more time."

Amazingly, this skeptical testing and looking for certainty is reported in several stories. This can only mean that the early action of the Spirit is accompanied *neither by complete subjective certainty nor by complete objective certainty.* The person upon whom God's Spirit comes is a person *seeking* for the certainty of God's presence and of God's action. The charismatics—even as bearers of political power—have no control over the action of God and of the Spirit.[39] The action of the Spirit, clearly directed at delivering Israel from overpowering enemies, aims neither at providing unmediated, heroic certainty for the charismatic, nor at a "spiritual" certainty of victory conditional on the success of an army. In fact, the intention is to work against a feeling of superiority and of certain victory in view of the powerful effect of the Spirit, so that after victory occurs Israel will not say, "My own hand has delivered me" (Judg. 7:2).

The bearers of the Spirit receive signs of being empowered, but are not supposed to rely on a power that they can control. The bearers of the Spirit even receive signs of their election as "ruler and deliverer"

---

38. Cf. §2.1.
39. Cf. the story in Judg. 7:1ff.

of the people, but this is connected with publicly recognizable forms of disempowerment. The persons whose services God enlists experience an annulment of their previous flow of experience, an annulment of their previous public self-presentation. This happens, for example, when Saul becomes caught up in the ecstatic state of the prophets.[40]

The situation is analogous with regard to public resonance. On the one hand, the descent of God's Spirit opens the door to public recognition that Saul is receiving another identity, that he has landed "among the prophets," that God wills to act in him and through him. On the other hand, this does not result in a personal gain in power and prestige. Instead it elicits dismay, perhaps even a certain scorn.

It is not easy to grasp precisely what is happening here. There is a *break* in both the self-experience and the public knowledge of a person. The crowd must ask itself whether this is still the "son of Kish" whom they know. The mighty Saul lies powerless all day long before Samuel. The Spirit's coming upon a person does not lead to a definite new

---

40. On the one hand, the texts single out the person upon whom the Spirit comes. On the other hand, they equate this person with the prophets who are in a state of ecstasy. The combination of these two perspectives is striking. See the observations of F. D. Goodman, *How About Demons?: Possession and Exorcism in the Modern World* (Bloomington: Indiana Univ. Press, 1988), 6ff. Goodman has investigated the forms of expression employed in different countries and cultures by people in a state of religious ecstasy. She discovered characteristics of accent, rhythm, and intonation that remained constant independently of the mother tongue of the speaker. In her opinion, this "suggests that we are dealing with a neurophysiological change that is instituted in all religious ritual when human beings speak in this nonordinary way" (6–7). On the basis of blood tests and electroencephalograms, Goodman concludes that "humans apparently utilize the same kind of trance for ritual purposes the world over, which suggests that it is part of our genetic endowment" (10). If these conclusions are accurate, they support the observation that the Samuel stories have the intention of both setting a character in relief and relativizing that emphasis, of both empowering a character and of introducing a break into the previous flow of experience by equating that character with other persons who find themselves in an ecstatic state. I am grateful to S. Brandt for pointing out that being equated with others could denote that the charismatics are not totally "carried away" into the numinous, the ghostly, and the undefinable. The logic and dynamic of their transformation of identity can be followed from outside—as a "loss of identity" with regard to the fact that they are only God's functionaries. Cf. also T. Spoerri, "Zum Begriff der Ekstase," in T. Spoerri, ed., *Beiträge zur Ekstase*, Bibliotheca Psychiatrica et Neurologica (Basel: S. Karger, 1968), 1ff.

identity that the person, or this person's environment, could utilize, regulate, and calculate. The new identity remains in the balance—in the balance between power and powerlessness, public recognition and public dismay. The new identity remains open for God to form as God wills.

This same thing is documented by an account of the descent of the Spirit who leads to the change in identity not only of an individual human being, but of a political structure.

The account of the "sharing of the Spirit of Moses" (Num. 11:14ff., 25ff.) expresses in a particularly striking way the interconnection between empowerment and disempowerment, between removal of the limitations on people's capacities and public uncertainty over the fact that their familiar appearance seems to have changed abruptly. Here as well, the point of departure is a politically relevant event. Although this event is not connected with a situation of acute distress, it is connected with a general mood of discontent and regret among the people of Israel on account of the state of their provisions in the wilderness. Looking at the flatbread prepared from manna, the people think not only about the "fleshpots of Egypt," but also about "the fish . . . the cucumbers, the melons, the leeks, the onions, and the garlic" (Num. 11:5). The people put Moses under public pressure, and he for his part complains to God.

> "I am not able to carry all this people alone, for they are too heavy for me." [God's answer consists in restructuring the political leadership.] So the LORD said to Moses, "Gather for me seventy of the elders of Israel . . . bring them to the tent of meeting, and have them take their place there with you. I will come down and talk with you there; and I will take and put on them some of the Spirit that is on you; and they shall bear the burden of the people along with you so that you will not bear it all by yourself." (Num. 11:14-17)

Considered so far, the gift and distribution of the Spirit is here, too, connected with the restoration of loyalty and unanimity among the people. Here as well, the people's unity and community is restored in a situation of unrest and complaint—in this case by means of "decentralized" leadership. By increasing the leadership circle a mutiny will hopefully be prevented, and the more difficult task of ensuring loyalty will hopefully again be achieved. It is at this point that strange things start happening. After Moses had gathered the seventy elders at the tent, with two of them remaining in the camp, "the LORD came down in the cloud and spoke to him, and took and put on the seventy elders some of the Spirit who was resting on him" (Num. 11:25). The Spirit comes not only upon those who are gathered, but also upon those who stayed back in the camp—in accordance with the total number of those whom God ordained to leadership and whom Moses selected at God's behest. Here as well, the text emphasizes that God's sharing of the Spirit is directed not according to the behavior of the people involved, but according to God's instructions and according to the corresponding selection procedures. Just as in the case of individual leader figures, the "oligarchy" of those who have received a share of the Spirit does not form an independently operating power. Here as well, the gift of the Spirit is first recognizable by the fact that the seventy elders, including those who stayed back in the camp, fall into an ecstatic state. Numbers 11:25b: "When the Spirit rested upon them, they fell into an ecstatic state. But they did not do so again." In this case, too, it is not only the enlightened commentaries,[41] but participants in the story who react with dismay at this immediate result of the sharing of the Spirit. An excited young man comes running out of the camp and tells about the two men who have fallen into an ecstatic state (who stand outside the established order in a double way, so to speak). Under these conditions Joshua does not foresee any lessening of the burden of political leadership and enjoins Moses, "Stop them!" Numbers 11:29: "But Moses said to him, '. . . Would that all the LORD's people were 'prophets,' and that the LORD would put God's Spirit on them!' "

How are we to understand this? Those who have been ordained to take some of the burden from Moses do not take over the affairs of government. They do not bring the people to order socio-therapeutically or morally. Instead they land in prophetic rapture. And Moses, to whom

---

41. "We are dealing with 'prophetic' exaltation, with a state of ecstasy from which come 'prophetic' words which are not comprehensible—or not necessarily so. This is very strange in the present context. Moses is supposed to be 'relieved of his burden' (vv. 14-17). How this goal is achieved by putting the seventy elders into a state of ecstasy is difficult to imagine; moreover, nothing is said on this subject" (M. Noth, *Numbers: A Commentary*, trans. J. D. Martin, OTL [Philadelphia: Westminster, 1968], 89).

anarchic-chaotic traits are otherwise truly foreign, is happy with the situation! He would be happiest if all the people were in a condition of prophetic agitation. Two opposed responses to the action of God's Spirit collide here head-on. On the one hand is distrust in the face of the change in people by means of the pouring out of God's Spirit, which does not occur within the framework of human preparations and dispositions. On the other hand is trust in the action of God's Spirit, which temporarily renders people apparently powerless, but which through this act draws their attention to the fact that God has enlisted their services, and which opens the door to their being recognized from the outside as God's deputies.

In all the cases discussed, the change of individual persons or of a number of people goes hand in hand with the dissolution and renewal of a *public* and of *public attention*. We do not at first know exactly what it means to say that Saul becomes "a different person." We hear only about the public reaction: "What has come over the son of Kish? Is Saul also among the prophets?" The observable abstractness and emptiness of the public reaction are further confirmed by the text when it comments that the reaction "Is Saul also among the prophets?" became a *proverb*. That is, it became a formula that fits different situations, whose use can be occasioned by different situations as long as the basic condition is met that an individual life shows a specific, considerable, publicly noticed discontinuity. In line with this is the reaction of informed political opinion, represented by Joshua: "What are we to do with these enraptured elders?"

In all cases of the Spirit's descent, the general *security of expectations* is called into question and changed. Sometimes this means that the danger, the distress, the expected annihilation—for example, by a superior army—is avoided. Other times it means that the routine of life in its daily round and of habitual expectations is disturbingly changed or interrupted. The individuals directly touched by the Spirit all have in common that they *become "beside themselves."* They draw attention to themselves; they become public. This commonality leaves open a variety of possibilities for their specific actions. Perhaps they exercise a specific *function*, even one that is highly necessary in its importance for the entire community: for example, they reunite the people, gathering them against the forces that oppress them. Perhaps those touched by the Spirit receive public loyalty and recognition. Or perhaps they seem only to give offense and to become curious, anomalous phenomena.

In any case, those persons who are touched and clothed by the Spirit go beyond themselves. They change their identity, fall into prophetic rapture, can hardly be recognized. They become angry, blow a ram's horn, cut oxen in pieces, become a leader of the people, become the center of a movement of deliverance. In every case it is obvious that their lives are no longer their own.

As a rule the early testimonies to the action of the Spirit[42]—testimonies that remain unclear and leave many questions unanswered—confine the change to individual political[43] or prophetic[44] models.

God's Spirit simultaneously empowers people *and* disempowers them.[45] The Spirit places them in an aura of public observation *and* public dismay. This action of the Spirit necessitates a clear knowledge that makes it possible to *distinguish* this action *from the action of other powers,* of other forces.

To what extent do the early insights into the action of God's Spirit contribute to clarifying the Spirit's action, to removing its ambivalence and ambiguity, to curbing its unsettling constitution? To what extent do even these early insights urge a "discerning of the spirits"?

---

42. Besides the story of the sharing of the Spirit of Moses, one should also note 1 Sam. 19:20. Concerning the development that does away with this monocentrism, see chap. 3 and §§4.5 and 5.1ff.

43. Cf. Num. 27:16ff. and Deut. 34:9, which bring out with particular clarity the connection between being "filled with the Spirit" and winning public loyalty. With regard to the problem that arises here concerning the interconnection and distinction between the "Spirit of God" and the "Spirit of wisdom," see §2.5.

44. Cf. 2 Kings 2:9ff. and Ecclus. 48:12ff. See §3.1 concerning the more complex constellation of the Spirit's "remaining" and "resting." This "remaining" and "resting" is asserted not only with regard to Moses, but also with regard to David (1 Sam. 16:13).

45. This interconnection receives a particularly drastic expression in numerous passages that emphasize the phenomena of being "lifted up" and "carried to another place" by the Spirit (several texts add by way of explanation that this occurs in a vision). See, e.g., 1 Kings 18:12; Ezek. 3:12ff.; 8:3; 11:1ff.; 37:1; 43:5; and passim.

2.4: In the act of making possible the recognition of evil spirits and lying spirits: Spirit and prophetic knowledge

The early biblical traditions are familiar not only with God's Spirit delivering out of distress, restoring unanimity among a people or preserving a people in affliction. They also report that God sends an *evil spirit* between people, or a spirit of recklessness and error. This evil spirit dissolves unanimity, or keeps it from ever arising. Or the evil spirit entices people to risky political enterprises. Judges 9:23 comes straight to the point: "But God sent an evil spirit between Abimelech and the lords of Shechem; and the lords of Shechem dealt treacherously with Abimelech." Isaiah 19:2-3 gives a particularly striking description of the process of political and social disintegration and destruction that confuses the spirit of a community or of a people:

> I will stir up Egyptians against Egyptians,
> and they will fight, one against the other,
> neighbor against neighbor, city against city, kingdom against
>   kingdom;
> the spirit of the Egyptians within them will be emptied out,
> and I will confound their plans;
> they will consult the idols and the spirits of the dead
> and the ghosts. . . .[46]

The action of an evil spirit is asserted not only with regard to a community, but also with regard to a person upon whom God's Spirit has previously come and whom God's Spirit has politically empowered.

---

46. On distinguishing and connecting the Spirit who comes "from outside" with the Spirit who works "within" persons and communities, see §2.5. Concerning the overcoming of this problem, see chaps. 4 and 5. Isaiah 19:14 speaks of a spirit "poured into" the Egyptians, which makes them dizzy and causes them to stagger around. 2 Kings 19:7 and Isa. 37:7 provide further clear evidence of the disintegrative "evil spirit" that leads into error, destruction, and self-destruction. The evil spirit, the "spirit of confusion," can come upon Israel's enemies as well as upon Israel itself. In Israel the evil spirit destroys above all the (prophetic) relationship of the people to God (Isa. 29:10): "For the LORD has poured out upon you a spirit of deep sleep; God has closed your eyes, you prophets, and covered your heads, you seers." Cf. Hos. 4:12; 5:4; 9:7; as well as Zech. 13:2; also the systematic connection made by Rom. 11:8.

"Now the Spirit of the LORD departed from Saul, and an evil spirit from the LORD tormented him" (1 Sam. 16:14). This evil spirit not only torments the one upon whom it comes, but also induces him to engage in hatred and aggressive behavior. Like God's good Spirit, this power is also perceived by outsiders. "And Saul's servants said to him, 'See now, an evil spirit from God is tormenting you. Let our lord now command the servants who attend you to look for someone who is skillful in playing the lyre; and when the evil spirit from God is upon you, he will play it, and you will feel better' "(vv. 15-16). As is well known, David is selected to drive out the evil spirit by means of music (see also 1 Sam. 16:23; 18:10; 19:9).

Up to this point, it seems plausible to conclude that the good Spirit of God is a Spirit who leads to the unity and community of a people or to the powerful, positive influence of an individual person. By contrast, the evil spirit leads to disintegration and destruction of a community. The evil spirit torments individual persons and induces them to act aggressively.

This conclusion, though, needs an important caveat. It is not always possible to distinguish immediately and clearly between the good Spirit of God and the evil spirit. The evil spirit can disguise its destructive might. The evil spirit can come on the scene and act as a "lying spirit," masking its destructive might. Against this, the *prophetic power of discerning spirits* must be summoned.

What is a lying spirit?

A "lying spirit" is not a picturesque expression for a lie that is not easily seen through, or for the mendacious attitude of an individual person. A lying spirit is the mendacious spirit of a community, of a people, which determines public opinion. "If the *Führer* knew that!"; "We don't know what is happening with the Jews"; "The miracle weapon will bring the ultimate victory!"—with public opinions and slogans of this sort, determined by a lying spirit, people attempted to stabilize public and private life in the Third Reich. "Water and air are inexhaustible natural resources"; "Dying forests are not connected to industrial and automobile emissions"; "With permanent armament we are making peace more secure!"—those were some of the many astoundingly resistant public opinions of the 1960s, '70s, and '80s that, as has become clear in the meantime, can be ascribed to a lying spirit. In many of these cases professionals and specialists have carefully discussed the theme and given their judgment. Public opinion is formed. "They" are agreed. Whoever says the contrary is someone who just likes to be contentious.

The story of the vision of Micaiah the son of Imlah (1 Kings 22 and 2 Chronicles 18) gives particularly striking expression to the problem and the drama of distinguishing God's Spirit from an evil spirit, the problem of distinguishing the Spirit of truth from a spirit of the lie.

In 1 Kings 22 the experts and representatives of public opinion are some four hundred prophets. Ahab, the king of Israel, has assembled them in order to question them. "'Shall I go to battle against Ramoth-gilead, or shall I refrain?' They said, 'Go up; for the LORD will give it into the hand of the king'" (v. 6, cf. 11ff.).

Four hundred prophets cannot be wrong. The battle forces would probably have set right out if the king of Judah, who happened to be present, had not been skeptical and asked for further prophets of God. The king of Israel concedes that there is one more prophet, but he says that he hates this prophet because he always prophesies only bad things, never good. Nevertheless Micaiah son of Imlah is brought by a messenger; while they are under way, the messenger recommends that Micaiah add his support to the opinion of the prophets: "The messenger who had gone to summon Micaiah said to him, 'Look, the words of the prophets with one accord are favorable to the king; let your word be like the word of one of them, and speak favorably'" (v. 13). What happens next is astounding. On the one hand, Micaiah answers the messenger, "As the LORD lives, whatever the LORD says to me, that I will speak" (v. 14). On the other hand, before the king he initially concurs with the universal opinion, which later turns out to be false and deceptive: "When he had come to the king, the king said to him, 'Micaiah, shall we go to Ramoth-gilead to battle, or shall we refrain?' He answered him, 'Go up and triumph; the LORD will give it into the hand of the king'" (v. 15). Only when the distrustful king adjures him in the name of God to speak the truth does the prophet unfold a vision that explains his first—false—answer. The vision draws attention to the lying spirit of the four hundred prophets as well as to the truth.

> "Therefore hear the word of the LORD: I saw the LORD sitting on God's throne, with all the host of heaven standing beside God to the right and to the left of God. And the LORD said, 'Who will entice

Ahab, so that he may go up and fall at Ramoth-gilead?' Then one said one thing, and another said another, until a spirit came forward and stood before the LORD, saying, 'I will entice him.' 'How?' the LORD asked him. He replied, 'I will go out and be a lying spirit in the mouth of all his prophets.' Then the LORD said, 'You are to entice him, and you shall succeed; go out and do it.' So you see, the LORD has put a lying spirit in the mouth of all these your prophets; the LORD has decreed disaster for you." (1 Kings 22:19-23)

The lying spirit is unavoidable, because it is sent by Godself. The four hundred prophets cannot help but fall victim to this lying spirit. The king as well is handed over to it. This is expressed by the fact that the king, albeit halfheartedly, uncertainly, and in disguise, goes out to battle, where he loses his life. It is also expressed by the fact that the prophets stand by their prognosis. They have no occasion to think that, against their better judgment, they are following a lying spirit, or are even propagating such a spirit of their own accord. They are simply sure of their specialty. "Then Zedekiah son of Chenaanah came up to Micaiah, slapped him on the cheek, and said, 'Which way did the Spirit of the LORD pass from me to speak to you?' " (v. 24). Micaiah's answer, unfolded in a vision, is that there is indeed a spirit sent by God among the prophets, but it is a lying spirit. Micaiah in fact claims for himself the very thing that Zedekiah calls into question. The Spirit of God mediates prophetic knowledge to him, which enables him to discern the spirits.

Micaiah's vision depicts the powerlessness and the blindness in which human beings are caught, in spite of their need to hear the Spirit of God speak.

What should the prophets do who are possessed by God's lying spirit? They are in the majority—four hundred to one—and resist Micaiah's claim to truth. But Micaiah responds to Zedekiah: Whether the Spirit of God has passed from you or not is something "you will find out on that day when you go in to hide in an inner chamber" (v. 25). And what should the king do, confronted with two prophecies? He chooses a middle road and enters the battle in disguise, after Micaiah has told him, "If you return in peace, the LORD has not spoken by me" (v. 28).

In what way can the Spirit of truth who speaks through the prophet be distinguished from the spirit of the lie? The obvious answer,

"By the fact that the prophet listens to God," is inadequate. Zedekiah, too, seems to consider himself accompanied and informed by God. There is in fact a spirit, even a spirit allowed and approved by God—albeit a lying one—with him and his fellow prophets. Is it possible to recognize and to put forward criteria for "discerning the spirits"? The story points to at least *three criteria,* which even in contemporary contexts of experience lose none of their persuasive force. These criteria are:

1. The readiness not to add one's support automatically to the ruling opinion, but to test *in constantly new ways* whether the spirit of the age, the spirit of the political leadership, of the consensus of the experts, or of other important influences agrees with the Spirit of truth or not.

2. The readiness to connect the publicly knowable truth of one's own prophecy with one's own existence and one's own destiny. That is, one's own credibility is made dependent on the factual occurrence of what is prophetically promised.

3. The capacity theologically to explain, to reconstruct, and thus to relativize a situation that has gone awry and that makes itself immune to the truth.

Micaiah is in accord with the first criterion not by actually seeking conflict with the ruling opinion and with the opinion of those who rule. He does not push his way to center stage; he must be summoned. Nor does he push his viewpoint on others. This is highlighted explicitly. The Spirit of truth is not tied to the attitude of one who speaks against the rest of the world with the loneliness of one crying in the wilderness. Yet the prophetic person also does not *shy away* from this conflict. The prophet does not *confuse* truth and consensus. The prophet does not confuse God's word with the word of those who happen to hold power at present, or with the opinion of the majority. This is because powerholders and the majority *can* fall victim to a lying spirit—and this means a power that actually seizes the majority of experts, the political leadership, and the public.

Prophetic persons who discern the spirits are not chronic faultfinders, loners, and eccentrics, looking for conflict and bent on proving that they are in the right. On occasion they may appear that way.

But in fact they are *free* in relation to the political and societal forces that hold power and that pressure people to fit in. This freedom of those who distinguish God's Spirit from a lying spirit does not mean that they have no commitments or obligations, or are fundamentally without political, practical loyalty. Micaiah pins himself down—here the second criterion comes into play—when he remarks to the king, "If you return in peace, the LORD has not spoken by me."

The prophets who distinguish God's Spirit from a lying spirit pin themselves down. This means not only that they are pinned down from outside on the basis of their prophecy, which can lead to their being ostracized, persecuted, bound and thrown into prison, or even killed.[47] They also themselves tie their own existence, their own destiny to the fulfillment of their predictions. By obligating themselves in this dangerous manner, they are free from the pressure of public opinion and of the ruling power. They are free in their view of the truth. They are free in their knowledge of what will actually occur. They both tie themselves to and are tied to the *knowledge of the truth* and the *definitive public* that will ineluctably recognize this truth: a future public that will recognize the realization of the truth.

A universal public will find their vision ultimately and definitively verified. To this corresponds the fact that, as will be shown later, their knowledge is already known in the heavenly public.[48] This does not mean that prophetic persons experience a correspondingly definitive earthly public, that they are assured of being able to consummate their triumph as individuals still living on earth. To be sure, these prophets who recognize the truth, who see through lies, and who are free in relation to the ruling power, political pressure, and the pressure of public opinion—these prophets know that the moment of truth will come, that truth will become reality. They know that the truth will be recognized and universally acknowledged, that it will cast off all doubt, all illusion, and all lies and show that these are in the wrong. But they have no assurance that *they themselves* will in their own time be among those experiencing the truth's becoming reality and the public acknowledgment of the truth. They cannot know themselves as the justified victors

---

47. Thus Micaiah is initially thrown into prison (1 Kings 22:26-27); prophecy costs Zecharaiah his life (2 Chron. 24:21).

48. See esp. §3.3.

of tomorrow. They cannot be sure of their earthly, public acknowledgment and honor. Perhaps they will be marked by care, persecution, and distress. Perhaps they will have died when what was promised occurs.

The third criterion for distinguishing the Spirit of truth from a lying spirit is not present in this story except in a very abstract manner: the reconstruction of a situation gone awry; the demonstration of the inevitability of the situation with its immunization against better knowledge. This reconstruction is scarcely comprehensible today without "translation aids" that open the path to a new understanding both of the conception of "heaven" and of politico-theological reflection in the forms of a "heavenly court."[49] Micaiah brings an outside perspective to the currently dominant viewpoint, which is supported by the absolute majority of all religious experts. Micaiah's outside perspective unmasks the dominant viewpoint as false, but Micaiah does not push any alternative. He describes the future reality that is already present in his superior view of the heavenly, definitive public. In contrast to the message of the lying spirit ("Go up to battle; God will grant you success!"), the future reality described by Micaiah will show itself to be *truth*. This truth runs as follows: "I saw all Israel scattered on the mountains, like sheep that have no shepherd; and the LORD said, 'These have no master; let each one go home in peace'" (1 Kings 22:17). Looking back from the perspective of this truth, it is possible to recognize that "the LORD has put a lying spirit in the mouth of all these your prophets; the LORD has decreed disaster for you" (v. 23). What the prophet predicts is not just some sort of abstract correctness, not the truth of the so-called twenty-twenty vision of hindsight, but a powerful, concrete truth whose reality is still obstructed but whose occurrence is imminent.

But what good is the prophetic discernment between truth and a lying spirit, and whom does this discernment benefit, if nothing about the given situation can be changed after all? Let us consider one more time the concrete case of the vision of Micaiah son of Imlah among

---

49. See P. D. Miller, "Cosmology and World Order in the Old Testament: The Divine Council as Cosmic-Political Symbol," in *Horizons in Biblical Theology: An International Dialogue* 9 (1987): 53ff.; M. Welker, "Über Gottes Engel: Systematisch-theologische Überlegungen im Anschluss an Claus Westermann und Hartmut Gese," *JBT* 2, ed. N. Lohfink and I. Baldermann (1987): 194ff.

the prophets and before Ahab. The prophet must go into prison (1 Kings 22:26-27). Zedekiah and his four hundred fellow prophets do not believe his words anyway, and according to Micaiah's own knowledge, they cannot believe him, since they are blinded and held captive by a lying spirit sent by God. In spite of Micaiah's words, the king goes out to battle and loses his life. This, too, is inevitable according to God's decree. The ruin of the royal house is thus decided from the outset. Even the prophets along with those who believed them will observe, when the military campaign to which they all gave their vigorous religious recommendation and blessing turns into a disaster, that it was not God's Spirit who was at work.

Under these circumstances, why does God have visions proclaimed at all? Why does God have the Spirit speak through prophets, even exposing them to affliction in the process, if ruin is decided regardless? What good is the knowledge and proclamation of the truth *now,* if no one believes it *now* regardless? What good is the knowledge and proclamation of the truth *now,* if *then,* later, everyone can experience—or will have experienced—the truth regardless?

It is important to recognize that the prophetic person, who brings the truth of God to bear, addresses *not only a contemporary public, and not even a homogeneous public.* The prophetic person of course speaks to the public that is spatially and temporally present to him—this is the internal view of the story. The prophet speaks to this public, although he knows that it will not believe him, that it is caught in a lying spirit. The prophet even speaks to those whom he knows to be destined for ruin. It is characteristic of the Spirit's action and of God's truth that they also establish their validity against those who do *not* accept them, who by all estimates do not even want to accept them and are not even able to accept them.

Yet the prophetic person who mediates God's truth addresses *not only his contemporary public,* which constitutes the internal view of this story. The prophet also addresses the public or publics that will look back on this story, the publics to which we too belong.

Put more precisely, it is the prophet by his vision who first gathers and constitutes this broad, asymptotically universal public that will adopt an external perspective on this story. The prophetic person addresses the public that will perceive without distortion the reality that the lying spirit depicts in a disguised and distorted manner. The prophet addresses the public that shall have a definitive knowledge of truth. For this public the prophet gives a valid description of reality: a description of reality that will last. But why is this important?

The prophetic vision preserves the story, making it worthy and capable of being remembered. The prophetic vision distinguishes the story from the countless suppressed so-called setbacks and misdirected developments of history, from the many advisory, political, and military miscalculations that disappear from view. In general the political, military, and other publics treat these setbacks according to the principle that it is best *to repress and to forget* them. After the military failure the four hundred prophets would presumably have simply withdrawn until sufficient water had passed under the bridge. Perhaps they would have changed their profession, gone to another ruler, or taken early retirement under the olive trees of their children. Perhaps they would have laid the mistaken prognosis at Zedekiah's doorstep, trying to rehabilitate themselves by dumping him. Then probably only Zedekiah would have behaved as Micaiah son of Imlah had predicted: You will learn that the Spirit of God has passed from you "on that day when you go in to hide in an inner chamber" (v. 25). Most likely one would not have been at a loss even for an explanation that would quell the uproar and lead back to normality. With the description of the remarkable death of the king, the story as it has come down to us even offers its own noteworthy initial explanation and justification of the false prophecy provided by the lying spirit. Ahab is struck by an arrow and commands his charioteer: "'Turn around, and carry me out of the battle, for I am wounded.' The battle grew hot that day, and the king was propped up in his chariot facing the Arameans, until at evening he died; the blood from the wound had flowed into the bottom of the chariot" (1 Kings 22:34b-35).

A mortally wounded king who nevertheless stands upright in his chariot—this is no place for a proper court prophet to have erroneous visions concerning his fate and the outcome of the battle! "In the Spirit I saw the king in battle. And behold, he stood unwavering in his chariot and did not fall!"

In contrast to all conceivable attempts at justification, repression, or forgetting, which would have brought the story below the threshold of what is worthy of remembrance for the participants and especially for succeeding generations, the vision of Micaiah son of Imlah records the fact that *the prophetic counsel was wrong*. It was wrong, as not only became clear *later*, but as was also recognized and could be known *beforehand* in God's presence and surroundings. The prophets of Ahab had no share in this truth and no access to it. They *had* to give false counsel because that is how God had disposed matters. Thus it is inadmissible to repress and to forget, as well as to rationalize and to justify. It was not by chance that the story went the way it did.

This means that Micaiah, to whom the Spirit of God "speaks" and who participates in the perception of reality that occurs in God's presence, is already announcing the *end of the Ahab era*. In distinguishing the Spirit of truth from a lying spirit, the prophet has a hand in making the collapse of Ahab's rule definitive and irrevocable. What is at stake is not a change in that rule, but the *preparation for its end and a new beginning*. What is intended is not just a break in the experiences with this era and this reality. At issue is a break in life processes; at issue is their being historicized and normatively evaluated. This is the goal of the prophetic speech of Micaiah son of Imlah. There are not to be any successors along the lines of Ahab. No Ahab Street and no Ahab Monument! No renaissance of Ahabism. No continuation of the "good old" court prophecy, which after all proved itself on the whole and has been purified of "extremist phenomena" like Zedekiah. God has decreed not the continuation of the status quo, but its end and a new beginning. This is the message of the prophecy. Its message is indeed primarily for succeeding generations. The prophecy orients the public that is formed anew after the disaster and that is seeking its own structure of values and of reality: Do not follow in these footsteps; you cannot build on this foundation; do not establish any continuity with this! This phase of history, this institution, this ideology, this public is not innocuous. It cannot be reformed. It cannot be classed under rubrics such as "inadvertently stumbled into war," "well-meaning but unfortunate," "small error of the party leadership," and the like. This phase of history, this institution, this ideology, this politics, this public is corrupt, destined for degeneration and disappearance. It is dangerous: one must not let oneself be infected by it. Even in attempts to learn from its mistakes, caution should be the watchword. A lying spirit brought it to the end willed and ordained by God.

The great significance—indeed, the vital necessity—of prophetic knowledge becomes comprehensible as soon as we ask what orientation for rebuilding is actually available when the cultural, political, and public life of a people collapses. The situation seems comparatively easy when various parties, various ideologies, various claims and proposals are present for the formation of public, political, and cultural life. After a lost war it can be expected that the superior, victorious power will impose its political and cultural structures on the defeated power. Alternatively, the victorious power may push through forms that are mixtures of the previously predominant spirit and of its own spiritual makeup. History is written by the victors. Not only history, but also the social construction of reality, the establishment of the boundary conditions for what is valid and what is not, for what is acknowledged and what is not, lie in the hands of those who prevail as the stronger party, the victors. Today the so-called global public is to a certain extent sensitive to the imperialistic destruction of cultures that goes hand in hand with this process.[50] This public laments, criticizes, and abhors the actions of imperialistic subjugation of smaller, weaker peoples and cultures by powers that are superior militarily, economically, and in terms of communications technology.

But what other choice is there with an Ahab regime[51] or a Nazi dictatorship, when a lying spirit rules the people and its political leadership, when elementary judicial, religious, and moral standards are transgressed, when militarily aggressive politics are carried out? Why should we not all breathe a sigh of relief when such a system, such a culture and history is simply blotted out, superseded by the intervention of a victorious power that is superior not only militarily, but also politically, religiously, and in humanitarian terms? Naturally we must

---

50. N. Lohfink provides an excellent illustration in *Great Themes from the Old Testament*, trans. R. Walls (Chicago: Franciscan Herald, 1981), 17–37.

51. The root of the spread of devastation and disintegration by this regime is to be seen in its attempt to make room for both the worship of Yahweh and the worship of Baal. This attempt, whose problematic can scarcely be understood in a culture that has differentiated politics and religion into separate subsystems, ultimately fails. Excavations show Ahab's "residence in full possession of the Canaanite culture of that day. But its Canaanite quality was greatly strengthened by the sanctuary that A[hab] erected in it not for Yahweh, the God of Israel, but for 'Baal'" (A. Alt, "Ahab," *RGG* 1, 189–90). See also the differentiated assessment of Ahab's religious politics by O. H. Steck, *Überlieferung und Zeitgeschichte in den Elia-Erzählungen*, WMANT 26 (Neukirchen-Vluyn: Neukirchener, 1968), esp. 65ff.

be careful that this argument not be employed for imperialistic power politics. Naturally it can happen that a militarily superior power suddenly begins to see lying spirits, realms of evil, and nests of terror everywhere in order to have a reason for violently replacing the systems of other lands. But are there not cases where the supersession of a corrupt system by another system is legitimate and even salutary? Is it not correct that, for example, in 1942 even a Little U.S.A. or a Little Russia on German soil would have been better than a continuation of Nazi rule?

For the persons upon whom God's Spirit has come, such considerations lead to an untenable position, even when they must conclude that the ruin of their contemporary culture has already been decided. This culture is ruled by a lying spirit. This culture must be blotted out, and there must be absolutely no toying with the idea of its continuation. God has decreed disaster for Ahab. The king shall die. The political system shall collapse. But the message is *not* that Israel shall become like *Aram.* "I saw all Israel scattered on the mountains, like sheep that have no shepherd; and the LORD said, 'These have no master; let each one go home in peace.'" Although the Ahab regime and the dominant lying spirit shall by no means continue their action, *the new beginning is not conceived as the Aramaizing of Israel.* The great significance of the prophecy that speaks in the Spirit of God becomes clear as soon as the extreme difficulty of the task is perceived. A *radical* break and new beginning is to be made, yet it is *Israel itself* that is supposed to *change.* Israel shall preserve, maintain—indeed, more precisely, restore— continuity with itself, with its good traditions. Passing through radical discontinuity, it shall come again to itself, to continuity with itself, on the basis of its good elements. The goal is nothing less than "resurrection." That which is valid before God shall arise anew.

Herein lies the great importance of this prophetic speech in God's Spirit—speech that brings to bear the truth that can be and is recognized in God's presence, speech that gives descriptions of reality that have definitive validity. This prophetic speech separates the politically and culturally dominant public, which is corrupt, irretrievably lost, and consigned by God to disappear, from the true identity of Israel, which is to be preserved and restored. The downfall is willed by God and limited. God's presence is not called into question by the catastrophe, but confirmed and proved by the prophetic vision, even if it becomes clear only in retrospect. God was always with and over Israel;

the evil spirit was sent by God; the disaster was intended. Therefore a new orientation according to God's word and will is necessary after the catastrophe.

Prophetic speech in God's Spirit allows the mediation of radical discontinuity in Israel's existence with the preservation of continuity. It allows the prospect of Israel's *regeneration*. The act of making possible the recognition of evil spirits and lying spirits aims at a regeneration, a renewal of the life held captive by these spirits. It envisages a new reality, renewed from its own roots. It addresses a definitive public. It thus concentrates on a reality that corresponds to God's will—on a reality that corresponds to God's presence. Not only does it speak at God's behest, it speaks from God's way of seeing things.

The prophet upon whom God's Spirit has come speaks with God's words, perceives in accordance with God's way of seeing things, and gives valid descriptions of reality. All this is confirmed by another story down to its very wording. The story, found in Numbers 24, belongs to the so-called Balaam stories (Numbers 22ff.).[52] In these stories, too, the ruin of Israel is decreed, but this time not by God, but by Balak, a ruler of the Moabites. This ruler, a low-level king, would like to bring an *evil spirit* upon Israel. He wants to bring this to pass with the help of Balaam, whose blessing and whose curse have the reputation of being infallibly effective. Thus in this story an evil spirit is solicited that will bring misfortune on Israel. Balak has Balaam (of whom the only thing one can say for certain is that he was neither Moabite nor Israelite) come in order to provide for a military victory by cursing Israel (cf. Num. 22:6).

The curses are unsuccessful because God places words of blessing in Balaam's mouth and Balaam obediently speaks the words given to him by God. His strength lies precisely in a remarkable mixture of power and powerlessness (cf. esp. Num. 22:18, 38; 23:26; 24:13).[53] Before the third of these pronouncements of blessing—which Balak interestingly seeks to manipulate by changes of place and perspective

---

52. See W. Gross, *Bileam: Literar- und formkritische Untersuchungen der Prosa in Num 22-24*, SANT 38 (Munich: Kösel, 1974).

53. For observations on this intertwining of power and powerlessness in the person upon whom God's Spirit comes, see esp. §2.3, as well as §§2.1, 2.2, 3.2, and 3.3.

(Num. 23:13, 17)—the Spirit of God, as is explicitly pointed out, comes upon Balaam. Numbers 24:2: "Balaam looked up and saw Israel camping tribe by tribe. Then the Spirit of God came upon him. . . ." The so-called vision does nothing less than glorify Israel's beauty, superiority, and power, as well as the fact that all this is willed by God. This vision is explicitly characterized as being grounded in *God's view* of things, indeed as being a rendering of God's view of things.

> "The oracle of Balaam son of Beor,
> the oracle of the man whose eye is open,
> the oracle of one who hears the words of God,
> who sees the vision of the Almighty,
> who falls down, but with eyes uncovered:
> how fair are your tents, O Jacob,
> your encampments, O Israel!
> Like palm-groves that stretch far away,
> like gardens beside a river,
> like aloes that the LORD has planted,
> like cedar trees beside the waters." (Num. 24:3-6; cf. 7ff.)

This story provides a series not only of confirmations and clarifications, but also of extensions of the insights that have already been gained. There is an even clearer highlighting than with Micaiah son of Imlah of the fact that the person upon whom God's Spirit comes acquires a share in God's way of viewing things, a share in the perception of true reality that is possible in God's presence. When the Spirit of God comes upon Balaam, he speaks as a man "whose eye is open . . . who hears the words of God, who sees the vision of the Almighty." When God's Spirit comes upon Balaam, he gives a striking definition of reality—against the interests of the ruler of the Moabites, who had solicited a different—and magically effective—description of the situation.

In this story, too, what is at issue is an interest in breaking off the cultural life of Israel. Israel is to be stricken and driven from the land. In this case, though, the ruler of another people would like to make use of the power that lies in God's Spirit. It is not said that it is impossible for Balak to lay hands on Israel because he is from another country. In the Ahab story, too, God leads into relative ruin not only by means of the lying spirit in the mouth of the prophet, but also by means of the army of the Aramaic people. Above all it is *not* said that God's Spirit can come only upon Israel or *only upon God's prophets.* Balaam is not an Israelite, but he hears God's speech, sees God's visions. A non-Israelite has a share in God's way of seeing things, a share in the truth that becomes reality, that prevails over public opinion and political power. The attempt of the Moabite to make use of this superior power of God's Spirit does not fail because Balaam's word is not a word of power, but because this word of power cannot be manipulated either by Balak or by Balaam. It is mediated by God's Spirit. Although what seems to be happening is an encounter between two non-Israelites who are obsessed and endowed with power, what is actually happening is simply the triumph of God's viewpoint and definition of reality. According to the testimony of these traditions, prophetic knowledge can do nothing more than give a report of this.

Naturally, this prophetic knowledge was and is pressed with questions about the criteria for its certainty and truth. As a matter of fact, a complex structural pattern of criteria exists for the action of the Spirit. This structural pattern is accessible to the knowledge of faith. In the process of coming to know this structural pattern, we should note several attempts—superficial and ambiguous, yet widespread and important in the biblical traditions—to nail down such criteria in a "natural" way.

2.5: In the concentration on the expected presence of God: The Spirit as a numinous entity and the ambiguity of cultic technology and of extraordinary insight

God's Spirit and its action were originally experienced in complicated and complex life relations, in great distress without the prospect of deliverance, in situations "between the times." The early experiences of the Spirit are unclear experiences in situations of which it is impossible to get an overview. These are situations in which only decay and disintegration of the society can be expected. In the midst of this hopelessness the Spirit, through the person upon whom the Spirit comes, elicits processes of gathering, uniting, restoring, and strengthening the community. Emergent processes that are difficult to grasp bring the people together again, bring the people "to themselves" again. Yet it is not only external tensions and conflicts that destroy all hope for maintaining unity, loyalty, and solidarity. Internal tensions and conflicts in the oppressed and threatened community do so as well. The Spirit preserves the community and makes it one in the midst of its being torn apart and laden with conflict. The Spirit takes those persons who are ordained to lead the people and brings them into a remarkable, indeed dismaying condition hovering between power and powerlessness. Precisely in this way they end up in an openness to God's creative power and effectiveness—an openness that can also be recognized by other people. In situations between dissolution and renewal of the community of the entire people, situations of which it is impossible to get an overview, the prophetic knowledge wrought by the Spirit recognizes a break in life processes that brings with it a new beginning and regeneration of a doomed community.

The domains in which the Spirit's action is initially experienced are unpredictable, unforeseeable emergent processes, breaks in life processes and in routines, and individual and collective situations of hovering in the balance. It is thus no wonder that the interconnection between Spirit, reception of the Spirit, perception of the Spirit, and so-called natural phenomena in which the Spirit can be seen at work could appear unclear and dubious. It is no wonder that the Holy Spirit and the Spirit's action were displaced into the clouds of indeterminacy. The chief difficulty in understanding the Spirit and the Spirit's action lay in mediating, on the one hand, the *undeniable evidence* of the Spirit's action and, on the other hand, the fact that it *cannot be predicted, calculated, or controlled.*

This structural pattern is manifested by the numerous passages that depict the *wind as bearer of God's action.* These passages record the fact that God's action is difficult to define. At the same time they highlight the undeniable evidence of this action. The frequent explanation that in most cases *rûaḥ* in the Old Testament means "wind" or "storm" is inadequate, even misleading, if one does not explicitly add that in the majority of passages this "wind" is anything but an event to be defined in solely meteorological terms. The "wind" sent by God is a power that defines and changes history and representative destinies.[54] The wind sent by God makes the waters of chaos recede (Gen. 8:1),

---

54. See also §3.5.

ends the plague of locusts decreed upon Egypt (Exod. 10:19), causes the ruin of those who persecute Israel (Exod. 15:10), or brings Israel nourishment in need (Num. 11:31).

The "wind" is both herald and medium of the process whereby God makes Godself present.[55] The word *rûaḥ* designates the power that accompanies God's word, the power or the image of the divine judgment at work in history.[56] It is also an obfuscatory formula for the destruction of a people or of the machinery of war.[57]

Only in a few cases that refer to *rûaḥ* is "wind" to be understood solely as a natural event. As a rule it means a power that makes it possible to recognize God, that mediates God's action. Since this power is difficult to grasp and cannot be either calculated or controlled, it is only too easy to block out the aspect of its evidence and palpable perceptibility. The expression that is an obfuscatory formula for the power of God or for the medium of that power can then stand just as well for "mere wind" in the sense of that which is incomprehensible, frail, and nugatory. As a matter of fact, in some prophetic texts and especially in wisdom texts we find *rûaḥ* for the experience of incomprehensibility, futility, and nothingness.[58]

If only these last passages are used as the starting point or guidelines for the attempt to understand the Spirit, this attempt fails from the outset. Indeterminacy, incomprehensibility—that is all that can be said about the Spirit. It is as numinous as the wind, if one disregards the manifest results of the wind! Such abstractions are comfortable because they immediately lead into the realm of what is indeterminate and arbitrary. These abstractions that reduce the Spirit to a merely numinous entity are unmasked within the biblical traditions themselves as a misleading misrepresentation. The increase in clarity in knowledge of the Spirit goes hand in hand with a *clearer recognition of the breadth and intentions of the Spirit's activities*. It becomes recognized that the action of the Spirit is not limited to Israel.

---

55. 2 Samuel 22:11; 1 Kings 19:11; Isa. 59:19; Ps. 18:11; 104:3.

56. Isaiah 4:4; 17:13; 27:8; 28:2; 29:6; 30:30; 41:16; Jer. 4:11-12; 10:13; 23:19; 51:16; Ezek. 13:11ff.; Hos. 4:19; 13:15.

57. Jeremiah 49:32, 36; Ezek. 5:2, 10, 12; 12:14; 17:21; Zech. 2:10.

58. Cf. Isa. 26:18; Hos. 12:2; Prov. 11:29; 27:16; Wisd. of Sol. 5:14; and naturally Ecclesiastes passim. A systematic connection between the aspects of nothingness and of judgment can be seen, for example, in Isa. 57:13 and 64:5.

It becomes recognized that the Spirit brings neither solely nor primarily deliverance from already existing distress. The actual intentions of the early and unclear action of the Spirit become clearer in retrospect. There is a subsiding of the impression, which the early action of the Spirit can certainly generate, of being one-sided, aggressive, arbitrary, and even magical.

To be sure, the clear testimonies to the action of the Spirit have structural continuities with the unclear and even ambiguous experiences of the Spirit. But the former call attention to the *clarity* of God's presence in the Spirit. They work against a cult of the indeterminate and numinous. An understanding of this state of affairs is to be developed in the subsequent chapters of this book.

The search for clear insights into the Spirit is admittedly not unproblematic. In contrast to the flight into an indeterminacy that dissolves the experience of the Spirit, there are isolated instances of fixed concentration on problematic, ambiguous determinacy and concretion. We find such instances, which mix God's Spirit and human spirit in an unclear way, in various biblical traditions—and not just in "early" experiences. An uncertain, unclear use of language is characteristic for these incipient forms of "natural theology." In analogous or identical contexts the Spirit can be designated as "Spirit of God" or "spirit of wisdom" or "spirit" (meaning "of human beings"). It is striking in this regard that this "experience of the Spirit" is predicated with particular frequency of non-Israelites.

Both of these problematic concretions of the experience of the Spirit stand in a thoroughly logical interconnection with the attestations to the Spirit that we have already investigated. We have seen that the Spirit mediates valid knowledge and definition of reality. *First,* the Spirit enables reality to be perceived from the perspective of God's presence. It therefore seems plausible to bring the cult, cultic sites, their erection and their function into an immediate interconnection with the Spirit of God and its action. *Second,* since in prophetic knowledge God's Spirit enables human beings to arrive at valid definitions of reality, it is to be expected that an extraordinary capacity for knowledge would not only be understood as a natural phenomenon, but at least occasionally be brought into interconnection with God's Spirit, and thus become a location for the mixing of spirits. Both problems in fact appear in the most varied biblical traditions.

The action of God's Spirit is brought in an *ambiguous way* into interconnection with the construction, reconstruction, and equipping of the temple. The presumably postexilic text Exod. 31.1ff. (as well as Exod. 35:30ff., which is in part identical) offers what is probably the clearest proof of the fact that God's Spirit is seen at work in the construction of the central cultic sites:

> The LORD spoke to Moses: See, I have called by name Bezalel son of Uri son of Hur, of the tribe of Judah: and I have filled him with the *Spirit of God,* with ability, intelligence, and knowledge in every kind of craft, to devise artistic designs, to work in gold, silver, and bronze, in cutting stones for setting, and in carving wood, in every kind of craft. Moreover, I have appointed with him . . . (Exod. 31:1-6)

The person filled with God's Spirit shall build the sanctuary and the most important cultic objects: the tent, the ark for the law, the cover on the ark (see Exod. 31:7), the altar of burnt offering, the priestly vestments—all the objects that are determinative for *the formation of the palpable environment of God's cultic presence, the formation of the palpably perceptible aura of God.*

At issue here are not only highly developed technical skills. At issue are not only a gift for invention and an understanding of art, although these and many additional endowments are regarded as characteristic of the person filled with God's Spirit (cf. Exod. 31:3; 35:34). At issue rather is an artistry that plans the coherent interconnection of the extensively described and very different artistic and technical labor processes. At issue is an artistry that sees the complex functional coherence of the entire cultic site and organizes the corresponding labor. In this regard the person filled with God's Spirit is also "inspired . . . to teach [others]" (Exod. 35:34). The technical and artistic planning and the construction of the site of God's palpable presence in every detail[59] are traced back to God's Spirit and to a person filled with this Spirit just as much as were the gathering of Israel in distress and the restoration of justice and internal unity. By entrusting the erection of a cultic site fitting for God and the production of the

---

59. Cf. Exod. 28:3ff.; 31:7ff.

objects necessary for cultic affairs to persons filled with God's Spirit, God cares—through the Spirit, the one filled with the Spirit, and that one's helpers—for the site of God's presence, the site of God's communication with the people, a site that is well-pleasing to God.

Ambiguity arises, however, inasmuch as in similar contexts one can speak of the gift of *God's* Spirit as well as of the gift of the "spirit of artistic skill" or of the "spirit of wisdom" (e.g., Exod. 28:3). In a similarly ambiguous manner the readiness to contribute to the fashioning or restoration of the temple is connected with "the Spirit/spirit" and the action of the Spirit/spirit, as well as with a condition of having one's spirit "stirred up." This clearly means that a contribution, an initiative to the fashioning or restoration of the temple is not something that individual persons or groups of people can undertake on their own impetus. Such different texts as Exod. 35:21; Hag. 1:14; Ezra 1:1, 5 (par. 2 Chron. 36:22-23) explicitly draw an interconnection between the action of "the Spirit/spirit" and the construction of the temple. It remains unclear, though, whether God "stirs up" God's Spirit in the person or another spirit is activated—and if so, which one?

Exodus 35:21: "And they came, everyone whose heart was stirred, and everyone *whose spirit moved him or her,* and brought the LORD's offering to be used for the tent of meeting, and for all its service, and for the sacred vestments."[60] In contrast to Exodus 31:3 and 35:31, this passage is not talking about the Spirit of God, but about people being moved by their own *spirit.* Yet this expression is too unusual and too striking to be read without religious emphasis and significance. One could hardly translate along the lines of "Every person who was motivated . . . ." The consciously religious connotation is still more clearly recognizable in those texts that speak of God's "stirring up the spirit." Haggai 1:14: "And the LORD stirred up the spirit of Zerubbabel son of Shealtiel, governor of Judah, and the spirit of Joshua son of Jehozadak, the high priest, and the spirit of all the remnant of the people; and they came and worked on the house of the LORD of hosts, their God." In Ezra 1 we find an emphasis on the "international cooperation" in the reconstruction of the temple, effected in and through a spirit stirred by God:

---

60. Emphasis added.

> In the first year of King Cyrus of Persia, in order that the word of
> the LORD by the mouth of Jeremiah might be accomplished, the
> LORD stirred up the spirit of King Cyrus of Persia. . . . [Cyrus is-
> sues an oral and written command throughout his entire empire:]
> "Thus says King Cyrus of Persia: The LORD, the God of heaven, has
> given me all the kingdoms of the earth, and he has charged me to
> build him a house at Jerusalem in Judah. Any of those among you
> who are of his people—may their God be with them!—are now per-
> mitted to go up to Jerusalem in Judah, and rebuild the house of the
> LORD, the God of Israel—he is the God who is in Jerusalem. . . ."
> (Ezra 1:1-3; cf. 2 Chron. 36:22-23)

Yet it is not only the spirit of Cyrus that is "stirred up," but the
spirit of all who are prepared to take part in the construction of
the temple: "The heads of the families of Judah and Benjamin, and the
priests and the Levites—everyone whose spirit God had stirred—got
ready to go up and rebuild the house of the LORD in Jerusalem" (Ezra
1:5). Victor and vanquished, friends and foes work together, after God
has stirred their spirit, in order to restore the place of the palpably perceptible presence of God, of the "God of heaven," as Cyrus says.

God's Spirit or the spirit stirred up by God or a spirit of human
persons is necessary in order to erect and fashion the site of God's
presence.

A similar wavering between "theological" and "anthropological"
statements about the Spirit/spirit is found in the area of "extraordinary
knowledge." If God's Spirit provides the capacity to give valid definitions of reality, it is plausible to see the Spirit of God at work in persons with extraordinary *knowledge* and *wisdom*.

We find what is probably the most striking support of this in
Gen. 41:38ff. After Joseph has interpreted Pharaoh's dreams, which
no one else had been able to understand, and then has given good economic and political advice that ensures the survival of Egypt, we read:

> Pharaoh said to his servants, "Can we find anyone else like this—
> one in whom is the Spirit of God?" So Pharaoh said to Joseph,
> "Since God has shown you all this, there is no one so discerning
> and wise as you. You shall be over my house, and all my people shall
> order themselves as you command. . . ." (Gen. 41:38-40)

We find structurally similar statements with regard to Nebuchadnezzar and Daniel.[61] It is repeatedly said of Daniel that the "spirit of the gods," the "spirit of the holy gods," or merely "an excellent spirit" is in him.

As was the case in connection with the construction of the temple, the wavering between a "theological" and an "anthropological" use of the expression "Spirit/spirit" is not all that is striking. It is also noteworthy that in both cases it is explicitly people from another country who are involved and who know the "Spirit of God" or the "spirit of the gods." The conscious combination of internal views (e.g., Israelites, Joseph, Daniel) and external views (e.g., Cyrus, Pharaoh, Nebuchadnezzar), of religious understanding and understanding appearing in a secular context, is located especially in wisdom texts.

Here we find several statements that clearly identify the "spirit of a mortal" with the "breath of the Almighty" in regard to "the person who has understanding." Job 32:8: "But truly it is the spirit in a mortal, the breath of the Almighty, that makes for understanding." Corresponding to this, the "Holy Spirit" is seen as standing in conflict with the unrighteous and those who lack understanding. Wisdom of Solomon 1:5: "For a holy and disciplined spirit will flee from deceit, and will leave foolish thoughts behind, and will be ashamed at the approach of unrighteousness." Here we observe the interconnection between God's Spirit, the "spirit of wisdom" and understanding, good sense, insight, and knowledge of how things are.[62] In prayer human beings can ask for the good sense mediated by the spirit of wisdom (Wisd. of Sol. 7:7): "Therefore I prayed, and good sense was given me; I called on God, and the spirit of wisdom came to me." Particularly in 7:17ff., the fruit of "good sense" and of the "spirit of wisdom" is strikingly and almost gushingly described as a superior, comprehensive, and at the same time fundamental *knowledge of creation*.

> For it is God who gave me unerring knowledge of what exists, to
> know the structure of the world and the activity of the elements;

---

61. Cf. Dan. 4:2ff., esp. 5-6; 5:11-12, 14; 6:3.

62. On the clear interconnection between the Spirit and righteousness, see §§3.1ff.

the beginning and end and middle of times, the alternations of the
solstices and the changes of the seasons, the cycles of the year and
the constellations of the stars, the natures of animals and the tem-
pers of wild animals, the powers of spirits and the thoughts of human beings, the varieties of plants and the virtues of roots; I
learned both what is secret and what is manifest, for wisdom, the
fashioner of all things, taught me. (Wisd. of Sol. 7:17-21)

Wisdom mediates knowledge of the differentiated structural patterns of creation. It gives "knowledge of creation" and makes possible
participation in the very process of God's planning and knowing, in
God's oversight and vigilance:

For wisdom is more mobile than any motion; because of her pure-
ness she pervades and penetrates all things. For she is a breath of
the power of God, and a pure emanation of the glory of the
Almighty; therefore nothing defiled gains entrance into her. For
she is a reflection of eternal light, a spotless mirror of the working
of God, and an image of God's goodness. Although she is but one,
she can do all things, and while remaining in herself, she renews all
things; in every generation she passes into holy souls and makes
them friends of God, and prophets. (Wisd. of Sol. 7:24-27)

It is astounding that these texts, on the edge of the canon, can treat
receiving wisdom and *receiving the Spirit* as one thing, or at least can
place them *parallel* to each other without a clear order of precedence.
For example, Wisd. of Sol. 9:17 asks, "Who has learned your counsel,
unless you have given wisdom and sent your holy Spirit from on high?"
Today it is only with great difficulty that we can make sense of this
interconnection between the gift of the Spirit, the gift of wisdom,
knowledge of creation, and prophecy. Gone are the days in which the
connection of technical-scientific knowledge of nature and prognostic
capacity could be given out as the interconnection between knowledge
of creation and prophecy. Through the history of the differentiation
and dichotomization of the knowledge of nature, on the one hand, and
of cultural insight, on the other hand, a complex, wisdom-centered
form of thought that could see the mediation of knowledge of creation
with experience of the Spirit has become an incomprehensible and archaic phenomenon. We do not possess a "natural theology" that would

be in a position to practice or even to justify this wisdom-centered form of thought. The ongoing confusion and lack of clarity that accompany the argument for and against "natural theology" may well be grounded in the inability to grasp clearly the theological intentions and forms of wisdom-centered thinking. It would be wrong, though, simply to trace this situation back to external forces (to "the" natural sciences, to the modern spirit, and so on) and thus to pass over the uncertainty and lack of clarity that lie in the knowledge of faith itself (and that are already to be observed within the biblical traditions).

On the one hand, the traditions in which we stand have given a primarily ethical-practical direction to the interconnection between knowledge and the reception of the Spirit[63]—inspired, to be sure, by the biblical traditions. On the other hand, the traditions in which we stand have in part supported the flight into the realm of the numinous and indeterminate, into the mystification of the experience of the Spirit. In the following discussion we will get to know insights and testimonies that in the midst of the unclarity of the Spirit's action make accessible the still greater clarity of this power of God and of its intentions.

---

63. Cf. texts such as Neh. 9:20, 30; Zech. 7:12; or Ps. 143:10, and esp. the interconnection between law and Spirit elucidated in §3.1.

CHAPTER 3

The Promised Spirit of Justice and Peace

3.1: Extending beyond justice and morality: The Spirit's resting upon the Messiah and the universal spread of justice, mercy, and knowledge of God

The Spirit of God was originally experienced as a power that overcomes the internal disintegration of the people and its political powerlessness in the face of external threats. Even these early experiences point to the fact that the Spirit is not something numinous, but a power that changes real life relations. They make it possible to know many characteristics of this power. They also provoke questions to which they cannot give any conclusive answer. Among other things, they raise the problem of how God's Spirit can be clearly distinguished from all sorts of demonic powers all the way to the spirit of militaristic enthusiasm. From this it follows that fundamental and universal intentions of the Spirit's action are not yet *clearly* perceived by the early testimonies. Those elements of the tradition that promise God's Spirit as a Spirit of justice and of peace bring clarity. Not only do they recognize the universal intentions of the Spirit's action. They also show that this power wills not only to put an end to disintegration and powerlessness of human communities, but also to forestall these problems, to prevent them. The promised Spirit of justice wishes to forestall conflicts, both internal and external, caused by human beings. By means of this knowledge the traditions that now lie before us work against a regression into the earlier ambiguities and lack of clarity.

Several "messianic" texts, above all in the Isaiah traditions, attest to the fact that God's Spirit is a Spirit of justice. These texts announce God's chosen bringer of salvation, upon whom the Spirit not only comes in a surprising way, but upon whom the Spirit also "remains." The understanding of the Spirit of God now appears to be settled in the truest sense of the word: The *Spirit of God "rests."* For the bringer of salvation, God's Spirit is an enduring endowment. What is effected by the person so endowed can be clearly understood by others.

The three most important texts in this regard, which leave their mark up to and into the New Testament traditions, are found in Isa. 11:1ff., 42:1ff., and 61:1ff. All three speak of God's Spirit remaining and resting. All three emphasize that God chooses and authorizes the one on whom the Spirit of God rests.[1] In addition, the descriptions offered by all three texts of what distinguishes the bearer of the Spirit chosen by God are analogous in terms of both structure and content.

The power and authority of the person who bears God's Spirit lie in the fact that this person establishes *justice, mercy, and knowledge of God* and gives them a universal extension. All three texts that have to do with the Spirit resting or remaining on God's chosen one talk not only about justice, not only about mercy, and not only about knowledge of God, but about the *strict interconnection* of all three. Justice, mercy, and knowledge of God are the three functional elements of God's *law*.[2] All three texts that promise the resting of the Spirit obviously have in mind the *fulfillment of the law* by the bearer of the Spirit.[3] What does this mean?

As far back as what is probably the oldest collection of laws accessible to us in the Old Testament, the so-called Covenant Code (Exod. 20:22—23:19), we find three different kinds of ordinances. There are the ordinances that treat matters of justice. There are the laws, framing the entire collection, that concern the cult: that is, the public, regulated, and accessible relation to God. And there are statutes that

---

1. The texts that talk about God's Spirit resting take up traditions of the interconnection between election, anointing, and imparting of the Spirit. 1 Samuel 10:1ff. reports that at God's behest Samuel anoints Saul "prince over God's heritage" and promises him that the Spirit of God will come upon him and that God will be with him. 1 Samuel 16:13 says that the Spirit of God *remained* upon David from the day of his anointing by Samuel onward. 2 Samuel 23 even asserts that the Spirit of God speaks through David, the anointed one of the God of Jacob.

2. See also §§1.3 and 5.3.

3. With regard to the following discussion, cf. M. Welker, "Security of Expectations: Reformulating the Theology of Law and Gospel," trans. J. Hoffmeyer, *Journal of Religion* 66 (1986): 237ff.; "Gesetz und Geist," *JBT* 4, ed. O. Hofius and P. Stuhlmacher (1989): 215ff.

cannot be simply classed with either the cultic or the judicial ordinances. This third group consists of laws whose goal is that people
forgo optimizing their own life relations on the backs of others, that
people even forgo insisting on their own rights and legally supportable
claims. According to the law, this act of forgoing the process of carrying through one's own interests and rights is supposed to occur for the
benefit of weaker and disadvantaged persons. Those named are *slaves*
(Exod. 21:2ff.), *strangers* (Exod. 22:20, 23:9), *widows and orphans*
(Exod. 22:21ff.), the *poor* (Exod. 22:24ff., 23:6), and fellow persons
with *neither influence nor power* (Exod. 23:1ff.).

These ordinances concerning mercy belong to the content of the
law. On the one hand, this means that as content of the law, mercy is
removed from the arbitrary, merely contingent behavior of individual
human beings, behavior guided by inclination. It is likewise removed
from dependence on mood and situation. Like judicial equity, mercy
shall be something that can be expected with a degree of certainty.
It shall become a socially established pattern; it shall become social
routine. On the other hand, the mercy laws do not regard the poor and
weak as passive recipients of patronizing charity. The mercy laws presuppose the participation of disadvantaged fellow persons in social,
economic, judicial, and other life relations. They assume this participation, even when reality speaks to the contrary. Because this participation is threatened and therefore in need of particular protection,
the mercy laws enter into operation.

Yet the anchoring of the mercy ordinances in the law accomplishes still more. The law presents a strict functional interconnection
of ordinances concerning justice, cult, and mercy. In doing so, the law
makes clear that justice without routinized protection of the weaker
party, that a judicial structure which is not constantly oriented toward
the integration of the weak and disadvantaged, does not deserve the
great name of "righteousness."[4] A publicly regulated and well-honed,
believable relation with God is not conceivable without the spread of
justice and mercy in the described interconnection. The early written
prophecy in particular makes this clear. Where mercy is lacking, there
the other elements of the law—namely justice and cultic life—also go

---

4. Beyond the following reflections, the place to present the diverse material
and systematic interconnections of justice and mercy is in a theology of law.

bad. A people that does not remain constantly sensitive to the poor and weak in its midst and that does not direct its judicial development toward their participation and integration begins to twist justice and to misuse the cult. This development leads to disintegration, decay, and destruction of the entire community. Conversely, a community acquires strength in all areas inasmuch as it, with the help of the mercy legislation, enables its people who are poor, weak, and in the position of outsiders to reach the general level of judicial, social, economic, and cultural relations of exchange and communication.

If we compare the great bodies of law in the Old Testament, we are struck by the fact that the *proportions* between the individual domains of the law shift greatly in the course of development.[5] Regardless of these shifts, the law remains a functional interconnection of ordinances that serve *the founding of justice, the routinization of mercy, and the cultivation of the public, universally accessible relation with God,* where this relation is ordered in a way that people can come to expect. The promises that speak of the Spirit's resting hold out the prospect of a fulfillment of this law—a fulfillment whose effects extend beyond Israel.

A shoot shall come out from the stump of Jesse,
and a branch shall grow out of his roots.
The Spirit of the LORD shall rest on him,
the Spirit of wisdom and understanding,
the Spirit of counsel and might,
the Spirit of knowledge and the fear of the LORD.
His delight shall be in the fear of the LORD.
He shall not judge by what his eyes see,
or decide by what his ears hear;
but with righteousness he shall judge the poor,
and decide with equity for the poor in the land;
he shall strike the earth with the rod of his mouth,
and with the breath of his lips he shall kill the wicked.

---

5. Thus the "differentiation of law" (see N. Luhmann, *Ausdifferenzierung des Rechts: Beiträge zur Rechtssoziologie und Rechtstheorie* [Frankfurt am Main: Suhrkamp, 1981], esp. 11ff., 35ff.) does not first occur in the modern period, as many sociologists of law today claim, but as early as in the course of the Old Testament traditions. Cf. Welker, "Gesetz und Geist," 215ff.

Righteousness shall be the belt around his waist,
and faithfulness the belt around his loins. . . .
They will not hurt or destroy on all my holy mountain;
for the earth will be full of the knowledge of the LORD
as the waters cover the sea.

On that day the root of Jesse shall stand as a signal to the peoples;
the nations shall inquire of him, and his dwelling shall be glorious.
(Isa. 11:1-5, 9-10)[6]

The bearer of the Spirit brings righteousness. The bearer of the
Spirit judges and decides what is right. Righteousness is the belt
around his waist; he establishes righteousness. This righteousness is of
a particular sort. The bearer of the Spirit does not judge by appearance
or by hearsay. He judges the helpless righteously; he decides for the
poor of the land. But this is to say that the bearer of the Spirit connects judicial decision-making with mercy. It does not mean that he
puts mercy in the place of judicial decision-making. He judges, and he
establishes justice. The bearer of the Spirit does not moralize at the
expense of the cultivation of justice. For example, he does not develop
an abundance of exceptions for the benefit of the weak without regard
for justice. The weak shall be treated with righteousness, and justice
shall adjust to protecting the weak. The messianic bearer of the Spirit
protects and cultivates the difficult *interconnection of justice and mercy.*
Yet the bearer of the Spirit not only brings righteousness by strictly
connecting justice and mercy. Isaiah 11:6ff. describes a universal *condition of peace*[7] *that even includes animals. The passage concludes with the
promise that nothing evil will be done and no more crimes will be committed, because the land will be filled with the knowledge of God.* Inasmuch
as the realization of justice and mercy is bound up with a knowledge of
God that fills the whole land, the third element of the law, the *cult,* is
taken up.

The cultic ordinances are to stipulate the public relation to God.
For the law—and also for a piety and theology oriented toward God's

---

6. With regard to what follows, cf. H. Wildberger, *Isaiah 1-12: A Commentary,*
trans. T. H. Trapp, Continental Commentaries (Minneapolis: Fortress, 1991), 459ff.
7. See §3.5.

Spirit—a public, communal, dependable relation to God is not conceivable without the realization of justice and mercy. An unjust people misuses the cult. A people in which neither justice nor mercy rules distorts and destroys its relation to God. Conversely, knowledge of God and the establishment of righteousness go hand in hand. Righteousness in the sense of justice, mercy, and knowledge of God is only attained when all three elements of the law stand in strict reciprocal interconnections. Whoever wishes to establish the knowledge of God in order subsequently somehow to effect justice and mercy has no more understood anything about God's law than has the person who wishes to practice justice and mercy in *an abstract manner* in order somehow to attain or to bring about knowledge of God on the basis of a good social condition.

The messianic promises that speak of the Spirit's resting hold out the prospect of the law being fulfilled. In addition, they hold out the prospect of the establishment of justice, mercy, and knowledge of God *not remaining confined to Israel*. Israel becomes conspicuous to the nations in a particular way. Filled with righteousness and knowledge of God, Israel directly attracts the nations: "On that day the root of Jesse shall stand as a signal to the peoples; the nations shall inquire of him, and his dwelling shall be glorious." Moreover, what seems to be a later addition[8] records that the outcasts of Israel are assembled and the dispersed of Judah are gathered "from the four corners of the earth." This, too, is bound up with a "signal for the nations."[9]

The establishment of justice, mercy, and knowledge of God is accompanied by a power of influence and attraction in relation to the nations. The revelation of God—not only for Israel, but also "for the nations"—is bound up with the strengthening of Israel, which is described both as the establishment of an eschatological condition of freedom in Israel and as the gathering of the dispersed. This revelation

---

8. See H. Barth, *Die Jesaja-Worte in der Josia-Zeit: Israel und Assur als Thema einer produktiven Neuinterpretation der Jesaja-Überlieferung,* WMANT 48 (Neukirchen-Vluyn: Neukirchener, 1977), 58.

9. Admittedly, imperialistic and militaristic traits come to the fore here: cf. Isa. 11:11ff. Nor are the later messianic promises free of such traits. The irreversible progress in the knowledge of the power of righteousness and of peace, however, is unmistakable in comparison with the early experience of the Spirit.

does not lead merely to the nations taking wide-eyed cognizance in one way or another. It leads rather to changes in orientation and in behavior. The nations seek out Israel, orient themselves toward Israel, and take as a model the people that reflects nothing less than divine glory.

These states of affairs are illuminated more precisely by the two other central messianic texts that speak of the Spirit's resting.

> Here is my servant, whom I uphold,
> my chosen, in whom my soul delights;
> I have put my Spirit upon him;
> he will bring forth justice to the nations.
> He will not cry or lift up his voice,
> or make it heard in the street;
> a bruised reed he will not break,
> and a dimly burning wick he will not quench;
> he will faithfully bring forth justice.
> He will not grow faint or be crushed
> until he has established justice in the earth;
> and the coastlands wait for his teaching [his law] (Isa. 42:1-4)[10]

> I am the LORD, I have called you in righteousness,
> I have taken you by the hand and kept you;
> I have given you as a covenant to the people,
> a light to the nations,
> to open the eyes that are blind,
> to bring out the prisoners from the dungeon,
> from the prison those who sit in darkness.
> I am the LORD, that is my name;
> my glory I give to no other,
> nor my praise to idols. (Isa. 42:6-8)

This passage emphasizes more strongly than Isaiah 11 that the justice brought by the bearer of the Spirit is established universally and—

---

10. K. Elliger's translation of *mišpāṭ* with "decision" [*Entscheid*] is too weak (*Deuterojesaja*, rev. ed., BKAT 11/1 [Neukirchen-Vluyn: Neukirchener, 1989], 198ff.). He probably chooses this translation in the interest of finding the middle road between *iudicium* and *ius*: i.e., legal justice that is actually decreed, active legal justice, spoken legal justice. Perhaps he is also shrinking back from a translation that seems too narrowly juridical.

recognized universally. God's chosen one brings justice to the ι.ations, establishes justice on earth (42:1, 4). He brings a righteousness for which the most far-flung areas of the world are waiting: "The coastlands wait for his teaching [his law]." This justice is marked by mercy, and thereby it proves itself to be real and effective justice: "A bruised reed he will not break, and a dimly burning wick he will not quench; he will faithfully bring forth justice." Mercy, the act of going to meet those who are weaker, the suffering, and the disadvantaged, is again emphasized in 42:7-8. The messianic bearer of the Spirit is called to open eyes that are blind, to bring prisoners out of the dungeon, and to free from prison all those who sit in darkness. Here the context shows clearly that mercy is applied not only to those who are socially disadvantaged, but also to those who are disadvantaged in terms of the knowledge of God.[11]

The bearer of the Spirit, who is also called God's servant, is created and ordained for the universally effective establishment and fulfillment of God's law.[12] The universal justice brought by the bearer of the Spirit is qualified by mercy. The universal knowledge of God is also qualified by mercy. God's revelation is an act of mercy; God makes Godself known as merciful.[13] The cultic aspect of the universal knowledge of God brought by the bearer of the Spirit is emphasized just as explicitly as the connection between justice and mercy.

The establishment of justice and mercy serves not only the encouragement[14] of the weak and those in misery, but also—and in strict interconnection with the former—the revelation and recognition, the

---

11. Cf. Isa. 42:6ff.; also Isa. 32:1ff.

12. Cf. R. Koch's excellent comparison of the servant of God with Moses, which at the same time perceives an element that points beyond Moses: i.e., the universality of the establishment of righteousness. "As Moses proclaimed to his people the Torah (Exod. 24:12) and the legal statutes (. . . Exod. 21:1; 24:3; Deut. 4:1) of God, so the ʿebhed yhwh will carry the Torah (Isa. 42:3) and the justice of Yahweh (Isa. 42:1, 4) to all the nations of the earth" (Geist und Messias: Beitrag zur biblischen Theologie des Alten Testaments [Vienna: Herder, 1950], 109). Cf. also Isa. 63:11.

13. Within the Isaiah traditions, some statements establish a relation to socio-judicial aspects, while others establish a relation to cultic aspects. Cf. Isa. 25:4; 29:19; 41:17; 49:13; 54:10; 57:15-16; 58:7-8; 65:15; 66:2.

14. "Establishment" and "encouragement" translate two different but related senses of the same German word, Aufrichtung—TRANS.

honor and adoration of God. The establishment of universal righteousness in interconnection with justice and mercy brings with itself a
knowledge of God that redounds to the benefit of Israel and the
nations.

If cult and mercy are really practiced, they have an effect not only
in marginal situations. They do not on the one hand serve only the
weak and the subjugated in the land and in all the world, and on
the other hand serve God and God's honor. God and God's bearer of
the Spirit act out of "righteousness": that is, with a purpose directed
toward the life relations of all persons. By no means does the messianic
bearer of the Spirit bring only peak religious experiences and relief
measures in special cases of distress. Together with the establishment of
mercy and knowledge of God, the bearer of the Spirit brings justice
and real righteousness for Israel and for the nations.

God's chosen one, on whom the Spirit rests, brings the fulfillment
of the law. Fulfillment of the law means the establishment of justice,
mercy, and knowledge of God in strict interconnection. This occurs
not only for Israel, but for the nations. The third central messianic text
also characterizes the bearer of the Spirit and his action in this way.

> The Spirit of the LORD God is upon me,
> because the LORD has anointed me;
> God has sent me to bring good news to the oppressed,
> to bind up the brokenhearted,
> to proclaim liberty to the captives,
> and release to the prisoners;
> to proclaim the year of the LORD's favor,
> and the day of vengeance of our God;
> to comfort all who mourn;
> to provide for those who mourn in Zion—
> to give them a garland instead of ashes,
> the oil of gladness instead of mourning,
> the mantle of praise instead of a faint spirit.
> They will be called oaks of righteousness,
> the planting of the LORD, to display God's glory.
> They shall build up the ancient ruins,
> they shall raise up the former devastations;
> they shall repair the ruined cities,
> the devastations of many generations.

Strangers shall stand and feed your flocks,
people from other lands shall till your land and dress your vines;
but you shall be called priests of the LORD,
you shall be named ministers of our God;
you shall enjoy the wealth of the nations,
and in their riches you shall glory.

. . . .

For I the LORD love justice,
I hate robbery and wrongdoing;

. . . .

Their descendants shall be known among the nations,
and their offspring among the peoples;
all who see them shall acknowledge
that they are a seed that the LORD has blessed.

. . . .

For as the earth brings forth its shoots,
and as a garden causes what is sown in it to spring up,
so the LORD GOD will cause righteousness and praise
to spring up before all the nations. (Isa. 61:1-11)

In this promise as well the specification of mercy is obvious and predominant. The bearer of the Spirit chosen by God brings good news to the oppressed, binds up those who are of broken heart, proclaims liberty to the captives, comforts those who are mourning, awakens a song of praise instead of a faint spirit. This mercy is not regarded as some sort of charitable good deed toward the weak, but as *an act of establishing righteousness* (cf. 61:3, 8, 11). The event is also universally perceived as such. The messianic bearer of the Spirit proclaims the "day of vengeance of our God." Israel, comforted and having gone from mourning to rejoicing, reflects God's righteousness for its surroundings. This is corroborated in 61:8 by the statement, "For I the LORD love justice, I hate robbery and wrongdoing." Here as well, a mercy practiced in connection with justice in order to establish righteousness is ultimately aiming at the universal knowledge of righteousness and of God among the nations.

Through the bearer of the Spirit, God brings forth righteousness and praise before all the nations (61:11), which is described in still more detail in Isaiah 62. Righteousness and praise of God before the nations have their center in the recognition of the justice and mercy established in Israel. "Strangers and people from other lands"—as the text puts it—will designate Israel as shoots of God's righteousness and glory. The strangers and people from other lands will call the Israelites "priests of Yahweh." Then follows a decisive, indeed dramatic expression: The strangers and people from other lands say to the Israelites, "*You shall be named ministers of our God.*" You are ministers of *our* God, of the God of nations not your own! The "strangers and people from other lands" identify the God of Israel as their own God, their own God as the God of Israel.

This means that the nations directly acquire a share in the messianic establishment of justice, mercy, and knowledge of God in Israel. The Gentiles are directly included in the event of salvation touched off by the bearer of the Spirit. Thus it is noted—already in the Old Testament traditions—that an establishment of justice, mercy, and knowledge of God in Israel that neglected the fulfillment of expectations for righteousness and the search for knowledge of God among the Gentiles, that did not mercifully include the Gentiles and did not mediate salvation to them, could not appeal to the messianic promises.[15] It is characteristic of the righteousness of God contained in the *messianic* promises that the creation of justice, mercy, and knowledge of God spreads to the nations, that the nations are given a part in Israel's experience of righteousness and in Israel's knowledge of God.

The fact that the nations are directly given a part in this event, the fact that the influence of this event is universal, does not signify any diminution of salvation for Israel—quite the contrary. The fact that the nations are mercifully given a part in the experience of God and in God's righteousness redounds purely to the acknowledgment, the honor, and the praise of Israel, as well as having many other positive repercussions for Israel. These positive repercussions are set forth so drastically in the framework of the Isaiah traditions that here, too, triumphalistic and imperialistic traits do not remain absent: "Strangers

---

15. See M. Welker, "Righteousness and God's Righteousness," trans. J. Hoffmeyer, in D. Migliore, ed., *The Church and Israel: Romans 9-11*, The 1989 Frederick Neumann Symposium on the Theological Interpretation of Scripture, *Princeton Seminary Bulletin*, suppl., no. 1 (1990): 124ff.

16. Cf. Isa. 61:5, 6.

shall feed your sheep . . . you shall enjoy the wealth of the nations."[16] All nations, all peoples will say with regard to Israel's descendants that "all who see them shall acknowledge that they are a seed that the LORD has blessed."[17] What is promised with regard to the Spirit's resting and to the messianic bearer of the Spirit chosen by God is a powerful, many-sided event that is bound up with broad powers of influence for Israel and for the nations.

The action of the Spirit and of the bearer of the Spirit thus re-ceives a more differentiated determinacy in comparison with the tradi-tions considered in chapter 2. But this does not mean that the action of the Spirit is to be understood as an event that wins people without any problems arising, that immediately makes sense to them and bene-fits them in an immediately recognizable manner. In the face of distor-tions that have in mind a quickly attainable harmony, a "reciprocity" that is indeterminately ("somehow or other") good, or something sim-ilar, we must try to imagine what *the obligation to practice mercy* means for a community, for a people.

Mercy—the sensitivity not only to the distress of other persons, but also to systematically disadvantageous arrangements and to unjust differentiation in a community, and the readiness to remove these wrongs—indeed cannot be confined to a circle of persons and to a field of problems that can be defined once and for all. Mercy must al-ways remain open and sensitive to new groups of weak, afflicted, and disadvantaged persons in a community, groups that become recogniz-able in unforeseeable ways. A community that is obligated to practice mercy thus becomes committed to constant self-change and self-renewal, to self-critical rethinking and reorientation. At the same time, mercy is to go hand in hand with the establishment of justice— and this means in any case with the establishment of forms and prac-tices of resolving conflict that can be *securely expected*.

On the one hand, what are required are sensitivity and the open-ness to revise and to relativize forms of orientation and of life, specifi-cally with regard to unjust differences, discrimination, and distress that are new on the scene, or the perception of which is new. On the other hand, what is required is the formation of a judicial security of expectations, and consequently of clear and unambiguous forms for

---

17. Isa. 61:9b; cf. also Isa. 62:1ff., esp. 62:12.

equitably disposing of conflict. It is not easy to unite the sensitivity of mercy and the stability of justice. Interest in a readily surveyable, well-honed, and secure judicial order can suppress the sensitivity and readiness to change of the living practice of mercy. The effort to practice a mercy sensitive to conflicts and capable of learning can render problematic the indispensable routines and the stability of the judicial order. In this situation there is a great temptation to leave mercy totally in the hands of *morality* and of public moral reasoning. Why is this a temptation and a danger?

Morality has to do with the process, continually readjudicated by an age, a culture, a tradition, or a group of participants, in which the conditions are laid down for the bestowal and withdrawal of respect. People exercise mutual influence on each other inasmuch as they lay down expectations for each other. If expectations are fulfilled, respect is bestowed. If they are not fulfilled, respect is withdrawn.[18] On this basis an impressive *market* of moral communication[19] develops. The bestowal and the promise of bestowal of respect, the withdrawal and the threat of withdrawal of respect accompany the reciprocal communicative relations. There is scarcely a theme conceivable that cannot essentially be "moralized." The moral market is extremely powerful. It is extremely active in a way of which we are for the most part only dimly aware. Why then is it not the force field wrought by the Spirit of God and by the messianic bearer of the Spirit? Why is the force field evoked by God's Spirit and by the messianic bearer of the Spirit more than morality?

Both the structural pattern of interdependence of justice, mercy, and knowledge of God and the differentiated universality of the action of the Spirit and of the Spirit's bearer transcend, correct, and orient well-established, vague, but powerful conceptions of morality, of the so-called common sense feel for justice, and of humanity.

---

18. For a treatment that can free one from illusions with regard to moral communication, see N. Luhmann, "Soziologie der Moral," in N. Luhmann and S. H. Pfürtner, eds., *Theorietechnik und Moral* (Frankfurt am Main: Suhrkamp, 1978), 8ff., esp. 43ff. From an individualistic perspective R. Bittner argues for replacing the moral specification of action with practical wisdom (*What Reason Demands*, trans. T. Talbot [Cambridge: Cambridge Univ. Press, 1989], esp. 111–39).

19. That is, a plurality of communications and of offers of communication that are defined by "values" that change rapidly or that are only relatively stable.

The recognition of this structural pattern of interdependence first sensitizes us to the fact that moral communication cannot be unambiguously defined, that moral communication can essentially be defined in highly arbitrary ways. Moral communication cannot automatically be identified with mercy. To be sure, mercy must be flexible and relative to the situation. But mercy remains bound to the experience of unjust and avoidable differentiation that discriminates against people. By contrast, we have the lived experience of ages and societies that stabilized their perverse moralities by taking as an important criterion for the bestowal of "respect" the possession of slaves, the disparaging of Jews or of blacks, hatred for other minorities, or contempt for "communists" struggling for the removal of relations of exploitation and for equitable relations of ownership. Have not these very ages denounced the people who did not comply with the morality of the age or of the day? Were not the people who deviated from such morality disparaged, for example, as "Jew-lovers" and "nigger-lovers," as "godless Reds," and with other titles designed to make their bearers the object of contempt? Have not these ages and these societies done everything to despise people who deviated from their morality, or to hold their fellow persons to the currently dominant morality, inasmuch as they threatened them with the withdrawal of respect for nonconformist behavior?

It could be objected that all of that was not morality at all. After all, morality is concerned with the true and the good, with freedom, equality, sisterhood and brotherhood, with respect for the worth of human beings, and so on.

In the face of this objection, it is easy to show the validity of the realization that *ideas* of morality can easily have more or less vague, positive notions as their content, but that in life as it is really lived the corruptibility and corruptness of morality cannot be excluded. In a fascist environment such as Germany after 1933, the anti-Semite will cynically conclude that it certainly would be "good" to make "the maxim of his or her will the principle of a universal legislation" and to treat the Jews accordingly. Racists in racist surroundings and anticommunists in environments hostile to communism will come to similar judgments.

In less strikingly ideological contexts, the corruptibility and corruptness of morality is less visible. For example, we are familiar with

societies in which into the 1970s scientific encyclopedias and professional literature could (with a subjectively good conscience!) propagate
the notion that air and water are "infinite resources." In these societies
the problems of the waste of energy and the production of garbage were
so successfully suppressed that large parts of the public initially reacted
to rising ecological sensitivity only with the withdrawal of respect from
the "nature freaks" and the "environmental alarmists."

All this is not to claim that morality and moral communication
are *unnecessary*. Moral communication is not only indispensable, it is
unavoidable. It is unavoidable wherever human beings not only seek to
connect their action and behavior with that of other human beings,
but also want to make sure that a community of respect is formed.

Nor is all this meant to claim that abstract and ideal viewpoints are
unnecessary for moral communication.[20] Yet in comparison with the
moral market and attempts to give it a definite form with the help of a
metaphysical grounding, the structural pattern of reciprocity of justice,
mercy, and knowledge of God represents a more realistic and specific
approach to shaping the life relations of human communities more concretely. This pattern of reciprocity is in fact more solidly embedded in

---

20. The Chicago ethicist Franklin I. Gamwell has recently put forward an impressive case for such an ideal viewpoint (*The Divine Good: Modern Moral Theory
and the Necessity of Good* [San Francisco: Harper & Row, 1990]). His thesis is: No
preservation of morality from relativism without grounding in a metaphysically and
theistically founded "creativity." Gamwell understands such creativity as the creative connection of unity and plurality. The orientation toward the creative connection of unity and plurality can of course be regarded as a very abstract formulation of
the purpose of the action of the Spirit (see the following sections of chap. 2). On
this level of abstraction, however, the definition is highly susceptible to being ignored or misused. It can be ignored, although "the entertainment of ideas is one of
the agencies through which human action and human communities are shaped," and
although, "at least in the longer run, . . . moral philosophies can hope to make a
contribution to the course of human events" (xi). This thesis can be misused due to
the need for limitation as soon as specific conceptions of unity and plurality must be
developed. All explicit and implicit visions of unity and plurality that guide the
course of individual and communal life must operate with limitations whose selection cannot be governed by morality alone. In this context see W. Schweiker's excit-
ing and instructive attempt to anchor the tasks of theology and ethics within the
bounds of definitions of reality that are capable of, and conducive to, solidarity
(*Mimetic Reflections: A Study in Hermeneutics, Theology, and Ethics* [New York: Ford-
ham Univ. Press, 1990], esp. 209ff.).

life as it is really lived, which inevitably brings with it instances of judicial communication and—at least sometimes unavoidably—questions about criteria for the development and perfection of judicial communication. The structural pattern of interdependence of justice, mercy, and knowledge of God provides answers to these vexing questions. At least one of these answers is not only a proposal or an ideal, but is, despite all misuse, deeply enculturated in many societies of this earth: No justice without routinized protection of those who are weaker. For nonreligious persons as well, this answer is difficult to reject. It is also scarcely to be relativized for those who—faced with the decision of choosing either a theistically grounded morality or an unfounded morality—decide in favor of an unfounded morality, an uncontrollably emerging moral market, or even an arbitrarily organized moral anarchy.

Justice, mercy, knowledge of God—these are not merely names for abstract ideal viewpoints. They are factors that are indispensable for human life together. We cannot avoid being constantly confronted with the judicial system and with conceptions of justice, because the judicial system has firmly established itself as a functional system of every society. It is equally impossible for us to avoid being confronted with weaker, oppressed, and marginalized people in our surroundings. Likewise we cannot avoid being challenged by these people. Nor can we escape the continually renewed question not only of how we individually, but of how—if at all—the entire society has reacted and ought to react to the charge to practice mercy. Today it is more difficult to understand the third element of the law, because secular cultures develop equivalents for valid definitions of reality and for the knowledge of God—equivalents whose structures, logics, and functions we have not yet sufficiently grasped (for example, the logic and function of mass media communication).

The field characterized by the Spirit's resting on the messianic bearer of the Spirit extends beyond morality inasmuch as it imposes a manifold determinacy on moral communication and at the same time leads moral communication beyond itself. This is not simply a matter of some sort of "religious grounding" of justice and morality, for which there are loud calls and an intensive search from time to time, particularly after instances of cultural collapse. Rather than giving some sort of "religious grounding," the action of the Spirit leads to *a knowledge of God compatible with justice and mercy and their reciprocal determination,*

*and to a corresponding specification of, and commitment on the part of, the
community.* The action of the Spirit aims at knowledge of God and at
an explicit understanding of self and of reality on the part of the community before God. This understanding of self and reality works
against the famous-infamous arbitrariness and vagueness of religion,
and against the less famous, but unfortunately no less dangerous, arbitrariness and corruptibility of morality.

Both the knowledge of God mediated by the Spirit and by the messianic bearer of the Spirit, and the community's explicit understanding of self and reality before God, are characterized by the struggle for
justice and mercy, the experience of justice and mercy, and the practice of justice and mercy. Moreover, they are never to be understood
exclusively (nationalistically or imperialistically, whether the imperialism be economic or cultural), but are open and sensitive to other traditions of the struggle for justice, mercy, and knowledge of God, for other
forms of this experience, and for other expressions of the corresponding practice.[21]

All this does not exclude—within the framework of this openness
and of this manifold determinacy—a free-flowing moral communication with its (often hardly conscious) values of the age and of the day.
But it does determine more precisely the conditions for the communication of respect, the conditions for holding out the prospect of respect, threatening to withdraw respect, and actually withdrawing it.
The moral market and the subjective sense of justice are not left to
themselves. They receive a rich orientation and a complex, differentiated standard.

3.2: Extending beyond the acquisition of political loyalty:
The Messiah "does not cry in the street"—The authority
of one who is publicly powerless and suffering

When the Spirit of God came upon the early charismatics, they gathered the people in situations of distress and led them through conflict
with people of other lands. The messianic bearer of the Spirit, on
whom the Spirit of God rests, aims at a universal condition of freedom,

---

21. See the more detailed discussions in §§3.3 and 3.4.

inasmuch as the bearer of the Spirit brings the "fulfillment of the law": that is, establishes justice, realizes mercy, and spreads knowledge of God—not only in Israel, but also among the nations. *Specific* judicial, social, or religious accomplishments are not named. No concrete program is proposed for a new configuration of "united nations" or of a "world society." How, then, does the messianic bearer of the Spirit win loyalty? How does the chosen one and servant, on whom God's Spirit rests, fulfill the law? How does the messianic bearer of the Spirit accomplish the law's fulfillment on a universal scale? How does the one on whom the Spirit rests concentrate the expectations and hopes of people, of the nations on himself? The way in which this universal acquisition of loyalty by the bearer of the Spirit is characterized in more detail is most astounding, indeed dismaying.

Isaiah 42:2—a text that Matt. 12:18ff. explicitly applies to Jesus and to Jesus' action[22]—explicitly notes that the bearer of the Spirit does not choose the usual forms and strategies for acquiring moral and political attention and loyalty: *He will not cry or lift up his voice, or make it heard in the street.*

The bearer of the Spirit does not make himself and his action prevail by means of a public relations campaign. He does not "plug" himself and his action. He does not even make use of a public proclamation of law or of judgment. He forgoes the usual forms for solidifying and pushing through political rule. The exegetical discussion has often brought out this act of forgoing the typical forms for laying claim to political rule. But in doing so it is easy to fail to notice that the bearer of the Spirit not only forgoes acquiring political loyalty "from above;" he also forgoes the strategies of so-called politics from below. This becomes clear from the fact that, of the three expressions employed ("He will not cry or lift up his voice, or make it heard in the street"), in any case the first, and perhaps also the second, are in the overwhelming majority of occurrences applied to *the cry of a victim.*[23]

---

22. See §4.1.

23. I am grateful to Patrick D. Miller (letter to author) for this extremely important observation, which carries with it profound consequences (see also §4.3): "It appears to me that in (Isaiah 42) v. 2, in at least two of the expressions that appear there, the point is that the spirit-empowered servant of the Lord will not cry out in the face of suffering. Where that is clearest is in the expression *lō' yiṣ 'aq*, 'he will not cry out.' As far as I can tell, the verb *sā'aq* always refers to the outcry of the

This would mean, though, that the bearer of the Spirit does not even call public attention to himself as a victim or as a person in suffering. The person who appears on the scene here is no typical ruler, nor anyone who represents an antitype to the typical ruler. The bearer of the Spirit does not simply engage in "opposition politics" and does not propagate a mere "counter-morality."

We must take note of the following dismaying fact. The chosen servant upon whom God's Spirit is laid generates public attention neither "from above" nor "from below" in the traditional forms of political public relations. *Nevertheless,* indeed precisely because of this, he attains universal attention and loyalty, and spreads justice, mercy, and knowledge of God on a universal scale. "He brings justice to the nations; he establishes justice in the earth; the coastlands wait for his teaching."

---

victim, someone in trouble or hurt. . . . The second expression is *velōʾ yiśśāʾ,* 'he will not lift up the voice'; it occurs seventeen times in the Old Testament. In thirteen instances, it is followed by *bākhāh,* 'to weep,' and thus in a context where the raising of the voice connotes sadness or distress. There are, however, at least three instances where the expression appears in juxtaposition to 'shout joyfully.' So the evidence is ambiguous. But 75 percent of the time it is a note of distress. I can only find one other occurrence of the third idiom, and it is not exactly the same. In Isa. 33:7, we have *sāʿaq ḥuṣāh,* 'to cry outside,' which J. Roberts translates in context as: 'But now the Arielites cry without, / The messengers of Shalem weep bitterly.' He comments as follows: 'the term *ḥṣh,* "without" does not mean "outside the city," as though these mourners were exiles, but "outside, in the streets," where public mourning customarily took place (Amos 5:16; Isa. 15:3; 24:11)' (J. J. M. Roberts, "Isaiah 55: Invitation to a Feast," in L. Meyers and M. O'Connor, eds., *The Word of the Lord Shall Go Forth: Essays in Honor of David Noel Freedman in Celebration of His Sixtieth Birthday* [Winona Lake, Ind.: Eisenbrauns, 1983], 27). This at least suggests that the third phrase may also have to do with one who does not cry out publicly or weep when oppression and suffering or even death come. We have assumed that in this Servant Song, the suffering that is clear in Isaiah 53 is not yet present. I think that is debatable. One at least should note that what is suggested above would be consistent with the clear word of Isa. 53:7."

The most important passages in support of this interpretation of Isa. 42:2 are still those provided by R. Marcus, "The 'Plain Meaning' of Isaiah 42:1-4," *Harvard Theological Review* 30 (1937): esp. 259; also important with regard to this theme is R. Boyce, *The Cry to God in the Old Testament,* Society of Biblical Literature Dissertation Series 103 (Atlanta: Scholars Press, 1988), esp. 77ff. The arguments of Elliger (*Deuterojesaja,* 208–9) are not very convincing.

This difficult state of affairs is articulated in two basic expressions of faith that are not easy to make sense of and to open up to understanding, but that prove to be thoroughly appropriate to the material. I am referring to the talk of the *"pouring out of the Spirit"* and to the attestation of *the rule of the powerless and despised servant of God*. Both things are spoken of repeatedly in the biblical traditions. Within the biblical traditions, interconnections between them and interconnections of both with the messianic promises of the fulfillment of the law are successively illuminated in increasing concentration. From the retrospective viewpoint of the New Testament traditions, a relatively stable picture results.[24] Yet even taken each on its own, both expressions, as difficult as it might be for us today to make immediate sense of them, distinguish themselves by their internal clarity and logic.

The image of the "pouring out" of the Spirit expresses in a complicated but appropriate manner the fact that the Spirit of God—proceeding from a more complex reality than our immediate surroundings can reflect—brings the unfolding of God's righteousness from the most varied foundations and surroundings. The Spirit of God acts in the same way as the rain, which, coming down from heaven, enables an entire landscape with the most varied living beings to burst into new life together, full of freshness and vitality.[25]

The "pouring out" of the Spirit is also an appropriate expression of the fact that the Spirit-bearer's fulfillment of the knowledge of God and of the expectations of righteousness will not remain confined to Israel, but will include "the nations." National, cultural, and other humanly erected boundaries can no more hinder the action of the Spirit than they can hinder the rain and the wind. The Joel promise will add that the knowledge of God and the knowledge of the reality intended by God for human beings are defined and mediated not only by upper-class circles, the circles that happen to be ruling at the moment. Men *and* women, old *and* young, male slaves *and* female slaves attain prophetic knowledge through the Spirit and mediate it to each other. Those who are politically and socially subordinated, even those who do not count in a society, will experience the righteousness and glory of

---

24. See M. Bucer, *De Regno Christi*, in W. Pauck, ed., *Melancthon and Bucer*, Library of Christian Classics 19 (Philadelphia: Westminster, 1969), 179–91.

25. For a more detailed discussion, see §3.3.

God and will reflect God's righteousness and glory for each other as well as for those social strata that previously alone had "weight."[26] Specific dominant values and systems of order cannot limit the action of the Spirit.

With the establishment of the messianically promised righteousness of God, the peoples who in Israel's perspective were previously religiously excluded are given an active part in the experience of righteousness and in the knowledge of God. The same is true for those groups of persons who belong to the people, but who previously were not "represented" in the vision and the practice of those who ruled. The *glory* of God's righteousness is revealed when the righteousness intended by God is depicted, reflected, and communicated in a plurality of ways from a variety of national, social, and cultural frames of reference. God's righteousness is defined by the interconnection of justice, mercy, and knowledge of God. God's righteousness is not bound up with a specific nation, a specific history, a specific morality, a specific politics, a specific form of administering the law. Under these conditions, who can draw loyalty to herself or himself? Is it even possible to conceive this plurality centered on a person and integrated by a person?

The answer is still more difficult to make sense of than is the talk of the "pouring out of the Spirit." The answer is that the bearer of the Spirit rules not by the use of force or by public relations strategies, but by powerlessness.

Isaiah 42:2 is no chance interpolation. The verse strengthens and renders more precise an emphasis that is also found in other texts that talk about the bearer of the Spirit. It strengthens, namely, the insistence that the bearer of the Spirit does not use the usual forms of exercising political and military might. In Isa. 11:4b we read that "he shall strike the earth *with the rod of his mouth,* and *with the breath of his lips* he shall kill the wicked." At least in retrospect, and definitively from New Testament perspectives, Isaiah 42 is to be seen in interconnection with the other so-called songs of the ʿebhed yhwh (Isa. 49:1ff.; 50:4ff.; 52:13ff.; the songs are difficult to delimit), which set forth in greater detail and clarity the *public powerlessness* of the servant chosen by God. According to Isaiah 49 as well, the servant is honored by God, but not

---

26. This is developed in §3.4.

by the politically "weighty" publics (49:3, 7). God has held him hidden and concealed (49:2). Neither the political publics nor the servant himself are aware at the outset of the power and influence granted him by God.

Isaiah 49:3-4a: "And God said to me, 'You are my servant, Israel, in whom I will be glorified.' But I said, 'I have labored in vain, I have spent my strength for nothing and vanity.' " The servant ordained to be "a light to the nations" and "a covenant-mediator to humanity" is initially "deeply despised" and "abhorred by the nations" (cf. esp. Isa. 49:6-8).

Isaiah 50:6 talks about the public aggression against the person stirred up and chosen by God, who shall proclaim God's mercy and make God's righteousness visible: "I gave my back to those who struck me, and my cheeks to those who pulled out the beard; I did not hide my face from insult and spitting."

Most strikingly and most disturbingly, the last Servant Song gives expression to the way in which the servant chosen by God bears powerlessness and suffering.[27] In this song, which "without a doubt was formed with reference to the first three songs of the ʿebhed yhwh,"[28] but which nevertheless deviates from them in many respects,[29] we again encounter the insistence that the servant centers public (aggressive) attention on himself *without saying a word*, that he does "not open his mouth" (Isa. 53:7). This passage emphasizes much more heavily than those in Isaiah 42, 49, and 50 that this servant orients people to himself *in the medium of contempt*. Many have shuddered at the sight of this figure marred beyond human semblance (52:14): he is unsightly, avoided, not esteemed, tormented, mistreated, and reckoned among criminals. A differentiated potential for scorn is concentrated on the servant who will "make many righteous."

The one who is silent and offensively despised brings God's righteousness; the servant establishes justice, mercy, and knowledge of

---

27. See O. H. Steck, "Aspekte des Gottesknechts in Jes 52,13-53,12," ZAW 97 (1985): 36ff.; W. H. Schmidt, "Die Ohnmacht des Messias: Zur Überlieferungsgeschichte der messianischen Weissagungen im Alten Testament," *Kerygma und Dogma* 15 (1969): 30ff.

28. Steck, "Aspekte des Gottesknechts," 47.

29. Cf. ibid., 48ff.

God—not only for Israel, but also for the nations. Why is salvation brought by a person who is publicly silent, even by one who counts for nothing, whom people have despised and abandoned? How can a person who is despised like this prepare the way for the *knowledge* of God's righteousness?

When faced with talk of "salvation," whoever is content with imprecise notions of "coming out on top" will not be able to answer these questions. The inclusion of the Gentiles, the inclusion of the nations, cannot be appropriately comprehended within the framework of a simple success story, be it the success story of a "bringer of salvation" with the power to impose his or her political will, or the success story of a people that practices exemplary justice. This is because the righteous access of the Gentiles to salvation is not grasped within the framework of a success story centered on *one* people.

What does it mean to say that God has *mercy* on the Gentiles? As truly as God is *righteous*, it cannot in any way mean that a lesser salvation is extended to the "families of the earth" (Gen. 12:3b), that the Gentiles experience so to speak a qualitatively subordinate treatment by God.[30] God also wills to extend Godself to the nations authentically and in all God's glory. This eliminates simple notions of inclusion that place the nations on a secondary level or merely on the horizon of the righteousness established in Israel, or that merely center the nations on a salvation that Israel experiences only *with regard to itself*. In spite of the emphasis on the historical and natural primacy of Israel, we are to comprehend the astounding aspect of the promise that the bearer of the Spirit also fulfills the Gentiles' expectations of righteousness and stimulates their knowledge of God. The Gentiles call the Israelites ministers of "our" God (Isaiah 61). Israel ministers inasmuch as it serves[31] its God, the God whom the Gentiles will recognize as their own.

This direct and authentic access to the God of Israel and to God's righteousness on the part of strangers, people of other lands, and Gentiles can be disturbing, indeed terrifying. God's mercy not

---

30. Romans 9:23 will insist that God wishes to demonstrate the "riches of God's glory for the vessels of mercy."

31. English usage requires employing two different verbs, *to minister* and *to serve*, where the German uses only one, *dienen*—TRANS.

only mitigates and makes more tolerable the situation of a disadvantaged person, a disadvantaged group, or a disadvantaged people. It also extends to them the glory, indeed the riches, of the glory of God. The experience that God's mercy does all this is overwhelming. As much as people may long for this experience, it is difficult to accept and to appropriate. The more tightly structured the religious tradition and one's placement of self within it, and the clearer the internalized normative structure, the more oppressively can the promised universalizing of salvation be experienced as a salvation that alienates, distances, uproots, and relativizes. This is due to the breaking open of the deeply rooted, proven, and familiar parameters of judgment by which piety specifies what is inside and what is outside, what belongs and what is foreign, what is nearer to God and what is further, what is stronger and what is weaker. New standards are set up.

To be able to recognize in this not an impoverished relativism, but the establishment of the glorious *righteousness of God*, which calls the parameters of human reckoning into question and transcends them— to be able to do so is to take seriously the promise of the publicly suffering, silent, and despised servant of God.

God does not rule the world through a "bringer of salvation" who secures the actual or fantasized political, judicial, and moral accomplishments of a people or of a group of persons.

The orientation toward the powerless servant of God leads persons and peoples with their various cultures of expectations and longings for salvation into a double situation that leads to their *transformation*, to their radical change. *The servant gathers the nations and places them in de facto bonds of solidarity in their shared negative, aggressive, and scornful relationship to the one who is suffering. Inasmuch as the peoples recognize this, they receive the capacity for rejection of their old identity, for transformation, renewal, and corresponding development toward each other.* Yet the powerless servant removes not only the peoples' ideologies of domination and the self-understanding tied up with these ideologies.

In the recognition that a person who was ostracized, despised, even persecuted and executed in the name of the prevailing orders is God's chosen one, people are opened to the recognition of God's righteousness. In an essential way this righteousness calls into question their previous conceptions and practices of righteousness and transcends them. It becomes possible to recognize that the most well-intended, apparently most proven, well-articulated, recognized forms and practices of righteousness are also corruptible and corrupted. They are called into question in favor of richer experiences of righteousness, clearer experiences of justice and mercy, and clearer knowledge of God. Even if the righteousness of a specific group of people, a specific tradition, a specific normative background is sensitized to mercy within the confines of its particular standards of reckoning, even if this righteousness is marked by conceptions of God, it is broken, relativized, and renewed. Bound up with this is a rejection of all attempts to establish one's own individual and collective well-being while making others pay the cost, a rejection of all attempts to stipulate within the framework of one's *own* judgment of justice and mercy the standard for what is due to those outside and for what is advantageous to them. Bound up with this is also a sensitization and vulnerability to new expectations of righteousness, expectations of mercy, and experiences of God. All this is—when it actually occurs and takes effect—very difficult to bear. The change that enables people to accept God's righteousness occurs in the process of knowing oneself and locating oneself in the domain of the Spirit-bearer, who "rules" through powerlessness. This change occurs by virtue of the fact that the bearer of the Spirit bears public scorn.

The silent, powerless servant of God does not bring a specific political or moral program to bear. In his sphere of power the experience of failure, of danger, and of the need for the renewal of human conceptions of salvation and righteousness has become the prevailing fundamental experience. It is with regard to the publicly silent, suffering, despised bearer of righteousness that this fundamental experience is raised up and spread.

The sovereignty of the God who elects this bearer of righteousness is characterized not simply by an infinitely powerful God prevailing from outside against all human claims to righteousness and against all human claims to have realized righteousness. The sovereignty of this God is characterized by the fact that God demonstrates God's own righteousness in the midst of diverse experiences of pressure being exerted for justice, mercy, and knowledge of God, in the midst of diverse experiences of the corruptibility of this pressure in view of the condition of being fallen under the power of sin, and in the midst of diverse experiences of renewal. God brings God's own righteousness to bear in the consonances and dissonances of these experiences and in their mutual critique and stimulation.

Inasmuch as God's sovereignty is mediated by the one who is publicly silent, ostracized, and despised, people become sensitized to the fact that *this God* builds the reign of God out of diverse and varied contexts, out of different traditions, and out of different cultures, each with its different experiences of community, each with its particular experiences of distress, each with its own expectations of deliverance, and each with its specific experiences of joy and liberation.

The faith that is directed toward this God and that waits for the action of the Spirit of this God cannot content itself with political and moral heroes, with established, tested, or ideal normative forms of power. Faith exposes itself in constantly new ways to the dissolution of the forms of order and of power of "this world."

It is in substantive accord with this relation to "reality" that, in the shared understanding of many exegetes, Isaiah 42 does not present God's chosen servant only before the nations or before Israel, but before the all-encompassing, definitive, *eschatological public* of the heavenly court.[32] This utterly universal public, which includes Israel and the nations—and not only of that day, but of all times—is concentrated on the servant chosen by God and endowed with God's Spirit.[33] Before this universal, eschatological public, God not only sets up a "relation of protection and patronage" to the chosen servant, but manifests the particular trust that God places in this person who is acting at God's behest, and makes known God's particular authorization.[34] Here is more than a political public. Here is more than a process of arousing attention and acquiring loyalty, as is customary in a political public.

It is no wonder that human beings, bound to specific natural locations, specific well-honed systems of order, and specific cultural contexts in specific times, react aggressively to the person who has received this authorization. This person does not fit political conceptions and images of power, rule, and success. Nor does this person fall on the spectrum stretching between the extremes of politics "from above" and

---

32. See also §§2.4 and 3.3.
33. Cf. Elliger, *Deuterojesaja*, 200–3.
34. Cf. ibid., 201–2, 204.

politics "from below." Likewise, this person does not fit the strategies for acquiring loyalty that build on that spectrum. No one who pledges herself to this servant can give herself up unqualifiedly to a specific public opinion, a general mood, an ideology, or a social routine.

Precisely for this reason the Spirit-bearer, who does not cry or lift up his voice or make it heard in the street, necessitates a particular *authenticity* of access to him. The bearer of the Spirit necessitates a readiness for critical engagement, change, and repentance—a readiness that abandons trust in the well-honed forms of power in which life is embedded, or which over and over are the objects of aspiration and longing. The bearer of the Spirit necessitates a new departure not only from dominant forms of political power, but also from dominant forms of judicial, religious, and moral power. God's Spirit of righteousness and peace acts through a Messiah who is "not politically practical," "not in tune with the public."[35]

3.3: Extending beyond the condition of being tied to a particular time and situation: What is meant by the "pouring out of the Spirit from heaven"?

The statement that God's Spirit is poured out *from heaven* or *from on high* is found repeatedly in the biblical traditions.[36] For secular cultures, this statement makes reference to the Holy Spirit a stumbling block from square one inasmuch as *heaven* is named as the starting place for the descent of the Spirit. Precisely the descent of the Spirit from heaven seems to put the doctrine of the Holy Spirit at a far remove from what secular environments can in general imagine as circumstances within the realm of truth and reality.

The claim that God also created heaven or the heavens, that God dwells in heaven, and that God's powers operate from heaven on human beings causes abundant difficulties for secular consciousness. "The heavens we shall gladly leave to the angels and the sparrows,"

---

35. Cf. the process of change described in Isa. 32:1ff.

36. Isaiah 32:15ff.; 44:3; Ezek. 39:29; Joel 3:1ff.; Zech. 12:10; Prov. 1:23; Wisd. of Sol. 9:17; in the New Testament in connection with the Pentecost event, as well as Acts 10:45; 1 Pet. 1:12, among others.

wrote Heinrich Heine[37] in opposition to a bourgeois religious culture that held out the prospect of vague heavenly joys after death, and that connected with this the requirement of patience and renunciation in life. Heaven as an obfuscatory formula for fantastic notions and empty consolations still counts in our own day as a symbol of an escapist form of religious life. Against this background people readily resonate to a summons such as John Lennon's "Imagine, there's no heaven!" It is indeed simpler not to complicate matters with conceptions of what religious life and faith speak about under the rubric of "heaven." It is simpler to take "natural heavens," "sky," as the only valid sense of "heaven." "Heaven" is the heavens of natural perception: the firmament with the sun, moon, stars, clouds, wind, snow, and rain, in which birds and, beginning with this century, airplanes are to be seen from time to time. Besides this, "heaven" at the most refers to the heavens of learned and scientific observation and calculation: the constellations of the stars, the Milky Way, and the many immensities of the universe that are inconceivable for common sense. By contrast, it seems that we land in numerous insoluble problems if we attempt to talk about the heaven intended by religious life and to understand this remarkable part of creation. We immediately think of Copernicus and Galileo, and of the humiliation of a theology that sought to push, against the scientific knowledge of its time, an understanding of the world that in its opinion lay in the Bible and that perhaps was taken for granted by medieval common sense.

The conception of "the ancients," who understood the world as something like the Toronto Skydome, in which the heavens are a half-sphere that covers the earth, thought of as a disk, still counts as a striking confirmation of their folly and of the progress we have made in the meantime. Yet in adopting this perspective we overlook *two things*. On the one hand, we overlook the fact that when, even today, for common sense the sun still circles the earth and rises in the east, common sense is correct relative to *sense* perception of the heavens. A. N. Whitehead has formulated a convincing justification for this:

---

37. H. Heine, *Germany: A Winter's Tale*, trans. H. Salinger (New York: L. B. Fischer, 1944), 5.

We are told by logicians that a proposition must be either true or false, and that there is no middle term. But in practice, we may know that a proposition expresses an important truth, but that it is subject to limitations and qualifications which at present remain undiscovered. It is a general feature of our knowledge, that we are insistently aware of important truths; and yet that the only formulations of these truths which we are able to make presuppose a general standpoint of conceptions which may have to be modified. . . . [Whitehead gives the following illustration from science.] Galileo said that the earth moves and that the sun is fixed; the Inquisition said that the earth is fixed and the sun moves; and Newtonian astronomers, adopting an absolute theory of space, said that both the sun and the earth move. But now we say that any one of these three statements is equally true, provided that you have fixed your sense of "rest" and "motion" in the way required by the statement adopted. At the date of Galileo's controversy with the Inquisition, Galileo's way of stating the facts was, beyond question, the fruitful procedure for the sake of scientific research. But in itself it was not more true than the formulation of the Inquisition. But at that time the modern concepts of relative motion were in nobody's mind; so that the statements were made in ignorance of the qualifications required for their more perfect truth. Yet this question of the motions of the earth and the sun expresses a real fact in the universe; and all sides had got hold of important truths concerning it. But with the knowledge of those times, the truths appeared to be inconsistent.[38]

On the other hand, we easily overlook the fact that in the biblical traditions (as well as in other traditions of antiquity), the understanding of heaven is significantly more complex than are the notions that make the rounds in our cultures today concerning the conceptions of those traditions. Most of the biblical traditions, when they talk about heaven, are namely connecting *different conceptual domains* and *different frames of reference,* and at the same time differentiating between them. To be sure, in many of the biblical texts "heaven" and "sky" are in fact almost identical. The heavens are the domain from which come wind and rain, and in which birds fly. In other texts the conception of

---

38. A. N. Whitehead, *Science and the Modern World* (New York: Macmillan, 1950), 262–63.

earth includes this domain, and the heavens are only the domain of the stellar constellations. In still other texts the entire observable cosmos is called "that which is visible" and distinguished from heaven,[39] which is invisible. This invisible heaven is probed and illuminated in images, in conceptions, and even in theories that are to be understood by us today in a secular perspective as images, conceptions, and theories of *power structures*.

To unfold the details of a doctrine of heaven is the task of a doctrine of creation.[40] Without anticipating this extremely important task —a task that is indispensable for urgently required changes in our conceptions of reality—we can at least say that in the biblical traditions we do not find exclusively conceptions of the natural constitution of heaven and earth that cosmology and the natural sciences have simply outdated and relativized. In many biblical texts heaven is described not only as the domain that from a human point of view lies above the earth. Heaven is also comprehended as a complex of uncontrollable powers that affect what happens on earth. Heaven is understood as a domain that is not accessible to human measurement and reckoning or to human manipulation.

In talking about heaven, what is at issue is not an abstract, indeterminate, otherworldly domain, but a domain that essentially and in a perceptible way determines life on this earth: for example, by bestowing

---

39. English generally uses the plural *heavens* for the first two senses presented in this paragraph, and the singular *heaven* for this third sense. German by contrast consistently uses the singular *Himmel* for all three senses. By having to choose in each particular case between *heaven* and *heavens*, the English translation systematically and misleadingly emphasizes one or another aspect of the broader sense of *Himmel*. Biblical Hebrew has only the plural form *šāmayîm*, while the Greek New Testament contains many instances of both the singular *ouranos* and the plural *ouranoi* (see n. 43 below)—TRANS.

40. For a preliminary treatment see M. Welker, "What Is Creation? Rereading Genesis 1 and 2," trans. J. Hoffmeyer, *Theology Today* 48 (1991): 56–71; M. Welker, *Universalität Gottes und Relativität der Welt: Theologische Kosmologie im Dialog mit dem amerikanischen Prozessdenken nach Whitehead*, 2d ed. (Neukirchen-Vluyn: Neukirchener, 1988), esp. 203ff.; and picking up on the latter work, J. Moltmann, *God in Creation: A New Theology of Creation and the Spirit of God*, trans. M. Kohl (San Francisco: Harper & Row, 1985), 158–84. See also C. McDannel, and B. Lang, eds., *Heaven: A History* (New Haven: Yale Univ. Press, 1988); and K. Barth, *CD* 3/3, 418–76.

and withdrawing light and water. Heaven and earth stand in a complex relation that is not symmetrically reciprocal. But the uncontested fact that earthly life is utterly dependent on a specific measure of light, air, warmth, and water, is only *one* sign of this relation.

Where the prejudice is abandoned that the cultures of antiquity were naive, it becomes apparent that even so-called archaic thought employs procedures that are very subtle, even thoroughly deserving of the name "scientific." In other words, this way of thinking takes complex structural patterns of which it believes it has come to a relatively good understanding, and extends their use by reinvesting them in domains of experience that it has not yet clearly understood but that appear to it to be analogous. The utter dependence on the heavens that give rain, light, and warmth is illuminated with the aid of experience. The understanding is employed symbolically in order to understand instances of utter dependence on *other* powers that are difficult to comprehend, overly complex, and overwhelming. By means of such a procedure, religious thought seeks to acquire insights into reality. Knowledge about unavoidable dependencies on *natural powers* and knowledge about ways to deal with such dependencies are employed in order to bring clarity to experiences with *cultural and social powers* at whose mercy human beings see themselves placed.

For example, a storm from the heavens is uncontrollable; its course and duration are unpredictable. Yet this storm is, in the strictest sense of the word, experienced. It is perceived with the senses, it is noticed, it imposes itself on sense perception. This situation is similar to experiences with social movements such as those set in motion by the early charismatic leaders, by "charismatic" persons on whom God's Spirit "descends." This situation is comparable to experiences of the gathering of the people Israel that go hand in hand with the descent of the Spirit *from on high*.[41] As in the case of the storm whose course could not be foreseen, this alliance, this gathering could not be predicted. Why could the people not be led together earlier? How long will solidarity and community remain? When will the action of the Spirit cease? In spite of these uncertainties and open questions, the action of these powers that cannot be calculated and controlled at will is as evident as the action of the power of the wind.

---

41. See §§2.1, 2.5, and 3.4.

It shows astounding systematic cogency to seek analogous structures in such different forms of power, of the concentration of power, and of the exercise of power, and to ascribe these structures to their own proper reality: namely, the complex reality of heaven. This reality connects the forces of nature and those socially and historically determined forces that likewise are totally or almost totally beyond individual and collective control. The reality to which both groups of forces are ascribed, heaven, cannot of course in this perspective be understood any longer in a purely *naturalistic* manner. Heaven must rather be understood as the location of natural *and* social forces and powers. In biblical traditions and in biblically inspired religious traditions, heaven is accordingly understood not only *spatially*, but temporally as well: as the future, the transcendence that lies temporally before us.[42] Finally, heaven is also represented in images and grasped in structures that we are totally unable to decode correctly, that we are not at all in a position to illuminate. It connects realities that are no longer or not yet accessible to our thought and imagination. For example, it holds onto past and future times and cultures that we are no longer able to include even in our broadest concepts of "the world."

Heaven is the domain of reality that is relatively inaccessible to us, which we cannot manipulate, but which exercises a determinative and even definitive influence on life here and now. Forces and powers of nature, forces and powers of social spheres, forces of history and powers of the future are for the biblical traditions localized "in heaven." Formulated for empirico-rationalistic and skeptical positions of consciousness, heaven is the domain of reality that allows us to grasp graphically and tangibly in their complexity the powers and forces that define our lives but that are not in our immediate perception and control. Heaven allows us to think through these powers and forces, or at least to assign them to an obfuscatory formula.

In this way the biblical traditions not only overcome a merely naturalistic understanding of heaven. They also resist the typically religious *divinization* of heaven and of its powers. Like earth, heaven is *created*. Heaven is a creature, not God or a divine power or a collection

---

42. Concerning the interconnection of future and transcendence, see J. Moltmann, "The Future as a New Paradigm of Transcendence," in *The Future of Creation: Collected Essays*, trans. M. Kohl (Philadelphia: Fortress, 1979), 1–17.

of potential energies that is to be termed "divine." This understanding of heaven is enlightening and of great theological significance. Although heaven is the location from which proceed overwhelming natural forces and uncontrollable social forces, it is created by God. It is a creature, indeed both a natural and a social creature., Like earth, heaven is destined to pass away, despite the fact that it is a collection of powerful and complex forces, and despite the fact that it remains relatively constant and appears relatively stable in comparison with the fleeting, perishable conditions of natural and political life on the earth. Heaven is a creature and not God. In a way that is difficult to comprehend "on earth," heaven brings together forces that on the earth diverge and are separated in space and time. In other words, when implausible, inconceivable concentrations of powers and forces appear on the earthly scene, the biblical traditions regard that process as an activity *that proceeds from heaven*.

In many cases this is no more than a code or an obfuscatory formula for what is happening. But in other cases it opens possibilities for exploring and even for understanding how hypercomplex forces shape and change reality on this earth.

In addition to this aspect there is a second of which we should take note. From early on, the biblical traditions are aware that the heavens perceived "above us" (the Skydome model) represent *only a section of heaven*. A certain level of perceptual development concerning the world knows that it can be raining on the mountain and sunny in the valley at the same time, that it is hailing there and snowing here. A certain level of experiential development also knows that on this earth it is simultaneously day and night, or that at the same time one part of the earth is subject to frost and another to a heat wave. The heavens not only change in their appearance, in the play and menace of the beneficial or devastating action of their forces over us. There is also a change from one perceived heaven to the next. The heaven over other people and landscapes is different. In particular it presents itself completely differently when we take other planets as our point of departure, when we take account of other cosmic systems of reference.[43]

---

43. Perhaps the combination of the pluralization and the unification of heaven that we encounter in several biblical texts is to be traced back to a hazy awareness, or in isolated cases even to a clear awareness, of this state of affairs.

What is important is that precisely the trust in the unity and con-stancy of the creaturely in spite of this evident discontinuity, in spite of these experiences of difference and strangeness, makes it possible to assume the enduring unity of heaven. Heaven can thus become the ba-sis and the field of reference of real, differentiated *universality*.

What is at issue is a field of reference that extends beyond peoples, cultures, climates, and times. Whatever may distance and separate creatures and regions from each other in space and time, they all have in common the fact that they live *under heaven* with its stars and their attendant orders and rhythms, which endure through various condi-tions of the world.

Although major achievements of abstraction are necessary in order to comprehend heaven as universal, or at any rate as universal in rela-tion to the earth, heaven can still be assumed as a reality in the most straightforward sense of perceptual realities. Here we have not a daring construct or an audacious idea, but a reality that is essentially ade-quately accessible in countless perceptual contexts, and that is in fact incorporated—albeit fragmentarily—into these perceptual contexts.

Although the dimensions and complexity of heaven are over-whelming, heaven can be adequately—although by no means exhaus-tively—incorporated into life on this earth. The creatureliness of heaven allows us to assume a continuity also in that domain of the world that is inaccessible to us. The creatureliness of heaven allows us to assume a fundamental familiarity with heaven despite our awareness of an abundance that is essentially impossible to perceive, take in, or measure. Heaven is—also outside our perceptual spectra—attuned to the earth, coordinated with the earth, created with an eye to earthly creatures, human beings, and their perceptual capacity. We find the Priestly creation account already moving along this line inasmuch as it differentiates, on the one hand, the separation of light from darkness, and on the other hand, the creation of the stars, which again separate light from darkness. The stars, namely, are located in the heavens of perception, which correspond to the Skydome model. Here in the Priestly account, absolute and relative conceptions of totality, a totality that overarches perceptual domains and totalities that are relative to perception, are seen in a differentiated interconnection.

This heaven, the domain of creation that is for us less defined and less accessible, is regarded by the biblical traditions as the location of the primary presence of God. Heaven, which forms specific, inevitable perceptual spheres yet remains uncontrollable, which inevitably exceeds our perceptual spheres and yet makes familiarity possible—this heaven is in a particular way the location of God's presence. It is precisely by way of "heaven the creature" that it becomes possible to conceive a coherent relationship between *the universality and the inexhaustibility of God's presence, on the one hand, and the powerful concreteness of God's presence, on the other hand*. The interconnections between universality and inexhaustibility and powerful concreteness—a concreteness that simultaneously touches and infuses *different* horizons of experience and *different* perceptual domains—are illuminated by the action of *God's Spirit*.

The talk about the pouring out of the Spirit "from on high" or "from heaven" that we encounter repeatedly in the biblical traditions is not merely an obfuscatory formula for a numinous power that breaks in "straight down from above." It is not merely an obfuscatory formula for this power's abstract capacity to gain access to everything and to overcome everything that would resist it. The reference to the pouring out of the Spirit from on high explicitly embraces both natural and cultural perspectives (for example, the Spirit brings both "life" and "righteousness"). The reference to the pouring out of the Spirit points to a process of emergence and thus to a plurality of ways of being affected and to reciprocal interdependencies of life in its diversity, sprouting up and being strengthened in many contexts simultaneously. The pouring out of the Spirit brings about an astounding and ungovernable interaction that cannot be one-sidedly initiated and controlled from individual sides and regions.[44] The pouring out of the Spirit brings about an emergent and surprising commonality and vitality. The texts of which we should most take note in this connection are Isa. 32:15ff. and 44:3. They describe an interdependent vitality that sprouts up from many contexts, a vitality that is both "natural" and "cultural":

---

44. A process that affects several contexts, and one that cannot be governed or kept in check, is also the focus of those passages that speak about the *pouring out* of anger: esp. Isa. 42:25; but also Jer. 6:11; 10:25; 14:16; Ezek. 7:8; 14:19; 20:8, 13, 21, 33-34; 21:36; 30:15; 36:18; Hos. 5:10; Ps. 69:25; 79:6.

. . . until a Spirit from on high is poured out on us,
and the wilderness becomes a fruitful field,
and the fruitful field is deemed a forest.
Then justice will dwell in the wilderness,
and righteousness abide in the fruitful field.
The effect of righteousness will be peace,
and the result of righteousness, quietness and trust
forever.
My people will abide in a peaceful habitation,
in secure dwellings, and in quiet resting places. (Isa. 32:15-18)

The text describes transformations of pristine nature into cultivated land, and the transparence of cultivated nature for uncultivated
nature. Nature and culture become permeable to each other. Nature
can pass over into culture; cultivated land can correspond to the power
and density of nature. This process does not produce some sort of peculiar hybrids. It becomes possible for different domains of life and of
experience to change into each other, and indeed to change back out
of each other. The result of earth having this "heavenly" constitution
is the spread of righteousness and peace. The openness and natural
changeableness of the domains of life are attended by experiences of
being sheltered by what is trusted and familiar. In spite of the greatest
permeability and changeableness, all the world does not become
strange and terrifying everywhere. Instead all the world becomes a
home, giving protection and security.

The pouring out of the Spirit from heaven not only provides the
conditions for flourishing growth, inasmuch as it realizes, under
earthly conditions, "heavenly" interdependencies that connect domains of life that are foreign to each other. With this flourishing
growth, the pouring out of the Spirit also furthers people's making a
commitment before God and their numbering themselves among those
who belong to God. Isaiah 44:1-5 clearly maps out how this all hangs
together:

But now hear, O Jacob my servant,
Israel whom I have chosen!
Thus says the LORD who made you,
who formed you in the womb and will help you:
Do not fear, O Jacob my servant,

Jeshurun whom I have chosen.
For I will pour water on the thirsty land,
and streams on the dry ground;
I will pour my Spirit upon your descendants,
and my blessing on your offspring.
They shall spring up like a green tamarisk,
like willows by flowing streams.
This one will say, "I am the LORD's,"[45]
another will be called by the name of Jacob,
yet another will write on the hand, "The LORD's,"
and adopt the [honor-bearing] name of Israel.[46]

Powerful, shared, flourishing growth that opens spheres of life to each other, in connection with the act of turning to God and allying oneself with God—this description of the working of the pouring out of the Spirit is also encountered in texts from Ezekiel. The interdependent springing up and revitalization of natural and cultural environments in connection with the pouring out of the Spirit is connected by Ezekiel with the gathering of Israel from the nations and with the nations' reactions to this process.[47] According to Ezekiel, the creation of "heavenly" relations on earth—permeability of different domains of life to each other, openness and changeableness of domains of life in favor of new commonality and new common life—not only goes hand in hand with people numbering themselves among those who belong to God. The new community and new vitality also stand in strict interconnection with the revelation of God, with the concentrated presence of God. With the pouring out of the Spirit, God turns God's *face* to human beings.

---

45. Cf. in Isaiah 61, esp. vv. 9 and 11, the interconnection between being honorably numbered among those who belong to God and the "springing up" of praise "before all the nations."

46. C. Westermann points out that what is meant in v. 5 is "not the natural increase in the generations to come, but an increase in and spread of the numbers of the worshippers of Yahweh due to the accession of non-Israelites, i.e., proselytes" (*Isaiah 40-66: A Commentary*, trans. D. M. G. Stalker, OTL [Philadelphia: Westminster, 1969], 136). This would speak for the growing together of different domains of life.

47. Cf. §3.1 as well as Ezek. 36:22ff.

. . . when I have brought them back from the peoples and gathered them from their enemies' lands, and through them have displayed my holiness in the sight of many nations. Then they shall know that I am the LORD their God. . . . and I will never again hide my face from them, when I pour out my Spirit upon the house of Israel, says the Lord GOD. (Ezek. 39:27-29)

By being "poured out from heaven," the Spirit effects new community in various structural patterns of life that are apparently foreign to one another. Nature and culture become open to each other. They enter into new, life-promoting, reciprocal interconnections.[48] Bound

---

48. This complex structural pattern is found in the so-called last words of David (2 Sam. 23:1ff.)—admittedly without the explicit "pluralistic" perspective of the pouring out of the Spirit. There the forces of life relations that have been made truly peaceful are illuminated through the Spirit. "Now these are the last words of David: / The oracle of David, son of Jesse, / the oracle of the man whom God exalted, / the anointed of the God of Jacob, / the favorite of the Strong One of Israel: / The Spirit of the LORD speaks through me, / God's word is upon my tongue. / The God of Israel has spoken, / the Rock of Israel has said to me: . . ." God speaks *to me and through me*—this connects David with Micaiah son of Imlah and with Balaam, as well as with later prophecy. In contrast to the visions that we have already examined, here the Spirit of God explicitly states criteria for the action of the "anointed one." Taken at face value, these criteria are familiar to us from Isaiah's promises of the fulfillment of the law (see §3.1): criteria for the correct political leadership as well as for the preservation of a people. Yet in addition there is a more precise characterization of the power of influence emanating from the righteous and God-fearing ruler: vv. 3b-4a: "One who rules over people justly, / ruling in the fear of God, / is like the light of morning, / like the sun rising on a cloudless morning. . . ." A second image depicts the prosperity granted by God to this ruler who is like the light of morning, ruling in righteousness and fear of God: v. 4b: "As green shoots from the earth / gleam from the rain, / so my house lives with God, / for God has made with me an everlasting covenant." Here, in a passage speaking about God's Spirit, criteria are stated that ensure the presence of God's Spirit and the absence of a lying spirit, as well as securing Israel's life in a prosperous order willed by God.

Rule in righteousness and fear of God not only makes the royal house appear like the light of morning that overcomes the power of chaos (cf. B. Janowski, *Rettungsgewissheit und Epiphanie des Heils: Das Motiv der Hilfe Gottes "am Morgen" im Alten Orient und im Alten Testament*, WMANT 59 [Neukirchen-Vluyn: Neukirchener, 1989], esp. 183ff.). The prosperity of the ruling house and of the people ruled by it goes hand in hand with this righteous, God-fearing rule over people. As is likewise portrayed by an image of flourishing vegetation ("green shoots"), God makes the house of David steadily flourish, quicken, and sprout up like watered grass. God

up with this is God's act of making Godself present: divine revelation. The interconnection of universal breadth and inexhaustibility, on the one hand, and of powerful concreteness and presence, on the other

---

thus ensures not only growth, but also sustenance and preservation. However insignificant the images may at first appear, they are very revealing. They bring to bear—this time "from below," as it were—the biblical perspective on heaven, the domain of creation that is relatively not at our disposition. The Spirit teaches that righteousness can be established in constantly new ways only in a steady, self-critical orientation toward God—which is precisely what the fear of God is. Without this self-critical orientation toward God, righteousness cannot be institutionalized, presupposed, or assumed as a matter of course. Only when it is grounded and constituted in this way does it shine forth new every morning. When it is so constituted, people greet it joyfully like the morning light. The preservation of the house of David, too, is not a matter of course—even against this background. Within the framework of the covenant and of the covenant's fulfillment, that preservation can certainly be expected ("Indeed, God made with me an eternal covenant, very much in order and protected"). Nevertheless that preservation needs preservation "from on high" and God's constant, renewed extension of Godself as much as grass is always in fresh need of rain.

Even the strongest notions of continuity (eternal covenant) do not assume the characteristics of an automatic process, of a routine no longer in need of constant attention. Israel is blessed when it is living in *constantly renewed preservation*. The continuity of public cultural and political life is life that is constantly in need of preservation and that is lived in the fear of God and in God's constant and renewed extension of Godself (cf. Isa. 59:21; Hag. 2:5).

Salvation, including the salvation that God grants within the well-ordered covenant, is characterized as "deliverance" (*yāŝaʿ*). The righteous ruler, the ruler who is like the morning light, is the ruler who remains dependent on God's delivering action, who remains subject to the powers of heaven.

These words from the perspective of the Spirit thus highlight the indispensable *vitality* of salvation and deliverance. The peace that the Spirit brings and the promised "rest" are not to be confused with processes that are rigidified or that run their course according to routine. Light, which brings forth enlivening life (green shoots as food) and which over and over again is greeted with renewed joy, is the appropriate image of the power of the Spirit that effects righteousness and enlivenment. This light is something not at our disposal, something heavenly. The power "from heaven" extends beyond justice and morality, forms of the acquisition of political loyalty, the condition of being tied to a particular time and situation, force fields of major cultures, cultural developments and misdirected developments, even nature. Yet the power "from heaven" is at work and effective in the midst of natural, cultural, time- and situation-bound, political, judicial, and moral relations. In the midst of these relations the power of the Spirit lifts life beyond its finitude.

hand, is what is characteristic of heaven. The pouring out of the Spirit as a power that is also at work on earth makes it possible to experience this characteristic interconnection.

A situation, a culture, a time is no longer the ultimate, encompassing framework of reality and experience. As the rain simultaneously affects different landscapes, God's Spirit simultaneously lays hold of and transforms incompatible domains of life and experience that obey different laws, as well as countries and cultures that are barely accessible to each other, or accessible only at isolated moments.

The experience of this power, which, coming from heavenly continuity and abundance, intervenes in earthly life relations, initiates processes of the specification of creatures before God and of creatures making commitments before God. It initiates processes of acknowledging and being acknowledged on the basis of belonging to God. This specification of creatures before God and this act of creatures making commitments before God do not remove consciously and unendingly renewed openness to God. They do not remove accepted dependence on God's action, which is always new. On the basis of the pouring out of the Spirit, the breadth, permeability, and familiarity of heaven, as well as the heavenly unquestionability of the acknowledgment of God's rule, can be and are imaged in an earthly way. Through the pouring out of the Spirit from heaven, God's inexhaustible power and presence, extending beyond specific times and situations, become recognizable in a manner that can be both experienced and described.

3.4: Extending beyond imperialistic monocultures: The promised interplay of the experiences of God and the perceptions of reality of men and women, old and young, female and male slaves

The classic Old Testament text that talks about the pouring out of the Spirit is found in Joel 2:28-32.[49]

---

49. The so-called Pentecost sermon of Peter quotes this text in its entirety and points out that what was prophesied by the prophet Joel is happening in the Pentecost event.

Then afterward
I will pour out my Spirit on all flesh;
your sons and your daughters shall prophesy,
your old people shall dream dreams,
and your young people shall see visions.
Even on the male and female slaves,
in those days, I will pour out my Spirit.

I will show portents in the heavens and on the earth, blood and fire
and columns of smoke. The sun shall be turned to darkness, and
the moon to blood. . . . Then everyone who calls on the name
of the LORD shall be saved; for in Mount Zion and in Jerusalem
there shall be those who escape, as the LORD has said, and among
the survivors shall be those whom the LORD calls.

The Joel promise is framed by words providing assurance of God's
manifest and delivering presence (cf. Joel 2:27, 32) in the midst of the
most monumental catastrophes. There is an interconnection between
God's concentrated, unobstructed presence, open to the address of human beings, and a pouring out of the Spirit that leads to an interplay
of the most varied attestations to God's presence—so varied that it
seems to be impossible to get an overview of their interplay. The contrast appears remarkable: on the one hand, the concentrated presence
of God; on the other hand, the pouring out of the Spirit, and recognition and attestation that in their variety are bound together in a manner of which it is impossible to get an overview.

The Spirit is poured out on "all flesh." According to Joel, this occurs in diverse concretion: men and women, old and young, male and
female slaves are touched by the pouring out of the Spirit. Today what
initially jumps out at us is the repeatedly emphasized granting of equal
status to women and men[50]—in contrast to many other biblical traditions. Hans Walter Wolff has called attention to the fact that the reference in Joel to the pouring out of the Spirit "on all flesh" highlights
in general "the weak, the powerless and the hopeless" as "recipients of

---

50. This equalization will also shape New Testament pneumatological statements (see Gal. 3:28). Concerning 1 Cor. 12:13, cf. E. Schüssler Fiorenza, *In Memory of Her: A Feminist Reconstruction of Christian Origins* (New York: Crossroad,
1983), 50, 218ff. Luke 2:25ff., 36ff. are also noteworthy in this connection.

new life with God." Indeed it is not only female and male slaves, but also the old and the young who are highlighted as recipients of new life. The old women and men are the people who are passing away, who no longer are present in full power, and who will soon belong to the past. Young persons are the people who are not yet powerfully present, whose effective activity lies in the future. Yet it is certain that "sons" and "daughters" mean not only young people, but the old, and to no less of an extent the powerful and hopeful men and women of the generation standing in the middle of life. They, too, are to receive the Spirit and thus "new life with God" and with each other.

This promise picks up and broadens the foundations in the mercy law and the impetus that is characteristic of the messianic promises of the Spirit.[51] It picks them up inasmuch as the explicit promise is made that male and female slaves will also receive the Spirit. The Joel promise, too, holds fast to the conviction that the action of the Spirit of righteousness occurs for the benefit of the economically weak and the socially disadvantaged. The Spirit remains a Spirit of righteousness who binds together justice and mercy. The Spirit remains a Spirit who mediates attentiveness to those who are weaker with the act of working toward equal status for all persons.[52]

This basic trait of the action of the Spirit is already familiar to us. It is fine-tuned and broadened inasmuch as there is a heightened sensitivity to privilege and discrimination with regard to men and women overall and with regard to generational differences. In response to the list of men and women, old and young, sons and daughters, and free

---

51. See §3.1.

52. H. W. Wolff, *Joel and Amos: A Commentary on the Books of the Prophets Joel and Amos*, trans. W. Janzen, S. D. McBride, Jr., and C. A. Muenchow, ed. S. D. Mc-Bride, Jr., Hermeneia (Philadelphia: Fortress, 1977), 67: "The promise regarding 'manservants and maidservants,' added by way of intensification, unmistakably introduces into the hope an element of social revolution. The ancient law of God in Israel had already accorded special attention to the rights of male and female slaves, providing that they, too, should freely share the joy to be found in the presence of Israel's God. Beginning with Amos, prophecy had raised its voice on behalf of all who were oppressed and unfree (cf. especially Jer. 34:8-22). In the coming age they shall be incorporated fully into the community of the free, by being deigned worthy of the highest distinction along with all the rest." See also J. de Santa Ana, *Good News to the Poor: The Challenge of the Poor in the History of the Church* (Geneva: World Council of Churches, 1977), 4ff.

and slave, both male and female, it would be wrong to take from this list nothing but an abstract concept of unity ("everyone") and to conclude that the point is only that "equality" somehow or other reign in the community. It is of the greatest significance to recognize that this promise represents a giant step beyond all communities that are indeed concerned about "equality," but in which only a specific group defines how unity and equality are to be understood concretely. This is because the promise remains no less sensitive to naturally given differences that can be misused than to differences that have been set up unjustly. It does not pass over the diversity of tensions nor does it pass over perishability. The community of the reception of the Spirit is to grow out of different experiences of God and out of different perceptions of reality.

The Spirit is poured out on all *flesh*: that is, frail, finite, and perishable life. This means not only that the Spirit also descends on population groups that do not yet stand in full possession of physical, spiritual, political, and economic powers, that do not have "a say," that do not constitute the "one" of "One thinks . . . ," "One believes . . . ," and so on, and that do not stipulate what shall count as "normal." Inasmuch as the text focuses on violent cosmic catastrophes, it makes possible the recognition of the essential frailty and vulnerability of all creatures, including those who enjoy a relative strength and superior position. Without leveling the differences, the text reckons all human beings to the category of "flesh": frail and perishable life. The "rulers" as well are in need of deliverance by God. They, too, are in need of the knowledge of God. Thus they are in need of the prophetic knowledge and prophetic instruction of the other members of the community who have been seized by the pouring out of the Spirit.

The pouring out of the Spirit results not only in a universal capacity to participate in the life processes of the community, let alone that participation being limited to the processes of judicial and economic communication. Inasmuch as all—sons and daughters, old and young, male and female slaves—attain *prophetic knowledge* through the Spirit, they are given the capacity to *open with each other and for each other the reality and the future intended by God.*

The pouring out of the Spirit gives to all—the members of the community who are apparently without influence and without significance, or at any rate are in fact subordinate, as well as those persons who have "a say"—the capacity to predict salvation and disaster, but also to recognize God's ways out of the danger, to recognize God's deliverance. Already the establishment of righteousness under the rule of the weak and suffering righteous person, occurring for the benefit of those who are weak and afflicted, was directed at a broadening and strengthening of individual and common life. Now the sensitivity to differences between human beings is heightened once again. Typical inequalities are comprehended more precisely, along with attendant focal points of conflicts, starting points for setting up and solidifying unjust relations. By contrast, what is being called for is not an abstract equality. Instead we are referred to the concrete, pluriform equality of "fleshliness" before God. In this fleshliness the Spirit gives life to the irreducibly many-sided prophetic community.

When the Spirit of God is poured out, the different persons and groups of people will open God's presence with each other and for each other. With each other and for each other, they will make it possible to know the reality intended by God. They will enrich and strengthen each other through their differentiated prophetic knowledge. From various perspectives and trajectories of experience, they will direct each other's attention to the agent responsible for their deliverance. But in this differentiated and pluriform community of testimony, not only is there a powerful continuation of the Spirit's working toward righteousness. In this differentiated and pluriform community of testimony, God becomes present in a concentrated way. What is striking is the only apparently paradoxical state of affairs that it is precisely in the differentiated abundance of prophetic attestation that God wills to make Godself knowable in a powerful and concentrated way.

The Joel promise is bound between declarations of God's unobstructed, powerful, delivering presence. This fact gives this promise a material connection with the biblical testimonies that attest to the interconnection between the presence of God's *Spirit* and God's act of turning the divine *face* to God's creatures.[53]

---

53. Cf. Ps. 51:12ff.; 139:7; 143:7, 10; and esp. Ezek. 39:29.

God's act of turning the divine face to God's creatures—an action that goes hand in hand with God's presence[54]—signifies that God is present in a concentrated yet most lively way. God can also be present in other ways: for example, through a personal representative who speaks and acts at God's behest, through an expression of God's will, or through God's word, however that word might be transmitted. In all these cases one can certainly speak of God's presence. But in all these cases problems of certainty also arise. Is this representative really authorized by God? Does this manifestation of someone's will really express God's will? Is this word really a valid word spoken by God? Is this image really an image of God?[55] In comparison with such forms of God's presence, the reference to God's face points to the fact that God is indubitably present. Moreover, God is present in a concentrated way. It is not only the hem of God's garment that is at work; it is not only a breath from God's lips that can be detected.

Why is God's face so central? Why does "God's face" bring God's "personal presence to expression"?[56] Why can God's face function by synecdoche for the entire person?[57] On what basis can one also claim with regard to human beings that because the essence of the human person is expressed in her or his face, "face" can in an extended sense function as a designation of the whole person? Why precisely the face? Why not the total bearing, why not the gait, why not the hands, why not the pattern of gestures, why not the voice, why not the speech?

In contrast to bearing and gait, voice and speech, the face is distinguished by the fact that it communicates *living* presence, not merely

---

54. See A. S. van der Woude, "*Pānīm* / Angesicht," *THAT* 2 (1976): 431–60; J. Reindl, *Das Angesicht Gottes im Sprachgebrauch des Alten Testaments,* Erfurter Theologische Studien (Leipzig: St. Benno, 1970); F. Nötscher, *Das Angesicht Gottes schauen, nach biblischer und babylonischer Auffassung,* 2d ed. (Darmstadt: Wissenschaftliche Buchgesellschaft, 1969). See also E. Lohse, "πρόσωπον," *Theological Dictionary of the New Testament* 6, ed. G. Friedrich, ed. and trans. G. W. Bromiley (Grand Rapids: Eerdmans, 1968), 768–80.

55. With regard to images made by human beings, it is clear from the outset for the Old Testament that they are not an *imago Dei.* Cf. the passages that trace the powerlessness of idols not only back to the fact that they are made by human beings, but also to the fact that there is *no spirit* dwelling within them: e.g., Jer. 10:14 and 51:17; Hab. 2:19.

56. Van der Woude, "*Pānīm* / Angesicht," 448.

57. Cf. ibid., 442.

presence in motion. The face can represent the entire person because, on the one hand, in communication it not only is active, but also comports itself receptively and reactively. The face not only provides an opportunity to cast some light on activity and reactivity; they can be *read off it directly*. Initial notice that the face has reacted and acted does not come from the effects that those who have been addressed by God experience with regard to themselves: for example, the terror that invades their members. On the other hand, we see in the face not only action and reaction, but also the *refusal* to act and the *refusal* to react. God not only causes the light of God's face to shine; God not only turns the divine face against God's enemies. God also hides the divine face, does not show the divine face, or lowers it.

With regard to God's face, God is grasped not only in God's independence and spontaneity, but also in God's uncontrollability and freedom. Specifically, God is grasped in God's independence, spontaneity, and freedom *in interchange* with human beings. Through God's face, God's vitality becomes manifest in God's communication with human beings.

How are we to understand the interconnection between the presence of God's face and the action of the Spirit? Alternatively, how are we to understand the interconnection between God's lively and powerful presence, open to being addressed by human beings, and the pouring out of the Spirit on all flesh?

First we must distinguish the perception of the face of God from the perception of a human face. On the one hand, the Old Testament knows that whoever looks at God must die.[58] On the other hand, the expression "to look at the face of Yahweh" or "to look at the face of God" is a fixed technical term of cultic language.[59] This form of contact with God is not an everyday, self-evident matter. It is a risky undertaking, out of the ordinary, and needs to be regulated by law.

To look at the face of God, to come before God's face—this process describes the cultic gathering of the community, the act of coming to the sanctuary. God's face is present and turned to human beings in a way that they can bear when that presence is bound up

---

58. According to Exod. 33:20, God says to Moses, "You cannot see my face; for no one shall see me and live." Cf. Deut. 18:16; Judg. 13:22.

59. Cf. Van der Woude, "*Pānîm* / Angesicht," 454.

with the *gathering and constitution of the community* in which the living presence of God's face is indirectly (with regard to the action and reaction of the members of the community) perceived. This interaction and interplay (which can certainly include fruitful contrasts, differences, and contradiction) is due, if it points to God's presence, to the action of the Spirit.[60]

The connection between the presence of the Spirit and God's act of turning the divine face to God's creatures releases the experience of God's presence from a domain defined and definable only by cultic law. The action of the Spirit is not bound to the cultic site and to the cultic assembly. Through the action of the Spirit Israel is gathered out of the nations. Through the action of the Spirit those persons who are of a broken disposition, a broken heart, are healed. Through the action of the Spirit daughters and sons, old and young, male and female slaves in Israel are given the ability to prophesy. This means that the power of God mediated to human beings also wills to act in everyday and even trouble-filled comings and goings of life, with their instances of obscurity, disintegration, and rupture. This means that the presence of God, which brings people together, sets them right, and heals them, wills to have its effect in the everyday, conflict-ridden comings and goings of human life. Neither the presence of God's face nor the community that experiences this presence and makes it present for each other is confined to the cultic assembly.

---

60. Karl Barth rightly comprehended this process insofar as in his entire work he defines the Holy Spirit and the Holy Spirit's action as the power in which God turns "the human person" to Godself. "The human person" is turned by God to God (cf. Barth, CD 1/2, 238ff.; CD 4/4, 27ff.). But Barth misrepresented this process insofar as the basic dialogistic structure of his theology over and over obstructed the perception of this power and pronounced the Holy Spirit to be the "subjective possibility of revelation" (cf. Barth, CD 1/2, 264–79). Reductionist thinking in the two-sided pattern "God and 'the human person,'" and a subject-object model that is fully inadequate for comprehending pneumatological matters hindered Barth from making a clear critical analysis of the intersubjective and objectifying powers of the Spirit. (Barth's attempt to impose these two formal structures also results in the repeated misshaping of his fine discussions concerning the gathering and sending of the community.) The Holy Spirit is not ultimately the power of the subjective, pious sense of what is right. This Spirit is just as little the power of a well-honed cultic or moral routine.

Bound up with this recognition is a compound fracturing of imperialistic monocultures together with their religious, nationalistic, racist, sexist, and other attempts to provide a grounding for themselves. The promised, concentrated presence of God in the midst of the reality illuminated in the pluralistic and prophetic manner described in the Joel promise means *first* that *every person who has become a participant in the pouring out of the Spirit can receive and mediate prophetic knowledge, can see through and help others see through the rupture and misery of people and the reasons for the rupture and misery. Every person who has become a participant in the pouring out of the Spirit can see and enable others to see what God is doing in and on the ruptured members of God's people not only to heal them for themselves, but to bind them together for each other and to revitalize them.*

The promised, concentrated presence of God in the midst of the reality illuminated in the pluralistic and prophetic manner described in the Joel promise means *second* that *on the basis of the connection between God's presence and the specific abundance and diversity of the prophetic attestations endowed by the Spirit, the gathering, building up, and vitalizing of the entire, diversely differentiated community and of its members will no longer be lost from view.* [61] A specific group of people, a specific stratum, a specific tradition, or a specific culture can no longer claim for itself alone God's presence, the reception of the Spirit, prophetic testimony, and true definitions of reality. God's presence, the reception of the Spirit, prophetic testimony, and true definitions of reality can also no longer be *repressed* by a group, a stratum, a tradition, or a culture.

The promised, concentrated presence of God in the midst of the reality illuminated in the pluralistic and prophetic manner described in the Joel promise means *third* that *God's presence is not grasped with metaphysical and other reductionist, abstract distortions, but is experienced in the complexity of diverse, concrete, mutually challenging and mutually enriching attestations to the reality intended by God.* This means that concrete and pluriform individuality and reciprocal mediation of this diversity are characteristic of the prophetic testimony to God and to God's presence, and to the reality intended by God. The individuality

---

61. These processes are presented by Barth as the gathering of "individual persons" (cf. Barth, CD 4/1, 643–739; CD 4/2, 614–726). This fails to make it possible to recognize the force field characteristic of the building up of the "body of Christ."

and diversity in question here are mediated by the Spirit. This individuality is not a private individuality that is to be consumed privately and that excludes other people. This diversity is not a mutually indifferent or even a hostile, disintegrative diversity.[62]

To the presence of God through the Spirit and to the pouring out of the Spirit corresponds a complex process of mutual illumination, strengthening, edification, liberation, and enlivenment of individual persons. To the particular complexity attendant on God's presence in the divine face corresponds the complexity of *that which is festive*, of the exuberance of joy, the polyphony of glorifying God, of doxology. Joy, the feast, and glorification are forms of experience, figuration, and self-communication that can be overwhelming without paralyzing, destroying, or being excessively demanding. This extravagance and complexity can certainly be incorporated into the vision and the experience of an individual person.

A series of texts, above all texts from wisdom literature, make clear that the presence of God's face presents an enlivening power that is also directly of great significance for the *individual* person. If God can communicate to persons what is right and just, the result is a revitalization of the individual person, a revitalization that is described as an experience of deliverance and as glorification of God in a situation of worship.

> "'Let his flesh become fresh with youth;
> let him return to the days of his youthful vigor.'
> Then he prays to God, and is accepted by God,
> at the festal shout he sees God's face,
> and God repays him for his righteousness.
> That person [who has been delivered] sings to others
> and says . . ." (Job 33:25-27)

The person enlivened by the Spirit, the person who at the festal shout is allowed to look at the face of God, thus not only prophetically recognizes God's ways with God's people and with God's community, including in the everyday world and even when God's people

---

62. Cf. §1.4.

are dispersed, disrupted, and threatened. The revitalized person who obtains a festal perception of God's face can also recognize her own unrighteousness and her deliverance out of her own subjugation to death. This person can acquire distance from herself, her old, past life. She is capable of recognizing and confessing her sins, her former unrighteousness, her unmercifulness, and her distancing of herself from God—a capacity that is by no means self-evident and that is also not a matter of moral sensitivity and contemplation. The delivered person, enlivened by God's Spirit, is capable of recognizing her own sins and of glorifying God. She can say, "I sinned, and perverted what was right, and it was not paid back to me. God has redeemed my soul from going down to the Pit, and my life shall see the light" (cf. Job 33:27ff.). This distancing from the old ego before God's face in the community assembled in the Spirit has extremely important consequences. In this distancing the person receives back life and righteousness. The renewed righteousness connects *acknowledgment by God, as well as a new self-respect, with respect from other people.*

This renewal of the interconnection between acknowledgment by God, self-respect, and respect from other people goes beyond all forms of religious self-assurance, beyond self-satisfaction, experiences of success, and experiences of good resonance. Between the recognition of sin and the glorification of God, between the recognition of one's own lostness, now overcome, and thanks for the deliverance that one has experienced, the objectively grounded consciousness of one's own worth can arise and develop.

Respect for the worth of a human being shall ensure the person's self-respect and the objective foundations of this self-respect, just as much as the capacity of this person to respect the worth of other people. This structural pattern is a fragile one, constantly threatened on many sides.[63] This structural pattern is solidified and cultivated through a process that cannot be staged: *the lifting up of human beings.*

---

63. Cf. esp. the problems of the corruptibility of a moral market as described in §§1.5 and 3.1. The prophetic consciousness of difference breaks the naive self-confidence of moral communication, and thereby creates space for the recognition of sin, on the one hand, and for growth beyond ideologically hardened notions of salvation and righteousness, on the other hand.

The action of the Spirit rescues people both out of deficient self-respect and out of the overestimation of self. It restores their capacity to give and to receive respect. Before the face of God, through the differentiated experience of God's reality as that reality is mediated for and through human beings, and through the experience of the reality intended by God, a renewal of human persons and of human life relations begins. This renewal is shared, mediated in prophetic knowledge, and communicated in diverse ways. In sensitive and subtle ways that correspond to the diversity of life as it is really lived, the same thing is accomplished through the Spirit as that which imperialistic monocultures seek in vain to secure in their one-sided, ideological way that, consciously or unconsciously, spreads destruction on every side. The complex interconnections of self-respect, respect for others, and respect from others are renewed and cultivated. People are freed from entrapments—both from those for which they bear the blame and from those of which they are innocent. They experience the lifting up of other people and the renewal of their worth, and are simultaneously given a part in this process.

Yet how can this renewal and lifting up again and again become a new event, if it cannot after all simply be one-sidedly implemented by specific persons, if it is as uncontrollable as the "pouring out of the Spirit from on high"?

3.5: Extending beyond nature: Creation, new creation, and peace through the Spirit

The question of how the "Spirit of creation" and the "Spirit of righteousness" are to be understood as the *one* Spirit of God is one of the greatest theological challenges. We shall seek an answer in the following discussion, bypassing many wrong turns that place false constraints on thought and decision.

How does God become present through the Spirit? The most important answers so far were as follows: (1) through the promised bearer of the Spirit, who brings the fulfillment of the law in the *universal establishment of justice, mercy, and knowledge of God*, without making use of the means of power politics; (2) through the *"pouring out"* of the Spirit from heaven—in other words, not only for *one*, but *for a plurality of politically, nationally, culturally, or otherwise definable "presents"* [64] *and environments;* (3) through action that steadily breaks down unjust differences between people, but at the same time remains open and sensitive to the variety and mutual challenge of prophetic perspectives and of expectations of righteousness, inasmuch as it cultivates the cross-fertilization and mutual enrichment of natural differences that do not rest on unrighteousness, and brings unjust differences again and again to consciousness. All these rich and differentiated forms are expressions of the action of God's Spirit and of God's living and concentrated presence. The action of God's Spirit and the presence of "the face" of God can therefore designate two aspects of the same thing.

By comparison, the intimacy and breadth of God's presence become manifest in a heightened way where there is explicit reference to God's *creative action* through the Spirit. Admittedly, the recognition of the differentiated interconnections between the "Spirit of righteousness" and the "Spirit of creation and new creation" is obstructed by many attempts to characterize the "Spirit of creation" by abstract reference to "ubiquity," "universal effectiveness," and "universal rule." In contrast to false abstractions of this sort, we shall recognize both that the Spirit of God acts in and through what is "fleshly," perishable, and finite, and how the Spirit does so.

In the statements about God's explicitly "creative" action, *rûaḥ* is as a rule translated with "breath." God gives fleshly, perishable, finite creatures a share in God's "breath" and thus in God's Spirit. This "breathing" grants to human beings the "breath of life" (cf. Gen. 2:7 and passim). God's Spirit takes effect in human beings and in other creatures as the breath of life.

Breath differentiates human beings who are alive from those who are dead. Correspondingly, the "breathing" God is shown to be the living God in contrast to wooden, stone, and other idols. The act of imparting God's "breath" is an expression of God's life-creating and life-preserving goodness. The gift and the withdrawal of *rûaḥ* are an expression of God's power over life and death. If God takes back their breath, creatures lose their life. They lose not only their individual life

---

64. The German word here is *Gegenwarten*, the plural form of *Gegenwart*. *Gegenwart* means both "present" (in the sense of "the present" as opposed to "the past" or "the future") and "presence" (in the sense of, e.g., "in our presence")—TRANS.

force, but also their participation in the medium common to that which is alive. To be alive thus means: through God's *rûaḥ*, to stand in a substantial pattern of interconnection, to have a part in a medium that is both individually enlivening and common to all that is creaturely. God's Spirit enlivens, is creatively and life-givingly effective, inasmuch as the Spirit produces this intimate, complex, and indissoluble interconnection of individual and common life.[65] If God withdraws the Spirit, if God takes back God's "breath," life loses this interconnection, and earthly life decays to dust:

Ps. 104:29-30:

When you hide your face, . . .
when you take away their breath, they die
and return to their dust.
When you send forth your Spirit, they are created;
and you renew the face of the ground.[66]

Similarly, Job 34:14-15:

If God should take back God's Spirit to Godself,
and gather to Godself God's breath,
all flesh would perish together,
and all mortals return to dust.

The "breathing," the sending out of God's Spirit, gives coherence, shape, and life (cf. Wisd. of Sol. 1:7). The taking back of the *rûaḥ* leads to death and decay. If the Spirit is held back by God, if God keeps to Godself, chaos must remain chaos.[67] If it is recognized that the

---

65. I have shown elsewhere ("What Is Creation?," 60ff.) that "creation" at a very general level, even according to the classical creation accounts, is not to be understood as a mere relation of production and dependence, but as the construction and maintenance of a coherent pattern of relations of interdependence among different realms of life.

66. Concerning the "gift" of the Spirit, cf. Gen. 6:3; Isa. 42:5; Job 33:4; as well as Job 12:10; Jth. 16:14.

67. This background lends support to the most persuasive interpretation proposed—that of O. H. Steck—for the difficult, unparalleled statement in Gen. 1:2: "But the earth was (still) meaningless and unserviceable, and darkness was over the primeval flood, and the breath of God was in movement over the waters." (The

creative action of the Spirit is not self-evident, that the activity of the Spirit is not "automatic," indeterminately "everywhere," and with an arbitrarily specifiable constancy, we can begin to call into question the careless and thoughtless totalizations that have caused great difficulty for theology and piety. The abstract reference to the Spirit's "ubiquity," "universal causality," and "universal effectiveness" can be corrected and replaced. The fact that God's Spirit "has filled the world, and . . . holds all things together" (Wisd. of Sol. 1:7; cf. Isa. 34:16) is not to be confused with abstract "ubiquity." The Spirit is present in that which is *held together* and *enlivened* by God—but not, for example, in that which is decaying to dust. God is present creating life and working righteousness. But through falseness and unrighteousness human beings can grieve and banish God's Spirit.[68] To be sure, God can send

---

translation follows that of O. H. Steck, *Der Schöpfungsbericht der Priesterschrift: Studien zur literarkritischen und überlieferungsgeschichtlichen Problematik von Genesis 1, 1- 2, 4a*, 2d ed., Forschungen zur Religion und Literatur des Alten und Neuen Testaments 115 [Göttingen: Vandenhoeck, 1981], 256.) On the basis of these textual investigations, Steck has suggested that we see that God's Spirit (*rûaḥ ʾelōhîm*) is not to be understood, as is frequently assumed, as a strong wind or a "wind of God" (whatever that might mean), but as the "breath" of God that indicates God's vitality and power. "It is unquestionable that *rûaḥ* [transcription M.W.] can also have this sense with regard to God. Naturally what is meant is not the breath of God that as such is already life-giving and effective. . . . What is meant is the breath of God that has an affinity to speaking, the breath of God that as such is not yet the effecting of creation, but which will form itself into the creative speaking of the ordering with which the process of creation begins in v. 3." (Ibid., 235–36. Steck refers [236] to the connection between God's *rûaḥ*, God's word, and creation in Ps. 33:6: "By the word of the LORD the heavens were made, and all their host by the *rûaḥ* of God's mouth," as well as to Ps. 147:18 and 148:8.) The "Spirit" that is moving over the waters of chaos expresses God's vitality, God's readiness to speak and to act, God's readiness to speak and to act "from eternity." (Concerning the background in the history of religions that illuminates Gen. 1:2, see M. Görg, "Religionsgeschichtliche Beobachtungen zur Rede vom 'Geist Gottes,'" *Wissenschaft und Weisheit* 43 [1980]: esp. 134ff.; as well as J. Assman, *Ägyptische Hymnen und Gebete*, Bibliothek der Alten Welt: Der Alte Orient [Zurich: Artemis, 1975], 268–69, 278, 292.)

68. Cf., e.g., Isa. 63:10; Wisd. of Sol. 1:5. It is striking that precisely in such cases of conflict the "holiness" of God's Spirit is emphasized by the Old Testament. For a critique of the abstract language of ubiquity and universal effectiveness with regard to the creative Spirit, see also M. R. Westall, "The Scope of the Term 'Spirit of God' in the Old Testament," *Indian Journal of Theology* 26 (1977): 29ff. The fact

the Spirit into, and thus enliven, the dead and the dust. Yet all notions of a ubiquitous, uninterrupted action of the Spirit that can be arbitrarily expected at every space-time location are foreign to the biblical testimonies. Such notions are due to mistaken dreams of security and perfection and to vague wishful thinking about God's omnipotence, not to the knowledge of faith.

The knowledge of faith says, rather, that God can take back God's Spirit and can turn away God's face, but that without God's will human beings are unable to activate the action of the Spirit.[69] There are no interconnections between the behavior of human beings and the action of the Spirit that automatically run their course and necessarily produce definitive relations. God and human beings stand in *asymmetric* causal and epistemic relations. These relations are not clearly brought into view by the abstract language of "the relation," "the relationship" between God and "the human person." Nor is this misunderstanding of the asymmetric relations between God and human beings corrected by emphatic insistence on the "drop-off" from God to the human person, on God's unconditional priority, or even by highlighting the movement "straight down from above" (Karl Barth). By contrast, Ps. 139:1ff. describes the complex relation of God and human beings in an illuminating way: God knows every human being precisely—indeed polyperspectivally, from all sides and in all situations and structural patterns of life, even before the person in question concretely experiences them and makes her way through them. A person who sees herself before God's face and God's Spirit knows that she is surrounded by God, but without possessing a correspondingly well-articulated knowledge of and about herself.

This simultaneously intimate and complex relation of God to creatures that is wrought by the Spirit, this knowledge of all structural patterns of life into which any creature could possibly enter, must not be replaced with conceptions of a "universal causality" and a "ubiquity" that are not more precisely defined. God is not interested

---

that "the Holy Spirit does not at all correspond to conceptions and expectations of omnipotence" is also emphasized by M. Plathow, *Heiliger Geist, Hoffnung der Schwachen* (Hannover: Lutherhaus, 1985), 17 and passim.

69. See Isa. 40:13: "Who has directed the Spirit of the LORD, or as God's counselor has instructed God?"

"in everything" in an indeterminate way; God is interested in a very determinate way in all—successful and endangered—*structural patterns of creaturely life*.

> O LORD, you have searched me and known me.
> You know when I sit down and when I rise up;
> you discern my thoughts from far away.
> You search out my path and my lying down,
> and are acquainted with all my ways.
> Even before a word is on my tongue,
> O LORD, you know it completely.
> You hem me in, behind and before,
> and lay your hand upon me.
> Such knowledge is too wonderful for me;
> it is so high that I cannot attain it.
> *Where can I go from your Spirit?*
> *Or where can I flee from your presence?* (Ps. 139:1-7)[70]

Here we see, on the one hand, God's power, God's concentrated vigilance and care for what is creaturely, and the interweaving of structural patterns of creaturely life with powerful creaturely community through participation in God's Spirit. On the other hand, there is the fragility, frailty, vulnerability, and mortality of what is creaturely. It is not easy to grasp how these two sides hang together.[71] It becomes impossible to understand how they hang together, if the creative action of the Spirit is abstractly totalized (universal causality, and so on). It also becomes impossible to know how they hang together, if one ignores the *fleshliness* of the creaturely reality in and through which God's Spirit acts.

The Spirit of God does not somehow or other act "everywhere." But God's Spirit does effect creaturely life. The Spirit does not act on abstract "eternal" entities, but on living beings. Fleshliness and the action of the Spirit are not to be separated from each other. But the correct recognition of the frailty and finitude of "the flesh," and the

---

70. Emphasis added.

71. Conceived in mechanical one-to-one relationships, the question (wrongly posed on the basis of incorrect theoretical presuppositions) arises again and again: How can the life wrought by God's Spirit be frail and finite?

diverse critiques of a false trust in "the flesh" that are found in the biblical traditions, have led to fatal attempts to abstract *fully* from fleshliness with regard to the action of the Spirit. The unclear notion of a totally numinous "action of the Spirit," fully removed from the flesh, has stood in the way of understanding either creation or new creation. The creative Spirit holds fleshly life together by giving a share in the medium common to all life. In this way the Spirit gives a share in nothing less than the Spirit. "Creation" and the creative action of the Spirit cannot be understood in total disregard of what is fleshly, frail, and perishable. But what happens in the "new creation"?

The *renewal* of creation by the Spirit also does not remove fleshliness. On the contrary, the renewal of creation goes hand in hand with a *renewal of and change in fleshliness.* This is made particularly clear by several texts from Ezekiel. In addition, we encounter in them descriptions that are already familiar to us of the Spirit's action aimed at righteousness.[72] Thus in connection with the gift and action of God's Spirit, Israel is gathered and brought together, Israel fulfills the law, and the whole process results in an inviolable relation between God and God's people.

> I will gather you from the peoples, and assemble you out of the countries where you have been scattered, and I will give you the land of Israel. . . . I will give them one heart, and put a new Spirit within them; I will remove the heart of stone from their flesh and give them a *heart of flesh*, so that they may follow my statutes and keep my ordinances and obey them. Then they shall be my people, and I will be their God. (Ezek. 11:17b, 19-20)

> A new heart I will give you, and a new Spirit I will put within you; and I will remove from your body the heart of stone and give you a *heart of flesh.* I will put my Spirit within you, and make you follow my statues and be careful to observe my ordinances. Then you shall live in the land that I gave to your ancestors; and you shall be my people, and I will be your God. (Ezek. 36:26-28)[73]

In comparison with the promises of the action of the Spirit that we have examined previously, what is new and illuminating in these texts

---

72. See esp. §3.1.
73. Emphasis added in this and prior quotation.

from Ezekiel is the more precise description of what concretely happens with the people touched by the Spirit's action. The conclusion is astounding: the granting of the Spirit, of the "new Spirit," of the Spirit of God, is attended by an *exchange of hearts*. Specifically, the heart of stone is replaced by a heart of flesh.[74]

In the structural patterns of associations familiar to us—deeply marked precisely by the biblical traditions—the statement that a heart of flesh is put in the place of a heart of stone sounds positive and promising. With such a statement we connect the overcoming of hardheartedness, of insensitivity, of rigidity, and of torpidity. But this first impression is called into question when we observe more precisely the negative meaning proper to the expression *flesh* (*bāśār*) in the Old Testament.

The flesh is exposed to frailty and to the process of perishing. The Egyptians' "horses are flesh, and not spirit" (Isa. 31:3). That is, in a war people should neither fear them nor depend on them. "Cursed are those who trust in mere mortals and make mere flesh their strength"— literally: "who make mortal flesh their helping arm" (Jer. 17:5; see also 2 Chron. 32:8). In Ps. 78:39 God reflects on the fact that human beings are "but flesh, a wind that passes and does not come again" (see also Ecclus. 14:18).[75]

Why is the gift of the Spirit attended by, of all things, the gift of a heart of *flesh*? Why is the gift of the Spirit not sufficient *by itself*? If not a heart of stone, why does not God nevertheless grant some sort of *firm* heart? Why does God not simply come out and grant the firm, *pure* heart for which Psalm 51 asks: "Create in me a clean heart, O God, and put a new and right Spirit within me"? Why does God not grant a

---

74. W. Zimmerli, *Ezekiel 1: A Commentary on the Book of the Prophet Ezekiel, Chapters 1-24,* trans. R. E. Clements, ed. F. M. Cross, K. Baltzer, and L. J. Greenspoon, Hermeneia (Philadelphia: Fortress, 1979), 262: "The heart, the seat both of thought and of the will, must be changed. Its hardness, described as a stony heart, must give place to a new genuine vitality, to a heart of flesh." H. W. Wolff, *Anthropology of the Old Testament,* trans. M. Kohl (Philadelphia: Fortress, 1974), 54: "The heart of stone is the dead heart . . . which is unreceptive and makes all the limbs incapable of action. The heart of flesh is the living heart, full of insight, which is at the same time ready for new action."

75. In the face of the granting of a fleshly heart, an obvious question is that of Job 6:11-12: "What is my strength, that I should wait? And what is my end, that I should be patient? Is my strength the strength of stones, or is my flesh bronze?"

"*new*" heart of whatever composition, but in any case not expressly a *fleshly* heart (cf. Ezek. 18:31)? Or why does God not simply come out and write the *law* on the heart—stone or not—as Jer. 31:33 characterizes the transformation to the new covenant, to the definitive knowledge of God and to the forgiveness of sins:

> But this is the covenant [namely, the *new* covenant] that I will make with the house of Israel after those days. . . . I will put my law within them, and I will write it on their hearts; and I will be their God, and they shall be my people.

Why, in the face of these possibilities, is the gift of the Spirit explicitly bound up with the gift of a *fleshly* heart? Why is the renewal and change of the *heart* important at all? Why cannot the action of the Spirit be accomplished without regard for flesh and heart, leaving them behind?

The *life* and *vitality* of creatures in general and of human beings in particular are apparently not to be conceived and understood by the Old Testament other than bound up with and bound into fleshliness. Fleshliness—in other words, sensitivity, vulnerability, frailty, and perishability—characterizes creaturely life.

A life that kept itself *untouched, untouchable,* and invulnerable, that remained insensitive to complex external influences—such a thing neither can nor should exist. The life created by God and effected and renewed through the Spirit is life in diverse structural patterns of interdependence. To be alive is to be sensitive in these structural patterns. To be alive is to be in need of stability, confirmation, and relationship, but also to react to the need for stability, confirmation, and relationship. To be alive is to be *capable,* in diverse frames of reference, of *self-withdrawal for the benefit of other living beings.* That is how what is creaturely is defined—through its own fleshliness and through its relations with other fleshly life. Fleshliness is a necessary condition of creaturely life. But fleshliness *alone* is no more a sufficient condition of life than is the Spirit *alone*. For the biblical traditions, a "pure" Spirit, a Spirit who does not enter into what is fleshly, is inconceivable.[76]

---

76. Cf. the general formal designation of spirit by E. Lessing, "Geist: V. Dogmatisch und ethisch," *TRE* 12 (1984): 218. The New Testament warns against letting

In order to effect life, the action of the Spirit needs that which is fleshly. This is not to say that the action of the Spirit needs orientation toward what is fleshly, trust in what is fleshly, or even desire for what is fleshly. What is fleshly is frail and perishable. It can—by the very attempt to counteract its frailty and perishability on its own—grow numb and die in the midst of life. The appearance of life is still maintained; the functional processes seem still to be intact; from an external point of view, it still looks like life. Yet as soon as it is addressed, as soon as an attempt is made to move it, to change it, it becomes clear that the heart is numb, the heart is of stone. The interchange with its surroundings, the exchange of internal and external perspectives no longer works. The processes that are still at hand are insensitive to changes coming from the outside. They are immune to such changes. They are incapable of behaving in a surprising, creative, lively manner and of influencing their surroundings. They are dead.

In order to overcome this death that seems like life, or in any case can sometimes seem like it, there needs to be a change. There needs to be a *renewal of that which is creaturely*—a renewal that corresponds to the action of the Spirit, that is not oriented and directed toward the flesh, that does not bet on and trust in the flesh, but that is in accord with the Spirit. In this way, though, *the flesh* is renewed in such a manner that it can correspond to the action of the Spirit and make room for it. This renewal cannot and ought not occur in a region "beyond the flesh."[77]

This fine but very important difference between an orientation of fleshly life toward the flesh, and the recognition that flesh renewed by

---

ourselves by *defined* by the flesh, living *according* to the flesh, *setting our minds* on the flesh (cf. Rom. 8:5ff.), yielding to the *desire* of the flesh and *trusting* the flesh (Gal. 5:16ff.; 6:8). But these warnings, too, must not be understood—in spite of Pauline dichotomizations—as if creaturely life and the action of the Spirit could be carried out in total disregard of the flesh. To be sure, the flesh must not become the center, the standard, the orienting agent. But the Spirit is poured out on all *flesh*—thus the citation of Joel 2:28ff. in Acts 2:17. The Spirit writes in hearts of *flesh*: "You are a letter of Christ" (2 Cor. 3:3). For a more detailed treatment of the relation and difference between Spirit and flesh, see §5.4.

77. In other theological perspectives, this state of affairs is emphasized by M. R. Miles, *Practicing Christianity: Critical Perspectives for an Embodied Spirituality* (New York: Crossroad, 1990), esp. 176ff.

the Spirit is indispensable for life, has been layered over by means of the simple dichotomy and abstract opposition of flesh versus Spirit. In contrast to a simple dichotomization of this sort, fleshly life is first of all to be understood not as a fixed entity, but as a *finite manifold*: "Like abundant leaves on a spreading tree that sheds some and puts forth others, so are the generations of flesh and blood: one dies and another is born" (Ecclus. 14:18). Through the creative Spirit, this finite manifold is given shape and coherence. If what is creaturely disregards these structural patterns of reciprocity wrought by the Spirit, if it acts contrary to them, this leads not only to devastation and destruction of other life, but also to endangerment and destruction of self. Vitality diminishes. Ossification and the closing off of self lead, in the midst of all attempts to counteract perishability, to death.[78] What is fleshly may attempt to elude death by solidifying itself, by means of its own power, in an orientation toward the flesh. But such attempts only achieve the opposite of that for which they are striving. To their detriment they break out of the coherence effected by the Spirit, out of the interdependent community of what is creaturely. This miscalculation that "trusts in the flesh," that orients itself toward the flesh, and that makes the flesh its center leads to death. A turnaround from this miscalculation presupposes that, through the action of the Spirit, a *renewal of fleshliness* in accord with the action of the Spirit also occurs.

Through this renewal—which requires a more precise exposition—fleshly, frail, and finite life is newly inserted into the community of that which is creaturely. Fleshly life is placed *in the service* of the action of the Spirit. Its finite forces of life can again radiate into the life that surrounds it. It itself can be empowered by the repercussions from other life. This renewal dissolves the ossifications that lead to external destruction and then, as a repercussion, to one's own desolate and fruitless death (heart of stone). This opens the way for a

---

78. E. Jüngel has frequently expounded this "pressure which drives towards relationlessness" (*Death: The Riddle and the Mystery*, trans. I. Nicol and U. Nicol [Philadelphia: Westminster, 1974], 78 and passim). Cf. also his reference to the "Spirit of the divine life, who already as Spirit is richly relational, and who creates new relations" ("Zur Lehre vom heiligen Geist," in *Die Mitte des Neuen Testaments: Einheit und Vielfalt neutestamentlicher Theologie: Festschrift für Eduard Schweizer zum siebzigsten Geburtstag*, ed. U. Luz and H. Weder [Göttingen: Vandenhoeck, 1983], 98ff.).

renewal of the power of the Spirit's action, a renewal of this action's influence on the surroundings of other creatures (cf. Psalm 51). Life—although as earthly life it cannot stop being fleshly—now orients itself toward the Spirit, is determined by the Spirit. It places its fleshliness in the service of the Spirit and thus in the service of the empowerment and spread of life.

Why does this renewal of creation by the Spirit extend beyond "nature"? Why cannot this structural pattern of vitality simply be left up to "nature" and to the play of nature's forces? To be sure, "natural" life also produces structural patterns and interdependencies, and cultivates the structural patterns in which it is embedded. But at the same time, what is steadily dominant in this comportment is the interest in one's own preservation, perfection, and extension.[79]

With the vitality of the new creation attesting to God's mighty action, more is attained than just any restoration and self-preservation of finite life. More also occurs than the restoration of the unimpeded, interdependent vitality of what is natural. Although the action of the Spirit does not happen in a way that bypasses the flesh, although the action of the Spirit also renews and restores life as fleshly and finite life, it would be erroneous to conclude that the action of the Spirit wills to bring the processes of life back to a condition of *accord with nature*. It would be erroneous to conclude that creaturely life should be carried out in accord with nature or that justice and social life should in some way correspond to "the" processes of nature. Such a Neoromantic understanding of nature, as obvious as it might seem today as a reaction to the devastating global destruction of nature, is neither provided nor supported by the texts referring to the Spirit. Not only do these texts know that "nature" as such can be the desert, the red-hot wind that destroys life, or an earthquake; they also

---

79. It is only in the last few years that the understanding of "natural" autopoietic self-organization has developed theoretical acuity. See H. R. Maturana, "The Organisation of the Living: A Theory of a Living Organisation," *International Journal of Man-Machine Studies* 7 (1975): 313–32; H. R. Maturana, F. G. Varela, and R. Uribe, "Autopoiesis: The Organisation of Living Systems, Its Characterization and a Model," *Biosystems* 5 (1974): 187–96; P. Dumouchel and J.-P. Dupuy, eds., *L'auto-organisation: de la physique au politique* (Paris: 1983), esp. 147ff. The situation is seen with an interdisciplinary orientation, but from the side of theology, in the works of H.-P. Müller: e.g., "Segen im Alten Testament," *ZTK* 87 (1990): esp. 29ff.

know that "natural" life preserves itself essentially at the cost of other life, indeed by destroying other life.

The most important image of life made possible and realized through the pouring out of the Spirit is not nature as such, but well-watered and enduringly *flourishing vegetation*. In order to attain enduringly flourishing vegetation, several preconditions must be fulfilled that go beyond a "back to nature" movement. Flourishing vegetation has peaceful natural *and* peaceful social relations as its preconditions.

The enduring preservation of flourishing vegetation presupposes peaceful relations between cultivated land and its uncultivated and unworked surroundings—relations that are mutually beneficial to the regeneration of each. But it also presupposes peaceful social relations. For this reason Isaiah 32 can use the indwelling of justice and righteousness in nature and culture, as well as transformations of nature and cultivated land into each other, to describe the effects of the pouring out of the Spirit.[80] The enduring preservation of flourishing vegetation is threatened just as much by unrighteousness between human beings and by the consequences of that unrighteousness, as by "conflictual relations" lying within nature itself: for example, wild animals, locust plagues, sicknesses, and natural catastrophes.

Nature that is truly *at peace* can thus be described in a visionary manner with relations that are not to be found under earthly conditions, as Isaiah 11 describes it: When the Spirit of God rests on the shoot from the root of Jesse, not only will there be a spread of justice, mercy, and knowledge of God,[81] but at the same time a condition of peace that transforms nature will be attained.

> The wolf shall live with the lamb,
> the leopard shall lie down with the kid,
> the calf and the lion and the fatling together,
> and a little child shall lead them.
> . . . .
> The nursing child shall play over the hole of the asp,
> and the weaned child shall put his hand on the adder's den.
> (Isa. 11:6, 8)

---

80. Cf. §3.3.
81. Cf. §3.1.

While these visions of conditions of "natural" peace come across as fantastic—although they follow a clear logic aimed at peaceful neighbor relations between "wild" and "civilized" creatureliness—the Old Testament traditions describe in a thoroughly realistic and plausible way the peacemaking that affects relations *between human beings.*

In Ezekiel 36 Israel is not granted a fleshly heart and God's Spirit in an *unmediated* way. The first step rather is this: "I will take you from the nations, and gather you from all the countries, and bring you into your own land. I will sprinkle clean water upon you, and you shall be clean" (vv. 24-25).

The renewal through the gift of a new Spirit and a fleshly heart occurs only after this act of cultic purification.[82] With this purification not only is an abstract relation to God changed. Old self-relations and old external relations are also changed. A complex beginning of *new internal and external relations* is thus brought to expression. The purified persons are in a new way attractive, accessible, worthy of trust, and capable of connecting with others. They also acquire a new self-relation, and the renewed complexes of relations—of self-relations and of external relations—are mutually strengthening.

The gift of a new Spirit and the renewal of the fleshly heart work the restoration of coherent structures of life even between persons who were "as good as dead to each other," who had "written each other off." That this is so can be made particularly clear with reference to Ezekiel 8–11.

The textual foundations are complicated. Ezekiel 8–11 has to do with a prophetic vision. In the Exile the "hand of the Lord GOD" falls upon the prophet, as Ezek. 8:1 puts it. The prophet sees a gleaming "figure that looked a human being," who grabs him by the hair.[83] Finally he is seized by the Spirit. The experience of the action of the

---

82. On the one hand, this act has been connected with the cultic ordinances of Num. 19:9-22. On the other hand, it has naturally been connected with Christian baptism. Cf. §§4.1 and 5.1.

83. Zimmerli, *Ezekiel 1*, 236: "Behind the seizure of the hair we may conjecture a basis in the experience of actual bodily pain (and giddiness) felt by the person concerned. The merging together of the subjects of the action: 1) the man 2) the Spirit 3) Yahweh himself . . . must not be separated in a logical division and torn apart by literary criticism. The one divine intervention is here experienced by the prophet under various aspects."

Spirit is attended by the certainty that it is *God* who is at work, and by a physical knowledge of being affected. The Spirit mediates a visionary experience and at the same time a consciousness of authenticity: what is at issue is simultaneously a fleshly-palpable experience and more than a palpable-earthly experience. Ezek. 8:3b: ". . . the Spirit lifted me up between earth and heaven, and brought me in visions of God to Jerusalem, to the entrance of the gateway of the inner court that faces north. . . ."

The Spirit makes possible the visionary presence of what is physically absent. In doing so, the Spirit connects—through the prophet—the Israel that has been torn apart: that is, Israel living in exile and Israel living in Jerusalem. In his vision, the prophet is led from the outer gate of the city into the temple grounds, and from there all the way to the inner sanctuary. In the process, several cases of idolatrous worship are—with a corresponding increase in degree—brought before his eyes. The inhabitants of Jerusalem are serving idols, and they are even doing so in the temple. The elders of the house of Israel justify and excuse this with the words, "The LORD does not see us, the LORD has forsaken the land" (Ezek. 8:12). In Ezek. 9:9 the crime of the inhabitants of Jerusalem is characterized in an even more comprehensive way: "The guilt of the house of Israel and Judah is exceedingly great; the land is full of bloodshed and the city full of perversity; for they say, 'The LORD has forsaken the land, and the LORD does not see [it].'" Lawlessness and misuse of the law are the order of the day across the board. God's judgment over Jerusalem is—to the consternation of the prophet—the obliteration of its inhabitants. Only those who sigh and groan on account of the abominations being committed in their midst shall be spared. It is unclear, though, whether there are such people besides the prophet himself (see Ezek. 9:8). *The residents of Jerusalem are thus doomed to death.*

Of course in the perspective of the inhabitants of Jerusalem, the reality looks different. For them *those who are living in exile are as good as dead.* The residents of Jerusalem say of those who are living in exile, "They have gone far from the LORD; to us this land is given for a possession" (Ezek. 11:15).[84]

---

84. Zimmerli (ibid.) has called attention to the fact that not only claims concerning objective rights of ownership are hiding behind this statement. To be sure,

On the one hand, people are saying, "God has forsaken the land, God does not see anything," in order to justify breaking the law and worshiping idols. On the other hand, the presence of God is denied those who are living in exile, in order to expropriate them both religiously and materially.

The inhabitants of Jerusalem and the exiles represented by the prophet (cf. Ezek. 11:25) see each other as sinners forsaken or given up by God who are doomed to death, or from whose lives the foundations have been withdrawn. For the prophet whom the Spirit has enabled to see visions, these *perspectives* of the ruptured parts of Israel become manifest and transparent *in relation to each other*. At the same time, he sees at work in those who are living in exile and in the inhabitants of Jerusalem a change that restores Israel in the eyes of the nations. In this change the Spirit becomes knowable as the power of God that creates new life relations and peace in situations of mutual enmity, foreignness, relationlessness, indeed in situations where each side has written off the other. People are brought into new relations to each other—and this goes hand in hand with the gift of a new, fleshly heart and of a new Spirit.

Yet at first the deficient existence of the exiles in their dispersion and brokenness is not disputed. "I have indeed removed them far way among the nations and scattered them among the countries" (Ezek. 11:16b). Nor is the interconnection between life in exile and dispersion and a deficient relation with God called into question. "Only to a small extent have I become a sanctuary to them in the countries where they have gone" (Ezek. 11:16c). Nevertheless, there is no confirmation of the judgment of the inhabitants of Jerusalem concerning the exiles: "They have gone far from the LORD." On the one hand, in

---

part of what is going on here is that the people of Jerusalem "out of very selfish motives reckoned upon the final removal of the exiles and finally settled themselves in the vacated properties. . . . The statement: 'They are far from Yahweh' is ambiguous. Beyond the literal fact that the exiles were far from Jerusalem, it hinted at the distance of the exiles from the place of the presence of God in a spiritual, and thus adverse, sense: those who have been deported are the sinners, who have gone far from Yahweh . . . and who therefore have been literally put away by him and robbed of the assurances of his presence. The land was the sacramental assurance of the favor of Yahweh. Whoever lost the land had visibly lost the sign of his favor and was far from Yahweh's salvation" (261).

their dispersion God has become "a sanctuary" to them—albeit in a limited way. God has taken over the place of the temple. On the other hand, through the prophet they are given the promise: "I will gather you from the peoples, and assemble you out of the countries where you have been scattered, and I will give you the land of Israel" (Ezek. 11:17).

This process of gathering out of dispersion and of giving back the land is bound up with a renewal of heart and spirit in Israel (Ezek. 11:19-20): "I will give them a new heart, and put a new Spirit within them; I will remove the heart of stone from their flesh and give them a heart of flesh, so that they may follow my statutes and keep my ordinances and obey them. Then they shall be my people, and I will be their God."[85] To be sure, it is impossible to make out with certainty whether the inhabitants of Jerusalem (more likely the case) or the exiles themselves are intended as the ones who shall receive a heart of flesh and a new Spirit. But in any case this process, the gift of a new Spirit and of a heart of flesh, is a process of a particular sort. This process is foundational for the understanding of new creation through the Spirit.

The granting of a heart of flesh and of a new Spirit is *not* a process that concerns *only* those who are immediately affected. God acts upon Israel in exile for the sake of the knowledge of God among the nations (cf. Ezekiel 36), and for the sake of this knowledge in sinful, idolatrous Jerusalem. The gathering of Israel thus also signifies *a change in the outside observers of this gathering*—whether the peoples of other lands or the inhabitants of Jerusalem. The peoples of other lands perceive not only the process of dispersed Israel being gathered out of their ranks, empowered, and led back into its land. The inhabitants of Jerusalem perceive not only that the land does not belong to them alone after all, that the exiles are not written off after all, that they are not far from God after all. The inhabitants of Jerusalem (according to Ezekiel 11) and the other nations (according to Ezekiel 36) are thus themselves confronted with God and with the knowledge of God. The process that elicits this knowledge of God—bound up with new self-relations,

---

85. On the continuities and discontinuities between Ezekiel and the Isaiah traditions, see W. H. Schmidt, "Ekstatische und charismatische Geistwirkungen im Alten Testament," in C. Heitmann and H. Mühlen, eds., *Erfahrung und Theologie des Heiligen Geistes* (Hamburg: Agentur des Rauhen Hauses; Munich: Kösel, 1974), esp. 92ff.

with new relations to social environments both near and far—is called the "gift of a heart of flesh and of a new Spirit."

The process of being changed for others as well does not diminish the significance of the process for those who are changed. Quite the contrary, it strengthens that significance. What happens to them affects not only them. It is not absorbed and consumed by them, as it were. It also benefits others, also affects others—and through the external perspectives of those others, it comes back to them, refracted, strengthened, and seen anew. *Through the connection with renewed fleshliness, the Spirit effects a witness both to the outside and from the outside, operating in a recursive manner in which those who bear witness are themselves recipients of witness borne to them by the concrete repercussions of their own witness.* The exiles are gathered and led home not only in order that things might go better for them and in order that they might personally again come to full knowledge of God. They are gathered and led home as God's self-demonstration in their eyes *as well as* in the eyes of the inhabitants of Jerusalem and in the eyes of the nations.

It is only this self-demonstration of God *through them in the eyes of others* that constitutes in the full sense the restoration of their relation with God, their vitalization, and their prosperity. By the same token, the inhabitants of Jerusalem are not initially threatened with annihilation and then renewed and established by the gift of a heart of flesh and of a new Spirit—for reasons that lie, so to speak, only between them and God. But their destiny is of direct significance for the exiles. It is not only dependent on how things go for the exiles, it also has a reactive effect on how things go for them. These structural patterns of interdependence are recognized by the prophet upon whom the Spirit has come. They are illuminated by the prophet who speaks in visions of the Spirit.

The *recognition of this recursiveness of the action of the Spirit* is indispensable if we want to understand the Spirit and the Spirit's *creative, recreative, and peacemaking power.* The Spirit acts so as not only to change people, but also in the process—revealing God's power in and through creaturely life—to work for others. This process of being changed for others as well reacts back on those who were changed. Not only does this strengthen the process, it is only thus that the action of the Spirit is completed. Those dispersed in exile are not only gathered so that they experience some good, but so that—through what happens to them, through their witness—the inhabitants of Jerusalem and the nations see God's glory. Those who have been gathered and led back thus demonstrate themselves to be not only people to whom God has done good, but also—precisely in their renewed fleshliness, placed in the service of the Spirit—*bearers and mediators of God's glory.*

This is not to say that they should not rejoice in their real blessing, that they should abstract from it and look only at their "missionary vocation." Their sensuality, naturalness, and finitude—in other words, their fleshliness—is *not* bracketed out or disparaged in this process. Instead God enlists its service. Just as the sufferings in a strange land and over life in a strange land are not glossed over or relativized, so the real, concrete, palpably accessible joys of returning and of being led back are not to be overlooked or disparaged.

Israel is to be touched and changed in its frailty, perishability, and finitude. In its fleshliness (and this means in a way that makes the change palpably recognizable and that awakens a sensitivity to the ongoing situations of distress in Israel's surroundings), Israel is to experience and attest to the process of the renewal of life relations. Where the Spirit acts on human beings, the experiences are firsthand ones. But these experiences are at the same time experiences for others, experiences that bear witness. The concrete process is essentially spiritual by virtue of the fact that others are necessarily given a part in it. The action of the Spirit, the revealed power of God, and the attestation to God's glory must not be sought any longer in the clouds or in realms of fantasy. They can be recognized in and through those persons, and in and through the influence of those persons, who have experienced the action of the Spirit firsthand, who have received not only a new Spirit, but also a heart of flesh.

A change that is carried out in the flesh and that is recognized from the outside is indispensable for the experience of the presence and glory of God. But on its own, without the action of the Spirit, it is not yet sufficient. On its own, what is fleshly has no capacity to bear witness. Even as fleshliness that has been delivered from the dead, it is not yet capable of bearing witness. Even the act of giving physical form out of the dust does not yet reach the level of vitality and of testimony to the Spirit. This is grasped very well and comprehensively depicted through a vision that gives a differentiated description of *deliverance from death,* and in so doing makes it possible to recognize both the *significance* and the *powerlessness* of the act of giving fleshly form. At the same time a differentiation is introduced that is overlooked in the conventional disputes about the "point of contact."[86]

> The hand of the LORD came upon me, and God brought me out by the Spirit of the LORD and set me down in the middle of a valley; it was full of bones. God led me all around them; there were very many lying [scattered] in the valley, and they were very dry. God said to me, "Mortal, can these bones live?" I answered, "O Lord GOD, you know." Then God said to me, "Prophesy to these bones, and say to them: O dry bones, hear the word of the LORD. Thus says the Lord GOD to these bones: I will cause Spirit to enter you, and you shall live. I will lay sinews on you, and will cause flesh to come upon you, and cover you with skin, and put Spirit in you, and you shall live; and you shall know that I am the LORD."
>
> So I prophesied as I had been commanded; and as I prophesied, suddenly there was a noise, a rattling, and the bones came together, bone to its bone. I looked, and there were sinews on them, and flesh had come upon them, and skin had covered them; but there was no Spirit in them. Then God said to me, "Prophesy to the Spirit, prophesy, mortal, and say to the Spirit: Thus says the Lord GOD: Come from the four winds, O Spirit, and breathe upon these slain, that they may live." I prophesied as God had commanded me, and the Spirit came into them, and they lived, and stood on their feet, a vast multitude.
>
> Then God said to me, "Mortal, these bones are the whole house of Israel. They say, 'Our bones are dried up, and our hope is lost; we are cut off completely.' Therefore prophesy, and say to them, Thus says the Lord GOD: I am going to open your graves, and bring you up from your graves, O my people; and I will bring you back to the land of Israel. And you shall know that I am the LORD, when I open your graves, and bring you up from your graves, O my people. I will put my Spirit within you, and you shall live, and I will place you on your own soil; then you shall know that I, the LORD, have spoken and will act," says the LORD. (Ezek. 37:1-14)

As spectacular as is the effect of the first speech of the prophet at God's behest, it does not yet overcome death. At best it generates the

---

86. Cf. §1.6, n. 90.

external illusion of life, only a reminder of life or a prospect of life. From the pile of bones, human forms have come into being. For outside observers, this restoration of still unenlivened fleshly forms can awaken the—shaky—*hope* that they will be enlivened.

This giving of life occurs in a second act, likewise externally effected. The prophet is summoned to speak to the Spirit. The essential externality and uncontrollability of the Spirit are highlighted by the fact that the Spirit is characterized as coming from the four winds.

The Spirit who comes from the four winds enables the dead forms to *stand up.* Out of the dead, Israel stands up again: "a vast multitude." The Spirit is treated as a power that comes from the four winds and unleashes processes of emergence that result in new spontaneity and new community. The power of the Spirit, which initiates processes of emergence, enables those affected by its action to engage in independent action that at the same time serves as an influential witness to their surroundings. Only with this step does the regained life, the new life delivered from the dead, make itself recognizable.

We thus need to take note of a graduated process. Through the Spirit, the prophet is enabled to have a vision of Israel's resurrection. The vision begins with an image that erases even the slightest hope: dry bones scattered in a plain demonstrate the power of death not only to extinguish life as it is really lived, but also to dissolve forms that could be remembered, externally observed, and identified. A power that totally destroys fleshly life and returns it to chaos is here as work. Death, not the Spirit, destroys fleshly form.

This oppressive picture is the point of departure for the interpretation of Israel's situation. Ezekiel 37:11: "Then God said to me, 'Mortal, these bones are the whole house of Israel. They say, "Our bones are dried up, and our hope is lost; we are cut off completely." ' " The image of the scattered bones reflects Israel's self-characterization: Our bones are dried up, and our hope is lost. In the prophetic vision this self-characterization is given palpable depiction. The condition of *real* death, the condition of real consequences of death, is placed before Israel's eyes. It is a condition that no longer even allows a self-characterization. Not only has hope foundered, the human bearers of hope—or the hopeless, one might better say—have also foundered to the point of no longer being recognizable. Israel is not only threatened, lost, and despairing. It is not even present. It has become unrecognizable. It is no longer even capable of a relation with itself. It is beyond sorrow, complaint, and horror. The prophet led by God in the Spirit perceives the dimensions of the catastrophe and the dimensions of the hopelessness. According to the vision, Israel is so lost, so destroyed, that it can no longer even perceive and lament its own downfall. The abyss of death, chaos, becomes visible. But with this it also becomes possible to recognize that if Israel is still capable of lament, it is still given space for renewal.

The prophet led by God in the Spirit is not only a spectator to this process. He is not simply a last survivor, a chronicler of the end. The prophet, who perceives the catastrophe in all its dimensions, is *given a share* in turning away this catastrophe. He does not just hear God's word. He does not just become an outside witness to the resurrection. Rather the prophet is commissioned to speak God's promise of life into the death that leads back into chaos.

To be sure, on its own this promise of life does not yet lead Israel to new life. It does, however, make Israel capable of *receiving new life*. The word spoken at God's behest *creates the fleshly "point of contact" for the life-creating action of the Spirit*—however poor and miserable this point of contact may appear in contrast to the enlivening action of the Spirit: the bones come together, but there is not yet any Spirit in them. Taken on its own, this point of contact is ambiguous. Without the action of the Spirit, it can quickly drive people from hope to despair.

Only now is *the situation of proximity to death or life brought about* that Israel seeks to express with its lament, "Our bones are dried up, and our hope is lost; we are cut off completely." Israel is still capable of lament, form is still present—the vision calls attention to that. The vision thus shows that the action of the word of God is needed even to provide the preconditions of fleshly forms necessary for the action of the Spirit who delivers from death.[87]

---

87. With regard to Ezekiel 37, J. Schreiner's formulation is on the mark: "Interpreted from the perspective of 'Spirit,' being alive means more than merely existing. It is not enough that God's people is merely present" ("Wirken des Geistes Gottes in alttestamentlicher Sicht," *Theologie und Glaube* 81 [1991], 11). Yet the vision emphasizes explicitly and at length that existing and "being present" are significant for the action of the Spirit. In so doing, the vision renounces all Docetic doctrines of the Spirit.

Israel needs the action of God's word merely in order to become *capable* of being made alive. It is not self-evident that those who have fallen victim to death are even *capable* of responding to the action of the Spirit. Analogously, the *gift of a heart of flesh* is needed for those who are in the terrible condition of being surrendered to chaos, far from the action of the Spirit and no longer capable themselves of perceiving the Spirit's action. Of course, the gift of a heart of flesh does not on its own lead to life. In itself it would be a gift that led to death, or that did not lead out of death. Yet *this gift provides the capacity* to enter expressly and with sensitivity to self into the situation between death and life. Without the palpably perceptible word and without a heart of flesh, Israel would not even experience, would not even fear the dried-out condition of its bones, the loss of hope. It *would be wholly incapable of becoming sensitive to itself and wholly incapable of becoming able to bear witness to others.*

The prophet whom God has commissioned and upon whom the Spirit has come is not only sensitive to decay and open to the action of the Spirit. The prophet appears as nothing short of having power over the Spirit. Of course the prophet for his own part is under commission and is only temporarily enabled to have this relation to the Spirit. But at God's behest he addresses the Spirit directly. He induces the Spirit to become present and active. The Spirit—difficult to grasp, coming from all four winds—becomes manifest by *giving life to the Israelites who find themselves between death and life.* Led in the Spirit, the *prophet can directly address the Spirit, inducing the Spirit to engage in life-creating action and thus to become knowable.*

For the Israelites who find themselves between death and life, or who have just been returned to this situation between death and life, the Spirit *comes upon them from outside* in a way that is not at their disposition. Through this process they are *returned to spontaneity and to vitality*: "They became alive and stood up."[88]

God's people are gathered not only out of distress, but out of death: they do not acquire vitality on their own. They do not acquire vitality

---

88. Ezekiel 2:2 and 3:24 also emphasize that the Spirit "puts people on their feet." Ezekiel 3:12, 14; 8:3; 11:1, 24; and 43:5 all record the fact that, in addition, the Spirit *lifts up*, that the Spirit makes it possible to adopt a perspective that transcends the earthly-natural capacity of perception.

on the basis of the form again given to them by God. Although this form is restored through the word, although the restoration precedes and must precede the enlivening action of the Spirit, this does not amount to a sufficient principle of vitalization or to a spontaneously active possibility of vitalization. The vitalization occurs by the Spirit who, coming from the outside, becomes present and knowable. This vitalization that comes from the outside results in the spontaneity of what is made alive.

Yet even a vitalization by the Spirit, by which those affected regain spontaneity, does not attain the goal of the process. Being led back into the situation between life and death, being enlivened with the Spirit, being *externally enabled to engage in spontaneous activity*—these are only the conditions of Israel's being brought back together and led back, and of the knowledge of God.

> ". . . say to them, Thus says the Lord GOD: I am going to open your graves, and bring you up from your graves, O my people; and I will bring you back to the land of Israel. . . . I will put my Spirit within you, and you shall live, and I will place you on your own soil; then you shall know that I, the LORD, have spoken and will act," says the LORD. (Ezek. 37:12)

In order for Israel to attain its full vitality and a peace that serves mutual empowerment,[89] several things must happen. Israel must be brought together and led back. It must be enlivened to a knowledge of God that is its own, is attested in relation to other peoples, and at the same time is awakened in others. Only then does all Israel attain the level of the knowledge of the prophet who recognizes God's word and God's Spirit, who is able to proclaim God's word and to address God's

---

89. Schreiner, "Wirken des Geistes Gottes," 14: "Many early Christian writers understood Ezekiel's vision as a vision of the event of the resurrection of the dead that will occur at the end of the world." Cf. W. Zimmerli, *Ezekiel 2: A Commentary on the Book of the Prophet Ezekiel, Chapters 25-48*, trans. J. D. Martin, ed. P. D. Hanson and L. J. Greenspoon, Hermeneia (Philadelphia: Fortress, 1983), 263–65. This interpretation is to be supported if "vision" can also be understood as "analogical imagination" (Tracy), that in specific finite life relations perceives restitutions that—reductionistically, but realistically—point ahead to events that cannot yet be adequately appropriated in images and concepts.

Spirit, and who in this way is given an active part in the process of the resurrection of Israel.

Fleshly-finite life is enabled to attest to God's action of new creation. In this way fleshly-finite life is led both subjectively and objectively beyond itself, beyond its own potential. It thus both attains and effects the joy and the peace that are given by the Spirit.[90]

---

90. See §§5.3 and chap. 6.

CHAPTER 4

Jesus Christ and the Concrete Presence of the Spirit

According to the judgment of Christian faith, there is no longer any need to seek the promised bearer of the Spirit, the deliverer on whom God's Spirit rests, in the clouds of indeterminacy. Christian faith sees an abundance of different testimonies agreeing on the fact that Jesus of Nazareth is this promised bearer of the Spirit. Accounts of Jesus' birth and baptism, as well as self-characterizations ascribed to him by various traditions, point back to the messianic prophecies and to the Old Testament promise of the bearer of the Spirit who is chosen by God and who delivers the world. Jesus' proclamation of the reign of God and his death on the cross can be brought into a differentiated interconnection with the promise of the bearer of the Spirit, with the promise of one chosen by God who attains universal loyalty through his very renunciation of political forms of self-promotion, indeed through a qualified public practice of silence and suffering. Jesus' healings and exorcisms show the conflict with the powers opposed to the action of the Spirit. Finally, the various promises of the sending of the Spirit, of the Paraclete, or of the sending of the Spirit by Jesus himself or on the basis of Jesus' intercession—these promises take up traditions that hold out the prospect of a "pouring out" of the Spirit from heaven upon a multitude of different people. Promises of the arrival of the messianic bearer of the Spirit and promises of the pouring out of the Spirit are thus connected precisely with regard to Jesus Christ.

Admittedly, the idea that the whole power of God's Spirit rests on Jesus, that by this power Jesus acts among human beings and gathers them, is dismaying and scandalous—and not just today, either. "For people of that time spirit is the greatest and strongest power there is."[1] Then how can the claim be made that this power is present in a concentrated and concrete manner over and in one human being? How can this power be present in a concentrated manner in one human person without acting in the spectacular fashion of the early charismatics—for example, Samson—or at least in the impressive fashion of the power politics of a Moses, a David, or a Cyrus?

"The power of God, God as giver of life, Spirit as the greatest power—all that now no longer remains 'behind' things, does not remain transcendent and only to be surmised. Now this power steps into the foreground so to speak at this one point, in Jesus Christ."[2] But how can this power of God become comprehensible *as power* precisely in this concrete extreme, precisely in this specific person? Does it not evade in this very concreteness every experience of power?

To what extent can one say that Jesus Christ, in whom according to the judgment of faith "all the fullness of God was pleased to dwell" (Col. 1:19), brings this fullness to bear through the Spirit in a concrete and concentrated manner in the midst of human life relations?

"It is a widespread opinion that the Holy Spirit is the 'unknown God,' the most hidden mystery within the Trinity. We place in contrast to this opinion the biblical conviction that the Holy Spirit represents the presence and reality of the salvation event in a way that can be experienced with the senses."[3] The more clearly this conviction is grounded theologically,[4] and the more clearly the power of the Spirit becomes recognizable in its palpability in the midst of creaturely life

---

1. K. Berger, *Hermeneutik des Neuen Testaments* (Gütersloh: Mohn, 1988), 279.

2. Ibid., 280. See also H.-J. Kraus, *Systematische Theologie im Kontext biblischer Geschichte und Eschatologie* (Neukirchen-Vluyn: Neukirchener, 1983), 359: "All the gospels answer the question of who Jesus is by referring to his anointing with God's Spirit" (cf. ibid., 359ff.). It should be noted that Kraus is reflecting on the power characteristic of God not with regard to a worked out pneumatology, but in his development of the conception of the reign of God. See also J. Moltmann, *The Way of Jesus Christ: Christology in Messianic Dimensions,* trans. M. Kohl (San Francisco: Harper, 1990), 73ff.

3. Thus F. J. Schierse in his excellent article "Die neutestamentliche Trinitätsoffenbarung," in *MySal* 2, 112.

4. Chapters 2 and 3 of this book were a grounding of this sort with regard to the Old Testament traditions.

relations, the more difficult it becomes initially to grasp that the "presence and reality of the salvation event" are supposed to have experienced their concentration in Jesus of Nazareth. The scope of the power of God directed to human beings precisely in this powerless person becomes visible only when we are able to recognize with regard to him a radicalization of the action of the Spirit. A power becomes recognizable that calls into question and removes one-sided, monocentric, and one-dimensional forms of power that can be readily reproduced, are quickly transferable, and provide comfortable access. It becomes recognizable that this bearer of the Spirit exercises an effect in a diverse concreteness of individual life and suffering, the fullness of which cannot be taken in from any one perspective. The Spirit-wrought power of testimony is to emanate from this fullness.[5] The community of those upon whom the Spirit has come is to grow out of a diverse concreteness of individual life and suffering, the fullness of which cannot be taken in from any one perspective. This community of those who have themselves become bearers of the Spirit is filled with the power of God. This community bears and reflects this power, lets it benefit others, and is itself strengthened in return.

4.1: The concentration of faith and hope: The public installation of the Christ

With regard to the New Testament traditions, it is not readily plausible that the Holy Spirit is the power that *publicly* installs the Christ. With regard to the Synoptic writers it is scarcely plausible at all.

In what public sphere does the one who "through the eternal Spirit offered himself without blemish to God" (Heb. 9:14) acquire authority and recognition? What "public installation" is meant when Paul says that Jesus Christ "was installed as Son of God with power according to the Spirit of holiness by resurrection from the dead" (Rom. 1:4)? If this

---

5. D. Ritschl articulates this state of affairs well when he speaks of Jesus' "minimal mode of existence; he lived his life in complete vulnerability, with no possessions, unmarried and without protection, taking each individual as seriously as God" (*The Logic of Theology: A Brief Account of the Relationship between Basic Concepts in Theology*, trans. J. Bowden [Philadelphia: Fortress, 1987], 174).

meant simply the "power of the public influence" of the Crucified and Resurrected One, as it becomes recognizable in the life and proclamation of the church, then the installation of the Christ through the Spirit would be a post-Easter event.

But in that case how should the relation between God's Spirit and Jesus Christ *before* the cross and resurrection be defined? Can we not yet perceive the Spirit here as the power of the public installation of the Christ? Indeed, do not the testimonies to the pre-Easter life of Jesus speak fundamentally against understanding the Holy Spirit as this power?

The Synoptic writers explicitly connect Jesus' birth, baptism, temptation in the wilderness, and healings and exorcisms with the Spirit of God, with the action of the power of God. But aside from the effect of the healings and exorcisms (which evidently were contested even in Jesus' day),[6] we have a hard time recognizing precisely in these contexts the *publicly* effective power that has become recognizable to us as the Spirit's identity in the Old Testament traditions. Do not these contexts connect the action of the Spirit precisely with an *exclusion of the public sphere?* Does not the so-called virgin birth resist all natural attempts to rationalize it or to solve its riddle, so that it is wholly unsuited to express a public installation of the Christ? Does not the Spirit lead Jesus to temptation "in the wilderness," and thus precisely out of all public spheres? Finally, the baptismal story contains a remarkable "thingification" and naturalization of the Spirit who descends in the form of a dove, and who perhaps is perceived only by Jesus or only by him and John the Baptist. Does not such a story speak against a publicly effective might and power of the Spirit?

Appearances can be deceiving, and this one is. The power of the public installation of the Christ becomes recognizable not only under post-Easter conditions, but also before Easter. It thus becomes recognizable as a power that is also effective beyond "this world," and thus beyond the limits set up and acknowledged by one group of people or by many groups living at a specific time in specific regions of the world as the "universal public."

According to the Synoptic writers, the Spirit leads Jesus into the wilderness (Mark 1:12-13; Matt. 4:1ff.; Luke 4:1ff.). To be sure, in so

---

6. See §§4.2 and 4.4.

doing the Spirit leads him out of human publics and to that extent into isolation. Yet the texts explicitly emphasize that this relative isolation at the same time signifies the presence of the devil, as well as the presence of wild animals (Mark) and of angels (Mark, Matthew). In this domain outside of any earthly-human public, the external signs of messianic power are directly offered to Jesus: "bread for the hungry masses, universal power through the renunciation of God and the worship of Satan, who can give this power; the messianic sign for the liberation of Israel in the temple of the holy city."[7] Against the background of the messianic promises, one will no doubt scarcely be able to join Jürgen Moltmann in the opinion that "through the temptations into which this same Spirit leads him (i.e., Jesus), he is *denied* the economic, political and religious means for a 'seizure of power.' "[8] Instead, in the temptation story Jesus *demonstrates* the power that he already has in relation to Satan by the very act of declining a spectacular moral or political seizure of power, bound to a particular time or a particular people, and by choosing the path of messianic suffering.[9] This demonstration of his power—mediated by the leading of the Spirit—remains unrecognizable and incomprehensible to the world all the way to the cross and resurrection. Yet there is no doubt that here is an installation of the Christ. This is true although the installation occurs in the domain of human isolation, in the domain of exposure to danger and to temptation, in the domain of "rulers and powers" that are difficult to comprehend with earthbound senses. It is true regardless of how this "wilderness" is to be conceived more precisely. Mark and Matthew give expression to the installation by pointing out that after the temptation, "the angels" "ministered" to Jesus.

The powerful installation of the Christ can be recognized more clearly in the birth accounts—contrary to the appearance of the extreme privacy and inaccessibility of the miraculous conception and birth of Jesus. The stories recounted in Matt. 1:18ff. and Luke 1:35ff., from which both fatherly and motherly activities of the Holy Spirit have been deduced,[10] pick up on Old Testament traditions in a variety

---

7. Moltmann, *Way of Jesus Christ*, 92–93.
8. Ibid., 93, emphasis added.
9. See also §4.3.
10. Cf. Moltmann, *Way of Jesus Christ*, 78ff., esp. 82ff.

of ways and depict the announcement of the Davidic Messiah.[11] Matthew 1:23 explicitly cites Isa. 7:14. Luke 1:32ff. and 48ff. refer in a substantively differentiated manner to the messianic promises, according to which God wills to establish justice and mercy "from generation to generation" and to fulfill the promise to Abraham.[12] Inasmuch as here the Messiah is born for all times and for all peoples, an event is occurring that cannot be adequately defined and comprehended in biological and political categories. It is not only through his action, not only through his suffering and death and through his overcoming of the world, but already as a person that Jesus is "installed" by the Spirit in publics that greatly surpass those of his time. He concretizes the fulfillment of the hopes and expectations of persons of all times and peoples. Without this universal relation to him, his person cannot and should not even be conceived.[13]

Just as every human being is born not as a merely biologically definable entity, but as the embodiment of a history and of a sphere of expectations,[14] so this child, too, is born as the embodiment of the messianic history and the messianic sphere of hopes and expectations. The marvelous birth announcement makes clear that what are determinative with regard to this child are not the expectations, wishes, and hopes of his parents, relatives, and friends, not even the hopes and cares shaped by the spirit of a particular time. Before birth and with birth, this person has *from the very beginning* gone beyond the memories, expectations, conceptions, and wishes of his own time, of his own both proximate and distant social surroundings. The fact that this is

---

11. See the subtle illumination of the interconnections by H. Gese, "Natus ex Virgine," in *Vom Sinai zum Zion: Alttestamentliche Beiträge zur biblischen Theologie,* BEvT (Munich: Kaiser, 1974), 130ff.

12. Cf. §3.1. See also R. Stronstad, "The Influence of the Old Testament on the Charismatic Theology of St. Luke," *Pneuma* 2 (1980): 39ff.

13. See §§4.5 and 6.2.

14. R. M. Liu has insistently drawn my attention to the fact that this is also true for those persons of whom we say that they were born into a "life unworthy of a human being." People who are *treated* as a merely biologically definable entity, or as a "merely statistical" value or as simply superfluous, the "tools that talk" of slaveholder societies, the "human rats" of Latin American garbage heaps, the victims of drugs and of traffic accidents—all these, too, embody a history and a sphere of expectations. Theologically, the history and the sphere of expectations that they embody are to be conceived as "judgment."

the case while at the same time this person is a concrete, historically and biologically comprehensible event, finds a fitting response in the statement, seen in a number of Old Testament passages, that here God has already acted "in the womb," or even before the person in question has been "formed in the womb."[15] The Christ is universally installed by the Spirit *before* becoming palpably present and public in any physical, social, concrete way. The Christ is not installed only for one time and one set of surroundings. He is the reference person for not merely *one* spectrum of experience and expectation. To be sure, the faith grounded by the Spirit through this public installation of the Christ, and the hope grounded through the action of the Spirit, are concretized within *specific* spectra of experience and expectation. At the same time, they go beyond these in intensity and breadth.

In contrast to these events—the temptation in the wilderness, the genesis in the womb, as well as in the vast sphere of expectations of the peoples encompassed by the promise to Abraham—Jesus' baptism is connected with concrete human publics. This story most readily makes clear how Jesus of Nazareth is installed under earthly conditions as the promised Chosen One of God, on whom the Spirit rests. Yet here, too, Jesus places himself not only in a specific group of people, a specific time, a specific culture. He has himself baptized. In other words, he consciously enters into solidarity with sinful human beings in need of repentance, purification, and the pouring out of the Spirit. In this very situation his messianic identity, rather than becoming fully unrecognizable, is highlighted. The Spirit of God comes upon him. The heavens open above him; his election and his identity as God's Son are pronounced "from heaven."[16]

The vision of the "open heavens" is a sign of salvation.[17] The open heavens and the "voice from heaven" point to the fact that this event is

---

15. Cf., e.g., the following passages, in part connected with pneumatological pronouncements: Isa. 44:24ff.; Jer. 1:5; Job 31:15; Ecclus. 49:7 and passim; as well as Luke 1:41ff. and Gal. 1:15.

16. Cf. Mark 1:10-11; Matt. 3:16-17; Luke 3:21b-22; see also John 1:32ff.; Acts 10:38. On the significance of theological discourse about heaven, see esp. §3.3.

17. Moltmann correctly calls attention to this: " . . . for the image of 'the closed heavens' is a way of describing the affliction and the forsakenness of human beings, and the barrenness of the earth" (*Way of Jesus Christ*, 89).

significant not only for the public in attendance. Admittedly, what in fact happens here is not fully comprehensible to the concrete public. The Messiah is not yet experienced in his power. Here the power of the Spirit does not yet demonstrate itself in a baptism in the Spirit that has the goal of bringing *all* persons into the messianic community. The descent of the Spirit on Jesus alone initially allows the Spirit to be perceived only in the enigmatic form of a dove.[18] The significance of Jesus' self-abasement in solidarity with sinful human beings and of the answer "from heaven" to this self-abasement are not yet fully evident to the immediate surroundings. Vis-à-vis "heaven" and the heavenly— the definitive and valid—public, it is already possible to recognize the installation of the Christ. What is still unclear in an earthly-concrete perspective is already realized for "all reality" and in the "fullness of time." The earthy-concrete, relative world of Jesus' presence—like other relative worlds—must still attain to the knowledge of God's Chosen One upon whom the Spirit has come. When this happens, it means nothing less than that that world has set out in a new direction, toward the recognition of its own lostness under the power of sin and toward saving participation in the pouring out of the Spirit.

Earthly life relations are preserved in spite of the opening of the heavens and the descent of the Spirit. The descent effects no visible, spectacular changes of the world. Jesus at the Jordan does not gather fighting armies behind him. Instead the action of the Spirit seems to accommodate itself in the form of a dove[19] to the seeming insignificance of "natural" relations of life and experience. Heavenly breadth and divine presence—and their action under the conditions of the earthly and the finite—are seen here in the context of natural

---

18. On this disturbing way of making it possible to recognize the one upon whom the Spirit has come, cf. §2.3. On the action of the bearer of the Spirit in diverse publics, cf. §2.2. On the significance of the "heavenly" public, cf. §§2.4 and 3.3. See also the reference to structural parallels in Judges 13, 1 Samuel 1–3 and Luke 1–3 in J. H. Raatschen, "Empfangen durch den Heiligen Geist: Überlegungen zu Mt 1,18-25," *Theologische Beiträge* (1980): esp. 272–73.

19. See S. Gero, "The Spirit as a Dove at the Baptism of Jesus," *NovT* 18 (1976): 17ff. See also the reference to Noah's dove that announces the end of the rule of chaos and the beginning of deliverance (Gen. 8:9ff.) in, e.g., J. Gnilka, *Das Evangelium nach Markus (Mk 1-8,26)*, EKKNT 2/1 (Zurich: Benziger; Neukirchen-Vluyn: Neukirchener, 1978), 52.

experience. The seeming insignificance and thus the relative hidden-ness of the descent of the Spirit in the form of a dove make it possible to recognize the Messiah as an individual person, and the person Je-sus of Nazareth as the Messiah. They do not yet make clear the effect of this person on the Gentiles.

With regard to the concrete person of Jesus in a concrete public, the action of the Spirit and the public installation of the Christ remain hidden.[20] The action of the Spirit is marked, but at the same time this action is not yet made universally functional. Precisely in being made palpably clear at a particular point, it is unclear and hidden.

The pre-Easter installations of the Christ in domains that go be-yond his contemporary public sphere are not yet very clear. Greater clarity is to be found in the interconnection between God's Spirit and Christ in those self-characterizations ascribed to Jesus and in those statements of other persons about him that refer back to the messianic promises.

The messianic promises of the Spirit-bearer who universally estab-lishes justice, mercy, and knowledge of God and thus brings the fulfill-ment of the law, the messianic promises of the Spirit-bearer who in silence and suffering acquires authority without exercising political vi-olence[21]—these promises are directly or indirectly applied to Jesus of Nazareth by several New Testament traditions. Contrary to the wide-spread opinion that the testimonies relating Jesus and the Spirit are sparse,[22] Matthew and Luke provide a considerable number of explicit quotations from the promises of the bearer of the Spirit, especially from Isaiah 11, 42, and 61, and apply these quotations to Jesus of Nazareth.

---

20. Cf. esp. §4.3.

21. Cf. §§3.1 and 4.2.

22. Cf. A. I. C. Heron, *The Holy Spirit* (Philadelphia: Westminster, 1983), 40. E. Jüngel is more precise: "The relation between holy Spirit and Jesus Christ, deci-sive for the early Christian experience of the Spirit, is determined less by the preach-ing of Jesus and his at best sparse reference to the Spirit (Matt. 11:4-6 as a cryptic reference to the one annointed with the Spirit according to Isa. 61:1ff.?), than by the Easter encounter with the resurrected Christ. It is from the perspective of this encounter that the earthly life of Jesus is then narrated as a life moved by the holy Spirit."

1. According to Matt. 11:5 and Luke 7:22, Jesus responds to the question of John the Baptist, "Are you the one who is to come, or are we to wait for another?" with a free quotation from Isa. 42:7 and 42:18 as well as 61:1: ". . . the blind receive their sight, the lame walk, the lepers are cleansed, the deaf hear, the dead are raised, and the poor have good news brought to them." Jesus also adds the beatitude, "And blessed is anyone who takes no offense at me" (Matt. 11:6; Luke 7:23).[23]

2. Still more detailed and direct is the reference to Isa. 42:1-4 and Isa. 11:10 in Matthew 12. In this text the Pharisees come to the decision, on the basis of Jesus' healing on the Sabbath, to kill him. Verses 15-17: "When Jesus became aware of this, he departed. Many crowds followed him, and he cured all of them, and he ordered them not to make him known.[24] This was to fulfill what had been spoken through the prophet Isaiah . . . ," at which point Isa. 42:1-4 is quoted at length.

> "Here is my servant, whom I have chosen,
> my beloved, with whom my soul is well pleased.
> I will put my Spirit upon him,
> and he will proclaim justice to the Gentiles.
> He will not wrangle or cry aloud,
> nor will anyone hear his voice in the streets.
> He will not break a bruised reed
> or quench a smoldering wick
> until he brings justice to victory.
> And in his name the Gentiles will hope." (Matt. 12:18-21)

Mercy on the sick and weak, righteousness for Israel and for the Gentiles, light and hope for the Gentiles—these traits are thus characteristic of the messianic bearer of the Spirit according to New Testament testimony as well. And Jesus of Nazareth is identified as this bearer of the Spirit.

---

23. Cf. Isa. 26:19; 29:18; 35:5-6.
24. For greater detail, cf. §4.3.

3. While Matthew quotes Isaiah 42 at length, we find in Luke[25] a long quotation from Isaiah 61, which, according to Luke, Jesus applies directly to himself.

> When he came to Nazareth, where he had been brought up, he went to the synagogue on the sabbath day, as was his custom. He stood up to read, and the scroll of the prophet Isaiah was given to him. He unrolled the scroll and found the place where it was written:
>
> "The Spirit of the Lord is upon me,
> because the Lord has anointed me
> to bring good news to the poor.
> The Lord has sent me to proclaim release to the captives
> and recovery of sight to the blind,
> to let the oppressed go free,
> to proclaim the year of the Lord's favor."
>
> And he rolled up the scroll, gave it back to the attendant, and sat down. The eyes of all in the synagogue were fixed on him. Then he began to say to them, "Today this scripture has been fulfilled in your hearing." (Luke 4:16-21)

4. In addition, the baptismal accounts of Matthew and Luke, as well as of Mark, pick up on Isaiah 11 and 42.[26] Isaiah 11:2 ("The Spirit of the LORD shall rest on him") and Isa. 42:1 ("Here is . . . my chosen, in whom my soul delights; I have put my Spirit upon him") are practically quoted or put into pictorial form in the Synoptic writers' accounts of Jesus' baptism.

5. Finally there is the passage about Simeon, endowed with the Spirit, waiting for "the Lord's Messiah." He had been promised that he would see the Messiah before his death. When he sees the child Jesus, he seems clearly to refer to Isa. 42:6 and 49:6. ". . . for my eyes have seen your salvation / which you have prepared in the presence of all peoples / a light for revelation to the Gentiles / and for glory to your

---

25. Cf. Stronstad, "Influence of the Old Testament," esp. 38ff.
26. Matthew 3:16-17; Luke 3:22; Mark 1:10-11; cf. also John 1:32.

people Israel" (Luke 2:30-32). The prophet Anna also recognizes in this situation the messianic event, proclaims it and praises God (cf. Luke 2:38).[27]

Most of these texts have in common that both *public* self-declarations attributed to Jesus (in relation to John and his disciples ["Go and tell . . . "], in relation to the Pharisees, in relation to those gathered in the synagogue) and outside characterizations refer to or play off of messianic promises of the bearer of the Spirit.

On the one hand, the Spirit need not continually be referred to by name in order to express the interconnection between God's Spirit and Jesus Christ.[28] On the other hand, it is important to pay attention to the consciously non-triumphalistic, indeed emphatically anti-triumphalistic traits of this bearer of the Spirit, which are grounded precisely in the action of the Spirit of God. Under pre-Easter conditions, they necessitate guarded, indirect talk of the Spirit's action, power, and public recognizability.[29]

Luke is the clearest and most direct in connecting, on the one hand, the public installation, the public effectiveness of Jesus, and the public resonance to that with, on the other hand, statements about the relation between the Spirit and Jesus: "Then Jesus, filled with the

---

27. It remains unclear—a sixth complex—whether Jesus' beatitudes both in the Sermon on the Mount (Matt. 5:3ff.) and in Luke 6:20ff. exhibit echoes of Isaiah 61. The first three beatitudes in Matthew concern those who are poor in a not merely economic sense, those who mourn, and those who seek righteousness. In these three beatitudes one can recognize the order of Isaiah 61: (1) God has sent me to bring good news to the poor; (2) to comfort those who mourn; and (3) they will be called trees of righteousness. Yet in any case the connections are loose both here and in Luke, while the other testimonies undoubtedly connect messianic promises of the Old Testament directly with Jesus and with the self-understanding attributed to him. J. D. G. Dunn opts more definitely for Luke 6 referring back to Isaiah 61 (*Jesus and the Spirit: A Study of the Religious and Charismatic Experiences of Jesus and the First Christians as Reflected in the New Testament* (Philadelphia: Westminster, n.d.), 55, 376.

28. Kraus correctly concludes that "in accord with the Old Testament Spirit-Messiah promise, the mystery of the Messiahship of Jesus of Nazareth is pneumatological" (*Systematische Theologie*, 359; cf. 359ff., 371ff., 407ff.).

29. For more detail, see §§4.2 and 4.3.

power of the Spirit, returned to Galilee, and a report about him spread through all the surrounding country" (Luke 4:14).[30]

Without question the bearer of the Spirit is also installed in the concrete public of his time and in his natural surroundings in order to bring help in an abundance of concrete, real situations of suffering, and in order to lead the weak and those "without a say" to the knowledge of God. But moral, therapeutic, political, time-bound, and group-bound forms of action and of publicity are insufficient. A "heavenly" power, or a power "coming from heaven,"[31] which can be adequately expressed and perceived only in the *fullness* of the power of the pouring out of the Spirit, is here at work.[32] *This* power expresses itself—and this conditions its mysterious hiddenness—in an earthly manner, concretely effective in diverse ways. Jesus of Nazareth acts under human and earthly-creaturely conditions as the promised Chosen One of God, on whom the Spirit rests. At the same time he is installed by the Spirit of God not only for a specific group of people, a specific age, or a specific culture. The interconnections of these apparently incompatible specifications are brought to expression by the accounts of his "birth by the Spirit" and "baptism in the Spirit," as well as by the accounts of his healings and exorcisms through the "Spirit of God."

4.2: Help in individual powerlessness: Driving out demons and liberation from entrapment with no escape

The Gospels are in agreement in reporting that Jesus of Nazareth not only proclaimed the reign of God, but also healed people and drove out

---

30. Cf. Acts 1:2: "until the day when he was taken up to heaven, after giving instructions through the Holy Spirit to the apostles whom he had chosen"; Acts 10:38: "how God anointed Jesus of Nazareth with the Holy Spirit and with power; how he went about doing good and healing all who were oppressed by the devil, for God was with him"; John 3:34: "He whom God has sent speaks the words of God, for he gives the Spirit without measure."

31. Cf. §§3.3 and 3.4.

32. Luke 10:21: "At that same hour Jesus rejoiced in the Holy Spirit and said, 'I thank you, Father, Lord of heaven and earth, because you have hidden these things from the wise and the intelligent and have revealed them to infants; yea, Father, for such was your gracious will.'" Cf. Matt. 11:25-27.

demons.[33] This "authority" is passed on to Jesus' disciples[34] and is to be given to all persons who come to faith.[35] Healing the sick and driving out demons are important signs that Jesus of Nazareth is the Messiah promised in the Old Testament traditions, on whom the Spirit of God rests, and that Jesus is the servant of God who bears people's sorrows and sicknesses.[36] Beyond the explicit references to Jesus being the messianic bearer of the Spirit, Matt. 12:18 emphasizes Jesus' words: "But if it is *by the Spirit of God* that I cast out demons, then the reign of God has come to you."[37] By the Spirit of God, demons are driven out. Accordingly, the Pharisees' reproach that Jesus is driving out demons not by the Spirit, but with the help of Beelzebul, the "ruler of the demons," is rejected as "blasphemy against the Spirit of God."[38]

How are we to understand the unclean spirits, the demons who make human beings "possessed"? Are not demons products of unbelief and superstition who in the sober, realistic, enlightened, scientific view of the world disappear like fog in sunlight? Would it not be a sign of reason to pass over the numerous passages in the Gospels that talk about Jesus' conflict with unclean and evil spirits, or at least not to conclude from their quantitative to their qualitative significance? Ernst Käsemann judges this kind of repression critically:

---

33. Cf. Mark 1:23ff., 34, 39; 2:3ff.; 3:11; 5:2ff.; 7:26ff.; 9:17ff., 25; 16:9; Matt. 4:23-24; 8:16, 32; 9:32-33, 35; 11:5; 12:15, 22ff.; 15:28; 17:18; Luke 4:18-19, 33ff., 40-41; 6:18; 7:21; 8:2, 27ff.; 9:39ff.; 11:14; 13:11ff., 32; John 10:21. It is important to note the explicit references to the increasing number of exorcisms among the Gentiles in the course of Jesus' activity (Mark 7:25ff.; Matt. 15:22ff. and passim).

34. Cf. Mark 3:14-15; 6:7, 13; Matt. 10:1, 7-8; Luke 9:1-2. But note also the insistence on the difference between Jesus' authority and that of the disciples in Mark 9:18b, 28-29; Matt. 17:19; Luke 9:40).

35. See Mark 16:17; cf. Luke 10:17; see J. Wilkinson, *Health and Healing: Studies in New Testament Principles and Practice* (Edinburgh: Handsel, 1980), esp. 159ff.

36. Cf. the explicit references to Isaiah 42 and 61 in Matt. 11:5; 12:18ff.; Luke 4:18ff.; 7:22; as well as the reference to Isa. 53:4 in Matt. 8:17.

37. Emphasis added; regarding the difficult parallel passage Luke 11:20, see T. Lorenzmeier, "Zum Logion Mt 12,28; Lk 11,20," in H. D. Betz and L. Schottroff, eds., *Neues Testament und christliche Existenz: Festschrift für Herbert Braun zum 70. Geburtstag am 4. Mai 1973* (Tübingen: Mohr, 1973), 289ff. Cf. Exod. 8:15; 31:18; Ps. 8:4.

38. See Mark 3:22ff.; Matt. 12:24ff., esp. 31; Luke 11:14ff.; 12:10; also §4.4.

But we need to ask seriously whether we are allowed to take central views of the New Testament in general and to cover them up or—to speak metaphorically—to shunt them off onto the wrong track in this way. To the extent that we talk about possession, we do no more than leave those New Testament views lying in a corner as inaccurate circumlocutions for mental and psychological disturbances—circumlocutions that our science has in the meantime corrected. This could not only unjustly trivialize biblical texts and historical traditions. It could also block insights that are truly illuminating and necessary for us.[39]

Käsemann has urged us not "to reduce the reality of possession merely to sicknesses of soul and mind." Instead we should uncover, as he puts it, the "metaphysical depth and cosmic breadth" of the New Testament stories.[40]

In the following discussion we shall take up Käsemann's intellectual initiative in an attempt structurally to grasp "possession" and demonic power.[41] The language of complex spirits and of possession refers to very complex, not readily comprehensible phenomena. The statements about demons and unclean spirits that are the most univocal for us today are probably those provided in the New Testament texts Mark 1:26, Luke 4:35, and Mark 9:17-18.

Mark 1:26: "And the unclean spirit, convulsing him and crying with a loud voice, came out of him." Luke 4:35: ". . . the demon had thrown him down before them." In Mark 9:17-18 we find the most medically significant information: ". . . I brought you my son; he has a spirit that makes him unable to speak; and whenever it seizes him, it dashes him down; and he foams and grinds his teeth and

---

39. E. Käsemann, "Die Heilung der Besessenen," in *Kirchliche Konflikte* 1 (Göttingen: Vandenhoeck, 1982), 189. See also D. Zähringer, "Die Dämonen," in *MySal* 2, 996ff., esp. 1000ff.

40. Käsemann, "Heilung," 193.

41. The most important works of M. Trowitzsch can be read as a still developing attempt, oriented on Martin Heidegger, to carry this through with regard to the cultures of Western modernity, possessed by the "spirit of technology." Cf. M. Trowitzsch, *Technokratie und Geist der Zeit: Beiträge zu einer theologischen Kritik* (Tübingen: Mohr, 1988), esp. 196ff., but also 83ff.

becomes rigid." This seems clearly to be a description of the symptoms of epilepsy.[42]

Whether it was a matter of epileptic attacks or of somnambulism (somnambulism conditioned either epileptically or in some other manner), in any event, the free formation of the will of the possessed person is suspended in the cases described. Without the free contribution of the affected person, he is controlled to his own harm and to his own endangerment. Mark 9:21-22 expressly mentions this involuntary self-endangerment and harm: "Jesus asked the father, 'How long has this been happening to him?' And he said, 'From childhood. It has often cast him into the fire and into the water, to destroy him.' "

In other cases as well in which people are possessed by demons, what is central is that *the free formation of their wills is excluded, that they inflict harm on themselves, and that their environment stands powerless in the face of this development.*[43] The symptoms elicited by the demon can be recognized with particular clarity in the story of the *healing of the Gerasene demoniac* (Mark 5:1ff.; Luke 8:26ff.; cf. Matt. 8:28ff.).

> They came to the other side of the sea, to the country of the Gerasenes. And when he [Jesus] had stepped out of the boat, immediately

---

42. Cf. Luke 9:29. The parallel text Matt. 17:15 could also be a reference to a case of epilepsy: "Lord, have mercy on my son, for he is lunatic and he suffers terribly; he often falls into the fire and often into the water." (The NRSV reads "he is an epileptic," but "lunatic," derived from *luna,* the Latin word for *moon,* is a closer semantic equivalent to the Greek *selēniazetai,* as well as to the German *mondsüchtig*— Trans.) J. Gnilka observes that "epilepsy was popularly called the holy sickness, probably because of the magnitude of the suffering connected with it or because it was regarded as suffering sent by a divinity. Relatively often it was connected with the moon goddess (cf. Matt. 17:15). Within the domain of Christianity the appraisal of epilepsy as a holy sickness was totally abandoned. It was understood as possession caused by demons" (*Das Evangelium nach Markus (Mk 8,27-16,20),* EKK 2/2 [Zurich: Benziger; Neukirchen-Vluyn: Neukirchener, 1979], 47).

43. In this context we ought not to think only of a demon coming on someone in an attacklike manner that cannot be directly anticipated. The New Testament traditions also ascribe chronic suffering of other sorts to demons: e.g., loss of linguistic capacity and the inability to walk upright (cf. Matt. 9:33; Luke 11:14; 13:11). We may leave undecided the question of whether there is in the background a relatively simple anthropology that defines language and upright carriage as the *essence* of the human person, and that thus sees demons attacking the essence of the human person.

a man out of the tombs with an unclean spirit met him. He lived among the tombs; and no one could restrain him any more, even with a chain; for he had often been restrained with shackles and chains, but the chains he wrenched apart, and the shackles he broke in pieces; and no one had the strength to subdue him. Night and day among the tombs and on the mountains he was always howling and bruising himself with stones. (Mark 5:1-5)

The demons, the unclean spirits, make it impossible for the persons possessed by them to live in a way corresponding to their creaturely possibilities and to take part in social life. To the detriment of the stricken persons, the demons unforeseeably incapacitate their will, bring them into a domain between death and life, and hold them in this domain. The Gerasene demoniac takes shelter in burial caves, in isolation.[44] He is helpless, restless, sleepless. He suffers and screams, harms and endangers himself (he strikes himself "with stones"). In addition, he draws the community into his woe and spreads anxiety and powerlessness around himself.

It is characteristic of the suffering caused by *demons* that woe and powerlessness are given a long-term status. The woe holds on tenaciously, and the possibility that it will reappear over and over again remains threateningly present.

The man possessed by an unclean spirit cannot live with his fellow persons, and they cannot live with him. They cannot even quiet him down with force. The unclean spirit is stronger than the community with its measures of restraint. Unclean spirits arouse so much fear precisely by virtue of the fact that they work so powerfully and evoke feelings of helplessness so offensively. They cause the people whom they possess to endanger themselves and to make themselves immune to help. In this way torment, suffering, and isolation are spread among those who are possessed, while anxiety and helplessness are spread among the others. The unclean spirit restricts the life possibilities of the persons stricken by it. Even when it grants extraordinary powers to the affected person, she can only waste them in a senseless, anxiety-spreading manner, or direct them against herself.

---

44. O. Böcher points out that places of death, burial caves and cemeteries, are the dwelling place of unclean spirits. Cf. Bocher, *Christus exorcista: Dämonismus und Taufe im Neuen Testament*, BWANT 96 (Stuttgart: Kohlhammer, 1972), 74–75.

It is in accord with the interest in stabilizing the suffering and torment that the unclean spirits vehemently resist being driven out. Mark
1:23-24: "Just then there was in their synagogue a person with an unclean spirit, and the person cried out: 'What have you to do with us,
Jesus of Nazareth? Have you come to destroy us?' "[45] Similarly Mark
5:6ff.: "When he saw Jesus from a distance, he ran and bowed down
before him; and he shouted at the top of his voice, 'What have you to
do with me, Jesus, Son of the Most High God? I adjure you by God, do
not torment me.' "[46]

Because those who are possessed cannot accept any help and thus
close themselves off from the community, but are also excluded from it,
one cannot speak here only of psychological suffering. The demonic
powers cause disintegration and dissociation of individuals and of
communities through the experience that people remain rejected and
foreign, that they scare off, depress, and condemn to helplessness the
fellow persons and communities who want to help them. The demonic
powers lead to *negative repercussions on all sides.* They are capable of re-
sisting and difficult to grasp, they universally understand healing as
torment and affliction, and they resist it or induce those whom they
possess to resist healing and liberation.[47] They thus disturb and destroy
coherent patterns of creaturely life in a long-term manner. Inasmuch
as those who are possessed resist every instance of the community's
extending itself to them, they cause anxiety in their fellow persons.
They *repulse their fellow persons.* This then rebounds upon them as
intensified isolation, even as hostility.[48] The demonic power that

---

45. Cf. Luke 4:33-34.

46. Cf. Matt. 8:29; also Mark 5:10; Luke 8:28, 31.

47. Changes of identity that are not altogether clear are found in several texts.
In Mark 5:7ff. it seems to be first the person who is possessed, then the demon who
says to Jesus: "I adjure you by God, do not torment me." Cf. Matt. 8:29ff.; Luke
8:28ff.; as well as Mark 1:23-24; Luke 4:33-34. The statement "My name is Legion;
for we are many," in the stories of the healing of the Gerasene (Mark 5:9 par.) also
expresses the fact that the demonic powers are difficult to grasp. To this multiplicity
that is difficult to grasp (cf. also the remarkable story of the "return of the unclean
spirits" in Matt. 12:43-45 par.) corresponds the ruptured, disintegrated, dissociating, isolating, and isolation-spreading identity of the person taken into possession
by an unclean spirit.

48. On the basis of the recognition that the structures present here can appear
in psychological, pathological, social, societal, and political contexts, Käsemann

paralyzes and disintegrates individual persons and their surroundings is directly opposed to the life-creating Spirit of God.

According to the testimonies that we have examined so far, the Spirit of God is a power that comes upon persons *for the benefit of others.* The Spirit changes Israel so that it may reveal God's glory to the Gentiles. Israel's change can then redound to the recognition of the bearer of the Spirit, and Israel can experience positive repercussions of its effect on the Gentiles. While the Holy Spirit causes gathering, building up, and strengthening of both the individual and the community through the integration of the weak and the outsiders, the demons are powers that isolate, separate, make people solitary, and disintegrate community. They labor in a variety of ways to weaken and dissolve coherent patterns of creaturely life.[49] They compel creatures to live in an agonizing manner below their life possibilities. Yet evidently the only way in which they are capable of relating to life and the living is by hindering, tormenting, and disfiguring. (They do this with mechanisms of negative reinforcement and of negative repercussions that we today must learn to see and to discover in other contexts than those of the witnesses of the New Testament traditions.)[50] Demonic powers can be "driven out." They may appear unavoidable and thus as destiny to

---

("Heilung," 194) has reflected on situations of our contemporary life and has diagnosed a situation of life "in panic": "Where today do human beings, communities, peoples and continents not live in panic? Whether it be panic about others or about the future; panic about the loss of their possessions . . . or about the loss of their power, of their jobs, of their freedom, of their next day's food; in fear of tyrants and exploiters and demons? The talk of an 'improvement of the quality of life' is bombast and hot air. It would be much more sober and much clearer if one were instead to ask how one finds a way out of either secret or undisguised panic." J. Moltmann and U. Bach show the way in which structurally demonic processes harm the relation between persons with disabilities and persons "without" disabilities in our societies. J. Moltmann, *Diakonie im Horizont des Reiches Gottes: Schritten zum Diakonentum aller Gläubigen* (Neukirchen-Vluyn: Neukirchener, 1984), esp. 42–51; U. Bach, "Der behinderte Mensch als Thema der Theologie," in ibid., 92–105.

49. Cf. §3.5.

50. While many of the diseases described by the New Testament traditions have lost their "demonic" aura for us, other forms of suffering can certainly be accompanied by "demonic" mechanisms of constraint that are analogous to those described here.

those who are directly affected and to their surroundings, but they have no essentially invulnerable power.

If we are seeking to identify corresponding situations today, we must ask where *situations of individual and collective suffering* are present that are perceived as agonizing and disintegrative, but at the same time are stabilized and stubbornly defended. For instance, addiction,[51] drug problems, epidemic greed, repression of life and self-anesthetization of consumerist societies on many levels of living, ecological exploitation, and excessive debt politics call attention to such "demonic" forms of human persons and human societies endangering and destroying themselves. A variety of structural patterns of life and experience are characterized by the fact that people in suffering make themselves immune to help, that their surroundings thus become powerless, that in this negative "interaction" all sides become paralyzed and disintegrated, and that the torment becomes long-term.

It is striking that in Jesus' pre-Easter activity, the demonic powers are not removed with one blow, but are "driven out" in a multitude of individual, concrete actions of liberation. The messianic bearer of the Spirit who drives out demons by the Spirit of God does not act by means of an "organized" liberation action, nor by means of a process that would be analogous to structural changes of a political, judicial, or moral sort. Instead he enters into a variety of individual, concrete stories and experiences of suffering. In the relative weakness and laboriousness of individual, concrete acts and encounters, the Messiah intervenes in disfigured, suffering, woe-generating life. No people of those liberated gathers here "as one person"; no "great army" of the delivered goes out to a messianic public relations event. On the contrary, all steps and tendencies that could go in this direction are, according to the testimony of the Synoptic writers, cut short by Jesus himself with the so-called "injunction of silence."[52] The liberation by the Spirit of God that goes hand in hand with the advent of God's

---

51. Cf. A. Wilson Schaef, *When Society Becomes an Addict* (San Francisco: Harper & Row, 1988), 37ff.; M. S. Peck, *People of the Lie: The Hope for Healing Human Evil* (New York: Simon and Schuster, 1983).

52. See §4.3; also W. Wrede, *The Messianic Secret*, trans. J. C. G. Greig (Cambridge: James Clarke, 1971); G. Bornkamm, *Jesus of Nazareth*, trans. I. McLusky, F. McLusky, and J. M. Robinson (New York: Harper & Row, 1960), 170ff.

reign is to take place in and through varied, individual, irrepeatable concreteness.

Specific case by specific case, concrete, individual, creaturely life is rescued from demonic powers. It is restored to unhindered creatureliness. It is not metamorphosed into a fantastic, somehow "superearthly" life, immune to sorrow and death. The persons who are liberated and healed remain earthly, finite, mortal beings. The liberation from demons by the messianic bearer of the Spirit and by God's Spirit *renews* earthly-creaturely life. God's power and God's glory are to be experienced and attested to from the perspective of this varied life in its earthly-concrete reality and of its renewal. The presence of the messianic bearer of the Spirit, the action of the Spirit, and the coming of God's reign are revealed in a variety of individual, concrete experiences of liberation from distress, captivity, and hopelessness, in experiences of deliverance and of the restoration of unimpaired, coherent patterns of life.

4.3: Gathering the people of God without public means of power: The injunction of silence and the "concrescent" public of the reign of God

In Jesus of Nazareth the messianic bearer of the Spirit is present as an individual human person in a concrete, "fleshly" manner. His action, action by the Spirit, is carried out upon individual, finite, concrete suffering human beings. Yet although we can certainly imagine that this action of removing suffering was concrete and striking *in those days*, it is questionable how this action—at first glance confined to specific points in time and space and extended only to individual persons—can be understood as the establishing of the *reign of God*. To be sure, the messianic bearer of the Spirit revealed in Jesus of Nazareth can no longer be confused with a mere ideal figure. To be sure, the action of the Spirit is no longer suspected of having been carried out in those days over people's heads, as it were, for it has shown itself to be palpably effective. Yet how is this action of the Spirit perceived by human beings after we "no longer know Christ according to the flesh" (2 Cor. 5:16)? Beyond the healings and the exorcisms performed by Jesus of Nazareth, might this action of the Spirit prove still to be perceivable in a bodily way today? If yes, *how* is it perceived concretely and objectively?

Such questions do not stem simply from an egoistic interest in salvation on the part of those who are born after the fact and thus in a certain sense too late; such questions do not stem simply from an egoistic interest in salvation on the part of our present, lying at such great distance from the immediate action of Jesus of Nazareth. Such questions are already included in the problem of how the action of the bearer of the Spirit and of God's Spirit, as this action is revealed in Jesus' healings and exorcisms, is to be understood as the establishment and arrival of the reign of God.[53] How is it conceivable that a sphere of power is constituted by means of this concrete, exorcistic action that influences diverse individual suffering?

These questions are provoked precisely by the heightened concreteness of Jesus' exorcistic action in comparison with the messianic promises of the Old Testament. We can certainly imagine a sphere of power built up through the promulgation of a new law, such as that spoken of in the text from Isaiah 42 cited in Matthew 12, into which we can "enter," in which we can participate and which we for our part can strengthen, which places a claim on us and makes us members of a change in life relations. But it is hard to conceive an analogous process in the face of the exorcisms. We have only vague notions of the people affected by this suffering. At best we can have only a fragmentary sense of their experiences of liberation and of joy. Even the relief of the persons affected along with them is so far removed from us that in any case those events do not seem to constitute a domain of power into which we could bring ourselves as into a public sphere structured by laws, moralities, and concepts of retributive justice.

Yet it is not only the concreteness of the healings and exorcisms that distances and isolates us, rendering us insecure, as soon as we start hearing that here the reign of God has come. It is at the same time the implausibility and incomprehensibility of the acts of driving out demons, and the problems in making clear sense of these acts—let

---

53. Picking up on the work of E. Schweizer, Kraus has defined the reign of God as a "sphere of power into which one can 'enter.'" For that reason, according to Kraus, *basileia tou theou* should be translated not only as the "rule of God," but also as the "reign of God."

alone repeating them—that make it difficult for us to think that the *reign* of God has come in this action. Establishment of righteousness for the benefit of the weak and afflicted—*that* we might still regard as realistic and conceivable even up to the present day. With this action of the Spirit we can still regard ourselves as subject to its claims and as having a part in the establishment of new structures of rule and of loyalty. But this is hardly the case with the accounts of healing and of exorcism.

The New Testament texts that talk about Jesus as the messianic bearer of the Spirit and about his exorcistic action cite at the same time those texts of the mercy law that concern the action of the Spirit of righteousness.[54] They do not annul these promises, but they sharpen them into diverse healings and exorcisms that do not make sense to us. Jesus' action on suffering and possessed persons goes beyond the typical cases—those that are classed by the law under particular types and that moralities could class under particular types—of action for the benefit of those who are weaker. Does not this action become "lost" in a multitude of individual cases, each of which is unique?

The New Testament strengthens our uncertainty and our hesitations concerning how a sphere of power can be built up through Jesus' action and concerning how God's *reign* can become present. They are strengthened by Jesus' repeated command "not to make him known" (e.g., Matt. 12:16), which picks up Isaiah 42: "He will not make his voice heard in the street." Confronted with this hostility to publicity and to public attention, how are we to imagine the establishment of a sphere of power into which people can "enter," and a corresponding presence of the *reign* of God?

The so-called injunction of silence is initially directed at the demons. Remarkably, the demons recognize that Jesus is "the Holy One of God" (Mark 1:24; Luke 4:34), the "Son of God" (Mark 3:11; Matt. 8:29; Luke 4:41), the "Son of the Most High God" (Mark 5:7; Luke 8:28), and they state it publicly. Luke 4:41 even says that "they knew that he was the Messiah."[55]

But this knowledge is no confession of faith and definitely not an instance of giving glory. Instead it is bound up with the rejection of

54. Cf. §§3.1 and 4.1.
55. Cf. Mark 1:34: "they knew him."

community with Jesus. In Mark 1:24 we read the explicit questions: "What have you to do with us, Jesus of Nazareth? Have you come to destroy us?" The unclean spirits who dominate and enslave people, making them anxious and driving them into suffering and distress, state their knowledge of Christ in a defensive, resistant manner.[56]

Why do these texts bring the demons together with the disclosure of Jesus' identity? Why should the pre-Easter revelation of Jesus' identity be seen in a bad light? Why does Jesus not make use of this publicity—in accord with the saying "To the pure all things are pure"? Why are these demonic voices silenced and separated from the fleshly, concrete life being held in their possession,[57] despite the fact that they are certainly in the right when they designate Jesus as the Holy One of God, as Son of the Most High God, or as the Messiah? "Be silent and come out of him!" (Mark 1:25). "But he sternly ordered them not to make him known" (Mark 3:12).[58]

All answers are inadequate that see in the injunction of silence merely an act of staving off the *demons* from making Jesus publicly recognizable. Instead Jesus wants to prevent his person becoming recognizable too soon and bound up with expectations that are too narrow. Not only the demons, but also the persons liberated by Jesus from the

---

56. The commentaries also emphasize that the address and the articulation of Jesus' name and mission are to be regarded as nothing less than an attempt at a counterexorcism. Gnilka is representative of many: "With the revelation of its knowledge the unclean spirit attempts to gain power over Jesus as if by a magic formula" (Gnilka, *Markus* 1, 80). Gnilka refers to a parallel in O. Bauernfeind, *Die Worte der Dämonen im Markusevangelium*, BWANT (Stuttgart: Kohlhammer, 1927), 15. Bauernfeind cites from a papyrus on magic: "I know you, Hermes, who you are and from whence you come."

57. Or the demons are allowed to enter life that is unclean in any case, as Mark 5 par. reports. The demons ask to be permitted to enter into the herd of pigs feeding nearby, and they induce the unclean animals to plunge into the water with them: an impressive demonstration of the divine removal of what is evil and unclean. Inasmuch as the destructive force is directed toward what is unclean, what is evil performs a good deed: it removes the unclean flesh that separates Jews and Gentiles or, alternatively, it leads to the unclean flesh removing itself. It is noteworthy that according to the narratives, Jesus' exorcistic action increasingly occurs in Gentile Christian territory. This also corresponds to the intentions of the messianic promises (cf. §§3.1, 3.3, and 3.4.).

58. Cf. Mark 1:34; Luke 4:35, 41.

violence of the demons,[59] as well as other witnesses of his healing and exorcistic action,[60] indeed even the disciples[61] are not supposed to surrender his identity too soon—not before the cross and resurrection.

Mark 7:36 emphasizes that "the more Jesus ordered them ['to tell no one'], the more zealously they proclaimed it." Nevertheless, there is no reason to understand the injunction of silence as a publicity tactic aimed at having the contrary effect. According to Matt. 12:16-19, the injunction to keep silent picks up on Isaiah 42, and with good reason:

> . . . and he ordered them not to make him known. This was to fulfill what had been spoken through the prophet Isaiah:
>
> "Here is my servant, whom I have chosen,
> my beloved, with whom my soul is well pleased.
> I will put my Spirit upon him,
> and he will proclaim justice to the Gentiles.
> He will not wrangle or cry aloud,
> nor will anyone hear his voice in the streets."[62]

Jesus does not want to act in such a way that his messianic identity is made known only in the light of healings he has performed, whether those making it known be demons, people who have been healed and liberated, or the disciples. Jesus' action is inseparably bound up with the proclamation of the coming reign of God and is not to be made public independently of this proclamation. The injunction of silence is to preserve the interconnection of the proclamation of God's reign, faith, the forgiveness of sins, and the experience of becoming whole. It is directed against universalizing the indispensable change of individual, concrete life and making it stand on its own.[63] What we today call public relations, the building up of a public image and of a public identity, public success and public recognition—*all this would, under pre-Easter*

---

59. Cf. Matt. 8:4; 9:30.

60. See Mark 5:43; 7:36; Matt. 12:16; Luke 8:56.

61. Cf. Mark 8:30; 9:9; Matt. 16:20; 17:9; Luke 9:21.

62. Cf. §3.2.

63. This point was emphasized to me by S. Brandt, with particular reference to Mark 6:1ff. Cf. W. J. Bittner, *Heilung—Zeichen der Herrschaft Gottes* (Neukirchen-Vluyn: Aussaat, 1984), esp. 37ff.

conditions, run fundamentally contrary to Jesus' messianic mission. Of
course, Jesus certainly acquires public resonance even against his will.
But the actual intention of his action is not to build up a specific, publicly recognized image as a wonder-working subduer of demons.

Nor is this contradicted by the charge to the healed Gerasene in
Mark 5:19 (par. Luke 8:39): "Go home to your friends, and tell them
how much the Lord has done for you, and what mercy the Lord has
shown you." To which follows: "And he went away and began to proclaim in the Decapolis how much Jesus had done for him; and everyone was amazed." To be sure, at first glance Jesus does seem here—in
direct opposition to the other texts considered—to be looking for public recognition through the report of the person whom has been
healed. But this is only at first glance, as Joachim Gnilka shows:

> The healed man is to go home to his people. The mercy of the Lord
> implicitly includes his people welcoming him back. By means of an
> appeal to the mercy of God that was revealed in the miracle, this
> mercy attains its goal in the full reincorporation of the previously
> excluded person into human society. Thus there is no reason to
> see in this charge a command of public proclamation. . . . The
> prospect of the reintegration of the excluded person is maintained,
> but the command to report the event to those of his own circle be-
> comes a particular form of the command of silence. When only
> those of his own house are the addressees of the report, this be-
> comes a restriction. Contrary to this, the healed man proclaims in
> the Decapolis what has happened to him, and thus breaks the
> "injunction of silence" (cf. 1:44-45).[64]

If according to this story as well Jesus is not looking to extend his
fame in the region east of the Jordan, the charge nevertheless remains:
"Go and tell your people, so that they will welcome you back." At what
public is Jesus' action aiming? *The publics growing out of concrete experi-*
ences of suffering and of liberation are those in which Jesus acts, those that
he centers and concentrates on himself. The goal is not to spread a catchy
image, a finished picture, an unequivocal success story, or a fixed and
unchangeable notion of salvation. The goal is to connect various experiences of concrete deliverance, of concrete liberation, the experiences

---

64. Gnilka, *Markus* 1, 206–7.

of concrete-individual, affected, and delivered life with Jesus' name and with the expectation and experience of the reign of God. These experiences of concrete suffering, of concrete pain, and the concrete experiences of liberation are bound up with the Messiah of whom it is said that "he has borne our infirmities and carried our diseases." They are bound up with the Messiah who does not want to make his voice heard in the street. This Messiah makes his appearance neither as a ruler, nor as one wishing to rule, nor as an opposition power, nor as an accuser. He is the middle of memories and expectations from which grows the community of those who suffer, who hope for liberation, and of those who have experienced liberation from sickness and pain. The demons who want to make Jesus' identity public all at once prohibit or at least hinder the coming into being, the growth, and the building up of this community. They act against the emergence, the growing together of the community characteristic of the action of the Spirit. They act against it by trying to render uniform and to homogenize the gathering of the community that is to grow out of a variety of experiences of concrete distress, powerlessness, captivity, and helplessness, and out of a variety of concrete experiences of deliverance and liberation.

Only on the basis of the experience and knowledge of the cross and the resurrection of Christ is it possible to publicize the identity of Jesus without distortion, without engaging in false concretions and false abstractions that hinder the coming and the growing together of God's reign. Only the event of the cross understood from the perspective of the resurrection makes clear that not only sick and suffering people in Jesus' day, or people with particular distresses and diseases in various historical and cultural situations, are to be liberated and gathered as God's people. Only with the cross does it become manifest that Jesus Christ, the bearer of the Spirit, wants to deliver persons and groups of people of all times, and historical worlds of all times, from the demonic clutches of sin.

The innocent righteous one who dies on the cross is executed in the name of judicial, political, and religious orders. Jews and Romans, Gentiles and Jews, the pious and the impious, the political and the apolitical, rulers and ruled, the reflective and the frenzied—in a unanimity that extends beyond their differences, they all bring the one chosen by God to the cross. After the revelation of Jesus' identity, human beings are to recognize themselves in this pluriform unanimity of the powerless and helpless world, captive to and blinded by sin. At the same time they are to have the liberating experience that, in the power of the Spirit, this Messiah both intervenes in their concrete, unique, perishable life and is present and effective in the "fullness of times" in an unimaginable diversity of paths of life and life worlds.[65]

Out of this universal community of those who are far from God, be it voluntarily or involuntarily, ignorantly or knowingly, God gathers and builds up God's people. In the deliverance of these people, the reign of God comes with the power that in the action of the earthly Jesus is still hidden, although it is already present through his *proclamation* of God's reign. Publicizing Jesus' identity too soon would dissolve the *interconnection* between the proclamation of God's reign and the healings of the sick. It would lead neither into the depths of human hopelessness nor into the breadth of God's reign.

Through the revelation of the identity of Christ on the cross, it becomes possible not only for human beings to recognize their pluriform lostness and the power—or powerlessness—that emanates from this lostness. It also becomes possible for them to recognize that this sacrifice took their place, that through the power of the Spirit people are to recognize their lostness as it reaches beyond their suffering and beyond their being affected by the suffering of others, and to be rescued from this lostness. Out of diverse concrete experiences of deliverance and liberation from the power of sin, which drives people far from God and demonically holds them there, the crucified and risen bearer of the Spirit gathers in constantly new ways the community of those who have been healed. This is the community of those who are to participate in life that has been rescued from death. Before this power of Christ has become clear through the cross, and before the power of the Spirit is "poured out" and is at work simultaneously in numerous life contexts, the identity of Jesus is not to become known. To publicize that identity too early arouses hopes and expectations that are too small and too narrow, and distorts and disfigures the salvation extended by God to human beings.[66]

---

65. See esp. §§4.5, 5.1, and 6.4.

66. See D. Schneider, *Der Geist des Gekreuzigten: Zur paulinischen Theologie des Heiligen Geistes* (Neukirchen-Vluyn: Aussaat, 1987), 109ff., esp. 124ff.

Yet not only the demons who want to make Jesus' true identity public too soon, but also the religious experts who purposefully distort Jesus true identity want to hinder his action. These are the experts whose judgment is that here a head demon is at work!

4.4: Why is blaspheming the Spirit unforgivable?

Mark 1:28 reports that after Jesus' exorcistic action, "at once his fame began to spread throughout the surrounding region of Galilee." This fame, though, is ambiguous. On the one hand, the "authority" of his action is acknowledged. On the other hand, people do not rightly know what they ought to make of it. Mark 1:27: "They were all amazed, and they kept on asking one another, 'What is this? A new teaching—with authority! He commands even the unclean spirits, and they obey him.' "

The general public, amazed and disturbed, comprehends only the rough outline of what is going on. The Pharisees, though, strive for *explanations,* which become accusations. The first explanation is that Jesus himself is possessed. The second explanation says that he is practicing magic.

Mark 3:22 (cf. 3:30): "And the scribes who came down from Jerusalem said, 'He has Beelzebul, and by the ruler of the demons he casts out demons.' "[67] Jesus himself is possessed. The Pharisees thus say what, according to Mark 3:21, Jesus' relatives, too, apparently are thinking when they conclude, "He has gone out of his mind."[68] In the judgment of the Pharisees and presumably of his own relatives, perhaps even in the judgment of parts of the public of the time, Jesus is at least temporarily regarded as himself possessed by an unclean spirit and as "crazy." When Jesus in the temple foresees his own death (John 7:19), the crowd answers (John 7:20), "You have a demon! Who is trying to kill you?" In John 8:48ff. as well Jesus is repeatedly reproached with

---

67. Similarly Matt. 12:24; 9:34. According to Luke 11:15 the reproach is spoken by some persons from "the crowds."

68. Gnilka compiles some of the proposed translations with the help of which people have tried to mitigate the harshness of the statement. Instead of "he has gone out of his mind," it might read, "he has lost all strength," "he is enraptured," and so on (Gnilka, *Markus* 1, 148).

being possessed by a demon. John 10:20-21 reflects the public uncertainty of the judgment: "Many of them were saying, 'He has a demon and is out of his mind. Why listen to him?' Others were saying, 'These are not the words of one who has a demon. Can a demon open the eyes of the blind?'"

In this situation of uncertainty, the judgment of the religious experts carries a lot of weight. This judgment attests not only that Jesus is possessed. It issues in the obscure reproach that he is complicit with the demons. On the one hand, it is acknowledged that Jesus rules over the demons in a certain way. On the other hand, he is characterized as being himself ruled by demons. Jesus is possessed in a particular manner, because he drives out the devil with Beelzebul. Here we seem to have demon against demon.[69]

The first response that Jesus gives to this reproach is so subtle that some interpreters have argued that it should be understood in light of Mark 4:12 par.: ". . . 'they may indeed look, but not perceive, / and may indeed listen, but not understand; / so that they may not turn again and be forgiven.'" The response meets the reproach head-on and points to its internal inconsistency. The reproach, "He drives out demons by the ruler of the demons," which is supposed to denounce Jesus as a magician and a devil's accomplice, is at odds with itself.

> "How can Satan cast out Satan? If a kingdom is divided against itself, that kingdom cannot stand. And if a house is divided against itself, that house will not be able to stand. And if Satan has risen up against himself and is divided, he cannot stand, but his end has come." (Mark 3:23b-26)[70]

Jesus' objection can be interpreted in two ways. First: "Even if I, in accord with your reproach, were driving out demons with their head

---

69. With reference to the following discussion, see C. Colpe, "Der Spruch von der Lästerung des Geistes," in E. Lohse, ed., *Der Ruf Jesu und die Antwort der Gemeinde: Exegetische Untersuchungen: Joachim Jeremias zum 70. Geburtstag gewidmet von seinen Schülern* (Göttingen: Vandenhoeck, 1970), 63ff., esp. 70ff.; Y. Congar, "Blasphemy Against the Holy Spirit," in P. Huizing and W. Bassett, eds., *Experience of the Spirit* (New York: Seabury, 1974), 47ff.; M. E. Boring, "The Unforgivable Sin," *NovT* 18 (1976): 258ff.; J. C. O'Neill, "The Unforgivable Sin (Matt. 12:31-32; Mark 3:28f; Luke 12:10)," *Journal for the Study of the New Testament* 19 (1983): 37ff.
70. Cf. Matt. 12:25-26; Luke 11:17-18.

demon, an inner conflict would take place in the reign of evil—a conflict that would lead to the annihilation of evil." The second possible interpretation reads the statement as a direct defense: "Your reproach is nonsense, since I certainly cannot be simultaneously promoting both an internal conflict in the reign of evil—a conflict that would lead to its annulment—and an establishment of the rule of the head demon." The reproach that Jesus is establishing the rule of demons by driving out demons, or that he is acting only in the interest of strengthening the rule of demons, is untenable.

The second objection in Mark 3:27 is simpler in itself: "But no one can enter a strong man's house and plunder his property without first tying up the strong man; then indeed the house can be plundered."[71]

The second objection rejects the interpretation of Jesus' action as an intrademonic affair. Jesus' action serves neither the solidification of the demons' rule nor a solely intrademonic disintegrative process, a battle of evil against evil, which would lead to evil's annulment. The second objection makes clear that here a power is at work that overwhelms and binds evil, which reduces evil's domain of rule and possession inasmuch as Jesus strips the demons of the life they have been holding in possession.[72]

This power that Jesus claims for his liberating action, the superior power that overwhelms the demonic powers, is the power of God that intervenes in earthly life relations: the Holy Spirit.

In Mark 3:28-30 this is expressed, in response to the reproach that Jesus is possessed by an unclean spirit, by appending the saying about the impossibility of forgiving blasphemy against the Holy Spirit: "'Truly I tell you, people will be forgiven for their sins and whatever blasphemies they utter; but whoever blasphemes against the Holy Spirit can never have forgiveness, but is guilty of an eternal sin'—for they had said, 'He has an unclean spirit.'"

---

71. Cf. Matt. 12:29; Luke 11:21-22.

72. Gnilka draws the direct conclusion that "the booty wrested away from the strong man are the persons who are liberated from disease and demons" (*Markus* 1, 150). Gnilka sees in the background the statement of Isa. 49:24-25: "Can the prey be taken from the mighty, or the captives of a tyrant be rescued? But thus says the LORD: Even the captives of the mighty shall be taken, and the prey of the tyrant be rescued; for I will contend with those who contend with you, and I will save your children."

The parallels, Matt. 12:31-32 and Luke 12:10, offer similar formulations, but in addition emphasize that even whoever speaks a word against the Human One will be forgiven, "but whoever speaks against the Holy Spirit will not be forgiven." Matthew adds, "either in this age or in the age to come." Moreover, Matt. 12:28 *explicitly* notes that Jesus drives out demons by the Spirit of God: "But if it is by the Spirit of God that I cast out demons, then the reign of God has come to you."

Jesus' action of driving out demons by the Spirit of God means that God's rule has come. This brings a complex state of affairs under consideration. This state of affairs must be illuminated in order to grasp the impossibility of forgiving blasphemy against the Spirit, and thereby to solve one of the greatest difficulties for theological understanding—according to Augustine even the greatest and most difficult problem of all presented by the Holy Scriptures.[73]

The dawning of the rule of God is *not* to be characterized by means of some sort of *displacement of demons by a superior power*. From a systematic perspective one would not be in error to think that way—and thus in a manner similar to the Pharisees ("by the leader of the demons he casts out demons"). Picking up on positions such as those which assert that God's Spirit infuses *all* spirits, or that *all* spirits are differentiated from God's Spirit by their limitedness and finitude, one could think that the Holy Spirit was something like a superior spirit, a spirit-structure that could not be outdone in terms of power and scope, one that put aside, removed, displaced, indeed annulled the other spirits. Blaspheming the Spirit would then consist in an absence of faith in such an ultimate, highest, perfect, insuperable force, and in the calling into question of such a force. Such totalizing conceptions and vague notions are familiar to us from religious and from philosophical positions of consciousness.[74]

Why is not such a conception of an ultimate, insuperable force and power either a chimera or—and here we follow the Pharisees' line of thinking—only a potentiation and hypostatization of forces and powers that come upon the human will? What speaks for qualifying as "good" and "divine" such a highest and most comprehensive power

---

73. Augustine, "Sermo 71: De verbis Evangelii Matthaei (XII 32)," *PL* 38, 449.

74. Cf. §§3.5 and 6.1.

over all the forces and powers that come upon the human will? Even suppose that such a highest force and power initially demonstrated itself to be something that did away with concrete instances of oppression and suffering. What would ensure that, seen over the long haul, this change of power did not lead from the frying pan into the fire, that indeed it did not drive out the demon with Beelzebul? After all, our life is full of experiences of ills being removed by greater ills. Our life is full of experiences of situations where what presents itself as the better solution, as new power or even as salvation, brings only an initially unseen deterioration, a greater captivity and oppression, more depressing consequences, and unforeseeable dangers. The breakdown of our optimism about progress, our skepticism concerning the promises that technologically unleashed environmental dangers and destruction can be taken care of technologically, our skepticism concerning the promises that the pauperization of the so-called Third World can be removed through a still more freely operating market economy, our skepticism concerning the promises that the crises of orientation of our cultures can be removed by providing more information—all these forms of disillusionment are ultimately to be traced back to such experiences. In today's promises to drive out demons and lying spirits, we frequently suspect that what are at work are only stronger demons and rulers of the lying spirits.

Jesus' critical engagement with the Pharisees does *not* call *this* skepticism into question. The sayings about blaspheming the Holy Spirit and about the impossibility of its being forgiven (Matt. 12:32; Mark 3:29; Luke 12:10) are not directed against suspicion toward religiously or otherwise introduced superior, "ultimate" structures and sources of power.

Neither some sort of action of power and might, nor some sort of event that apparently brings "total, unbeatable solutions to problems," but a multitude of concrete experiences of the removal of wrong, a multitude of diverse concrete experiences of liberation are indicative of the action of the Spirit. A multitude of experiences of help in concrete powerlessness, experiences of deliverance from entrapment with no escape point to the liberating Spirit of God. These various actions of liberation and deliverance are elicited and activated by a power and a person who claims nothing for self. Here no hero image, no success story, no power apparatus is to be institutionalized. The one who is

publicly silent and suffering, who will allow himself to be identified
definitively as the Crucified One, is the one who drives out demons:
"But if it is by the Spirit of God that *I* cast out demons, then God's rule
has come to you." The fact that the rule of God has come is characterized by the binding of the action of the Spirit to this concrete person
and by the evident selflessness of the Spirit, which helps others, delivers others, and sets others right. The manifest selflessness and the
manifest action of deliverance for the benefit of others condition the
impossibility of forgiving blasphemy against the Spirit.

Compared with the messianic prophecies,[75] now not only does the
bearer of the Spirit become concretely recognizable, but also through
him specific concrete, individually untransferable *experiences* of the effect of this Spirit-bearer and of the action of the Spirit are released. In
the progressive individuation that we perceive here, more is happening
than a change of religious, political, social, or—if we can understand
this word neutrally—ideological structures. Centering on the messianic Spirit-bearer, who shows himself to be a suffering righteous person who withdraws himself for the benefit of others, not only generates
a different religious, political, or social *climate*. What happens is not
only a *change of orientation* by means of, say, justice and righteousness
being established for the benefit of the afflicted and weak, judicial development being oriented on the mercy law, and pressure being exerted
to build the mercy ordinances into law.

Not only is the bearer of the Spirit himself now recognizable individually, the *experience of the effect of the Spirit* also immediately acquires varied, individual-concrete support. The action of the bearer of
the Spirit by the Spirit of God initially manifests itself in the *removal
of the concrete suffering of individual human beings.* Individual sick, suffering human beings palpably experience, in their own bodies, in insuperable concreteness and certainty, the action of this bearer of the
Spirit. They experience in their own bodies that their possession is
healed: in other words, that the power that is uncontrollably determin-
ing their will and hindering and destroying their individual and communal life is taken away. By Jesus' action and by the action of the
Spirit, these suffering, possessed persons become the persons on whom

---

75. Cf. esp. §3.1.

God shows God's glory.[76] In a bodily way, in the most extreme concreteness, these possessed persons experience God's acting upon them inasmuch as their lives are changed in an unimaginable way. Their fellow persons also experience through them the concrete, bodily action of the Spirit's presence. For on the one hand, the action of the Spirit becomes manifest to them in pluriform concreteness in their fellow creatures: that is, in a way that can be experienced in closest proximity. On the other hand, this action of the Spirit is not to be confused with human efforts to bring about recovery. However and wherever we identify the demonic in our present-day cultures, inasmuch as the action of the Spirit is directed at *demonic* forces, it intervenes in situations of the greatest helplessness, beyond all human attempts to bring help.

As we have seen, by "demonic action" we are to understand the massive impairment of the individual and thus also of the social living out of life—an impairment that harms both those who are directly affected and their fellow persons, that endangers and destroys them, but that can be turned away neither by those directly affected nor by their fellow persons. Demonic action brings about situations in which we see ourselves condemned to total helplessness, where patience is of no use and where time does not heal. Nicely worded attempts to soothe and encourage stick in our throats. Feelings of powerlessness, apathy, and outbreaks of anxiety and despair follow one after the other. Demonic powers bring about situations that in retrospect we call "hopeless" or "tragic," ones we are relieved to see succeeded by death, or ones we repress because it is unbearable to live in the presence of their horror and cruelty. Or it is a matter of situations of apparently "natural" life, situations of bondage and powerlessness to which we have with resignation accustomed ourselves: muteness, visual impairment, paralysis, and other physical and mental disabilities—forms of suffering that we also apply metaphorically to unhappy situations of understanding gone awry in the community.

---

76. It is noteworthy that Jesus' healings and exorcisms are expressly reported with regard to *all* the groups envisaged by the promises of the Spirit: men and women, old and young, free and slave, indeed even—as the texts attest with a certain hesitation—Jews and Gentiles!

The saying about the impossibility of forgiving blasphemy against God's Spirit is directed against those who disregard the undeniable experience of diverse deliverance out of distress from which there is, by human standards, no escape. It is directed against those who do not want to recognize the demonstration of God's power in God's selfless help to those who are suffering without prospect of deliverance. It is directed against those who take the last hope away from others and who obstruct their own access to a last hope. The saying about "blaspheming the Spirit" contemplates nothing less than the "impossible possibility" that people might go against the obvious experience of liberation and deliverance and might block, both for themselves and for others, the view of God's delivering power.[77] Inasmuch as Jesus demonstrates that the Pharisees' claim is obviously inconsistent, ineffectual, and self-contradictory, he calls attention to this "impossible possibility."

Blaspheming the Spirit becomes a problem precisely because through the action of the Spirit, the divine power enters *into human life, suffering, and experience.* Blaspheming the Spirit is unforgivable because it is in the Spirit's action under the conditions of human life that the divine glory shows itself. Nowhere do we experience the action of God's Spirit, the power of the present reign of God, more authentically than here, attuned to the relations of our individual and communal lives.

This means that we can and must perceive God's action and the presence of God's reign under the conditions of human finitude, and only under such conditions. It is an error to seek an unearthly, abstract, and in this sense "pure" knowledge of God. It is possible that human beings who have had the clear and concrete experience that God's Spirit liberates, nevertheless speak against the Spirit. Perhaps they do so because they are seeking a *pure* action of the Spirit that is

---

77. See Dunn, *Jesus and the Spirit,* 52: "If the critic had failed to recognize the source of Jesus' power and was criticizing only Jesus, *bar nasa,* his sin was forgivable. But if he was willfully ignoring the plain evidence of his eyes, that the power was God's Spirit, then he was putting himself in a position where forgiveness could not reach him." Hebrews 6:4ff. is also to be understood in the sense of this "impossible possibility." Cf. Heb. 2:2ff.; 10:29ff. For another treatment of this theme, see C. Gestrich, *Die Wiederkehr des Glanzes in der Welt: Die christliche Lehre von der Sünde und ihrer Vergebung in gegenwärtiger Verantwortung* (Tübingen: Mohr, 1989), 248ff., esp. 249.

not concrete, not performed on real people. Perhaps they do so because they are asking for an action of the Spirit that does not liberate, does not build up God's reign, does not gather, does not activate God's salutary will. For such people, this search leads nowhere. It is indeed impossible to help people who, after and in spite of the experience of the Spirit, seek and ask for a Spirit and an action of the Spirit that are not divine or not favorable to human beings.

Blaspheming the Spirit thus means not wanting to perceive and to take seriously the clear and concrete demonstrations of divine action under the conditions of earthly life—even though they have already been experienced.[78] It is immaterial whether this blasphemy occurs because human beings want to disregard God or because they want to leave concrete human life and suffering behind. Blaspheming the Spirit means disregarding God's already experienced intervention in the world of human beings. It means, *contrary to better experience*, not taking either God or oneself and suffering and liberated people seriously—and to do one is always to do the other.

4.5: Witness and Comforter—the Spirit of truth and of love

The promised Spirit of righteousness and of peace takes shape as the power that installs the messianic bearer of the Spirit. The Spirit thus acts as the power of deliverance out of countless concrete captivities and distresses as well as the power of the emergent and partly manifest, partly hidden gathering and building up of the people of God. In the judgment of Christian faith, this power of deliverance acquires and retains its clarity inasmuch as the Spirit of God is experienced, recognized, believed, and defined as the Spirit of Jesus Christ.[79] The power

---

78. Cf. E. Käsemann, "The Beginnings of Christian Theology," in *New Testament Questions of Today*, trans. W. J. Montague (Philadelphia: Fortress, 1969), 102–7; A. Schlatter, *Der Evangelist Matthäus: Seine Sprache, sein Ziel, seine Selbständigkeit*, 5th ed. (Stuttgart: Calwer, 1959), 408: "Here is not a case of grumbling against an absent god. Rather here divine action becomes manifest in human experience. 'Spirit' means the reception of divine action with its creative power into human life."

79. Perhaps no one has driven this home like Karl Barth.

of God's Spirit, the power that creatively brings righteousness and
makes peace, becomes recognizable from the perspective of Jesus' selflessness, from the perspective of his action of healing and liberating
concrete, suffering human beings, from the perspective of Christ's action and suffering: that is, from the perspective of his announcement
and establishment of the reign of God, from the perspective of his
death on the cross, and from the perspective of the lostness and deliverance of the world as they become manifest in this process.

The Holy Spirit is the Spirit of Jesus Christ—this statement can
admittedly degenerate into an indeterminately held correctness that
justifies diverse relations of domination and forms of structural violence. Without protection against false abstractions, the statement
could be misused religiously, politically, and morally, and has in fact
been so misused.[80] All sorts of theologies and forms of piety have made
their peace with a numinous and opaque "Spirit of Christ": nationalistic, chauvinistic, patriarchal, sexist, and racist, scornful of the old and
the sick, hostile to children, justifying and stabilizing exploitative and
unmerciful relations, and in all cases de facto hostile to the Spirit. In a
variety of ways the attempt has been made to dampen or to extinguish
the power of the Spirit by means of a "Lord Jesus" drawn either consciously or unconsciously along ideological lines.

In contrast, it must be made clear that the Spirit of Christ is a
power that:

- brings help in various forms of individually and communally experienced powerlessness, captivity, and entrapment;
- in total selflessness and without public means of power thus
  gathers people to the universal, emergent public of the reign of
  God;
- acts as the Spirit of deliverance from human distress and sin,
  and the Spirit of the restoration of both solidarity and the capacity for communal action;
- acts as the Spirit of preservation in the midst of ongoing affliction in the most varied contexts of life;

---

80. Embittered women in the United States have been attempting in recent
years to pillory this misuse as "Christofascism."

- transforms and renews people and orders, and opens people to God's creative action;
- makes it possible to recognize evil spirits and lying spirits;
- provides a concentration on God's presence in the midst of the impossibility of getting an overview of the world and of life.

In contrast to all abstract-theistic, metaphysical, mystical, or dialogico-personalistic theological "concentrations" and means of supplying orientation in name only, the Spirit of Christ acts as a power that:

- persistently works toward the universal establishment of justice, mercy, and knowledge of God in strict reciprocal interconnections;
- grants authority to the person who is publicly powerless, suffering, and despised;
- extends beyond imperialistic monocultures and the condition of being tied to a particular situation and time, and makes possible the prophetic community of experience and of testimony of women and men, old and young persons, ruling and oppressed persons;
- enlists the services of this finite and perishable community, and changes and renews it in order to make God's power of creation and of new creation manifest and effective through and for this community.[81]

The Spirit of Christ is not a power that centers in a reductionist and totalistic way on an "ultimate point of reference."[82] Rather the

---

81. Cf. §§4.1–4.4, 2.1–2.5, and 3.1–3.5.

82. G. D. Kaufman has with particular clarity developed a theology that understands God as the "ultimate point of reference, transcending every finite position and thus making it possible to judge and criticize them all" (*God the Problem* [Cambridge: Harvard Univ. Press, 1972], 34; cf. 33–34, 265ff.). See also G. D. Kaufman, *The Theological Imagination: Constructing the Concept of God* (Philadelphia: Westminster, 1981), 80ff., 103ff., 266ff., 274ff. He has run into great difficulties in trying to give a substantive grounding to this primarily negatively and defensively formulated religious principle (cf. *Theological Imagination*, 123ff.). Without such a

Spirit is recognized as the selflessly delivering power of the Crucified One, exercising an effect in the most diverse contexts of life, reshaping them, and making God's presence recognizable through them and from them. This "multipresence" of the Spirit, or alternatively the Spirit's diverse acts of making Christ present, are made clear by the New Testament traditions in a variety of ways. The most striking of these are no doubt the talk of the "pouring out of the Spirit" by Christ or by Christ's mediation,[83] and the talk of the "Paraclete." In both cases the concentrated presence of Christ's power is grasped in diverse structural patterns of life and experience. The language of the "pouring out" of the Spirit emphasizes more strongly the *power* granted by Christ, which is expressed in diverse but specific ways, and which serves the attestation to, and extension of, community with Christ. By comparison, talk of the Paraclete emphasizes that the power sent by Christ is the power of community with *Christ*, the power of *Christ's* presence, which at the same time enters into diverse structural patterns of life and experience.[84]

The Paraclete assumes the place of the "fleshly," physical-finite presence of Jesus in the world. In total selflessness the Paraclete represents Jesus, drawing attention to Jesus and to Jesus' words. The Paraclete is sent in Jesus' name by the Father (John 14:26; cf. 14:16) or by Jesus "from the Father" (John 15:26, cf. 16:7). The Paraclete will teach the disciples everything and will remind them of all that Jesus has said to them (John 14:26), "testify" on Jesus' behalf (John 15:26), and "not speak on [the Paraclete's] own" (John 16:13ff.). The Paraclete will glorify Jesus, because the Paraclete will take what is Jesus' and declare it to them (John 16:14; cf. 16:15).

---

grounding, Kaufman's religious interest in defending against religious imperialism and religious arbitrariness appears to be only an inconsequential variant of the criticized positions, which to be consistent would have to give way to agnostic relativism, but in so doing could not prevent forms of religious fundamentalism from relativizing it as mere religious skepticism.

83. See §5.1.

84. See L. Ragaz, "Der Paraklet," *Neue Wege* 39 (1945): 217ff. H. Schlier emphasizes that, according to John, the Spirit empowers "human beings to be bearers and givers of the Spirit" ("Zum Begriff des Geistes nach dem Johannesevangelium," in J. Blinzler et al., eds., *Neutestamentliche Aufsätze: Festschrift für Prof. Josef Schmid zum 70. Geburtstag* [Regensburg: F. Pustet, 1963], esp. 236–37).

Through the Paraclete, Jesus and Jesus' word are made present in *many* experiential contexts in an authentic and concentrated manner. Unlike the fleshly-earthly Jesus, this advocate—and through this advocate, Jesus—can be with the disciples "in eternity" (John 14:16-17).[85] If we bear in mind this differentiated structural pattern of Jesus' diverse yet authentic presence through the Spirit,[86] we will not be disturbed by the observation that with the Paraclete in John 14:16 "Jesus himself is also implicitly" meant, or that with the Paraclete in 1 John 2:1 the exalted Christ is meant.[87] Nor will we be disturbed by the ascertainment of diverse analogous statements about Jesus and "the Spirit" in the Johannine writings.[88] Through the Paraclete Jesus and Jesus' word become and "remain" present[89] in diverse structural patterns of life and experience—without giving up the concentration and authenticity of Jesus' palpable proximity. In this way Jesus' powerful, "heavenly" manner of existence[90] can be present in an earthly way. Through the Spirit Jesus is not, to be sure, "ubiquitous" in an indeterminate, indifferent way.[91] But through the Paraclete Jesus does indeed

---

85. F. Mussner makes an unconvincing attempt to differentiate between, on the one hand, the Spirit received by all believers and, on the other hand, a gift of the Spirit that provides the capacity to bear witness to Christ and that is reserved for "those who have the 'office' of witness" ("Die johanneischen Parakletsprüche und die apostolische Tradition," *Biblische Zeitschrift* 5 (1961): 67, 69.

86. R. Schnackenburg puts it nicely when he says that in the Paraclete "the *Christus incarnatus* becomes the *Christus praesens* for believers" ("Christologie des Neuen Testaments," in *MySal* 3/1, 348.

87. G. Klein, "Paraklet," *RGG* 5, 102. Klein rightly notes that the "controversy about the origin in the history of religions of the figure of the P[araclete] is to be overcome through the following insight. The ancient Jewish (Behm), the heterodox Jewish (Cross) and the Gnostic (Bultmann) domains are not mutually exclusive. Rather, in the P[araclete] characteristics of the Jewish 'advocate' figure, of the Messiah, of the Human One (Bornkamm), of the precursor-fulfiller pattern, and of the Mandaean 'helper' converge (Schultz)."

88. Cf. G. Bornkamm, "Der Paraklet im Johannesevangelium," in E. Wolf, ed., *Festschrift Rudolf Bultmann* (Stuttgart: Kohlhammer, 1949), 12ff.

89. See John 16:7: "It is to your advantage that I go away, for if I do not go away, the Paraclete will not come to you." John 14:12 is also to be understood in this connection. Cf. §5.2.

90. For an explanation of the "realism" of this manner of existence, see §3.3.

91. See the critical engagement with false, superficial metaphysical conceptions of totality in §3.5; further, see G. W. Locher, "Der Geist als Paraklet: Eine

simultaneously enter in full authenticity into environments that are far removed from each other, and foreign to each other, in time and space.[92] This experientially accessible presence of the Spirit both creates individual certainty *and* at same time can enable the presence of the Spirit to be expected and to be valid without restrictions in other structural patterns of life and experience, including those that are foreign and inaccessible.

The consciousness of this presence of the Spirit is extremely powerful.[93] This consciousness can understand and interact with the rational, empirical, ideological, and other forms of communication and of generalization of "the world," and at the same time go beyond these forms.[94] On the one hand, the "presence of the Spirit" signifies acceptance of the (mere) certainty and perspectival character bound up with the finitude and concreteness of life as it is really lived. It likewise signifies acceptance of the attendant need to become complete. People who receive the Spirit are enabled to bear *witness*; it is the Spirit who, through those human beings whose services have been enlisted, bears witness to Christ.[95] To bear witness means to place value on certainty and authenticity, but also on perspectival and fragmentary perception, and on a rendition in accord with such perception.[96] It is not the role of testimony to aim at a "total vision," a comprehensive theory, an intelligent "reconstruction" or something similar. To that extent it is powerful in its very limitation.

---

exegetisch-dogmatische Besinnung," *EvT* 26 (1966): 565ff.; as well as D. Bonhoeffer, *Christ the Center*, trans. J. Bowden (New York: Harper & Row, 1966), 45–46.

92. See the analogies in §5.1, but also already in 2.3 and even in 1.2. Concerning the tie-in with the messianic promises, see Bornkamm, "Paraklet," 18ff.

93. Cf. §§5.1 and 5.4.

94. See the statements in John 14:17, 19 about the inability of "the world" to receive the "Spirit of truth" and to perceive Jesus' "heavenly" presence. See also 1 Cor. 2:15: "Those who are spiritual discern all things, and they are themselves subject to no one else's scrutiny."

95. Cf. Acts 1:8; John 15:26. Cf. also R. E. Brown, "The Paraclete in the Fourth Gospel," *New Testament Studies* 13 (1966–1967): esp. 129ff.; C. Dietzfelbinger, "Paraklet und theologischer Anspruch im Johannesevangelium," *ZTK* 82 (1985): 400ff.

96. I owe to an unpublished lecture held in Tübingen by Hans-Georg Gadamer the recognition that the fragmentary quality of testimony is consciously willed and accepted. Cf. K. Barth, *CD* 1/2, 440ff.

On the other hand, the "presence of the Spirit" leads to a community of testimony that reveals a *truth* that is not simply a matter of a certainty or of a plurality of certainties. The "Spirit of truth" (John 14:17; 15:26; 16:23) will—precisely because this Spirit is also the "Spirit of testimony"—lead human beings "into all the truth" (John 16:13). The Spirit is the form of address and invocation that is appropriate to God, that corresponds to God in God's fullness and glory (cf. John 4:23-24). Precisely because this Spirit attests to the suffering and crucified righteous one who claims nothing for himself, precisely because the Spirit will not speak "on the Spirit's own,"[97] but is the Spirit of the community of testimonies,[98] the Spirit both can give people power and steadfastness in their testimony, relative as it is in every case, and can bring them in this community to clearer knowledge of the truth.[99] In the presence of the Spirit, existential steadfastness and openness to one's own completion in the knowledge of God as well as in the practice of righteousness and of love of one's neighbor are not mutually exclusive. Yet the generalization of the subjective and individual perspective, and the power that lies in this generalization, by no means adequately express the power of the *Spirit.*[100]

The Spirit also acts in structural patterns of life and experience that are still foreign and distant. The Spirit exercises an influence on them, and by acting in turn through their reactions wills to lead to a

---

97. See §6.1. See in this connection John 3:34 and G. T. Montague, S.M., *The Holy Spirit: Growth of a Biblical Tradition* (New York: Paulist Press, 1976), 343–44; also—in a christological perspective—Kraus, *Systematische Theologie,* 407ff.

98. This corresponds to the sensitivity to differences that is also important in other pneumatological contexts, and to an orientation to emergent processes. Against this background of a *differentiated* community of witnesses, statements such as Rom. 9:1 and 1 John 4:6 lose the appearance of being religious glorifications of subjective certainty and self-righteousness. Concerning the "inspired community," see also G. Johnston, *The Spirit-Paraclete in the Gospel of John,* SNTSMS 12 (Cambridge: Cambridge Univ. Press, 1970), 46ff.

99. Cf. the description in John 16:13 of proclamation by the Spirit and of this proclamation's openness to the future. Cf. also the reference in John 16:8ff. to the Spirit's "proving the world wrong."

100. See J. T. Beck's thoughts about the interconnection between the power of bearing witness and the power of bearing new life in *Vorlesungen über christliche Ethik,* vol. 1, *Die genetische Anlage des christlichen Lebens,* ed. J. Lindenmeyer (Gütersloh: Bertelsmann, 1882), 123ff.

fuller revelation and knowledge of truth. The certainty that this is the will and action of the Spirit also gives, on the one hand, steadfastness and trust in the face of and in the midst of foreign, even hostile life relations. This gift of this steadfastness—not just one or another form of appeasement or mollification—is accurately characterized as "comfort." The Spirit is the "Comforter" precisely because the Spirit not only gives me steadfastness in my current situation and in the face of the relative openness of the future, but also because the Spirit comes to give me strength in unfamiliar situations, and acts out of them for my benefit.[101] Trust in the Spirit in situations of public persecution is founded on this power of "comfort." Mark 13:11: "When they bring you to trial and hand you over, do not worry beforehand about what you are to say; but say whatever is given you at that time, for it is not you who speak, but the Holy Spirit" (cf. Matt. 10:20; Luke 12:12).

In the presence of the Spirit this steadfastness, this comfort is not only received in both familiar and foreign structural patterns of life. This steadfastness is also established for other people. The Spirit enables people to give strength and steadfastness to other people who are distant, foreign, even hostile, not only giving them some "free space," but allowing them to develop in the way that is best for them. By doing this the Spirit becomes manifest as the Spirit of love. Love furthers the powerful self-development of the beloved fellow person, and thus perceives the connected self-withdrawal not as a loss, but as a strengthening of the lover. In love the developmental possibilities of the beloved persons are "felt passionately as a claim that [they] find [themselves] in a friendly universe."[102] Those who are beloved are to develop beyond their own conceptions. Their surroundings are to be friendly and beneficial to them.[103] In the power of the Spirit this love, both experienced and given, experiences a powerful strengthening, because the fear of powerlessness and of the boundaries of one's own love and of others' love is taken away. The experience of comfort and

---

101. The Heidelberg Catechism (1563) expresses this well, particularly in the first question, although admittedly in a perspective that is primarily christological and only secondarily pneumatological (A. O. Mills and M. E. Osterhaven, trans., *The Heidelberg Catechism with Commentary* by André Péry [New York: Pilgrim Press, 1962], 17).

102. A. N. Whitehead, *Adventures in Ideas* (New York: Free Press, 1933), 289.

103. Cf. in more detail §5.3.

of steadfastness is due to a love that does not lie only in individual hearts and on individual shoulders. This love is "poured out" (cf. Rom. 5:5). It thus comes upon us out of an overwhelming number of life contexts, and from innumerable other structural patterns of life it strengthens the love given by us.

The Spirit of God thus generates a force field of love in which people strive so that all things might "work for good" for their "neighbors." In an international situation in which whole countries are politically and judicially neglected, in which the ideology of scarceness triumphs and in which the struggle to prevail economically is the order of the day, this "Comforter" may appear to be an illusion. Yet in truth the Spirit acts in such an international situation as the revealer of "judgment" on the powers that rule this world. From the perspective of structural patterns of life plunged into misery, the Spirit bears witness that *this* international situation has no staying power, no validity, that contrary to all self-righteousness of both the "pious" and the "impious," it is marked by unbelief, distance from Christ, and nothingness, and is dependent on the delivering power of the Spirit.[104]

---

104. Cf. John 16:8ff. In this way the church is led "under the cross" in constantly new ways. Concerning the interconnection between the accusation of the Paraclete and the trial of Jesus, see E. Bammel, "Jesus und der Paraklet in Johannes 16," in B. Lindars and S. S. Smalley, eds., *Christ and Spirit in the New Testament: Studies in Honour of C. F. D. Moule* (Cambridge: Cambridge Univ. Press, 1973), 211ff.; Dietzfelbinger, "Paraklet im Johannesevangelium," 392ff.; D. A. Carson, "The Function of the Paraclete in John 16:7-11," *JBL* 98 (1979): 547ff.

CHAPTER 5

The Pouring Out of the Spirit: Its Action of Liberation and of Overcoming the World

The powerful action of the Spirit, that which is characteristic of this "power by which God accomplishes the divine will,"[1] comes to expression through the "pouring out" of the Spirit. The pouring out of the Spirit means that the Spirit not only comes upon individual persons and groups of people in a surprising manner in order to become effective in and through them as well as to influence both their proximate and their distant environments. The Spirit also influences people by coming from both their proximate and their distant environments, inasmuch as the Spirit at the same time enlists the services of other people with them. The persons seized, moved, and renewed by God's Spirit can know themselves placed in a force field that is seized, moved, and renewed from many sides—a force field of which they are members and bearers, but which they cannot bear, shape, be responsible for, and enliven alone.

This force field wrought by the pouring out of the Spirit forms not a homogeneous unity, but a differentiated one. The force field and the unity of the Spirit can therefore appear to people as insignificant, as impossible to encompass in a single overview, or even as an illusion, but they are no less real than the church of Christ, which

---

1. In the words of E. Jüngel, "the holy Spirit is the power by which God accomplishes the divine will" ("Zur Lehre vom heiligen Geist," in U. Luz and H. Weder, eds., *Die Mitte des Neuen Testaments: Einheit und Vielfalt neutestamentlicher Theologie: Festschrift für Eduard Schweizer zum siebzigsten Geburtstag* [Göttingen: Vandenhoeck, 1983], 99). §6.1 in particular makes clear that this is not to be thought of as an assertion of *self* in the usual sense.

extends beyond particular cultures and epochs. On the contrary, the force field of the Spirit is also effective where, in general, a community of people that attests to God's action and, in particular, the church of Christ are still in the emergent process of becoming, not yet fully concretized and not yet clearly recognizable.

The power of God comes to expression in a variety of ways that often move people toward each other in a surprising manner, and thus causes the attestation and extension of God's people, of the unity of people with Christ, and of their deliverance from lostness, powerlessness, and dejection. It is this power of the Spirit that is articulated by talking about the pouring out of the Spirit. The talk of the pouring out of the Spirit articulates the influence that persons seized by the Spirit exercise in their own proper person on both their proximate and their distant environments, whether those persons are directly conscious of that influence or not. The talk of the pouring out of the Spirit also articulates the powers of influence caused by the Spirit, whether the people seized by the Spirit are conscious of them or not, that act and react on them from people in both their proximate and their distant environments. Thus the talk of the pouring out of the Spirit articulates the powers that are the real basis for the joy and the calmness, the trust, and the power of persistence of those persons who are seized by the Spirit and placed in the community of the Spirit.

The pouring out of the Spirit, the descent of the Spirit, or baptism with the Spirit is no once-and-for-all event. It did not occur only at Pentecost. The Acts of the Apostles alone reports several instances of the Spirit being poured out or several descents of the Spirit.[2] Of course the Pentecost event seems to give the determinative orientation for the recognition that in each case it is the *Spirit of God* that is poured out, that the baptism is carried out with the Spirit of God. What happened at Pentecost?

---

2. Acts 2:1ff.; 4:31; 8:15ff.; 10:44ff.; 11:15ff.; 15:8ff.; 19:2ff. See also Titus 3:6 as well as §§3.3 and 3.4. For a closer specification of the reception of the Spirit, see M. M. B. Turner, "The Significance of Receiving the Spirit in Luke-Acts: A Survey of Modern Scholarship," *Trinity Journal* 2 (1981): 131ff.

5.1: Pentecost miracle and baptism in the Spirit: A ruptured world begins to grow together

The Pentecost event is a "miracle of languages *and* of hearing."[3] It is the event of the essentially worldwide proclamation of "God's deeds of power," which is made possible by an unforeseeable universal understanding. The disintegration and dispersion of human beings, the Babylonian confusion of languages (Genesis 11), and the connected rupture of the world are removed. But in this removal cultural, national, and linguistic differences are not set aside, but retained. The entire, differentiated representative world of a given time in its differentiation not only is addressed, but also understands the proclamation of God's action of deliverance carried out on human beings. At great length and with the help of a quotation from the Joel promise of the universal pouring out of the Spirit, the account of the Pentecost event emphasizes that the representative world in its differentiation into many peoples, into Jews and Gentiles, into men and women, young and old, female and male slaves, is an active witness of this event.

The "frank" *proclamation*—an open and public proclamation, unafraid and borne by joyful confidence—of God's "deeds of power" is just as much the result of the pouring out of God's Spirit as is a new community of diverse persons and groups of people. The community of Jews and Gentiles touched by the pouring out of the Spirit is particularly emphasized—a community that evidently surprises and disturbs again and again.[4]

What is decisive in this story, what is "miraculous" about the Pentecost event, is not the fantastic and ominous characteristics of the Pentecost story—the "sound from heaven" and the divided tongues of fire[5]—nor the "speaking in tongues" that initially evokes only incomprehension. The miracle of the baptism in the Spirit lies not in what is difficult to understand or incomprehensible, but in a totally

---

3. R. Pesch, *Die Apostelgeschichte (Apg 1-12)*, EKKNT 5/1 (Einsiedeln: Benziger; Neukirchen-Vluyn: Neukirchener, 1986), 104.

4. Cf. Acts 10:45; 11:18; 15:8. See also 1 Cor. 12:13; Rom. 15:16.

5. On these audible and visible signs of the Spirit's descent, see Pesch, *Apostelgeschichte 1–12*, 103.

unexpected comprehensibility and in an unbelievable, universal capacity to understand and act of understanding:

> When the day of Pentecost had come, they were all together in one
> place. And suddenly from heaven there came a sound like the rush
> of a violent wind, and it filled the entire house where they were sit-
> ting. Divided tongues, as of fire, appeared among them, and a
> tongue rested on each of them. All of them were filled with the
> Holy Spirit and began to speak in other languages, as the Spirit
> gave them ability.
>
> Now there were devout Jews from every nation under heaven
> living in Jerusalem. And at this voice [this sound] the crowd gath-
> ered and was bewildered, because each one heard them speaking in
> the language of each. Amazed and astonished, they asked, "Are not
> all these who are speaking Galileans? And how is it that we hear,
> each of us, in our own native language? Parthians, Medes, Elamites,
> and residents of Mesopotamia, Judea and Cappadocia, Pontus and
> Asia, Phrygia and Pamphylia, Egypt and the parts of Libya belong-
> ing to Cyrene, and visitors from Rome, both Jews and proselytes,
> Cretans and Arabs—in our own languages we hear them speaking
> about God's deeds of power." All were amazed and perplexed, say-
> ing to one another, "What does this mean?" But others sneered and
> said, "They are filled with new wine."
>
> But Peter, standing with the eleven, raised his voice and ad-
> dressed them, "Men of Judea and all who live in Jerusalem, let this
> be known to you, and listen to what I say. Indeed, these are not
> drunk, as you suppose, for it is only nine o'clock in the morning.
> No, this is what was spoken through the prophet Joel:" [here the
> Joel promise is quoted].(Acts 2:1-16)[6]

It is extremely important to see that what is happening here is not
some indiscriminate event occurring "from heaven," as a consequence
of which people "speak in tongues" in an incomprehensible manner,
or at least in a manner that is in need of interpretation and translation, all of which causes their fellow persons to be astounded and dismayed and to engage in flippant mockery of them, and which Peter
finally explains by drawing on a biblical text. The people upon whom

---

6. Joel 3:1-5; cf. Chapter 3.4.

the Spirit has come, the people touched by the Pentecost event, do not speak in an incomprehensible manner. Instead they speak of God's deeds of power in a way that at most is to be called "overcomprehensible." This unbelievable comprehensibility is what deeply confuses and frightens those around them.[7]

Those who do not understand *each other*—Parthians, Medes, and Elamites—and those who live in Mesopotamia, Judea, Cappadocia, Pontus, and the province of Asia, Phrygia, and Pamphylia, Egypt, and the parts of Cyrene in Libya, and residents of Rome, Jews as well as proselytes, Cretans and Arabs—they all understand what is spoken and attested.[8] They all understand what is being said: they do not just catch some piece of it, connected with the impression that others also somehow would be catching the same thing. No, they understand the point of it all in the language in which they have grown up. Without dissolving the variety and complexity of their backgrounds, without setting aside their forms of expression and understanding as these forms are marked off in relation to other forms, an unbelievable commonality of

---

7. The Pentecost story describes not a case of glossolalia, but of "xenolalia," of speaking in foreign languages. Pesch argues that Luke has reinterpreted a case of glossolalia (Acts 2:4)—see §5.5 for a more detailed discussion—as a case of "xenolalia" (Acts 2:6, 8ff.) (*Apostelgeschichte 1–12*, 104–5, 107–8). I must admit that the text seems to offer no compelling support for Pesch's viewpoint. But even if Pesch were right, it should be remembered that the point of the story, developed in the greatest conceivable detail, is the prophetic testimony as well as the international capacity for, and act of, understanding. What is occurring here is not incomprehensible "speaking in tongues" in need of interpretation, but a speaking in universally comprehensible "tongues." Nor do the other accounts of the descent of the Spirit in the Acts of the Apostles give support worth mentioning to a thesis of reinterpretation. Either they do not even give a closer description of the consequences of the pouring out of the Spirit, or they highlight the act of proclamation. Even in the two cases in which glossolalia is named as a consequence of the pouring out of the Spirit, the accounts couple it with externally identifiable praise of God (Acts 10:46) or with prophetic speech (Acts 19:6). Cf. J. Roloff, *Die Apostelgeschichte*, NTD 5 (Göttingen: Vandenhoeck, 1981), 42–43. See also D. L. Tiede, "Acts 2:1-47," *Interpretation* 33 (1979): 65: "Efforts to limit the 'gift of the Spirit' to ecstatic experiences or to equate it with a particular manifestation are frustrated by the data of the text."

8. Pesch, *Apostelgeschichte 1–12*, 105: "The *list* 'represents' in an exemplary selection or a particular sequence . . . all peoples." Roloff emphasizes with greater precision that the list "illuminates the horizon of the Jewish world" (*Apostelgeschichte*, 42–43).

experience and of understanding occurs. And this *difference between the experience of plural inaccessibility to each other* and of *enduring foreignness*, and unfamiliarity, on the one hand, and of *utter commonality of the capacity to understand*, on the other hand—this is what is truly spectacular and shocking about the Pentecost event.[9]

To the "miracle of hearing" corresponds the "miracle of languages": namely, the experience that the Galileans speak not just to those who belong to their people and who share their language, that they make themselves understood not only within the boundaries of their culture and their language, but that they can attest to and proclaim God's deeds of power in a way that is nothing less than *universal*.

An astounding, indeed frightening clarity in the midst of the received complexity and variety, a dismaying familiarity in the midst of the received inaccessibility and unfamiliarity—this is what is miraculous and wonderful about the revelation at Pentecost. The Pentecost event connects intense experiences of individuality with a new experience of community—albeit an experience that is difficult to understand. These experiences of individuality do not correspond to those of modern ego consciousness. Instead one's own particularity is experienced in the midst of a consciously perceived polyindividuality and polyconcreteness, in the midst of a diversity which, while foreign to the individual human person, through the Pentecost event allows and makes possible commonality and common experience and knowledge. In the midst of this foreignness familiarity with self is preserved: the language of one's background is not removed, the fact that one belongs to a particular people and to a particular history is not called into question. The experience of community is likewise differentiated. Although no natural preconditions for successful understanding are present, the people who have been led together can hear clearly and in common what is being said about God's deeds of power. The stable typologies of understanding are retained, and in them, in the forms that establish commonality with specific people and difference—indeed,

---

9. W. H. Willimon rightly observes that this is a story "about the irruption of the Spirit into the community and the first fruit of the Spirit—the gift of proclamation" (*Acts, Interpretation: A Commentary for Teaching and Preaching* [Atlanta: John Knox, 1988], 30). It should be said, though, that the heterogeneity and universality of this community, emphasized by Luke in a twofold perspective, is essential.

impossibility of understanding with regard to other people—God's action is understood by all sides.

The experience of the power of the Spirit is reflected by that experience which shows itself in every good proclamation, on the basis of every good sermon. It is the experience of a power which enables persons of different background, education, interests, and expectations to pay attention and to understand, and which enables them to have shared experiences of commonality, including challenging experiences of commonality, that do not originate with themselves. These are not diffuse or external experiences, like those that might come from a homogeneous disturbance or from shared dismay. The connecting power is not strangeness, such as the strangeness of an instance of speaking in tongues that is in itself incomprehensible and in need of interpretation. The connecting power is not a power that "connects" only in a shared inability to understand. Instead the miracle of the Pentecost event is constituted by unexpected, universal, but not homogeneous clarity.

The Pentecost event includes the previously occurring forms of experiencing the Spirit. In addition it activates the promises of the pouring out of the Spirit, in particular Joel's promise of the Spirit. Going yet one step further, it surpasses the previously experienced effects of the Spirit and the previously awakened expectations of the Spirit. The Pentecost event gathers a community that becomes a bearer of, and a witness to, God's deeds of power. We have encountered this process of gathering—as an effect of God's Spirit—in diverse contexts. The Pentecost event gathers a differentiated community that includes various groups of people: a community in which unimpeded communication is not to be expected and mutual enrichment is not foreseeable, is no longer or not yet part of the picture. This much is also announced by the Old Testament promises of the "pouring out of the Spirit." But the Pentecost event not only touches people in situations that individuate them—such as sickness, possession, or the individually experienced captivity of sin. It also exerts an influence on an experience of objective powerlessness, of mutual foreignness, speechlessness, and inability to achieve understanding: the experience that every person is confined within her own background, language, and culture. The Pentecost event goes beyond the previous experiences and expectations of the action of the Spirit inasmuch as it not only effects a mutually enriching prophetic understanding between men and women, male and female slaves, old and young, but also, in the midst of the experienced impossibility of mutual understanding, gives rise to experiences of connectedness, of commonality, of totally unexpected familiarity.

The Pentecost event not only removes individual experiences of isolation and separation, as well as their social consequences, as in Jesus' healings and exorcisms.[10] It produces a powerful public in which there is the possibility and the reality of *diverse* experiences of the removal of isolation and of individual and collective separation coupled with the preservation of cultural, historical, and linguistic diversity. The universal public is not constituted by some sort of sensational event, a catastrophe, a festival, or a fireworks display, although the Pentecost event also exhibits traits of all of these. The powerful, public, and terrifying experience of the pouring out of the Spirit is mediated by a "sound like the rush of a violent wind" (Acts 2:2), which differentiates itself as speaking and understanding in many languages and then is called "this voice" (Acts 2:6). This demonstration of the public power of the Holy Spirit, mediated by those who, on the basis of the descent of the Spirit, speak in "other tongues," is what is spectacular about the Pentecost event. The concrete course of the event reported in Acts 2 cannot be repeated and directly adopted as one's own. Yet it can be understood, along with the promise present in it.[11]

In the center of this event stands an inconceivable shared understanding of "God's deeds of power," an understanding considered impossible. An understanding of talk about God's action, an understanding that is both individual and shared worldwide, becomes the foundation of the recognition of the Spirit's might. Through the *pouring out of the Spirit, God effects a world-encompassing, multilingual, polyindividual testimony to Godself.* In this way God attests to Godself in a process that unites people in a way that causes them both wonderment and fear.

In this way a force field is created with the pouring out of the Spirit. The people on whom the Spirit is poured out, who thus receive

---

10. Cf. §4.2.

11. Today we find formally analogous—and only formally analogous—processes in the worldwide relation, mediated by the mass media, to electronic entertainment music and to high-level competitive sports, both of which take on a "religious" quality for many people.

baptism in the Spirit, become members of this force field. They can
have a part as both givers and recipients in the universal community
created by the Spirit.[12]

This force field is insufficiently perceived when "baptism in the
Spirit" is supposed to be comprehended within a form of thought that
operates with only two sides (God and "the human person") and two
directions (from God to the human person, from the human person to
God). Karl Barth chose such an approach and depicted baptism in the
Spirit as the "first step" proceeding from God, through which "the human person" is "turned" toward God, to which "the human person"
can with gratitude "answer" in water baptism, and to which the person can give assent.[13] Barth's concentration on "the human person"
and on the person's "turning"[14] is certainly clear and readily encompassed in a single overview. But it is a false abstraction grounded in the
dialogistic approach of Barth's theology. This intellectual model comes
across as "totally concrete and plausible" only in a superficial way, for
a specific time and culture. Its reductionism and power of distortion
become clear precisely with regard to baptism in the Spirit. In this pattern baptism in the Spirit is reduced to the renewal and repentance of
"the human person."[15] According to the biblical testimonies, the universal and public power that lies in the pouring out of the Spirit, which

---

12. For emphasis on the effective and perceivable power, cf. Acts 1:8; 8:17ff.
Cf. also 1 Thess. 1:5-6; 1 Cor. 2:4; Rom. 15:19 and passim.

13. K. Barth, CD 4/4, 3ff., 41ff.

14. "Our gaze must be focused upon it." Cf. Barth, CD 4/4, 6; for the language
of "turning," cf. ibid., 6ff. (Instead of *turning*, the English translation of CD renders
the noun *Wendung* with *change*. But it translates verbal forms of the same root with
turn, thus obscuring the connection between the two. Precisely this connection is
important for Barth's argument—TRANS.) G. Haufe shows that "the correlation between baptism and the Holy Spirit is not always of one kind in early Christian texts,
but rather is carried out in different forms" ("Taufe und Heiliger Geist im Urchris-
tentum," *TLZ* 101 [1976]: 565, 561ff.). J. D. G. Dunn observes a confession-relative
"correlation" (*Baptism in the Holy Spirit: A Re-examination of the New Testament
Teaching on the Gift of the Spirit in Relation to Pentecostalism Today*, Studies in Biblical
Theology, 2d ser., 15 [Napierville, Ill.: Alec R. Allenson, 1970], esp. 224ff.

15. This point was first called to my attention by LaDonna France Huizinga.
For a consciously ecclesiological perspective on baptism in the Spirit, see, e.g.,
K. McDonnell, "The Holy Spirit and Christian Initiation," in K. McDonnell, ed.,
The Holy Spirit and Power: the Catholic Charismatic Renewal (New York: Doubleday,

in baptism in the Spirit is granted and appropriated to human beings, cannot be comprehended in an essential and structure-giving manner within the framework of this theological model.

Barth of course *means* with his talk of "the human person" both the individual and "the human person in general." Yet in the form he has chosen, he cannot in a basic way give expression to the indispensable internal differentiations of the "collective person" or of the species "human being." This leads to one of two possibilities. Either the differentiated power of the pouring out of the Spirit is reduced to God's primacy over "the human person," where this primacy is defined only in terms of space and time (God acts "first" and "from above"). Or that power is highlighted only in passing, without exercising an influence on the approach taken by theological reflection or on the experiential forms of faith.[16]

By contrast, it is important to recognize that with baptism in the Spirit the fullness of the Spirit's action—accessible and comprehensible to the human person in only a limited way, perhaps even totally inaccessible and incomprehensible to her, but nevertheless persistently benefiting her—is really present and effective.[17] This fullness of salvation is not something diffuse and numinous that remains otherworldly

---

1975), 57ff.; as well as H. Berkhof, *The Doctrine of the Holy Spirit* (Richmond: John Knox, 1964), 22–29.

16. Cf. Barth, *CD* 4/4, 24–25. There, on the one hand, the demonstrations of power in the resurrection and in baptism in the Spirit are not clearly differentiated and related to each other. On the other hand, the uncertainty of the argument is unmistakable ("In this light one may see how it can come about that . . ."). Cf. the explicitly individualistic articulation of the "work of the Holy Spirit" (ibid., 27 and passim).

17. With Dietrich Bonhoeffer and picking up on Martin Luther, this can be described by saying that it is "the office of the Holy Spirit" to bring Christ to individual persons (Cf. Eph. 3:17; 1 Cor. 12:3) and thus to build up the community (D. Bonhoeffer, *The Cost of Discipleship*, rev. ed., trans. R. Fuller and I. Booth [New York: Macmillan, 1963], 272–74). This same state of affairs is expressed in a christocentric perspective (cf. §4.5) by saying that Christ baptizes with the Holy Spirit (cf. Mark 1:8; Matt. 3:11; Luke 3:16). John articulates the strict interconnection between the multipresence of Jesus Christ *in the Spirit* and the authentic presence of *Jesus Christ* in the action of the Spirit in the following way. On the one hand, John expressly emphasizes that the gift and the reception of the Spirit occur only *after* the "glorification" of Jesus (John 7:39). On the other hand, John depicts the gift of the Spirit as the "breathing" of the resurrected Christ (John 20:22).

or can only be incorporated into indeterminate, mystical "experience." Instead it is mediated in and through the community of testimony of people who have been "washed . . . sanctified . . . justified" by the name of Jesus Christ and the Spirit of God.[18]

The constitution of this universal community, which extends be-yond specific times, cultures, and world situations, and of the real force field in which this community stands and which it embodies, is not the work of individual persons. Nor is it simply the fruit of shared efforts and arrangements. This community and this force field are es-tablished out of the fullness of realities, worlds, and times, and that means out of the "heavenly" domain.[19] People are also drawn into this community and this force field independently of their knowledge of the Spirit (cf. Acts 19:2), independently of their works (see Titus 3:5), but also in and with their readiness to let themselves be filled by the Spirit (cf., e.g., Eph. 5:18). Although the constitution of this commu-nity and of this force field is not something that human beings can make happen, it is clearly recognizable and identifiable. It is bound up with universal understanding concerning "God's deeds of power." For its part, this understanding is concentrated on the proclamation of the Crucified and Resurrected One, on the reception of the Spirit poured out by this messianic bearer of the Spirit, and on the proclamation of the gospel of God's deliverance of human beings.[20]

Various forms of expression and of understanding can precede or accompany the concrete perception, experience, and making present of this community and of the force field that bears and embodies it.[21] On the basis of the particular constitution of this force field, each per-ception, experience, and making present of the Spirit and of the Spirit's action remains conscious that it is unable to exhaust the full-ness of the Spirit. It remains conscious of having received only a

---

18. 1 Corinthians 6:11; cf. Titus 3:3-7; Heb. 10:21-25.

19. See the various perspectives of Acts 2:33; Heb. 6:4; 1 Pet. 1:12.

20. Cf., e.g., 2 Cor. 11:4. G. Sauter accurately notes that "the work of the Holy Spirit . . . has the goal of bringing God's reality to bear in our time, thus of *glorifying God in our time*" ("Zur Theologie des Heiligen Geistes im Blick auf die Pfingstpredigt," in *In der Freiheit des Geistes: Theologische Studien* (Göttingen: Vandenhoeck, 1988), 105, cf. 106ff.

21. The Acts of the Apostles alone names prayer, petition for the Spirit, preaching, hearing of the word, laying on of hands, and water baptism. Cf., e.g., Acts 2:28; 4:31; 8:15; 10:44; 11:15; 19:6.

"share," indeed a "first installment" of and by the Spirit who makes the fullness of salvation really present under earthly conditions.[22] This is not to say that what is at issue here is a fragmentary gift of the Spirit or a merely "subjective" appropriation. In the force field of the pouring out of the Spirit, the Spirit is validly experienced.

Nevertheless, the fullness of the Spirit and the fullness of the Spirit's real, powerful effect cannot be exhaustively perceived, experienced, and mediated by the finite world and the finite beings on which the Spirit acts. But what prohibits the action of the Spirit from being perceived—or caricatured—in an exclusively reductionist and distorting manner, or as a dismaying event?

God is at work on this ruptured world, on this world that is suffering under the power of self-endangerment, self-destruction, and sin, under the power of demonic forces and powers, under the illusion of being distant from God and abandoned by God. How are God's action and God's presence through the Spirit experienced and mediated in such a way that God's action in this ruptured world becomes clearly recognizable and can have a liberating effect?

5.2: Faith and hope as public force fields: God and life in God's presence become known

According to the testimony of the biblical traditions, the fact that the force field[23] of the Spirit possesses "heavenly" complexity and is not at the disposal of human beings excludes neither individuals being certain

---

22. Cf. 2 Cor. 1:22; 5:5; Eph. 1:14-15; Heb. 6:4; Berkhof, *Doctrine of the Holy Spirit*, 105–7.

23. On the previous use of the field concept in the doctrine of God, theology of law and pneumatology, see O. A. Dilschneider, *Geist als Vollender des Glaubens* (Gütersloh: Mohn, 1978), 65; M. Welker, "Security of Expectations: Reformulating the Theology of Law and Gospel," trans. J. Hoffmeyer, *Journal of Religion* 66 (1986): esp. 245ff.; M. Welker, "The Holy Spirit," trans. J. Hoffmeyer, *Theology Today* 46 (1989): 17ff.; W. Pannenberg, *Systematic Theology*, vol. 1, trans. G. W. Bromiley (Grand Rapids: Eerdmans, 1991), 382–84; I. U. Dalferth, *Kombinatorische Theologie: Probleme theologischer Rationalität*, QD 130 (Freiburg: Herder, 1991), 132ff. The following discussion will demonstrate the material and theological necessity of using the model of a field whose elements are themselves fields. Only in this way can the relation between the Spirit and faith be defined in a way that is materially convincing and that is in accord with the complexity of the biblical traditions.

of the action of the Spirit, nor this action becoming recognizable in a publicly powerful manner.[24] The Spirit effects and makes use of particular forms of understanding so that people in finite structural patterns of life and experience can relate themselves to the fullness of this power of the Spirit and can attest to its real presence and action. The New Testament traditions particularly highlight "faith, hope, and love" as such forms of understanding (often misleadingly designated "cardinal virtues"). In these forms the force field of the Spirit concretizes itself in such a way that human memories and expectations, human contacts and human understanding, human attentiveness and human self-withdrawal become possible *in the Spirit*. Through such "gifts" or "gifts of grace" or charisms, God's Spirit gives human beings a share in the Spirit[25] in such a way that they become members and bearers of this force field. The gifts of grace, the charisms, are elements of the force field of the Spirit, and at the same time they themselves constitute force fields, through which the action of the Spirit is realized and spread in the finite and shared life of human beings.[26]

---

24. Cf., e.g., 1 Thess. 1:5-6; 1 Cor. 2:4, 13; Rom. 15:19; as well as 1 Cor. 7:40; Rom. 9:1.

25. Thus God's Spirit also gives them a share in the power of Jesus Christ (cf. esp. §§4.5 and 5.1) and in the power of the Creator (see esp. §§2.5 and 3.5, as well as the reference in John 3:5-6 to Genesis 1). The connections with a theology of the Trinity are not yet developed in this book. They are only considered as the subject comes up from time to time "from below," from the perspective of attested *experiences* of the Spirit. An adequate exposition of the interconnection between pneumatology and the doctrine of the Trinity requires the development of new forms of thought on the basis of the contents of faith. Here nothing more than an initial step in that direction is proposed. Neither the dialogistic versions of the doctrine of the Trinity nor a vague "social" mutualism are in a position to give an adequate exposition of this interconnection.

26. Elements of a force field that themselves constitute force fields can be compared to a system differentiated into subsystems, a structure composed of structures, or—more graphically—a complexly structured network whose component parts themselves form nets. A theology that does not wish to remain below the level of the biblical traditions' great powers of conception will have to learn again to work with such forms. This does not exclude efforts to popularize such forms and to render them plausible; on the contrary. On the following discussion, cf. B. Spörlein, "Das Charisma im Neuen Testament," in A. Resch, ed., *Mystik* (Innsbruck: Resch, 1975), 175ff.

The charisms are substantively grounded forms in which the Spirit becomes knowable and effects knowledge, forms in which "the manifestation of the Spirit" is given to specific people "for the common good" (1 Cor. 12:7): in other words, in order to benefit others, which then has beneficial repercussions for themselves. Through the charisms—which nowhere are listed completely, but are characterized in their intentions in lists that in part agree with each other and in part diverge from each other (cf. Romans 12, 1 Corinthians 12, but also Isa. 11:2ff.)—force fields are built up; force fields can emerge in which differently endowed people can attest to and open up the reality of the Spirit for each other and with each other.

Individual persons with their particular endowments are thus enlisted to serve. They enter into force fields and help to constitute them: fields that in turn are elements of the force field of the Spirit. The one Spirit, the one Christ, the one God makes use of diverse gifts of grace, diverse deeds and services (cf. 1 Cor. 12:4-6) and of their interplay in order to reveal and to attest to God's presence. These gifts and deeds are given to individual persons in order for them to mediate to each other God's revelation and attestation. To be sure, the Spirit enlists the services of individual persons, and in the understanding caused by the Spirit effects personal certainty. Yet the charisms are not private gifts, let alone gifts for private consumption. They all serve inclusion and participation in the knowledge of God mediated by the Spirit. This knowledge unfolds as the knowledge of the divine Creator, the delivering Christ, and the liberating and enlivening Spirit. It works toward the glorification of the God who acts on human beings in this differentiated structural pattern.

Through the action of the Spirit, God and life in God's presence become known in a differentiated way. Knowledge of God and of the reality intended by God are made accessible.

In 1 Cor. 12:8-9 the charisms of "the utterance of wisdom," "the utterance of knowledge," and faith are named before the power of rectifying creaturely life in a physical-palpable way by "healing." But healing the sick and the "working of miracles" that are not more closely defined are also put forward as powers (1 Cor. 12:9-10) that attest to the Spirit and to the Spirit's action through human beings and under creaturely conditions. These charisms are followed in the list by "prophecy," "the discernment of spirits," "various kinds of tongues," and "the interpretation of tongues" (v. 10).[27] On the one hand, Paul seems to have in mind certain hierarchies of the gifts of the Spirit (see, for example, 1 Cor. 12:31; 14:1). On the other hand, he explains in detail that *all* gifts serve and should serve diverse, reciprocal knowledge of the *body of Christ*, which is composed of many different members (cf. 1 Cor. 12:12ff., Rom. 12:5-6, 10, 16; Eph. 4:2ff.) All the gifts remain dependent on each other. Paul warns against constructing hierarchies, which leads to divisions. He insists that precisely the members who seem to be weaker are indispensable. He insists that all members together form a community of suffering and of joy, from which they could not disengage themselves without loss of their identity. He insists that God has given greater honor to those members who find themselves disadvantaged, in order to maintain the consciousness of their significance.[28]

The Spirit is a force field that constitutes public force fields. In turn, people can enter these fields or be drawn into them as bearers and as borne, as constituting and as constituted. Here we have before us a structure that has the capacity to remove numerous so-called riddles that have confronted theological understanding.

First, it becomes undeniably clear that the charisms—for example, faith—are not simply individual postures and attitudes, but forms of participation and of inclusion in public powers. The fact that faith can be publicly known and perceived, as Paul indeed emphasizes in almost every one of his letters (cf. 1 Thess. 1:8; 2 Thess. 1:3-4; Rom. 1:8 and passim), and the fact that faith has "come" with Christ (Gal. 3:24-25), forbid every form of essentially individualizing, privatizing, and irrationalizing faith.[29] This is not to say that faith always and everywhere becomes recognizable as a matter of necessity. A person or a group of people can be "standing in faith" and in the process be

---

27. See H. Thielicke, *The Evangelical Faith*, vol. 3, *Theology of the Spirit: The Third Article of the Creed: The Manifestation of the Holy Spirit in the Word, the Church, the Religions, and the Last Things*, trans. and ed. G. W. Bromiley (Grand Rapids: Eerdmans, 1982), 73ff.

28. The systematic undergirding of this is the interconnection of justice and mercy in the interest of a living community in righteousness. For discussion, see §§3.1 and 5.3.

29. Cf. Jüngel, "Zur Lehre vom heiligen Geist," 110, 112ff. See esp. the nicely formulated thesis: "The God who comes to the world brings faith along" (110).

carried by the faith of others or strengthen other people in faith, without being able at the moment to consciously appropriate this. The use of *sown seed* in 1 Cor. 9:11 as an image for spiritual gifts (*pneumatika*) is illuminating. But those who believe can also know that they are in a domain of resonance, extending beyond particular times and cultures, even when they experience the gifts of the Spirit and the influence of these gifts as seemingly insignificant, or even as regionally hidden and unrecognizable. This domain of resonance also carries them when they themselves find no *direct* resonance, when they personally encounter absolutely no understanding of, assent to, or agreement with "their faith." The power of the Spirit extends further than particular instances of concrete individual and communal structural patterns of understanding and communication. This is not to deny, though, that the "gift of the Spirit"[30] expresses itself in the communicative gifts of grace and is perceived, experienced, and mediated in them.

The Spirit becomes manifest as "gift" in the spiritual gifts that the Spirit bestows. In the gifts of grace the Spirit becomes recognizable through the process of human beings receiving a share in the Spirit. Of course these gifts of grace are not emptily operating forms of communication, but themselves point to Christ, Christ's proclamation and Christ's action: they draw people into the community of Christ, and thus bring God closer to human beings and human beings closer to God.[31] The Spirit is received through the "message of faith,"[32] although the Spirit is the power of God that creates faith.[33] This only appears "paradoxical" and incomprehensible if we start from a basis of abstract, one-to-one relations of "Spirit and faith," and if we repeat

---

30. Cf., e.g., Acts 2:38; 10:45.

31. For a detailed discussion, see esp. §§6.2ff., but also 3.5 as well as H. Dörries' illuminating treatment, picking up on the work of Basil, of the strict connection between faith, baptism, and doxology (*De Spiritu sancto: Der Beitrag des Basilius zum Abschluss des trinitarischen Dogmas*, Abhandlungen der Akademie der Wissenschaften in Göttingen: Philologisch-Historische Klasse 39 [Göttingen: Vandenhoeck, 1956], esp. 133ff., 177ff.).

32. Cf. Gal. 3:2, 5, 14; the list in 2 Cor. 6:4ff.; as well as Eph. 1:3.

33. Cf. 2 Cor. 4:13, and more specifically the Augsburg Confession, art. 5 in T. G. Tappert, ed. and trans., *The Book of Concord: The Confessions of the Evangelical Lutheran Church* (Philadelphia: Fortress, 1959), 31.

again and again the old familiar question of who—under these conditions—brings and effects whom.

As soon as we see that the Spirit becomes recognizable in the gifts of the Spirit and thus in force fields that allow people to participate in and to impart the Spirit, the relation of theological priority between Spirit and faith becomes clear, although the Spirit is received and accepted in faith.[34] It also becomes comprehensible that the "Spirit of faith" presses faith to engage in proclamation[35] in order to demonstrate and confirm faith as a force field, to activate it as an element in the field of the Spirit, and to fill this overarching field. Further, it becomes comprehensible that testimony and proclamation can never be privately shaped, individually attempted undertakings risked at one's own initiative. And it becomes comprehensible why this is the case. The established forms of proclamation, which often appear offensive to many people precisely in individualistically decomposed cultures, have their basis in the fact that proclamation cannot step out of the force fields generated by the Spirit: "no prophecy ever came by human will, but men and women moved by the Holy Spirit spoke from God" (2 Pet. 1:21).

This "being moved" by the Spirit is not, however, blind and scornful of human beings, but on the one hand aims at strengthening people whose services have been enlisted, even when for themselves this does not become clear and capable of being experienced—and definitely does not become so on a steady basis.[36] On the other hand, this "being moved" by the Spirit aims at universal communication and commonality of the knowledge of faith (corresponding to Pentecost's pouring out of the Spirit), at a steady increase in the knowledge of God and of

---

34. See also the reference to the pouring out of God's love through the Spirit (Rom. 5:5), or to the increase in hope by the power of the Spirit (Rom. 15:13). Cf. 2 Tim. 1:7, 13-14.

35. 2 Cor. 4:13; cf. 1 Cor. 14:1. See also the references in Acts 6:5; 11:24 to people being full "of faith and the Holy Spirit" or "of the Holy Spirit and of faith."

36. Cf., e.g., Eph. 3:16, as well as 2 Tim. 1:7. In confession and in the search for knowledge, faith contends against this lack of clarity. Faith thus strives for both subjective and objective acknowledgment. For a detailed treatment of this differentiation, see M. Plathow, *Heiliger Geist, Hoffnung der Schwachen* (Hannover: Lutherhaus, 1985), 58ff.

God's action,[37] and at commonality and endurance in temptation by unbelief, both one's own and others'.[38]

Like the other force fields generated by the Spirit, the public force field of faith is not a closed system. It also does not have an absolute place in a fixed hierarchy of gifts of grace. The charisms of the mediation of knowledge, of faith, and of prophetic speech that are highlighted in 1 Corinthians 12 are (along with mercy and martyrdom) relativized in 1 Corinthians 13 in comparison with the gift of love.[39] Somewhat less clearly, in this connection a privileged position is awarded to hope in comparison with the still imperfect knowledge of faith, or at any rate in the condition of being oriented to the path from faith to eschatological sight.[40] Hope, too, is a force field that at the same time is an element of the force field of the Spirit.[41]

Hope is a form of experience and of understanding. It is the form in which faith is related to the experience of the world that is still apparently unredeemed. For its part, hope grows out of experiences of patience and of proof in affliction (Rom. 5:3ff.), as well as out of experiences of love given and received in a loveless world marked by the law of struggle for one's own survival. Although hope is "sown" by concrete human beings and is strengthened by concrete experiences of their standing the test, it is not merely the result of these experiences. It is a universal force field, directed toward the experience of God's glory and the universal demonstration of God's righteousness (cf. Rom. 5:2-3). It is a force field of which human beings can even "boast." This force

---

37. Cf. Col. 1:9 and the more detailed discussion in §5.3.

38. In this connection a semantics of battle is sometimes chosen that is definitely not to be understood in a militaristic manner, but has been misused again and again in this way in the history of the church. See Philem. 1:27 or—perhaps picking up on Isa. 11:4b and 49:2—Eph. 6:17.

39. Love can be understood and characterized as a "fruit of the Spirit" and thus not as a form of communication, but as a condition of the psyche and a community condition. Cf. §5.3.

40. See 1 Cor. 13:9-10, 12-13. See also J. Moltmann, *Theology of Hope: On the Ground and the Implications of a Christian Eschatology*, trans. J. W. Leitch (London: SCM Press, 1967), 19ff.

41. Cf. Rom. 15:13; Eph. 4:4; as well as Rom. 5:5; Gal. 5:5. See M. Welker, "Hoffnung und Hoffen auf Gott," in H. Deuser et al., eds., *Gottes Zukunft—Zukunft der Welt: Festschrift für Jürgen Moltmann zum 60. Geburtstag* (Munich: Kaiser, 1986), 23ff.

field increases in intensity and spreads by the experience of "joy and peace" in faith (Rom. 15:13). Joy and peace, these "fruits of the Spirit," thus give nourishment to hope. But the force field of hope is—like faith as well—not continually dependent on our individually confirming and being confirmed by our own concrete experiences of joy and peace. By their "God of hope," people are filled with joy and peace. God, who is love, pours out love "into our hearts through the Holy Spirit" (Rom. 5:5). Even in experiences of lovelessness and hopelessness, even when frightened by their own lovelessness and the hopelessness they themselves have spread, people can and should know that the Spirit wills to make them bearers and members of the universal community of hope and of love, to renew the perishing world for them and through them.

With great theological sensitivity, the reformers comprehended the interconnection between, on the one hand, a concrete, individual knowledge of being affected by the Holy Spirit and, on the other hand, an action of the Holy Spirit aimed at worldwide gathering and renewal. Martin Luther puts it this way in his explanation of the third article in the Small Catechism:

> I believe that by my own reason or strength I cannot believe in Jesus Christ, my Lord, or come to him. But the Holy Spirit has called *me* through the Gospel, enlightened me with his gifts, and sanctified and preserved me in true faith, *just as* he calls, gathers, enlightens, and sanctifies *the whole Christian church on earth* and preserves it in union with Jesus Christ in the one true faith. *In this Christian church* he daily and abundantly forgives *all my sins, and the sins of all believers,* and on the last day he will raise *me and all the dead* and will grant eternal life *to me and to all who believe* in Christ. This is most certainly true.[42]

Me, as well as the whole Christian church; all my sins, and the sins of all believers; me and all who believe; me and all the dead—this emphatic differentiation articulates precisely the public that we have observed, the public effected by the Spirit. It is the public that in Jesus' action grows in secret and manifests the coming reign of God. It is the public that at Pentecost breaks forth in power in a terrifying and

---

42. M. Luther, *The Small Catechism*, in Tappert, *Book of Concord*, 345, emphasis added.

confusing manner—acting upon me as upon "the whole Christian church." It is extremely important to note that the action of the Spirit is to be understood neither pluralistically in the sense of a dissociating pluralism nor individualistically in the sense of an abstractly unifying individualism.[43] Both misunderstandings not only obscure the action of the Spirit—they are nothing less than corrosive of it. The action of God's Spirit constitutes me not as the abstract ego, the abstract individual, as consciousness, or self-consciousness "in general," in which I am totally the same as all other egos, individuals, consciousnesses and self-consciousnesses. The action of the Spirit does not simply make us uniform egos before God, pure individuals, naked self-consciousnesses or some other instances of inner life.[44] The action of the Spirit touches me as a concrete individual, which is to say, as a human being with a specific background and language, from a specific country, a specific culture and landscape, and a specific natural and spiritual climate, with specific experiences and expectations, cares and notions of happiness, compunctions and experiences of success, perhaps at the moment calm, responsive, and open to the world, alert and healthy, or perhaps at the moment sick, tormented, closed, distrustful, out of synch with myself and with the world. The action of the Spirit touches me in the unique and irrepeatable concretization of this "here and now." At the same time, though, the action of the Spirit is bound in a diversely differentiated way into specific shared forms of life and experience. At the same time the action of the Spirit affects me *as well as all believers*, as well as the whole Christian church, as well as the whole community that streams together at Pentecost. It affects me as a member, as an element, as a representative and bearer of this community, but also as someone borne by this community.

This connection to which the reformers call attention, this connection between concrete, unique individuality and ecumenical universality, founders in an individualism structured around abstract unity as well as in unqualified, dissociative pluralism.[45]

---

43. Cf. §1.4.

44. Cf. F. Gogarten's magnum opus *Die Verkündigung Jesu Christi: Grundlagen und Aufgabe* (Tübingen: Mohr, 1948), esp. 405ff.

45. In spite of the individualistic edge he gives to his exposition, this is recognized by E. Herms, *Luthers Auslegung des Dritten Artikels* (Tübingen: Mohr, 1987), esp 15ff., 39ff.

By contrast, it is the Holy Spirit—as is also emphasized by the Heidelberg Catechism—who brings about the trust that binds together *me and the whole church of Christ:* ". . . that, *not only to others, but to me also* God has given the forgiveness of sins, everlasting righteousness and salvation, out of sheer grace solely for the sake of Christ's saving work."[46]

The Holy Spirit is given "to me also," "not only to others."[47] The object and fruit of the action of Jesus' "Spirit and word" is the "congregation chosen" "from among the whole human race," which "from the beginning to the end of the world" is gathered, protected, and preserved "in the unity of the true faith." In this chosen community *I, too,* am present, because due to the action of the Spirit "I am and forever will remain a living member of it."[48]

In the force field of the Spirit, concrete individuality and world-overarching universality are held together. This holds true not only for faith and hope, but also for the other gifts and powers of the Spirit.

5.3: Love and peace: God's righteous and merciful will can be fulfilled

The Spirit of God is not only a power that existentially affects human beings, bringing them into a universal community. The Spirit effects not only forms of the experience of God and forms of the exchange of experiences. The Spirit effects not only powers that make it possible for human beings to strengthen each other in body and soul. The Spirit also effects *conditions* of the psyche and the community, conditions that Paul calls the "fruit of the Spirit." Galatians 5:22-23 enumerates these conditions of the psyche and the community: "love, joy, peace, patience, kindness, generosity, faithfulness, gentleness, and self-control."

Paul thus names more or less complex and far-reaching conditions that are defined by *free self-withdrawal and self-giving for the benefit of*

---

46. A. O. Mills and M. E. Osterhaven, trans., *The Heidelberg Catechism with Commentary* by André Péry (New York: Pilgrim Press, 1962), 53, answer to question 21; emphasis added.

47. Cf. ibid., 95, answer to question 53.

48. Ibid., 97, answer to question 54. See also J. Calvin, *Christliche Unterweisung: Der Genfer Katechismus von 1537* (Gütersloh: Mohn, 1978), 45.

other creatures, whether given in a liberating manner or received in a liberating manner.[49]

Free self-withdrawal for the benefit of others gives fellow creatures open space and possibilities of development that surprise and delight them. It does not pin them down, does not make claims on them, but gives them space for their own development. This free self-withdrawal can express itself in strained relations as patience and gentleness. In the act of taking an interest in other people, it can unfold as kindness and generosity. But free self-withdrawal for the benefit of fellow creatures finds its most complete expression in love.

Love rejoices in the free self-development of the beloved fellow persons. Love works toward the goal that all things might work together for good for these persons.[50] For the person who loves, the free self-withdrawal that characterizes the relation to the beloved persons is not perceived as a burden or a loss. The acceptance of love is a joy for her because it makes possible the continuation and increase of love and of the freedom mediated by love. To be sure, love is given wings by being reciprocated, but it is not dependent on that. It can survive the death of the beloved person. It can even survive the other person's shunning love.[51]

---

49. Cf. W. Huber's reflections on an "ethic of self-limitation" in *Konflikt und Konsens: Studien zur Ethik der Verantwortung* (Munich: Kaiser, 1990), 204ff.; W. Huber and H. R. Reuter, *Friedensethik* (Stuttgart: Kohlhammer, 1990), 243ff.

50. Karl Barth put it this way: love "in the sense of Agape" is a "sovereign seeking of the other. . . . This seeking is sovereign because it is directed and oriented not to the sovereignty of the one who loves but to the sovereignty of the beloved one" (*Evangelical Theology: An Introduction*, trans. G. Foley [New York: Holt, Rinehart and Winston, 1963], 201). This of course is in the framework of Barth's thinking in terms of I-Thou correlations—a way of thinking that provokes either/or decisions.

51. On "cognitive love" cf. N. Luhmann, *Love as Passion: The Codification of Intimacy*, trans. J. Gaines and D. L. Jones (Cambridge: Harvard Univ. Press, 1986), 175, translation altered: "What is important is to find meaning in the world of someone else. As this world can never be unproblematical, so, too, the meaning affirming it can also never be unproblematical. . . . It [i.e, the meaning affirming the world of someone else] has to run the risk of winding up not knowing what is good for the other person and holding on to love *instead* of such knowledge." This is the case when love seeks to maintain and to strengthen itself by recursiveness. Otherwise it is more realistic in this situation for love to stick to the act of according the appropriate "honor" to the beloved person, in the sense of "honoring the beloved's memory"—an act that is in itself loving.

Through loving self-withdrawal, the person whose love is not directly reciprocated also surpasses her previous limits and comes to rejoice in the self-development of the beloved person. In the force field of the Spirit, the love of the person who is not directly loved in return does not remain without resonance. In this force field the giving and experiencing of love are moved beyond simple I-Thou relations. Love becomes a power that both reaches out and draws in, one that defines, reshapes, and creates diverse webs of relationships. Love thus infuses complex relations of social life.

Love as a fruit of the Spirit, as a condition of the psyche and a community condition that precedes and underlies relations of communication, is a world-changing force field. It relates individual diversity of self-withdrawal to individual diversity of life strengthened and enhanced by being loved. Where love defines not only person-to-person relations, but also relations of sociality and of community, it concretizes the force field of the Spirit in the most complete way. One can readily see with one's own eyes that love is the most complete of the forms of expression and communication in accordance with the Spirit. For in a differentiated way, love corresponds to the promised Spirit of righteousness and of peace.[52] Love overcomes hostilities, mutual foreignness, and indifference. Inasmuch as love is oriented to specific, individual life, love undermines normative forms that stand in its way. Love is a master in inventing exceptions that provide deliverance and promote life. Because love not only immerses itself in the beloved person, but also exercises a beneficial influence, both directly and indirectly, on that person's environment, love is continually building up new forms of life, both individual and communal. With its free self-withdrawal, love is contagious. In a way unmatched by any other power granted to human beings, love promotes life. Love promotes the quickening and renewal of life relations (cf. 1 Cor. 13:1ff.).

In this enlivening power, love as a fruit of the Spirit corresponds to the creative Spirit. It corresponds to this Spirit by virtue of the fact that it both infiltrates imperialistic monocultures and dissolves them in favor of freer, more complete forms of community. Love as a fruit of the Spirit tolerates no division into hostile camps and vilification of the other side along racist, sexist, and other lines. Love dissolves these

---

52. With regard to the following discussion, cf. chap. 3.

polarized and hostile divisions as well as hierarchical social formations. It is only in *opposition* to the power of love that ideologies of class and race can maintain themselves. Sexist, nationalistic, and other "chauvinisms" can prevail only by suppressing the power of love, only by damping the Spirit whose gift *and* fruit love is. In constantly new ways, love—"poured out" like the Spirit as well—grows out of diverse, individual life and effectively enters into diverse, individual life (cf. 1 Cor. 13:8). Love as a charism is indeed a "heavenly power."[53]

In its unremitting concreteness, in its arising from diverse individuality, and in its relatedness to diverse individuality, love admittedly appears to be something of which it is impossible to get an overview, something that is impossible to regulate, something that is indeed continually endangered and vulnerable. Love cannot be arranged by politics or by moral conditioning. It "grows," it forms itself as a force field in emergent processes. Yet the fact that love cannot be reduced to an abstract unity, homogenized, commanded, or decreed constitutes its power in the midst of its seeming public insignificance.[54] Inasmuch as love as a gift of the Spirit overcomes racist, sexist, nationalistic, and other barriers, it works toward a more comprehensive righteousness, a more sensitive justice, and a more effective practice of mercy, in accordance with the messianic promises. In a way that can be precisely defined, love acts as the "fulfilling of the law" (Rom. 13:10), shaping and defining conditions of the pysche *and* of the community.

Love, which becomes reality by an emergent process, activates a plural, mutual liberation, enhancement, and empowerment. Love does this by working out of diverse, individual, and concrete structural patterns of life and into diverse, individual, and concrete structural patterns of life. It effects the *culture of free self-withdrawal for the benefit of fellow creatures* and enjoyment of the free self-withdrawal of fellow creatures, which in turn issues in free self-withdrawal for the benefit of others. Inasmuch as this love influences judicial, moral, and political processes without letting itself be taken captive, functionalized, and fit into them, and inasmuch as, in its boundless freedom and power of renewal, it radiates out into these processes, it changes situations of

---

53. Cf. §3.3.
54. See also Sauter, "Zur Theologie des Heiligen Geistes," 111–12.

community and the atmospheres of communities. It doing so, it makes peace.

"Peace" is that relation of persons and communities to each other and to their surroundings that is defined by love: in other words, by the strengthening of life and of its developmental possibilities that occurs in free self-withdrawal for the benefit of others. In this sense "peace is a successful form of human life together. In particular, it is a successful political order."[55] But peace is also a *self-relation* mediated by simple or complex experiences of the self's surroundings.[56] Both the self-relation of an individual and the self-relation of a relative world can be defined by the form of peace. This "inner peace" (admittedly inconceivable or at least deceptive without "successful" life together) is the fruit of the awareness and of the experience that free self-withdrawal for the benefit of others evokes—whether directly or circuitously and indirectly—infectiously loving self-withdrawal. "Inner peace" is the fruit of the awareness and of the experience that love, with its either direct or circuitous paths of action, and with its indirect repercussions, is for its part borne by love, or will be so borne. Real peace therefore goes hand in hand with the spread of calm and the consciousness of dynamic completion.[57]

In a world that is exposing itself to massive danger and that is marked by a diversity of forms of the absence of peace, the merely positive definition of peace is insufficient. The loving enhancement of strength through free self-withdrawal will have to be defined and experienced in such a way that it is not merely left up to individual discretion on a case-by-case basis, and to mere diverse hope for powerful emergent processes of completion. As "indicators" of the "quality of human life" that is deserving of the designation *peace,* Wolfgang Huber has highlighted "the dismantling of distress, the avoidance of violence, and the diminution of bondage."[58] He has thus articulated three interdependent aspects that are indispensable to the strengthening of one's own development in the sense of the love described above. As long as

---

55. Huber and Reuter, *Friedensethik,* 21.

56. A. N. Whitehead calls attention to this in *Adventures of Ideas* (New York: Free Press, 1967), 286ff.

57. See also §6.5.

58. Huber and Reuter, *Friedensethik,* 22, cf. 22ff.

an Aristotelian spirit and Aristotelian concepts of freedom define this world,[59] it will not be enough to take account of those perspectives on oppressed life that are those of the oppressive surroundings. It will also be essential to bring under *explicit* consideration life that needs to be liberated from distress, violence, and bondage—specifically, to consider the active relationship of such life to its surroundings. This would mean that, according to what we know so far, the steady development of ecological and multicultural sensitivity would have to be named explicitly as a fourth characteristic.

Inasmuch as the biblical traditions recognize that love fulfills "the law," they take it seriously as a power that extends beyond politics, justice, and morality. They see that the promise of the "Spirit of righteousness and peace"[60] is universally yet concretely (polyindividually) fulfilled by the Spirit whose gift and fruit love is.[61]

The inability to understand this is one of the greatest hindrances on the way to the development of a realistic pneumatology. This inability has often reduced the concept of love to the spectra of experience, knowledge, and effects of I-Thou relations. This inability has hindered the recognition and practice of the interconnection between love and peace (cf. 2 Cor. 13:11). Underlying this inability are fatal, abstract oppositions of "law" and "Spirit" as well as, bound up with those oppositions, definitions of "law" and of "love" that are reductionist to the point of being caricatures.

Apparently clear and univocal New Testament statements about the relation between "law and Spirit" block the recognition of this inability.[62]

At first glance the situation seems to be unambiguous and to speak for "separate worlds" with regard to the Old and New Testaments.[63] From this perspective, law and Spirit relate to each other as life and death, disaster and salvation, sin and deliverance. The law brings

---

59. Cf. §6.1.

60. Cf. chap. 3.

61. Cf. Gal. 5:22; Rom. 5:5; Col. 1:8.

62. Cf. M. Welker, "Gesetz und Geist," *JBT* 4, ed. O. Hofius and P. Stuhlmacher (Neukirchen-Vluyn: Neukirchener, 1989): 215ff. The following discussion takes up the insights at which that article arrives.

63. And thus for the incompatibility of the insights at which chaps. 3 and 5 of this work arrive!

death; the Spirit brings life. "The letter kills, but the Spirit gives life" (2 Cor. 3:6b; cf. Rom. 8:2; 1 Cor. 15:56).

The "law of sin and of death," the law that Paul can even characterize as the "power of sin"—one can hardly conceive a sharper contrast to God's Spirit, who creates life, makes alive, and liberates from the power of sin. This viewpoint seems to find complete support in the following statements: the Spirit was not received on the basis of "works of law" (Gal. 3:2; cf. 3:14); those who "are led by the Spirit . . . are not subject to the law" (Gal. 5:18); "through the Spirit, by faith," Christians "eagerly wait for the hope of righteousness" (Gal. 5:5); "now we are discharged from the law . . . so that we serve in the new reality of the Spirit" (Rom. 7:6). This viewpoint seems to find similar support in Paul's attempts to portray those "who worship in the Spirit of God" as "the circumcision" (Phil. 3:3), and to present true circumcision as that which "occurs to the heart through the Spirit, not according to the letter" (Rom. 2:29).

Yet the clarity attained with the simple dichotomization and abstract opposition of (negatively characterized) "law" and (positively characterized) "Spirit" is deceptive. This becomes evident even if one looks only at texts of Paul. Romans 7:14 says explicitly that "the law is *spiritual.*" Romans 8:2 sets in opposition to the "law of sin and of death" not simply the Spirit who makes alive, but the liberating "*law* of the Spirit of life in Christ Jesus." These formulations would be incomprehensible if Paul thought that a merely negative characterization of the law and the naked opposition of law and Spirit were appropriate to the material. In addition, it would be impossible to explain why Paul speaks not only of the "*law* of the Spirit," but also of the "*law* of faith" (Rom. 3:27) and the "*law* of Christ" (Gal. 6:2; 1 Cor. 9:21), if his point were to set up an abstract opposition between the negative law that leads to ruin and the positive forces and effects of the Spirit.

Admittedly, the converse position does not provide any way out of the difficulties. If we place our bets only on Paul's insistence that "the law is holy, and the commandment is holy and just and good" (Rom. 7:12), and if we then add that Paul repeatedly underlines the goodness of the law, we find ourselves in a no less perplexing situation. The problem is that we must then make comprehensible why the good law, which Paul names in a series with the great gifts of "the adoption, the glory, the covenants . . . and the promises" (Rom. 9:4), can also be characterized as "the law of sin and of death."

Why is the law able not only to arouse our "passions" and to go so far as to bring "sin" to life (Rom. 7:5, 7-8)? Why can it even be characterized as "the power of sin" (1 Cor. 15:56)? As long as this state of affairs is not explained and the *difference* between law and Spirit is not comprehended, the differentiated *interconnection* of law and Spirit cannot be grasped. As long as we do not get past unclear mixtures of law and Spirit, the abstract opposition that reduces the law to the "letter that kills," to something misused by sin and works righteousness, will reassert itself again and again.

The law's powerlessness against sin and the corrupting power of the law under the might of sin cannot be summed up in one concept and described in one word. Against its own intentions, the law can stimulate evil and multiply disaster (Rom. 5:20), because the very forms of misguided behavior and misdeeds named by the law become a spur to sin. The law can be misused on the basis of perspectival and selective perception and fulfillment. Thus people can concentrate in diverse ways on tithing "mint, dill, and cummin" as the law requires, but disregard the "weightier matters of the law: justice and mercy and faith" (Matt. 23:23).

Even concentration on "the weightier matters of the law," on justice, mercy, and relationship with God, can become a power that sin can misuse. This is a lesson we can learn from the intrabiblical critique of collective and individual "self-righteousness" and "works righteousness." Those connections between concrete expressions of justice, mercy, and knowledge of God that are optimal according to human standards can turn into forms of pious or moral deception of self and others. In the hands of human beings, God's good law can be misused for machinations that are consciously or unconsciously, subjectively or objectively evil. The law thus acts as a power of palliation, concealment, deceptive self-pacification, appeasement, and empty consolation of others, and as a force for systematically leading people astray.

With the best intentions, with the greatest naiveté, in the most earnest moralism, and in the most deeply felt piety, sinful human beings pervert the law. The law is made into a machinery of deception that generates the illusion of righteousness, of mercy, and of a well-ordered relation with God both on the individual level and on the public-cultic level. This illusion can impose itself as a source of paralysis and corruption on an entire society, an entire time and culture, indeed on an entire world situation. It can lead them to ruin, despite

their operating all the while with the consciousness that they are doing
and experiencing what is right, good, and pleasing to God.

The law becomes a *power of sin*: not only a power of some sort of
misguided behavior or false self-orientation of a judicial, moral, or religious nature, but also a power that destroys renewal, new beginning,
restoration, and fundamental change of behavior, or even the mere
prospect of such.[64] The law becomes a "power of *sin* "because it permits
every imaginable form of judicial, moral, and religious sensibility to
be "built into" a self-righteousness that is concealed, "consensually"
agreed on and, under certain circumstances, large-scale. Under the
power of sin the law systematically conceals selfishness, self-deception,
and the fact that human beings are constantly distancing themselves
from the justice intended by God, from mercy, and from true knowledge of God. Under these conditions, how can the law still be called
good? How can Paul insist that the law is and remains "*spiritual?*" Why
does he talk about the "*law of the Spirit*" and expressly relate the *action
of the Spirit* to the fulfillment of the law's intentions of righteousness?

It is not theological willfulness, but the recognition of the power of
the Spirit and of this power's determinacy that underlie Paul's only
apparently contradictory statements. The Spirit of "the God of love
and peace" (2 Cor. 13:11), the Spirit who brings love and peace, is the
promised "Spirit of righteousness."[65] This Spirit presses to realize the
intentions of the law.[66] By simultaneously universalizing and individualizing the law's intentions to establish justice, mercy, and knowledge
of God, the Spirit works toward the fulfillment of these intentions.

---

64. Cf. the more detailed discussion in §6.3.

65. Cf. esp. §3.1, as well as J. Comblin, *The Holy Spirit and Liberation*, trans.
P. Burns (Maryknoll, N.Y.: Orbis, 1989), 51–55; L.-J. Suenens and H. Camara,
Charismatic Renewal and Social Action: A Dialogue (Ann Arbor, Mich.: Servant
Books, 1979).

66. Continuity and potentiation in the relation of law and Spirit are also indi-
rectly emphasized by, for example, Heb. 10:28ff.; Acts 5:32. See also E. Lohse, "ὁ
νόμος τοῦ πνεύματος τῆς ζωῆς: Exegetische Anmerkungen zu Röm 8,2," in H. D.
Betz and L. Schottroff, eds., *Neues Testament und christliche Existenz: Festschrift für
Herbert Braun zum 70. Geburtstag am 4. Mai 1973* (Tübingen: Mohr, 1973), 279ff.;
P. W. Meyer, "The Holy Spirit in the Pauline Letters: A Contextual Exploration,"
Interpretation 33 (1979): esp. 7ff.; E. Reinmuth, *Geist und Gesetz: Studien zu Voraus-
setzungen und Inhalt der paulinischen Paränese*, Theologische Arbeiten 44 (Berlin:
Evangelische Verlagsanstalt, 1985), esp. 73–74, 94ff.

The intentions of the law are universally realized by the Spirit inasmuch as "the Gentiles," too—as was depicted by the messianic promises—with their experiences of righteousness, with their hopes for righteousness and mercy, and with their striving after knowledge of God, receive "access to God."[67] This universalization only appears to activate a relativizing of the law. Rather, what are relativized are all substantive claims, advanced in an absolute and universal manner, to fulfill the law or to have fulfilled it. The different forms of striving after righteousness enter here into fruitful tensions of mutual challenge and correction.

In this process it is love, free self-withdrawal and self-giving for the empowerment of others, that is the standard completely compatible with the intentions of the law, which at the same time concretely and constantly corrects all sinful perversions of these intentions. Love not only practices mercy, but is sensitive to anything that endangers or disadvantages the beloved persons. Love does everything within its power to remove these dangers or disadvantages. Love not only procures justice for those in its environment, but uses every power at its disposal to strengthen and increase their life possibilities. The strength of love consists in the fact that it acts out of innumerable concrete, individual situations into concrete, individual situations. This strength turns love into a power that persistently acts against sin's ideological ossifications and perspectival distortions of the law. Admittedly, this strength goes hand in hand with a characteristic powerlessness. Without the power of the Spirit, love neither causes nor finds peace. Love remains in polyindividual disintegration, scattered and contingent, incapable of causing the law's intentions of righteousness to prevail even regionally, much less fulfilling them universally.

By contrast, love in the power of the Spirit is the power of God's self-demonstration, the power by which God rules the world. This power is of course obstructed and covered over in diverse ways. But with regard to the Crucified and Resurrected One, this love is recognized and experienced in constantly new ways as the common, connecting standard, as the power that changes people and worlds: the love that not only strengthens individual life, but that is directed to and for a world that closes itself to God's will. The Crucified and

---

67. Cf. Gal. 3:14; Eph. 2:18; 3:5-6 and passim.

Resurrected One reveals a love directed to and for a world that seeks to defend itself with all religious, political, judicial, and moral means against this love. This world makes itself totally immune to God and plunges itself collectively into ruin. It is to this world that God extends the power that—"poured out" (Rom. 5:5) into the hearts of human beings—arises out of diverse life contexts to serve a more complete righteousness.

In the power of the Spirit, love fulfills and transcends the intentions of the law that are directed toward justice and mercy. Love both serves to strengthen the concrete neighbor through free self-withdrawal and spreads itself out in such a peacemaking way that conditions of the psyche and of the community are marked and defined by it. In this love, God's righteous and merciful will can be fulfilled.

The action of the Spirit neither begins with the letter of the law nor builds on the works of the law. Even specific forms of the law cannot claim to be instituted by the Spirit. Nevertheless, the law retains an orienting function even in the midst of the pouring out of the Holy Spirit and in the midst of the action of the Holy Spirit. Among human beings and in the midst of world conditions that, dominated by sin, can misuse, distort, and obstruct righteousness, mercy, and knowledge of God, the Spirit establishes God's righteousness and mercy and provides demonstrations of God's presence. In this way the Spirit enlists the services of people in constantly new ways and under the most varied conditions in order to fulfill the law and God's will through love.

5.4: Vocation of freedom: Spirit and world no longer need be distinguished according to an escapist model; Spirit and flesh no longer need be distinguished neurotically

Persons defined by the Spirit fulfill God's will and correspond to the intentions of God's good law without compulsion, without being anxiously tied to the "letter," without overemphasizing their own works and achievements or those of other persons (cf. Gal. 5:18). These persons act in accord with God's will in love, which strengthens one's neighbors through free self-withdrawal. In the community of these persons, peace is created in the power of the Spirit by the diverse spread of love. In this love and in this peace, persons defined by the Spirit acquire a truly free relation to themselves and to their relative world. The distinctions between "Spirit" and "world"—more precisely between "the Spirit of God" and "the spirit of the world" (1 Cor. 2:12ff.), and between "Spirit" and "flesh"—call attention to this process of enabling people to be free in relation to themselves and in relation to the ruling powers in a given situation, the ones who define "reality."[68]

The freedom acquired by persons defined by the Spirit is difficult to comprehend within the limits of the metaphysics of spirit that still predominates in the West, and within the limits of the conceptions of "self" and "world" shaped by this metaphysics.[69] According to this metaphysics, a free relation to oneself and to the world is to be conceived and realized *only within* the self-relation and the world-relation. "World" (in the sense of the totality accessible to human beings) and "flesh" (in the sense of the psychophysical unity of finite living beings) are inescapable for human beings. As long as finite beings exist, they exist "in the flesh" and "in the world." "The world" is the totality of all events that are or can be experienced. Within the perspective of the Western spirit, to abstract from the world, to oppose oneself to it "in the Spirit" or to go beyond it "in the Spirit," seems to lead to erroneous relations to reality. Only a conscious flight from the world or an unhappy, unsustainable retreat into domains of fantasy can distance itself from this continuum. Things are different with the individual unity of our life and with each structural pattern of experience, with the psychosocial self. With regard to the psychosocial self, decisive and enduring distancing from "oneself" is certainly possible, along with the connected change in personality. Yet whatever the cause of these conditioned deviations from oneself, from the life situation assumed as "original" and "natural," the effect, the result of such forms of interference is as a rule experienced as a defect and designated a "neurosis."

---

68. Cf. Jüngel, "Zur Lehre vom heiligen Geist," 97–98. On the problematic of false totalizations and abstract oppositions of "flesh" and "Spirit," see also §3.5.

69. Concerning these conceptions, see §6.1; concerning the theological-pneumatological alternative, §§6.2–6.5. Concerning the difficulty of mediating Hegelianizing definitions of Spirit with the proper recognition of the "ontological selflessness" of the Spirit, see Jüngel, "Zur Lehre vom heiligen Geist," 107, 109.

Neuroses arise as soon as the "attitudes and life goals of an individual" do not lie in the spectrum of her psychological and physical possibilities.[70] The deformed self and a flight into an "other world" seem to be the "fruits" of an effective religious spirit and of the conjuration of this spirit's superior power.

The biblical traditions have something in common with this distrustful approach: namely, that the biblical traditions also conceive "the world" and "the flesh" (more precisely, the condition of being defined by "the flesh") as *forms of power*.[71] Yet the biblical traditions do not understand these forms of power as inescapable, self-referential systems. Above all they do not identify these forms of power with the totalized and individual fundamental forms of conscious life ("the world" and "the human person"). As surely as all human beings are fleshly and as surely as they live in the domain of the power of the world (or of a world), just as surely are these powers not the only factors that shape them. Nor do these powers necessarily play the *primary* role in shaping them. To be sure, these powers strive to do this, indeed to be that which *alone* defines human beings. If they succeed in doing so, human beings are threatened with extreme danger and bondage. According to the understanding of the biblical traditions, the person who—in the perspective of the Western spirit—is adjusted and attuned only to "herself," in the sense of her fleshliness, and to "reality," in the sense of her world, has by no means finally "found her identity" and attained "peace with the world." She has arrived neither at self-knowledge nor at maturity.

The person who has come under the domination of the flesh handed over to sin, and under the power of the "law of the world," is a person handed over without protection to "being-toward-death." Such a person is incapable of self-withdrawal, of love, and of experiencing peace. She must without respite struggle for self-preservation and against a diminishing life force. In a world in which "life" is always

---

70. Cf. J. Wolpe, "Neurose," *Lexicon der Psychologie* 2/2 (1976): 646ff.

71. Cf. E. Brandenburger, *Fleisch und Geist: Paulus und die dualistische Weisheit,* WMANT 29 (Neukirchen-Vluyn: Neukirchener, 1968), esp. 226ff.; G. Gutiérrez, *We Drink from Our Own Wells: The Spiritual Journey of a People,* trans. M. J. O'Connell (Maryknoll, N.Y.: Orbis, 1984), 55–61.

also robbery,[72] this person struggles in vain for self-preservation. The person *defined* by the flesh has been "sold" to sin (cf. Rom. 7:14).

By appealing to trust in the delivering power of the Spirit, the biblical traditions are not conjuring up a second world "up above" and a separate, removed, unrealistic existence. By appealing to trust in the enlivening power of the Spirit (John 6:63), the biblical traditions concentrate on God's power, which in the midst of the rulers and powers of the world enlists the services of fleshly life in such a way that this life is not lost and does not fall victim to what is null and invalid. The liberating power of God's Spirit protects life from spreading its own anxiety and insecurity, and from heightening—always conscious of the futility of the effort—its own assertion of self at the expense of others. The liberating power of God's Spirit protects life from solidifying and spreading its own perplexity and joylessness until death and the passing away of a relative world put an end to this frantic hither-and-thither. When human beings surrender themselves to the power of the flesh, which asserts itself as an orientational power, they experience powerlessness. We need to keep in mind this powerlessness and the meaninglessness of life dominated by the power of the flesh if we are to understand the sharp words against "the flesh," more precisely against letting oneself be defined by the flesh, as well as the oppositions between "Spirit" and "flesh," which often have the sound of abstract, reciprocal negations.

In itself, the flesh is powerless. In truth, it is granted its power only by sin. As long as what is fleshly is under the power of sin, it cannot attain freedom on its own. Without the action of the Spirit, what is fleshly is helplessly handed over to the power of sin. Indeed it executes this power by itself defining the human person, subjugating the human person herself to the "mind-set of the flesh" (Rom. 8:2-7). The "mind-set" of the flesh is an aggressive and defensive posture of

---

72. A. N. Whitehead, *Process and Reality: An Essay in Cosmology*, corrected ed., ed. D. R. Griffin and D. W. Sherburne (New York: Free Press, 1978), 105: "All societies require interplay with their environment; and in the case of living societies this interplay takes the form of robbery. The living society may, or may not, be a higher type of organism than the food which it disintegrates. But whether or no it be for the general good, life is robbery." This state of affairs is generously overlooked by all those contemporary theories and theologies that promulgate naive, mutualistic conceptions of "life" and of "sociality."

self-preservation that seeks to make one's own self-relation and self-development—limited as they are by one's own finitude and by death—as strong as possible. In the process, this posture of self-preservation fails to connect with life that is valid and beneficial to life. "By potentiating itself, the flesh presses toward the relationlessness of death."[73]

The Spirit of God is *not* a force that erodes, squelches, impairs, and deforms life *in* the flesh. Rather, the Spirit of God is a power that liberates life *in* the flesh from the power of sin. The Spirit of God is a power that liberates from the condition of being surrendered to the—futile—attempt to assert oneself at the expense of others and to preserve oneself by means of a "self-potentiation" oriented to oneself. The Spirit is a power that leads life *in* the flesh, precisely as such, to the "resurrection of the flesh" and to participation in "eternal life" (Gal. 6:8).[74]

Through the Spirit, the loving, free self-withdrawal of self for the benefit of others lets accrue to human beings the very thing that they vainly attempt to attain through trust in the flesh, through an orientation toward the flesh.[75] Persons defined by the Spirit acquire a freedom that procures freedom for other persons and that is the opposite of neurotic, stereotypical, internalized self-limitations and self-deformations. The vigilance and sensitivity wrought by the Spirit

---

73. Jüngel, "Zur Lehre vom heiligen Geist," 98.

74. Cf. §§6.4 and 6.5. See also the fine works of D. Müller, "Geisterfahrung und Totenauferweckung: Untersuchungen zur Totenauferweckung bei Paulus und den ihm vorgegebenen Überlieferungen" (doctoral diss., Univ. of Kiel, 1980), esp. 222ff.; and D. L. Dabney, "Die Kenosis des Geistes: Kontinuität zwischen Schöpfung und Erlösung im Werk des Heiligen Geistes" (doctoral diss., Univ. of Tübingen, 1989), esp. 233ff. Dabney has attempted to supplement J. Moltmann's early theology of the cross with the pneumatology that it lacks—but not with the doctrine of sin that it also lacks. For this reason the steps he has taken toward further developing this theology—steps that are correct and acknowledged as such by Moltmann—remain at the level of programmatic theses. The pluriform power of the new creation by the Spirit is brought out by the meditations of O. Noordmans, *Das Evangelium des Geistes* (Zurich: EVZ-Verlag, 1960). He rightly insists again and again that the characteristic action of the Spirit cannot be understood without a grasp of the "overpowering character" of the "pouring out" of the Spirit (ibid., 39, 41, and passim). See also A. Geense, "Pneumatologische Entwürfe in der niederländischen Theologie," *TLZ* 106 (1981): esp. 790–91.

75. Cf. Gal. 3:2ff.; 5:13ff.; 1 Cor. 3:1; Phil. 3:3.

enable life to become a power source of righteousness and mercy, and a mirror of God's glory in the midst of the earthly world. Life ordained by the Spirit to resurrection becomes for its part life-promoting seed (cf. 1 Cor. 15:42ff.).

The action of the Spirit does not flee from the world, but overcomes the world, delivering and renewing life. The Spirit does not cause a flight from the world, but rather the resurrection of the flesh and participation in eternal life—and thus a reformation and transformation of that which is perishable (cf. 1 Cor. 15:49-50). God's power acts on earthly life so that it becomes a bearer and a mirror of God's glory, and so that it acts in turn on other earthly life. For the person who is "fleshly"-minded, this action of the Spirit is incomprehensible. Since this action is not supported by earthly forms and demonstrations of power, it can come across as incomprehensible and insignificant. It is endangered in diverse ways. Although by this power the coming of God's reign can be activated under the conditions of the earthly world, this action of the Spirit can appear of negligible significance in comparison with the ruling powers that define the world in a given situation. The power of the Spirit is in fact superior to the world, changing the world. But this power of the Spirit and the freedom attendant on life in the Spirit's force field appear unclear and not "fitted" to this world. It is in this regard that the occasionally unnuanced oppositions between "Spirit" and "world," "the spirit of the world" and "the Spirit of God" can be grasped. But the criteria for recognizing God's Spirit, for opening oneself to the action of God's Spirit, or for discerning the spirits, is not a tendency to flee from the world, not hostility to the body and to life, not envy and a deranged relation to all forms of *joie de vivre*, especially to sensuality.

Instead, the statements that distinguish the Spirit of God from the spirit of the world, occasionally escalated to the point of misleading, abstract oppositions, have the goal of emphatically communicating a major insight of faith. Specifically, they have the goal of communicating the insight that human life is liberated from the contorted struggle against a meaningless existence. Human life need not engage in the vain attempt to iterate and to potentiate its self-preservation by orienting itself to the perishing powers of the world or by surrendering itself to the power of sin. It need not surrender itself to a power that makes the renewal of life impossible, that generates only the illusion of a renewal of life, and in so doing obstructs and blocks the paths to a life with validity. The call to freedom in the Spirit denies the claim that there is no alternative in this life to the struggle for self-preservation. By calling attention to the action of the Spirit who is present, this call to freedom invites people to lay hold of this freedom and to live in it.

5.5: Speaking in tongues and the inspiration of Scripture

On the basis of the understanding acquired thus far, it is possible to clarify two of the most controversial pneumatological themes of the last two decades. The first is so-called *speaking in tongues* and the question of the position and significance it should receive in the life of the church. The second is the problem of how to understand the *inspiration of Scripture*, and of what its consequences are for piety, theology, and proclamation. The first question is a point of controversy above all between members of Pentecostal churches and the Charismatic Renewal, on the one hand, and Christians who do not belong to these churches and movements, on the other hand. The second problem generates tensions between evangelicals, fundamentalists, and biblicistically oriented Christians, on the one hand, and other believers, on the other hand. In the unenlightened form in which both themes are currently subjected to polemical treatment, they are an offense to persons who are not believers. Both themes seem to show with particular clarity that the Christian faith is outdated and lives in superstitious, authoritarian postures that are hostile to rationality, postures that in general no open and honest person could wish on himself.

In contrast to these prejudices, the following discussion shall, on the basis of the understanding acquired up to this point, present in the right light the limited function of speaking in tongues and the positive sense of the notion of the "inspiration of Scripture." To this end we need to lay bare that which for the biblical testimonies themselves is the determinative justification and critique of the phenomena that have caused such an uproar:

Why Is Speaking in Tongues the Most Problematic among the Gifts of the Spirit? So-called speaking in tongues as a consequence of the pouring out of the Spirit and of baptism in the Spirit is attested numerous times in the New Testament. Mark 16:17 talks about speaking "in new tongues";[76] Acts 10:46 and 19:6 and 1 Cor. 12:30, about speaking "in tongues"; 1 Cor. 13:8, simply about "tongues"; 1 Cor. 12:10 and 12:28, about "various kinds of tongues." Besides the Pentecost account, 1 Corinthians 14 provides the only detailed and graphic depiction. Here Paul describes speaking in tongues as incomprehensible speech that occurs in a state of rapture and that is in need of explanation and translation. It is, further, a prayer directed to God that in praise and thanksgiving serves to build up those who are praying in tongues—but only those who are praying in tongues. As described in 1 Corinthians 14, speaking in tongues throws the individual back on himself and awakens the need for interpretation. Between the successful understanding that occurs in the Pentecost event and the form of glossolalia on which Paul is critically focusing in 1 Corinthians 14, there are obviously differences that must be noted.[77]

It is undisputed that the descent of the Spirit is not necessarily bound up with the gift of speaking in tongues, or even only with the gift of that form of speaking in tongues that is generally incomprehensible and in need of interpretation. In two cases—Acts 10:44ff. and 19:6ff.—it is reported that after the descent of the Spirit, people spoke in tongues. While Peter is proclaiming Christ, the Spirit descends on the Gentiles and they begin "speaking in tongues and extolling God." After the Spirit has descended on John's disciples, who had not even heard that there was a Holy Spirit, they "speak in tongues and prophesy." One cannot clearly ascertain whether these are cases of speech that is comprehensible in a miraculous way, as described in the Pentecost account, or whether they are cases of speech that is initially incomprehensible and in need of interpretation. Thus we should not speculate about whether precisely the Gentiles and those who knew nothing of the Spirit are depicted as at first being capable only of "speaking in tongues." Both texts indeed also emphasize features of comprehensibility when they speak of people being enabled to

---

76. Those who have come to faith will be accompanied by these signs: "by using my name they will cast out demons; they will speak in new tongues."

77. See F. Stagg, "The Holy Spirit in the New Testament," RevExp 63 (1966): esp. 145: "Modern 'glossolalia' movements confuse Pentecost and Corinth."

"prophesy" and of the fact that the Gentiles come to praise God in a way that is recognizable to outsiders.[78]

Acts 4:31, 8:17, 9:17, and 11:15 show that the descent of the Spirit is not necessarily connected with the gift of "various kinds of tongues" —whether they are comprehensible or in need of interpretation. These passages provide accounts of people being filled with the Holy Spirit or of the Spirit descending on them without their being given the gift of speaking in tongues. That itself argues against the claim that the descent of the Spirit and speaking in tongues are to be necessarily connected. It also argues against privileging speaking in tongues over other gifts of the Spirit. This provides a basis for assigning speaking in tongues a relative position among the diverse gifts of the Spirit.

To be sure, according to a number of New Testament testimonies, the different kinds of speaking in tongues—to which both glossolalia and xenoglossia belong[79]—are regarded as a gift of the Spirit. Yet the different gifts of speaking in tongues are not the central, the first, or the highest gift of the Spirit, and still less the only and decisive gift of the Spirit.[80] Instead, 1 Corinthians 12:8-9a first names those gifts that lie along the line drawn by extrapolating from the Pentecost event: the sharing of wisdom, the mediation of knowledge, and faith.[81] Next (1 Cor. 12:9b, 10a) follow those gifts that stand in continuity with Jesus' messianic action: healing, the working of miracles, prophetic speech, and the discernment of spirits.[82] Finally (1 Cor. 12:10b) come the gift of speech in various kinds of tongues and the gift of interpreting speech in tongues. This is in accord with Paul's famous critical

---

78. Cf. B. Van Elderen, "Glossolalia in the New Testament," *Journal of the Evangelical Theological Society* 7 (1964): esp. 54–55.

79. On the differentiation, see A. Bittlinger, "Die charismatische Erneuerung der Kirchen: Aufbruch urchristlicher Geisterfahrung," in C. Heitmann and H. Mühlen, eds., *Erfahrung und Theologie des Heiligen Geistes* (Hamburg: Agentur des Rauhen Hauses; Munich: Kösel, 1974), esp. 29ff.; for a general treatment, W. E. Mills, ed., *Speaking in Tongues: Let's Talk about It* (Waco, Tex.: Word Books, 1973); H. N. Malony and A. A. Lovekin, *Glossolalia: Behavioral Science Perspectives on Speaking in Tongues* (New York: Oxford Univ. Press, 1986).

80. On the general skepticism regarding a fixed concentration on signs following baptism in the Spirit, see M. Ramsey, *Holy Spirit: A Biblical Study* (Grand Rapids: Eerdmans, 1977), esp. 130–31.

81. Cf. §5.1.

82. Cf. §§4.2–4.4.

analysis of the practice of overemphasizing or even absolutizing speaking in tongues (1 Corinthians 14).

On the one hand, Paul notes that speaking in tongues is a gift of the Spirit. Those who speak in tongues speak to God, speak mysteries in the Spirit, and *build up* themselves. "I would like all of you to speak in tongues" (14:5). In tongues the spirit of a person prays, and a blessing is spoken with the spirit (cf. 14:14, 16). "I thank God that I speak in tongues more than all of you" (14:18). "Do not forbid speaking in tongues" (14:39).

Yet the gift that is thus esteemed is at the same time sharply relativized inasmuch as it is made *subordinate to prophetic speech*: that is, to comprehensible speech that builds up the community.[83] Already in the first five verses, Paul repeatedly emphasizes that prophetic speech and the person who speaks prophetically are more important and stand higher than speaking in tongues and the person who speaks in tongues. "How will I benefit you unless I speak to you in some revelation or knowledge or prophecy or teaching?" (14:6). Then come several sharp formulations: If you speak only in tongues you are making meaningless noise; you are talking to the wind (14:7-9). You remain strangers to each other (cf. 14:11, 16); your mind remains without fruit; the blessing that you speak remains incomprehensible (14:14ff.). Collective speaking in tongues goes so far as to generate the impression in outsiders that the community is crazy: "If, therefore, the whole church comes together and all speak in tongues, and outsiders or unbelievers enter, will they not say that you are out of your mind?" (14:23).

The most severe reproach is that made with reference back to Isa. 28:11ff., that speaking in tongues is a "sign for unbelievers," by which is said nothing less than that speaking in tongues provokes those who do not believe to persist in unbelief.[84] Paul's conclusion in

---

83. See the illuminating dissertation of T. Gillespie, "Prophecy and Tongues: The Concept of Christian Prophecy and Pauline Thought" (Ph.D. diss., School of Theology at Claremont, Calif., 1971). See especially the differentiated demonstration of the interconnection between prophetic speech and proclamation of the gospel (72ff. and passim).

84. See F. Lang, *Die Briefe an die Korinther*, rev. ed., NTD 7 (Göttingen: Vandenhoeck, 1986), 196; H.-D. Wendland even speaks of a "means of hardening the heart" (*Die Briefe an die Korinther*, 15th ed., NTD 7 [Göttingen: Vandenhoeck, 1980], 129).

weighing the various factors is unequivocal: "in church I would rather speak five words with my mind, in order to instruct others also, than ten thousand words in a tongue" (14:19).

Why is speaking in tongues nevertheless taken so seriously in many churches of the Pentecostal movement as well as in some communities of the more recent Charismatic Movement? Why is it regarded not merely as a subordinate gift of the Spirit, but rather as a central and thus indispensable one?

The reasons for this mistaken evaluation certainly lie in part in an understanding of God's Spirit that sees the Spirit as something numinous.[85] In part they lie in a deficient understanding of what happened at Pentecost.[86] Or they lie simply in unclear notions of what the Holy Spirit wills to bring into effect. If God's Spirit is regarded as a force that evokes numinous feelings and corresponding "experiences," it is no surprise when gifts and impressions that remain correspondingly numinous—such as mystical gifts and impressions—are placed at the center of piety and of ecclesial life. If the only things retained from the Pentecost event are those that cause wonderment and dismay, if people abstract from the fact that in this event the very thing that evokes wonderment is an *understanding and clarity* that could not be expected at all, the result must be a false understanding of the Spirit's action and a mistaken evaluation of the gifts of the Spirit.

Yet in addition, the centering on glossolalia is also to be understood and taken seriously as an effort to respond to faith's need for concretization and as a protest phenomenon—not only as a protest against the total exclusion of this gift of the Spirit from the traditional churches.[87] Liturgical ossification, theological abstraction, and integration of spirituality into specific secular life-styles and forms of moralism led to a state of affairs where what is specific to the experience of faith, what is particular, what stands out or is even offensive

---

85. Cf. §2.5.

86. Cf. §5.1.

87. K. McDonnell rightly says that "tongues, the lowest of the gifts, is still a gift of the Spirit" ("The Function of Tongues in Pentecostalism," *One in Christ* 19 [1983]: 347. See also the discussion of the Special Committee on the Work of the Holy Spirit in *Minutes of the General Assembly of the United Presbyterian Church in the United States of America*, ser. 7, vol. 4 (Philadelphia: Office of the General Assembly, 1970), 146ff.

in relation to a given secular culture, could no longer be rightly known. Here speaking in tongues, as a phenomenon that diverges with particular clarity from the normal forms of experience, offered the very kernel around which a countermovement could crystallize.

Yet the explanation must be sought still deeper. The experience of the power of the Spirit and life in the force field of faith are threatened by abstractions that dissolve this force field and by a number of reductionist views. If we recognize and understand these dangers in their complex interconnection, the fixed concentration on speaking in tongues can be regarded as nothing less than an attempt to stand against these dangers. The experience of the power of the Spirit and life in the force field of faith are threatened by the abstraction from concrete individuals, on the one hand, and by the reduction to a concrete[88] individualism, on the other hand. The Spirit enlists the services of real, individual human beings. The force field of faith is generated with them, through them, and for them. If abstraction is made from them, if a faith "in itself" or an "otherworldly" action of the Spirit is sought or assumed, the power of the Spirit and the force of faith degenerate into ghostly entities.

The abstract individualism of modernity seems to work against this inasmuch as it propagates the force field of a self-relation that is common to all human beings yet proper to each: namely, one's own self-relation "as spirit."[89] Yet inasmuch as this abstract individualism assumes the place of polyconcrete individualism, the specific, enlivening power of the pouring out of the Spirit, the rich world of the Joel promise and of the Pentecost experience cease to be recognizable. This is not to say that pluralistic, polyconcrete individualism on its own constitutes and reflects the power of the Spirit and the force field of faith. Mere polyconcrete individualism cannot comprehend the unity of the Spirit and the coherence of faith. It disregards the diversity of characteristic forms, and their interconnections, released by the Spirit through the charisms. The place of the demonstration of the power of the Spirit and of faith is assumed by an unspecifiable reciprocity and

---

88. To be more precise, we should speak of a "concretional" individualism that moves toward a multiplicity of concrete individuations.

89. Cf. the more detailed discussion in §6.1.

by a juxtaposition that at best is interlaced in a numinous, marketlike manner.

In the face of this structural pattern of problems, speaking in tongues as the center, beginning, and goal of experience of the Spirit seems to work not only against the reduction to an indeterminately pluriform individualism, but also against the abstraction from the concrete individual as well as the abstraction from the diverse, polyconcrete community. It not only arouses the individually interested attention of many—whether in enthusiasm or in dismay. It also places the concrete, Spirit-endowed individual in the center of the community. It fosters the growth of the need for concrete experience of this gift of the Spirit, and in any case it gives rise to concrete attestations to the presence of the Spirit, albeit in obscure form. It thus seems to ward off abstract individualism, differentiates persons gifted in speaking in tongues from those gifted in interpretation, and opens up depth dimensions of the capacity for feeling and expression that go beyond all standardizations and typologies. In this differentiation it confronts both the abstraction from diverse, polyconcrete community and the concentration on a merely individual, concrete experience of the Spirit. It is essentially a process that includes different forms of involvement and that generates and binds essentially public attention.

In this manner it seems to prevent collapse into a disintegrative pluralism and relativism. It gives to the community, to the assembly gathered for worship, and to individual religious experience a basic form that both enables and requires experiences and communications that are of a strange and concrete sort. In addition, public speaking in tongues with its need for interpretation excludes in any case the possibility of the community of the Spirit becoming egoistically absorbed. It excludes the possibility of religious experience being confused with a subjective sense of power and of justice. It excludes these possibilities by virtue of the fact that it is essentially uncontrollable and incomprehensible, and that its operation is unforeseeable and unpredictable.[90]

This reconstruction cannot be more than an attempt to make comprehensible why the Pentecostal communities centered on speaking in

---

90. See J. Koenig, *Charismata: God's Gifts for God's People*, Biblical Perspectives on Current Issues (Philadelphia: Westminster, 1978), esp. 108ff. (on "Individuation and Incorporation through Charismata").

tongues are convinced, on various levels of feeling and of awareness, that they are placing at the center of their piety a form and experience that is not only powerful, but also appropriate to and in accord with the Pentecost event. On closer examination, though, speaking in tongues proves to be ill-suited to being loaded with this much freight, and the Pauline warning against privileging speaking in tongues appears fitting and justified.

Giving preeminence to speaking in tongues places in the center of a community's attention a form of presentation and experience that in itself is indeterminate, and that is as ambivalent as indeterminate or empty mystical consciousness. Its indeterminacy and need for interpretation are by no means a guarantee of a rich experience of faith.

In opposition to the Joel promise and the Pentecost event, as well as to the action of the Spirit in Jesus' healings, speaking in tongues takes those who are involved in it out of familiar life contexts and forms of experience, out of the plurality of experiences of suffering and liberation, and out of the plurality of cultures and languages. Like mystical "experience" or modern ego-consciousness, speaking in tongues is a form that can be used and employed *either* in a manner that individuates *or* in a manner that makes connections, *either* in a manner that brings about disintegration *or* in a manner that fosters solidarity.

Speaking in tongues is an expressive religious form that in itself is empty, indeterminate, and in need of interpretation. As such it cultivates a *latent* pluralism that can assume *either* an upbuilding form *or* a disintegrating one. In this connection it is open for the controllable or uncontrollable formation of hierarchies of persons capable of interpretation.

The consequence of all this is not an across-the-board rejection on the basis of anxieties about strangeness and irrationalism, but merely a calling into question of the overemphasis on speaking in tongues, a calling into question of its being highlighted among the gifts of the Spirit, and a calling into question of the practice of centering on it as the sign of being endowed with the Spirit at all. This calling into question rests on an orientation to the Pentecost event in the context of the other actions of the Spirit to which the biblical traditions attest. It is thus not a mere repetition of what is said in 1 Corinthians 14. The fact that the privileging of speaking in tongues is to be called into question does not mean that the significance of baptism in the Spirit is to be relativized. On the contrary, a sober comprehension of the significance of speaking in tongues works against an overly restricted perception of baptism in the Spirit and of its consequences.[91]

On the Problem of the Inspiration of Scripture. On the basis of a developed doctrine of the Holy Spirit, it must also be possible to answer the controverted question of whether or not the Bible is inspired. Specifically, it must be possible to do so on the basis of a clarification of how the notion of inspiration is actually to be understood. The concept of inspiration is viewed in vastly differing ways in the Bible. Applying "inspiration" to the authors of the biblical texts constitutes a shift of meaning. It is in this shift of meaning that the doctrine of inspiration has achieved fame and notoriety and has turned into a "theological bogeyman."[92]

The act of inspiring the authors of the biblical texts is viewed as an event in which God implanted the precise wording of the text in the authors, indeed even dictated the text while they wrote it out: the Bible—dictated directly by God. On this basis the Bible can be understood *throughout* in the manner in which the prophetic oracles were understood: "Thus says the Lord . . . ." Each individual word is of equal significance; every word is "the" word of God; every word is

---

91. To be sure, an across-the-board agreement with the viewpoints advanced by Paul in 1 Corinthians 14 is not among the results of correcting the perception of baptism in the Spirit along the lines I have been discussing. Precisely with regard to baptism in the Spirit, the patriarchal statements at the end of the chapter (33b-35) are untenable. See the subtle interpretation of E. Schüssler Fiorenza, *In Memory of Her: A Feminist Reconstruction of Christian Origins* (New York: Crossroad, 1983), 230–33. Cf. also B. Dominy, "Paul and Spiritual Gifts: Reflections on I Corinthians 12–14," *Southwestern Journal of Theology* 26 (1983): 49ff.

92. Barth, CD 1/2, 526. Concerning the following discussion, cf. ibid., 514–26. I concur in Barth's critique and evaluation of the doctrine of inspiration. His own proposed solution, though, needs to be developed pneumatologically if the "sovereignty of God" is not to remain opaque and subject to authoritarian misuse. Barth is certainly right that the Bible, "grounded upon itself apart from the mystery of Christ and the Holy Ghost . . . became a 'paper Pope,' and unlike the living Pope in Rome it was wholly given up into the hands of its interpreters. It was no longer a free spiritual force" (525). But it is equally true that the insistence on the sovereignty of God's word—without a development of the mystery of the Spirit—can become a theological sledgehammer no less subject to being instrumentalized.

immediately a "message." On this basis a simple theory of the authority of Scripture can be developed. The Bible is the direct reproduction
of what God directly said. The Holy Spirit, or God by the Holy Spirit,
dictated *every word,* and *this* means: the Bible is inspired. This conception is attributed in exemplary form to Protestant scholasticism of the
sixteenth and seventeenth centuries. In any case it is very much a part
of the scene in many forms of popular piety up to the present day.

Daniel L. Migliore provides a good summary of the intentions that
lie behind this understanding of inspiration:

> Enlightenment, secularization, and the new emphasis on human
> autonomy in the modern era challenged all traditional authority.
> Anxious to protect the insights of the Reformation, Protestant
> theologians became increasingly defensive and strident in their
> claims about the supernatural character of Scripture. Every book,
> every chapter, every verse, every word was directly inspired by
> God. The doctrine of inspiration became a theory of the supernat-
> ural origin of Scripture. Various ideas about how this took place
> were advanced.[93]

As Migliore makes clear, this position is naturally not up to the level
of what prominent theologies have to say concerning the doctrine of
Scripture, including those that take the Bible very seriously and that
develop a sharply defined understanding of the authority of the word.[94]

It is no secret that biblical criticism has totally destroyed all attempts to divinize Scripture or to attribute any form of "supernaturalness" to it. It has become possible to see that the attempts to conceive

---

93. D. L. Migliore, *Called to Freedom: Liberation Theology and the Future of
Christian Doctrine* (Philadelphia: Westminster, 1980), 24–25. Cf. G. Siegwalt's in-
sightful elucidation of conceptions of inspiration in *Dogmatique pour la catholicité
évangélique: Système mystagogique de la foi chrétienne,* vol. 1, *Les Fondements de la
foi,* pt. 2, *Réalité et Révélation* (Geneva: Labor et Fides; Paris: Cerf, 1987), 269ff.,
esp. 279ff.

94. One only need think of the famous *sola scriptura.* We need to join Luther in
supplementing his "Scripture alone" and in understanding it more determinately.
For example, Scripture alone shall be *queen*—see M. Luther, *Assertio Omnium Artic-
ulorum, WA* 7, 94ff. This entails, though, that Scripture is not Godself. The position
of queen is attributed to Scripture in relation to all other texts written by human
beings.

of the Bible as a word-for-word record of the directly dictated word of God are defensive religious ideology. The critical approach thus has also pulled the rug out from under the credibility of the doctrine of the inspiration of Scripture. It has destroyed the popular conception of inspiration as "inspiration of the *authors* of the biblical texts," by which is meant that God dictated the precise wording of the text to them. Regrettably the baby has been thrown out with the bath water, so that along with this conception of the inspiration of Scripture, *every* understanding of scriptural inspiration has been destroyed. In addition, this model produces a simplistic and reductionist conception of the Spirit and of inspiration.[95] Is it possible to regain an understanding of the inspiration of Scripture that does not lead to absurd conflicts with realism, rationality, and historical sensibility?

According to the testimony of the biblical traditions, the Spirit of God has been experienced as a power that restores a community in the midst of distress and disintegration, reactivating solidarity, loyalty, and the capacity for action in this community. This holds true not only in situations of external danger, but also in situations of internal danger. The messianic traditions describe the Spirit as a power that induces or enables the bearer of the Spirit to restore righteousness and mercy for the benefit of the poor and weak in a people. In this way this people is able to attain great universal influence, to acquire strong loyalty, and to reflect God's glory. In this process the bearer of the Spirit does not make use of *one* specific code, be it moral, political, or otherwise publicly established. But *how* does this bringing together, strengthening, and vitalizing of God's people occur? How is this universal shining forth of God's glory through God's people possible? How does the mission that it promises, *mission that acts by the power of attraction*, become possible? If we pose these questions, we are confronted with words that say that God's Spirit was *poured out,* and is poured out in the present. But the pouring out of the Spirit effects a process in which the services of a multitude of people who receive the

---

95. Let it be noted in passing that Isaiah 6, Jer. 1:9, and Ezek. 3:2—texts that are sometimes appropriated for this theme—say nothing about a prophet writing down a biblical text according to the simplistic model of inspiration.

Spirit are enlisted in diverse ways—in a multitude of locations at the same time. The pouring out of the Spirit is bound up with a diverse process of both knowable and hidden renewal and revitalization in a way analogous to that by which a garden or a whole land is revitalized and refreshed by the descending rain.[96]

The people touched by the pouring out of the Spirit unlock reality and the future for each other in a variegated partnership thoroughly deserving of the name *pluralistic*, and in emergent cooperation. In this polycentric variegation, the fullness of God's presence becomes experientially present as it is made manifest by the Spirit. Where persons are differentiated and separated by language, race, gender, age, and social stratum, the pouring out of the Spirit "from heaven" signifies that these persons—removing unjust differences and cultivating natural, creative differences—produce with and for each other a trusting intimacy with God's will and, mediated by that intimacy, a trusting intimacy in and with a world that they cannot attain in their natural-finite perspectives.

On the basis of this recognition, it appears not only meaningful and correct, but also materially necessary to say that *Scripture is inspired*. As in the community of the Joel vision or of the Pentecost event, *a plurality of testimonies are present in the biblical traditions*. These testimonies speak out of various times, out of various experiential and educational backgrounds, out of various situations of distress, out of despair, out of joy, and out of experiences of deliverance. They speak out of various notions of history and of the future, as well as out of various perspectives on the world. They reflect in a variegated manner the fullness of God's concrete and living presence, if the Spirit is acting through these testimonies.

It is the Spirit who through the texts produces a charged field of experiences. The experiences of God that the texts communicate are not homogenized, not stereotyped. Sometimes they appear to be in conflict with each other or incompatible with each other. To be sure, in many cases they do conflict with each other, and sometimes they simply are incompatible with each other. But this is not a weakness of

---

96. See the more detailed discussion in §§3.1ff.

Scripture, as a narrow-minded rationality might think. It is, rather, one of Scripture's strengths, for in this way *the biblical texts are clearly subordinated to the reality to which they relate themselves and to which they attest.* The reality of God and of the world intended by God, the reality to which the biblical texts and traditions attest, is richer and more lively than could be presented by *one* text or one structural pattern of experience alone, or than could be articulated by *several* texts. In their diversity and variegation, the biblical texts give expression to the fact that they are nothing more than *testimonies* to the reality and presence of God.

As *testimonies* they refer to experiences that are concrete, partial, and in this manner fragmentary. As testimonies they cannot help but declare this concrete, partial, and fragmentary perception of what has happened, of what they have seen and heard, of what they regard as significant and important. The Bible is a multitude of such testimonies. These testimonies are certainly defined by interpretations, interests, even by theories and conceptions of the world. Yet the texts are testimonies by virtue of the fact that no text and no tradition offers *the* view, *the* encompassing theology, *the* only authentic perception of God's presence.

It is, rather, the Holy Spirit who causes these testimonies—the partial, even fragmentary and conflicting experiences and insights—*to point to* the reality of God, to reflect it. As soon as this happens and to the extent that it happens, we are justified in speaking of an *inspiration of Scripture,* even compelled to speak of it. It is the action of the Spirit that makes these testimonies to be true and living testimonies. It is the action of the Spirit that through these testimonies brings together, renews, and strengthens the people of God. It is the action of the Spirit that enables the people of God to recognize and to confess the presence of God in their midst.

The Holy Spirit not only brings together the testimonies of the biblical traditions in ever-renewed ways and concentrates them so that they can point to the presence of God. Or, to say it with a different emphasis, the Holy Spirit is not only the action of God in which God concentrates the biblical testimonies on Godself and enables them to become true and life-promoting. The Holy Spirit is also the action that enables these testimonies to speak out of various contexts and experiences. In various historical, cultural, social, intellectual, and other contexts, these testimonies can find their voices.[97] These contexts can also be in conflict with each other. They appear incompatible with each other. They may not even provide the capacity to understand each other directly, as the persons of various languages in the Pentecost event were not in a position to understand each other, and yet they all in their own languages heard the proclamation of "God's deeds of power." These persons were even confused, were seized by fear, became the victims of irony and scorn, because they and outsiders could not help but notice that other people whom they did not understand and by whom they themselves were not understood, nevertheless were able with them to hear and to grasp the same message.

The action of the Spirit through Scripture that can be summarized in the expression "inspiration" thus also means the fact that the action of the testimonies of Scripture can arise from different and even heterogeneous contexts, and can act on different and heterogeneous contexts. This action of the Spirit that leads to God's word being heard, meeting with a response, being taken up and producing fruit[98] has, following Calvin, been called the *testimonium Spiritus Sancti internum*. This "internal testimony of the Spirit" has also been designated "the secret testimony" (*testimonium arcanum*). It effects, it attains the unity of personal certainty and thus corresponds on the human side to the unity of God's presence. Talk of the inspiration of Scripture thus applies first of all to the action of God in and through which the various testimonies of the biblical traditions, either individually or communally in more or less complex interconnections, point to God's presence and to God's glory. Second, talk of the inspiration of Scripture applies to the action of God through which the testimonies of Scripture evoke in individual human beings or communities experiences,

---

97. Accordingly, the "fulfillment of Scripture" or passages of Scripture applied to a later time are frequently traced back to people speaking "by the Spirit," to the Holy Spirit "speaking," or to the Holy Spirit speaking "through" David, Isaiah, Jeremiah, etc. Cf. Mark 12:36; Matt. 22:43; Acts 1:16; 4:25; 28:25; Heb. 3:7; 9:8; 10:15; 1 Tim. 4:1; 1 Pet. 1:11ff.; 2 Pet. 1:21.

98. See also the differentiated case made by F. Mildenberger for a theological use of the word *inspiration* (*Biblische Dogmatik: Eine Biblische Theologie in dogmatischer Perspektive*, vol. 1, *Prolegomena: Verstehen und Geltung der Bibel* [Stuttgart: Kohlhammer, 1991], esp. 93ff.).

answers, and reactions to that presence of God to which they attest.[99] Without this inspiration, both the texts of the Bible in itself and the community in itself are nothing but "dead letters" and "dead bones." Through the Spirit, the Bible—inspired—attests to the presence and glory of God. Through the Spirit, inspired testimonies and inspired readers of the Bible become capable of experiencing, expressing, and communicating the presence and glory of God.

---

99. J. Calvin highlights two aspects of the testimony of the Holy Spirit: "For as God alone is a fit witness of himself in his Word, so also the Word will not find acceptance in men's hearts before it is sealed by the inward testimony of the Spirit. The same Spirit, therefore, who has spoken through the mouths of the prophets must penetrate into our hearts to persuade us that they faithfully proclaimed what had been divinely commanded" (*Inst.* vol. 1, 1/7, 4, 78. Cf. ibid., 1/7 and 9 as well as 2/5, 5. Cf. also vol. 2, 3/24, 1 and 4/14, 8. Illuminating in this context are W. Krusche, *Das Wirken des Heiligen Geistes nach Calvin*, Forschungen zur Kirchen- und Dogmengeschichte 7 (Göttingen: Vandenhoeck, 1957), 167ff., 202ff.; T. Preiss, *Das innere Zeugnis des Heiligen Geistes*, ThSt[B] 21 (Zollikon-Zurich: Evangelischer Verlag, 1947), esp. 12ff.; G. W. Locher, *Testimonium internum: Calvins Lehre vom Heiligen Geist und das hermeneutische Problem*, ThSt[B] 81 (Zurich: Evangelischer Verlag Zurich, 1964). M. Brecht casts light on the theological efforts to preserve the tension between both aspects of the Spirit's testimony ("Beobachtungen zur Vorstellung vom Heiligen Geist in der lutherischen Orthodoxie und im frühen Pietismus," in J. Heubach, *Der Heilige Geist im Verständnis Luthers und der lutherischen Theologie*, Veröffentlichungen der Luther-Akademie Ratzeburg 17 [Erlangen: Martin-Luther, 1990], 46ff.); for a Reformed perspective, see C. W. Hodge, "The Witness of the Holy Spirit to the Bible," *Princeton Theological Review* 11 (1913): 41ff.

CHAPTER 6

The Public Person of the Spirit:
God in the Midst of Creation

The Western world has been shaped and defined by a spirit that exhibits another constitution, other interests, other goals, and other power structures than the Spirit of God. This spirit has also spread over the rest of the world. It has, for example, defined and regulated what counts as the essence of the human person, what counts as the ground of certainty, or what count as meaningful interests in development and as meaningful forms of development for human beings and for cultures. The accepted conceptions of order, rule, reason, harmony, and peace are still dictated by this spirit, or at least are decisively influenced by it. They are, as that which is unquestioned and self-evident, unobtrusively inscribed in psyches, forms of thought, and constructions of "reality," inasmuch as this spirit asserts *itself* in all domains of life and experience.

In a manner that seems highly self-evident, this spirit acquires plausibility and trust and possesses an almost boundless power of expansion. Because this is the case, this spirit—whether it became explicitly recognizable or remained as an all-infusing medium underneath the threshold of consciousness—has been frequently confused with the Spirit of God.[1]

---

1. On the practice of lumping together *pneuma* and *nous*, cf. N. Berdyaev, *Spirit and Reality*, trans. G. Reavey (New York: Charles Scribner's Sons, 1939), 15–31; on the fusion of the Holy Spirit and Aristotelian spirit, W. Kern and Y. Congar, *Geist und Heiliger Geist*, Christlicher Glaube in moderner Gesellschaft 22 (Freiburg: Herder, 1982), 90ff.; on distinguishing the two, G. Sauter, "Geist und Freiheit: Geistvorstellungen und die Erwartung des Geistes," *EvT* 41 (1981): esp. 217ff.; G. Sauter, "Ekstatische Gewissheit oder vergewissernde Sicherung: Zum Verhältnis von Geist und Vernunft," in *In der Freiheit des Geistes: Theologische Studien* (Göttingen:

Hybrids were developed—in significant theologies as well—that identified the spirit that dominates the Western world and the Spirit of God.[2] On the one hand, religious and moral countermeasures were mustered against the spirit of the Western world with the help of these hybrids. Admittedly, these countermeasures had only limited scope. On the other hand, these hybrids obstructed and distorted the clear knowledge of God's Spirit. With regard to the Spirit and to experience of the Spirit, these hybrids generated, or at least had a hand in causing, the uncertainty and lack of orientation that we have had to assume as our point of departure throughout this book.

The insights acquired in this theology of the Holy Spirit allow us to work against this troubling state of affairs at a basic level by discerning the spirits. They allow us to discern, on the one hand, the Spirit who does *not* bear witness to the Spirit, but who makes present the self-withdrawing and self-giving Crucified One.[3] They allow us to discern, on the other hand, the spirit that cultivates and spreads individual and community self-relations in the sense of self-certainty, self-possession, and the constant increase of this self-relation that serves self-production.[4] Further on we shall be presenting an exposition of

---

Vandenhoeck, 1988), esp. 41ff.; A. M. Aagaard, "Die Erfahrung des Geistes," in O. A. Dilschneider, ed., *Theologie des Geistes* (Gütersloh: Mohn, 1980), 9ff. On the problem of discerning the spirits precisely with regard to the philosophical conceptions discussed on the following pages, see W. Kasper, "Aspekte gegenwärtiger Pneumatologie," in W. Kasper, ed., *Gegenwart des Geistes: Aspekte der Pneumatologie*, QD 85 (Freiburg: Herder, 1979), 15ff.

2. Here we should highlight H. Zwingli's concept of the Spirit, which is marked by a conception of "freedom as God's pure self-determination and self-communication," as has been shown by B. Hamm, *Zwinglis Reformation der Freiheit* (Neukirchen-Vluyn: Neukirchener, 1988), 42, cf. 41ff., 117ff., 127ff. In the twentieth century, K. Rahner's "transcendental" pneumatology with its "mysticism of everyday life" comes very close to the Western conception of spirit (cf. Rahner, *Theological Investigations*, vol. 16, *Experience of the Spirit: Source of Theology*, trans. D. Morland [New York: Crossroad, 1979]; vol. 17, *Jesus, Man, and the Church*, trans. M. Kohl [New York: Crossroad, 1981]. With regard to a substantive pneumatology, these volumes are astonishingly devoid of insight).

3. Cf. esp. §4.5.

4. This self-relation in relationship with others was not only attributed to the Spirit of God, but regarded as the form of the personhood of God's Spirit. As far back as K. v. Lechler (*Die biblische Lehre vom heiligen Geiste*, pt. 1 [Gütersloh: Bertelsmann, 1899], 254ff.) we find the attempt to assert the "personality" of the

this spirit. The insights that we have acquired allow us to discern, on the one hand, God's Spirit, who becomes manifest and enables human beings to have a share in the Spirit by—having been "poured out"—exercising an influence that reaches into diverse contexts and by enabling people from diverse contexts to strengthen each other and to serve each other, promoting what is best for each other. They allow us to discern, on the other hand, the spirit that gives power over all that is experienced and encountered, inasmuch as this spirit subsumes it under and integrates it into the unity of this spirit's self-relationship. To be sure, the spirit of the Western world also includes *the moment of the giving up of self through self-externalization*. But it includes this moment only as a point of transition on the way to heightened self-development. To be sure, the Spirit of God is also a thoroughly *powerful* force in the weak and in human beings capable of free self-withdrawal (cf. 2 Cor. 12:9). But the two forms of exercising power and of withdrawing self are fundamentally different.

The difference between the spirits evokes a differentiated understanding of self, reality, and validity. In order to show this, let us orient ourselves to the most intellectually informed and culturally influential understandings of "the spirit" of the Western world: namely, the understandings that we owe to the philosophers Aristotle and Hegel. We will see that this spirit aims at the cult of the abstract, private person and of the stratified, monocentric institution, as well as at the cognitive or cognitively controllable domination of the world. It will become clear

---

Spirit with regard to a "being-for-self" that is precisely not supported by the biblical texts. V. Lechler can see "one ego besides other egos" in the Spirit only because he carelessly defines subjectivity and personality as "an ego," standing "over against [others] and effecting self-differentiation in relation to them, yet also exchanging relationships with them" (ibid., 260). Besides the major philosophical tradition to be presented in the following pages, S. Kierkegaard's reductionist definition of spirit has surely exercised a formative influence. See *Kierkegaard's Writings*, vol. 16, *The Sickness unto Death: A Christian Psychological Exposition for Upbuilding and Awakening*, ed. and trans. H. V. Hong and E. H. Hong (Princeton, N.J.: Princeton Univ. Press, 1980), 13: "A human being is spirit. But what is spirit? Spirit is the self. But what is the self? The self is a relation that relates itself to itself . . ." By contrast, see H. Mühlen, *Der Heilige Geist als Person: In der Trinität, bei der Inkarnation und im Gnadenbund: Ich—Du—Wir*, 4th ed., Münsterische Beiträge zur Theologie 26 (Münster: Aschendorff, 1980), 156ff.; F. J. Schierse, "Die neutestamentliche Trinitätsoffenbarung," in *MySal* 2, 121ff.

that this spirit establishes forms of domination that must seek to suppress and to erode alternatives to itself. These forms of domination can experience the process of undergoing a fundamental (not a self-substitutive) transformation of the self only as "ruin" and "catastrophe." On the borders of each and every relative world and reality of this spirit, *imperialistic grasping and an anxiously defensive posture* are essential to this spirit. *Only in coming "to itself" can this spirit go "beyond itself"; only for the sake of producing itself more completely can it withdraw itself.*

By contrast, the Spirit of God places people in the community of conscious solidarity, the community of responsibility and love of persons who can accept their own finitude and perishability, who can live with the clear consciousness of the perishability of their relative world and reality because they know that in and beyond this perishability, they are ordained to participate in the divine glory and in its extension. These persons are aware of their public significance and worth in view of the significance and worth of their fellow creatures, and in view of God's glorification. They experience themselves as members of a community effected by the Spirit, a community of persons who change themselves, each other, and the world by *free self-withdrawal for the benefit of their fellow creatures.* These persons, too, spread out a force field; they, too, constitute a domain of power in the Spirit of shared participation. Yet this "expansion" is guided by an empathetic sensitivity to life in suffering, and to life that is still hostilely opposed to this expansion. It is guided by the search for liberation of merely private and cognitive identity, for liberation from the dangerous self-stabilizations and self-immunizations of monocentric forms of order.

In contrast to the spirit of the Western world of the past, the Spirit of God provides familiarity—for the sake of the liberating truth—with painful experiences of the collapse of certainties solidified by frequent use. This Spirit provides familiarity with fear of the power of the self-imposed endangerment and blindness caused by sin. The Spirit provides this familiarity for the sake of the experience of the love in which, in a manner that is not at our disposal, we are placed into structural patterns of life that are friendly and beneficial to us. This Spirit liberates from the paralysis caused by the power of sin, so that in free self-withdrawal we go beyond ourselves inasmuch as we resituate other creatures into, or enable them to move into, structural patterns of life that are beneficial to them. This Spirit provides familiarity with suffering on account of the finitude of one's own life and one's own lifeworld. This Spirit provides this familiarity for the sake of the joy that can be and is experienced in having a share in a life that is and remains valid, that carries us in and beyond our finitude, and that thus transforms our finite life and maintains it as transformed.

A truth that is not dominated by the search for mere certainty and self-certainty, a love that is foreign to the predominant spirit of Western culture, and a life that is not defined according to the standard of one's own finitude are in action here, influencing human certainties and experiences of community and of life. In substantive terms, the Apostles' Creed calls these forces the communion[5] of saints, the forgiveness of sins, the resurrection of that which is perishable, and the life everlasting.

6.1 Self-referential self-production and selflessness of the Spirit: On overcoming the predominant metaphysical concepts of Spirit (Aristotle and Hegel)

The decision to understand God's Spirit or the divine Spirit with the aid of Aristotle's metaphysics is one of the major theoretical decisions in Western intellectual history that have defined the basic formations of Western culture, and in addition have marked the forms for shaping life on this planet. This theoretical decision did not rest on an individual act of will, but on the discovery of a complex interconnection of experiences that provided mutually reinforcing evidence. This discovery enabled the interconnection between the continuity of sure self-relation and the activity of increasingly putting what is other at one's own disposal, as well as—in the context of this interconnection—the feeling of heightened pleasure, to become one of the most important, complex intellectual driving forces of human development.

---

5. Whereas the usual English version of the Creed uses the word "communion," the German uses *Gemeinschaft*, the word that is standardly translated "community." In the present text "communion" will appear in those passages that are exploring the meaning of the phrase from the Creed—TRANS.

This interconnection, which I shall attempt to clarify in the following discussion, became equally important for the definition of "God" and of God's intentions for the world, as well as for the definition of "the" human essence and of the living and striving worthy of human beings.

Inasmuch as the biblical statement that "God is Spirit" (John 4:24) was interpreted and understood in the sense of this theoretical decision, this statement was unhinged from the context of the biblical traditions and of the insights into God's Spirit contained in those traditions, and made to "fit" the spirit of the Western world. Religion and theology also were made to serve in paving the way for this spirit. They, too, were made to serve the development of a history—a history of culture, institutions, reason, and consciousness—that many people have come to regard as fateful for humanity and as fatal to the natural surroundings of human beings.

"God is Spirit"—this statement, comprehended with the aid of Aristotelian metaphysics, made possible a clear concept of the *person* of the Spirit or of the person of the divine: *self-referential, outside the world and yet related to it, comprehending everything and thus perfect, controlling everything and at the same time at one with itself.* This "person" could serve as the standard and the ideal for human personhood. At the same time it could be comprehended as a form in which the divine imparted itself to the human and the human could participate in the divine. In Book XII, 7 of his *Metaphysics*, Aristotle ingeniously develops this concept.[6] Hegel picked up the concept and with no less genius developed it further. What is at issue?

---

6. The following discussion employs the text Aristoteles, *Metaphysik XII*, ed. with a translation by H.-G. Gadamer, 3d ed., Klostermann Texte: Philosophie (Frankfurt am Main: Klostermann, 1984). Gadamer's translation is adopted only in part. (The English rendering of the Aristotle passage here follows in part *The Works of Aristotle*, vol. 8, *Metaphysica*, trans. W. D. Ross [Oxford: Clarendon Press, 1928]—TRANS.). The formulation ὁ Θεὸς . . . νοῦς ἐστιν, which has been translated into German both as *Gott ist Geist* ("God is spirit") and as *Gott ist Vernunft* ("God is reason"), is found only implicitly and not explicitly in *Metaphysics* XII, 7. It is found explicitly in the fragment "On Prayer," in *Aristotelis Fragmenta Selecta*, ed. W. D. Ross, 3d ed., Scriptorum Classicorum Bibliotheca Oxoniensis (Oxford: Oxford Univ. Press, 1964), 57. This was first pointed out to me by Michael Jacob. (In the English translation of the *Metaphysics* cited above, Ross renders νοῦς as "thought." It

The Aristotelian starting point may at first glance come across as insignificant and as pretty far out on a speculative limb. Yet it develops a form of power with the capacity to exercise the greatest conceivable influence. According to Aristotle, spirit—an ancestor of the modern *cogito*—is *the power that thinks itself insofar as it takes part in and receives a part in what is thought.* The medium in which this spirit lives is thought, and the form of this spirit is relation to itself *in* the relation to another. Spirit is the power that does not lose itself in the relation to another, but acquires and maintains itself in the "thinking" relation. The thinking of what is thought is an actual[7] activity in which spirit actualizes itself. This self-actualization is heightened by the expansion and intensification of this thinking that relates itself to another. This thinking self-actualization is good. Indeed, it is divine. In the words of Aristotle,

> thinking in itself deals with that which is best in itself, and the more it is thinking, the more it deals with that which is best. Spirit thinks itself by participating in that which is thought. Spirit becomes itself an object of thought by grasping and thinking that which is thought, so that spirit and that which is thought are identical.[8]

Aristotle explicitly emphasizes that the power that both produces and is this identity of thinking and of what is thought, is *spirit*.

---

is helpful to remember here that the sense of the German word *Geist* is broad enough for it frequently to serve as the translation of "mind" as well as of "spirit." For instance, the German translation of G. Bateson's *Steps to an Ecology of Mind* is entitled *Ökologie des Geistes*—TRANS.)

7. The German *wirklich* corresponds to both "real" and "actual" in ordinary English. In most cases *Wirklichkeit* should be translated into English as "reality." Such has been the practice up to this point in this text. But it is standard in German-language discussions of Aristotle's philosophy to use *Wirklichkeit* as a technical term, corresponding to the use of "actuality" in English-language discussions of Aristotle's thought. Hegel's use of *Wirklichkeit*, although presenting a strong *substantive* critique of Aristotle, is *terminologically* dependent on Aristotelian usage. Therefore, in the discussion of Aristotle's and Hegel's thought, *Wirklichkeit* and related forms will be translated with "actuality" and related forms. "Reality" and related forms will still appear occasionally in this context, translating the German *Realität* and related forms—TRANS.

8. This and the following quotations are all from Aristotle's *Metaphysics* 1072b, 19–32.

Aristotle likewise insists that "the divine" lies in the active appropriation of what is thought, and in the self-actualization bound up with
this appropriation.

> For that which is capable of receiving that which is thought and
> which is, is also spirit, to be sure, but it is in actual activity only
> when it has [that which is thought]. Thus actually active thought,
> more so than the capacity to think, is the divine element that spirit
> seems to have.

Spirit is the activity of thinking. It exists only in this manner and
is only when it is active by thinking, taking part in what is thought
and thus actualizing itself. Although in thought that which is spirit
penetrates that which is thinkable, it is unmixed with that which is
bodily. Nevertheless—to the great enthusiasm of philosophic thought
—the active spirit is in its activity objective to itself. The active spirit's
making itself objective to itself and *becoming objective to itself* in the relation to that which is thought is regarded by Aristotle as "the divine."
     This self-experience of spirit is what is best and the high point of
all imaginable pleasure. This pleasure is realized in philosophic thinking, in speculation, in *theoria*. Here human beings attain a share in
divine pleasure and well-being.

> Intellectual contemplation (philosophic thought) is what is most
> pleasant and best. If, then, the Divinity is always doing as well as we
> sometimes [are], this compels our wonder. If the Divinity is doing
> still better, this compels our wonder still more. And the Divinity
> indeed is doing better.

There is thus proper to *divinity* a more complete, heightened *manner* of the same *spiritual self-actualization and self-experience* of which we
partake in philosophic contemplation, in the thinking of thought. The
divine is the spirit that, in the relation that partakes of what is thought
and appropriates it for itself, makes itself objective to itself and becomes objective to itself. In its heightened, complete well-being it is
divinity. Aristotle also understands this thinking activity and self-
production as "life." He defines this activity as determinative life, as
"divine" life, as "best and eternal" life. "Life also naturally belongs to

the Divinity, for the activity (*energeia*) of spirit is life. And the Divinity is activity. This activity is itself the Divinity's best and eternal life."

Some translations have rendered the expression *energeia* as "self-actualization." This is thoroughly appropriate with regard to the substance of the matter. This *self*-actualization includes both the activity, the "en-act-edness" of thinking, and that which is brought forth, that which is made objective, to which thinking relates itself. But what is made objective is the very thinking of what is thought, for in thinking what is thought, thinking becomes sensible of its very self. In thinking what is thought, thinking does not become foreign to itself, but instead receives itself, generates and enjoys itself. This process of becoming active, of producing itself, of becoming sensible of itself, of receiving itself, of enjoying itself is the "best and eternal life of divinity." This is spirit as divinity, divinity as spirit.

"God is spirit"—this is summarized and elucidated by Aristotle in the following manner: "We assert therefore that the Divinity is a living being, eternal and complete, so that life and continuous and eternal existence belong to the Divinity, for this is the essence of the Divinity."

But God's vitality is active thinking that grasps what is thought, participates in it and appropriates it, and thereby produces itself, becomes sensible of and knowable to itself, relates itself to itself. In this active thinking that produces itself and becomes thematic to itself, in this self-actualization of thought, we human beings also participate in the divine spirit, in the divine life, in the divine self-relatedness.

One of the simplest interpretations of spirit's divine self-relation is that here *the unity of the subjective and the objective* is present. According to this interpretation, this spiritual unity, the spiritual life, is defined by a thinking self-relation of spirit. The thinking spirit relates itself to the thought spirit, and in doing so is at one with itself, as we are at one with ourselves in the relation of "I am I." This interpretation, though, is reductionist. It cannot distinguish a mute, empty entity that revolves only around itself, a vacuous, tautological "I-am-I-am-I-. . . ," from the life of the spirit described by Aristotle.

In order to comprehend the life of the spirit perceived by Aristotle, it is necessary to consider the following: Spirit is the capacity, in the act of thinking, of participating and receiving a share in that which is *thought* and in that which *is*. Further, spirit is the capacity of being actively related to oneself *in this process of participation*. Spirit is thus not merely openness to that which is thought and to that which is; spirit is also *active appropriation*. Only *in this active appropriation* does the divine spirit become *sensible of itself*. In other words, spirit relates itself not only to itself, but rather *inasmuch* as it actively relates itself to that which is and is thought, it relates itself to itself. Inasmuch as it heightens its intellectually operative control over that which is thought, it heightens its self-production and its intimacy with itself. This remarkable self-relation—self-relation inasmuch as it relates itself to another—occurs in thinking. In thinking it is not only that which is thought, but also thinking itself that becomes thematic to itself. Those who think not only know what is thought; they also know that it is *thought*. They know about their *self*-relation to what is thought. They thus know that they themselves are thinking beings. This is latently and concomitantly the case in every act, more precisely in every activity of thinking. Every instance of thinking thus has two objects: the more or less explicitly thematized object and, at least implicitly, itself. Aristotle is persuaded that "spirit" is this thinking that in its self-actualization takes part in and has a part in what is thought and what is.

An important, interesting, and complex operation is initiated inasmuch as thinking completes itself and potentiates itself in its self-relation: "the more it is thinking, the more it deals with that which is best." In this potentiation, not only must thinking disengage itself more and more strongly from the externally assumed object of thought in order to become more sensible of itself and more active. Not only must it disengage itself more strongly from external impressions: in other words, from thinking this and that and the other, and from lingering with that which is thought. Not only must it avoid scattering its activity and attention in the ebb and flow of whatever occurs to it. *Thinking must also disengage itself from a merely latent continuity with itself. It cannot content itself with the dim certainty of somehow* always being present, of somehow being a participant, of somehow accompanying what is thought. It must—continuing with the metaphor—not only break loose from external impressions, but *also let itself loose, wrest itself loose from itself*, free itself, release itself. In this act, thinking must create the precondition for becoming more clearly thematic to itself. The phenomenon that has fascinated even the most sophisticated philosophical reflection again and again is this: In this heightened abstraction from what is thought and in this breaking loose from the torpid stream of its *own* intellectual activity, thinking acquires *itself* and attains the most concrete kind of certainty.

This basic movement of simultaneous self-bifurcation *and* self-acquisition, of abstraction from self *and* of concrete experience of self, of bifurcation *and* of the attainment of conscious intimacy with self is fascinating not only to philosophical speculation. This basic movement also has driven cultural development up to and including modern society's processes of differentiation. This process of producing itself, of wrenching itself free, and at the same time of becoming knowable to itself, of becoming intimate with itself, is according to Aristotle the life of spirit, the divine.

Without question, we have here a complex and impressive principle, striking in its subtlety and in its wealth of facets and of possibilities for development. Most of the theological and philosophical speculative efforts directed toward "the identity of subject and object," "the dialectic," or "the Spirit" are only poor caricatures of this profound *dialectical* understanding of Aristotle's.

Aristotle's understanding, which connects several different pieces of evidence, was extended and completed by Hegel. Hegel is correct when he notes with sadness that the "speculative consideration and knowledge of the nature and activity of spirit has declined . . . in recent times, even to the point of losing even a vague notion of it. . . . Thus Aristotle's writings clearly remain the only writings that [contain] truly speculative developments concerning the being and the activity of spirit."[9] The passage that we examined from Aristotle's *Metaphysics*, Book XII, is in Hegel's words "the highest point of Aristotle's metaphysics, the most speculative thing there can be."[10] Hegel concluded his great *Encyclopedia* by citing this text.[11]

---

9. G. W. F. Hegel, "Fragment zur Philosophie des Geistes," in *Werke*, Theorie-Werkausgabe, ed. E. Moldenhauer and K. M. Michel, vol. 11, *Berliner Schriften (1818–1831)* (Frankfurt am Main: Suhrkamp, 1970), 523–24; this edition will be cited henceforth as *Werke*.

10. G. W. F. Hegel, *Vorlesungen über die Geschichte der Philosophie 2, Werke* 19, 219.

11. G. W. F. Hegel, *Hegel's Philosophy of Mind*, trans. W. Wallace and A. V. Miller (Oxford: Oxford Univ. Press, 1971), 315.

Hegel saw the task of philosophy in general, and the achievement of his own philosophy in particular, in the removal of an essential deficiency of Aristotelian theory. In Hegel's view, the great achievement of Aristotle lies in having called attention to the fact that *thought which thinks itself is the acme of concreteness and certainty*, and in having identified this extremely concrete and certain self-relation as "the divine."

Yet now that philosophy with Aristotle has comprehended self-thinking thought as that which is concrete, and has recognized the divine in this self-thinking thought, there is a need "for knowing, spirit . . . to objectify itself, to return to objectivity, to reconcile with itself *the world* that it has abandoned. . . . For spirit is not merely pure thinking, but thinking that makes itself objective, and *in this objectification maintains itself*, has itself in a manner adequate to itself, *is at home with itself.*"[12]

On the one hand, Hegel emphasizes the genius and the fundamental status of the Aristotelian understanding of divine spirit: "*As spirit I am only insofar as I know myself.* . . . *Know thyself*, the inscription over the temple of the knowing god at Delphi, is the absolute commandment that expresses the nature of spirit."[13]

On the other hand, Hegel lodges the criticism that Aristotle comprehended *only a principle*, that he remained in the element of *abstract thought*. In doing so he comprehended spirit reductionistically, failing to grasp spirit in its true activity.

"But this element of thought itself is abstract. It is the activity of an individual consciousness. Spirit, though, is not only as individual, finite consciousness, but as spirit that is universal and concrete in itself."[14]

In contrast to Aristotle, Hegel sees that the Western spirit's self-comprehension in the act of thinking is a process and progress filled "by developed, total actuality." In the spirit and as spirit it is *not only an individual who becomes certain of herself.* Communities, institutions,

---

12. Hegel, *Werke* 19, 412, cf. 410, 412ff.; emphasis added.

13. Hegel, *Vorlesungen über die Geschichte der Philosophie* 3, *Werke* 20, 480–81; emphasis partially added; cf. 481.

14. Ibid., 481. The following quotations are also from here. The fact that the young Hegel admittedly employs a concept of Spirit that still depends quite heavily on Aristotle is documented by his *Jenaer Systementwürfe* 2, *Gesammelte Werke* 7, ed. R.-P. Horstmann and J. H. Trede (Hamburg: Meiner, 1971), 174ff.

states, conditions of the world—in short, *a world becomes conscious of itself in a step-by-step manner.* Spirit as universal, concrete spirit not only "runs through the thinking of an individual and presents itself in an individual consciousness." Spirit is comprehended abstractly, one-sidedly, and insufficiently as long as it is not recognized as the "universal spirit that presents itself in the wealth of its figuration in world history."

Just as in thinking the individual wrenches himself loose from himself and from his environment—a process rightly seen and presented by Aristotle—so *a world* comprehends itself inasmuch as it concretizes, manifests, presents, and recognizes itself in cultural achievements and cultural institutions. Therefore Hegel can say that in world history spirit is "in its most concrete actuality," that "world history . . . is the exposition of spirit as it laboriously acquires and makes accessible to itself the knowledge of that which it is in itself."[15] Inasmuch as spirit in its knowing itself simultaneously manifests itself both subjectively and objectively, both cognitively and practically, world history is to be understood not only as the exposition of spirit, but at the same time as "the actual becoming of spirit."[16]

Spirit, which Hegel also terms "that which is common to all peoples," is thus not only the power in which the thinking human individual relates herself to herself. It is also the power in which a varied culture, a culture that is intellectually active in diverse ways and that grasps itself in thoughts—indeed, an entire world—not only comes to an understanding about itself and about its own actuality, but also presents itself, manifests itself, and in this reality comprehends itself.[17]

At this point it is relatively easy to elaborate on the basis of Hegel's insight what is inadequate about the Aristotelian conception. With his conception of divine spirit, Aristotle offers an extremely reductionist understanding of joy and of life, and above all a highly reductionist understanding of *actuality.* He comprehends spirit and the life of spirit as a *merely intellectual relation* and form of behavior. Above all

---

15. G. W. F. Hegel, *The Philosophy of History,* trans. J. Sibree, Great Books in Philosophy (Buffalo: Prometheus, 1991), 16, 17–18, translation altered.

16. Ibid., 457, translation altered.

17. Hegel, *Werke* 11, 149; see also B. Taureck, "Geist / Heiliger Geist / Geistesgaben: VII. Der philosophische Geistbegriff," *TRE* 12 (1984): 250ff.

he comprehends pleasure, actuality, and life only as cognitive self-production and self-possession. Although the activity of spirit *passes through the moment of self-distancing*, it attains again and again only what is its own and what it has appropriated in thought.

Both self-relation that occurs *only in thinking* and mere *self-possession* make the life of divine spirit celebrated by Aristotle into an essentially powerless and dismal affair, in spite of all the impressiveness of its internal dynamic.

Were this way of talking about spirit proffered as the content of a *theological* pneumatology, as an answer to the problems presented to us by the biblical texts concerning God's Spirit, it would appear to be simplistic, both avoiding the challenges and offering naive solutions. To name only the simplest problems one could pose, it is impossible for *intellectual* self-possession to be the answer to a real, community-destroying situation of distress. It is impossible for intellectual *self-possession* to bring change and redemption, for example, to a society defined by the principle of egotism that disintegrates community, and by the principle of the deception that masks this egotism.

At this level, Hegel's philosophy of spirit, articulating and describing as it does the forces of sociality and the developmental dynamics of material conditions of the world, offers a vastly superior alternative. Spirit is to be understood not only as intellectual self-relation, but as *real, material processes of producing self and of becoming thematic to self*. Spirit is to be conceived not only as a self-relation of the individual, but as the complex *self-relation of a historical world*. To this extent spirit is the true and complete principle of community. Spirit can be defined, in the words of the *Phenomenology of Spirit*, as "'I' that is 'We' and 'We' that is 'I.'"[18] The task is to comprehend "spirits" of differing complexity, from friendship to global society, in their differences and their hierarchical interconnections.

In spirit, in the spiritual relation, the community and the world lose all foreignness for the "I," because it recognizes its own structures of life and knowledge in this reality. By the same token, the community recognizes itself in the individual self that it produces and shapes. To put the matter in terms of simple, direct examples, the civil community

---

18. G. W. F. Hegel, *Phenomenology of Spirit*, trans. A. V. Miller (Oxford: Clarendon Press, 1977), 110.

reproduces, recognizes, protects, and maintains itself in the individual citizen; the association, in the associate; the faith-community, in the community member.

Hegel is convinced that the *Christian religion* provides one of the most complete ways of laying bare this spiritual structure of reality, indeed one of its most complete revelations. The Christian, so-called manifest religion reveals both that and how the absolute spirit that brings forth and infuses the world relates to spirit: that is, to itself. This religion reveals how the spiritual world perceives the divine in an individual spirit, in a human "I."[19] Finally, the Christian religion reveals how the spiritual world recognizes and acknowledges this spiritual relation as its own real divinity. The form of reality makes it accessible to humanity and to the act of knowing, and the human person has the power to know and to shape reality. Of course, with this insight religious consciousness raises itself to philosophic consciousness.

It is the responsibility of this philosophic consciousness to unveil the "essence of spirit" in the *reconstruction* of the relation of "nature and 'I' "—a task already set down by the young Hegel.[20] Philosophy reconstructs, regulates, and stimulates spiritual self-relation and spiritual life in individual, communal, cultural, and world-historical frames of reference.

In doing so, philosophy must do something that, at least on an initial reading of Hegel's writings, is very confusing: it must control a whole hierarchy of "spirits," which are sublated into ever-more complex and comprehensive structures of spirit. Has the Aristotelian spirit thus been poured out on the flesh? Have the recognized difficulties been overcome? Does Hegel's insight provide a key to theological pneumatology? Is Hegel's insight itself already the act of unlocking?

Hegel has doubtless grasped the "life" of the spirit of the Western world: its force and its freedom in entering into that which is finite, manifold, and perishable. Yet he also grasps this vitality and freedom only as vital and free *being-at-home-with-self*. Even if spirit enters into what is finite and perishable, even in union with what is finite and

---

19. According to Hegel, it is quite incidental that this human "I" is called Jesus of Nazareth.

20. Thus G. W. F. Hegel, *Faith and Knowledge*, trans. W. Cerf and H. S. Harris (Albany: SUNY Press, 1977), 177–180.

perishable, spirit is only "in itself and at home with itself"; "spirit is being-at-home-with-self."[21] Spirit is the "reconciled return to itself out of its other."[22] This does *not* mean that spirit is only an abstract, *merely intellectual self-relation* that leaves behind that which is other, finite, and perishable. It does not mean that spirit does not get involved with what is other. It does not even mean that spirit does not establish a community and does not materially form a world. Instead Hegel repeatedly describes the "divine spirit" as a force that produces real human community and real unity in real life relations, a force that shapes nature and culture. Yet this force is to be understood as the "infinite return into self" that connects and unites human beings.[23] That which "binds individuals together is also what constitutes their true self-consciousness, what is innermost and most proper to them."[24]

To be sure, Hegel calls this return into self that mediates unity and community "love" and "*God as present.*"[25] Yet it is hard to see why this "love," "God as present" does not essentially push us back to the Aristotelian conception. It is hard to see why this spirit should not be the power, the realization, and manifestation of a collective and individual egotism. It is hard to see why spirit should not be the power of the potentiation, extension, and completion of an egotism of that sort.

It is impossible to see how this spirit could be a power for change, reversal, and new beginning in a situation of spreading individual and collective self-closure and self-production, relatively adjusted and veiled in their brutalities and deficiencies. "Spirit is only this perceiving of itself."[26]

---

21. Cf. Hegel, *Philosophy of History,* 17, translation altered; emphasis in original omitted.

22. G. W. F. Hegel, *The Philosophy of Fine Art* 2, trans. F. P. B. Osmaston (New York: Hacker Art, 1975), 309, translation altered.

23. G. W. F. Hegel, *Lectures on the Philosophy of Religion* 3, trans. E. B. Speirs and J. B. Sanderson, ed. E. B. Speirs (New York: Humanities, 1962), 107.

24. Ibid., translation altered.

25. Ibid.

26. G. W. F. Hegel, *Geschichte der Philosophie* 1, *Werke* 18, 93. Cf. ibid.: "There is only *one* Spirit, the universal divine Spirit—not that it merely is everywhere. It is not merely in many as commonality, as external 'all-ness' . . . but as that which permeates, as the unity of itself and of a show of its other . . . [as] overarching its other [e.g., ununited, unreconciled diversity], its other and itself in one."

Where the danger and power of the evil spirit and of the lying spirit, where the danger and power of distress and disintegration that are communally caused and perpetuated, and thus at the same time denied and veiled, have been recognized, the Spirit of God is definitely expected as something other than self-generation, self-attestation, perception of itself, and return into itself in otherness. The same is true where the hope is awakened for real enlivenment that renews the diversity of life in its concrete reality.

"Spirit engenders itself. . . . It is only inasmuch as it engenders itself, bears witness to itself and shows itself, manifests itself."[27] If this is articulated and presented only in the medium of self-relation and self-production, of return to self, if spirit only brings this structure into the "other of itself," if spirit lays bare in reality only this perception of itself, this spirit *certainly* does not articulate the *Holy* Spirit. The Spirit of God does not deliver, preserve, and renew by engaging in a mere self-perception that creates the unity of an all-infusing self-attestation and return into self.

The Hegelian conception only appears to overcome the naiveté of classical metaphysical pneumatology. To be sure, Hegel corrects the formality, abstractness, and reflexive distance from reality of classical metaphysical pneumatology. Yet in view of the efforts to experience the presence of the Spirit in the midst of the conditions of a finitude that suffers under the power of sin, the Hegelian pneumatology also *remains* simplistic and barren.

A theology of the Holy Spirit must see through the fixed concentration, common to both Hegel and Aristotle, on the unity of (1) self-relation capable of potentiation, (2) intellectually operative control, and (3) pleasure. A theology of the Holy Spirit must make clear that the "person" of the spirit that can be grasped in this unity hardly has anything in common with the Spirit of God attested in the biblical traditions. A theology of the Holy Spirit must work in an enlightening manner against the cult of this spirit and against the respect that has become habitual at the global level for this spirit's power. A theology of the Holy Spirit does this effectively, true to its subject matter, by aiding in the recognition of the specific *selflessness of the Spirit of God*, and in the recognition of what are bound up with this selflessness: the public

---

27. Ibid., 94.

personality, the power and effectiveness, and the deliverance and renewal of the world.[28]

By contrast to the spirit that rules the Western world by fixed
concentration on self-consciousness and heightened control, the selflessness of the Spirit of God can appear unclear and numinous. Yet
the Spirit of God is anything but an incomprehensible entity, dissi-
pating into indeterminate shapelessness. Even where the Spirit initially only "comes upon" individual human beings, the Spirit
immediately forms a *domain of resonance*. The person upon whom the
Spirit comes acts directly or indirectly, consciously or unconsciously
for the benefit of other persons. The persons immediately affected by
the Spirit's action are for their part so "touched," or their services are
so powerfully enlisted, that they likewise orient themselves to acting
for the benefit of others. The Spirit of God effects a domain of liberation and of freedom (2 Cor. 3:17), a domain not determined by
self-relation exercising control, or even merely by intellectual self-
relation. People are liberated for action that liberates other people.
This can lead to positive repercussions within their own domain of
experience, but it need not do so. In any case the persons upon whom
the Spirit comes experience themselves as withdrawing themselves in
freedom, as creating for others, as acting for the benefit of the development of others. In doing so they are equipped with great powers.
Great powers of what is lovable and trustworthy proceed from them.
At an essential level they *awaken* pleasure in strangers, even if this is
covered over by shame and on occasion turns into aggression and
hatred against them.

The persons upon whom God's Spirit comes and whose services
God's Spirit enlists cannot rest content with relating cognitively to
themselves and with presenting themselves in their surroundings in

---

28. See K. L. Schmidt, "Das Pneuma Hagion als Person und als Charisma:
Eine lexicologische und biblisch-theologische Studie," *Eranos Jahrbuch* 13 (1945):
esp. 224ff. See further H. Schlier's description of the process in which human be-
ings are concretely placed in the eschatological domain of God's action ("Herkunft,
Ankunft und Wirkungen des Heiligen Geistes im Neuen Testament," in C. Heit-
mann and H. Mühlen, eds., *Erfahrung und Theologie des Heiligen Geistes* (Hamburg:
Agentur des Rauhen Hauses; Munich: Kösel, 1974), 118ff; H. Mühlen, "Soziale
Geisterfahrung als Antwort auf eine einseitige Gotteslehre," ibid., 253ff.

ways that can be cognitively integrated and controlled. They cannot be satisfied with bringing *themselves* into, and finding themselves in, other life relations in such a way that these relations, and thus they themselves, are at their disposal. Their own pleasure does not depend on constant self-identification and the connected maximized control. Their pleasure is bound up with the liberating opening of new life possibilities for other persons, with the experiences of overcoming, for the benefit of others, powers and forces that are oppressive and hostile to life. Their own pleasure is bound up with the experience of a power that also acts through them; a power that leads them beyond their own experiences, conceptions, and ideals; a power that has enlisted their services in order to protect, liberate, renew, and enliven other creatures. In the orientation to the crucified and risen Christ, the power of the Spirit acquires clarity as Christ's form of attraction and influence: as the Spirit of Christ. This power is expressed in the constitution of the community of the body of Christ, in liberation from paralysis by sin, and in liberation for valid life.

The critique developed in this theology of the Holy Spirit of the Western concept of the Spirit and God essentially influenced by Aristotle concurs with the intention of a critique exercised by Eberhard Jüngel on the basic Aristotelian approach of Western metaphysics. Inspired by Martin Heidegger, Jüngel has rightly called into question the understanding of actuality built on the basic Aristotelian approach.[29] He has accurately noted that this understanding of actuality, which is bound up with a certain idea of God, is incompatible with the God of Christian faith and with this faith's understanding of actuality. The critical analysis of the Aristotelian approach and of a theology influenced by it constitutes one of the most important contributions of Jüngel's major work.

Jüngel argues that what is temporally imperishable, which Aristotle sees expressed in the active, intellectual self-relation of the divine spirit, "is traditionally defined as 'the actual and only actual,' as pure actualization in the form of having been actualized . . . as the

---

29. Cf. E. Jüngel, "Die Welt als Möglichkeit und Wirklichkeit: Zum ontologischen Ansatz der Rechtfertigungslehre," in *Unterwegs zur Sache: Theologische Bemerkungen*, BEvT 61 (Munich: Kaiser, 1972), 206ff.

actualized without possibility: self-actualization in the sense of being self-actualized."[30] Jüngel adds that

> based on this metaphysical decision whose consequences appear to have become our fate, the tradition has consequently thought God as pure actuality, as the purest act of self-actualization in the sense of one who has always and already actualized himself. In that sense, God is thus and not otherwise; he has, so to speak, always already made himself necessary.[31]

Jüngel claims that *Christian faith* needs *to give up this idea of God* both on the basis of God's word and on the basis of the internal aporias of this idea of God.[32] Without question we ought to concur with Jüngel in this critique of the idea of God or of the Spirit as pure actuality in the manner of *actus purus*, as the pure activity of having always already actualized oneself.[33] Yet the execution of this critique and the conceptual alternative stay within the limits of the Aristotelian approach. Unlike Hegel, Jüngel does not see clearly the intellectualism of the Aristotelian approach and the inadequacy of the connected conception of "actuality." He does not contest the Aristotelian definition—or the definition that appeals to Aristotle's basic model—of "actuality" as such. He does not contest that the "self-actualization in the sense of being self-actualized" that Aristotle comprehends as *intellectual self*-possession is appropriately defined *as actuality* at all, or that actuality is sufficiently comprehended in this model. While Hegel calls this basic approach itself into question, Jüngel develops only an external critique. In other words, without calling *this* understanding of actuality itself into question, Jüngel seeks to subordinate this understanding of actuality to the primacy of possibility.

A questionable, abstractly and intellectualistically articulated so-called actuality thus remains presupposed and taken over in Jüngel's

---

30. E. Jüngel, *God as the Mystery of the World: On the Foundation of the Theology of the Crucified One in the Dispute between Theism and Atheism*, trans. D. L. Guder (Grand Rapids, Mich.: Eerdmans, 1983), 213–14, translation altered.

31. Ibid., 214, translation altered.

32. Jüngel, "Die Welt als Möglichkeit und Wirklichkeit," 209–10.

33. The idea of God being criticized—God as *actus purus*—is paradigmatically expounded by Thomas Aquinas, *Summa Theologica* 1, 3, 1, c; 2, c; and passim.

conception, even if its priority, its ontological primacy over possibility is contested.

Yet Jüngel not only remains below the level of insight provided by Hegel into the conceptual weakness of the Aristotelian understanding of actuality. He also does not do justice to the intellectual subtlety of the Aristotelian approach. Jüngel formulates his program thus:

> For that reason we think God in unity with perishability. And in doing so we oppose the fundamental Aristotelian approach of Western metaphysics, which ascribed to pure actuality an ontological primacy over possibility and thus assigned necessarily an exclusively negative ontological quality to perishability.[34]

Since the Aristotelian conception of "actuality" has not been criticized in itself, this programmatic formulation can be integrated into Aristotle's metaphysics as soon as the basic approach of this metaphysics is perceived in its dialectical power.

Jüngel imputes to Aristotelian metaphysics a conception of actuality as "self-actualization in the sense of always and already having actualized oneself."[35] By contrast, Aristotelian metaphysics conceives the intellectual self-actualization that stands at its center as a *living power* that can *definitely* claim to stand *in union with perishability and with possibility.*

Intellectual self-relation indeed "is" only *in* its en-acted constant activation and renewal. As we have seen, pure thinking must break loose from external impressions and contents *as well as from itself.* It must tear itself away from itself, release itself from itself. It thus must split itself in two in order to lay hold of itself and to acquire itself. One would need to show why this activity of self-actualization does *not* necessarily bring with it the moment of passing away, why it does not in this manner subordinate itself to the "primacy of possibility." Independently of Aristotle's own answer, the question of primacy that is important for Jüngel remains open at this level, since Aristotle's *intellectual* en-actedness, which in principle is able to take up all contents of thought into itself, latently holds all contents of thought co-present.

---

34. Jüngel, *God as the Mystery of the World,* 214, translation altered.
35. Ibid., translation altered.

The Aristotelian conception thus provides all the preconditions necessary to carry out Jüngel's program by its own means and within its own
boundaries. The "highest point" (Hegel) of Aristotle's metaphysics is
not at odds with defining the living, intellectually active divine spirit as
holding the fullness of possibility present and as standing in differentiated unity with perishability.

Without abandoning the Aristotelian model, one can understand
it in the sense of Jüngel's program. Jüngel's critique offers no objection strong enough to prevent the continued use of Aristotelian conceptions of actuality, spirit, and God, or to prevent renewals of these
conceptions.

On the one hand, the unsharp articulation of the basic Aristotelian model prevents Jüngel from perceiving what it can achieve and
how it can be interpreted in the sense of his own program. On the
other hand, the insufficient critical sensitivity to a merely intellectual-
ist understanding of actuality prevents Jüngel from comprehending the
problematic of a theory that makes merely *intellectual* self-possession its
center and standard.

On this level neither the essential abstractness and escapism of a
pneumatology oriented on Aristotelian foundations, nor the relative
strengths, the possibilities for gradation and concretization on the basis of Aristotelian theoretical foundations, can be comprehended and
critically controlled, not to mention replaced.

By contrast, Hegel did not shortchange the basic speculative structure of the Aristotelian understanding of actuality. He reproached
Aristotle for saying that "possibility and actuality are identical."[36] He
clearly recognized both the dialectical strengths of the Aristotelian
conception as well as the decisive *weakness in his understanding of actuality*. Although Hegel can be regarded as the most important precursor
of contemporary academe in its enthusiasm for "thought" as such, he
had a sober perception of the problematic of an understanding of actuality that is reduced to *intellectual self-possession*. The "task of thought"
cannot be to think "more" than *this* actuality, but rather to grasp the
concept of "actuality" more clearly and more broadly. Hegel concedes
that Aristotelian metaphysics grasped *that which is concrete and the*

---

36. Hegel, *Werke* 19, 164.

principle of certainty. Yet this is not to say that Aristotelian metaphysics offers a conception of actuality that can simply be presupposed and accepted, that then in a second step could be externally criticized and superseded.

Hegel's conception of a substance infused with spirit, of an actuality that is historically concretized by spirit and that historically expresses spirit, *changes* Aristotle's understanding of spirit and of actuality. Hegel conceives spirit not only as the power of self-producing and self-maintaining thought, but as *the power of the real self-production of all entities infused with thought*, be they human individuals, or states of communities or of the world. Only by doing so can Hegel claim to *make good* philosophically on the program to think God in unity with perishability.

Spirit's process of self-production and self-manifestation, or more precisely, the process in which spirit presents and demonstrates itself in the production of reality, is conceived and described by Hegel as a historico-cultural process of higher and higher development. Spirit is united with perishability, submerged in the world and in the diversity of life, and at the same time is thoroughly divine. This spirit brings forth what is actual, makes actuality knowable and thematic, and at the same time sublates these manifestations into higher forms. It thus is permanently outstripping itself. On the path of its self-comprehension, spirit presents actuality in ever more complete ways. But at the same time spirit is withdrawing itself; the less complete manifestations of spirit are being sublated. They are showing themselves to be "being which also has the significance of not being."[37] This being, though, is *possibility*. With Hegel's theory one is thus clearly justified in saying that spiritual actuality outstrips itself by becoming the possibility for a more comprehensive actuality.

As surely as a figure of spirit recedes, is sublated as a historical phenomenon, so surely does it form the material out of which spirit can produce more complete manifestations of itself. In this sense, no completion of actuality whatsoever can be conceived, realized, or

---

37. Hegel, *Elements of the Philosophy of Right*, ed. A. W. Wood, trans. H. R. Nisbet, Cambridge Texts in the History of Political Thought (Cambrige: Cambridge Univ. Press, 1991), 69, translation altered.

understood without possibility. This is a consistent, powerful, and persuasive contestation of the basic Aristotelian approach of "Western metaphysics, which ascribed to pure actuality an ontological primacy over possibility."[38]

Hegel's conception provides a critique of the doctrine of the primacy of *pure* actuality. Specifically, it provides not merely an external critique, but a change and sublation of the conception that underlay the Aristotelian conviction. Hegel transforms Aristotle's abstract doctrine of spirit, a doctrine that remained in the medium of thought, into a doctrine that draws the logical consequences of grasping spirit as the "spirit that reconciles the world to itself," as self-objectifying spirit that infuses and shapes objectivity.

Spirit has thereby *entered into perishability*. It has abandoned the sphere of merely *pure* actuality. Aristotelian spirit is recognized as an abstract essentiality that is unable to make good the claim to comprehend, present, and shape actuality. The remote and lifeless illusion of spirit in intellectual self-possession is seen through, historicized, sublated, and outmoded.

In *one* central respect Hegel does indeed overcome the ingenuousness of metaphysical pneumatology. He overcomes the remoteness and abstraction from experience that belong to metaphysical pneumatology's understanding of spirit and of actuality. He provides one way of making good the claim to think this spirit in union with perishability. In this respect many theologies, too, can learn from Hegel.

Nevertheless this philosophical doctrine of spirit, striking and powerful in itself, remains theologically unsatisfying, indeed unacceptable. It articulates the vitality and freedom of spirit only as vital and—in all relations to an other—free being-at-home-with-self, as self-production and as return to self. It thus remains unilluminating and naive in the face of the consciousness, attested by the biblical traditions, of the systematic, powerful, yet veiled destruction of human forms of understanding and structural patterns of life. It likewise remains unilluminating and naive in the face of the expectations directed toward the Spirit of God in this situation of destruction.

---

38. Jüngel, *God as the Mystery of the World*, 214, translation altered.

6.2: The Spirit of Christ and the communion of the sanctified in a world that is endangering itself

The perception of the predominant forms in which the world is endangering itself is constantly shifting. According to all indications, at the end of the twentieth century the concentration on the danger of humanity's nuclear self-destruction[39] will pass the baton—without the nuclear threat being banished—to the awareness that the worst way in which human beings are endangering themselves is the erosion (no longer creeping, but now galloping) of their biological-natural environments.[40] In less than half a century, the earth has lost almost a fifth of its productive land and a fifth of its tropical rain forests, as well as tens of thousands of plant and animal species.[41] Nonrenewable resources and sources of energy are being depleted and consumed at a breathtaking pace, and the fish populations of the world's oceans are being plundered to the point of desolation. Through political, economic, cultural, and moral negligence—indeed, criminal indifference concerning the consequences of pauperization and need—the world has accepted a population explosion that has more or less doubled the world's population in half a century. Through criminal indifference and greed, the world has accepted the pauperization of large parts of its population and has systematically either allowed this pauperization to occur, or actively worked at bringing it about. "For decades now the terms of trade—the relation of export and import prices—have put at a massive disadvantage the countries of the Third World exporting raw materials." The

> suppliers of raw materials [must] spend disproportionately more for the necessary imports than they can take in through their exports. They are thus dependent on marketing their raw materials to a

---

39. Good examples in this regard are G. Kaufman, *Theology for a Nuclear Age* (Philadelphia: Westminster, 1985); and D. Henrich, *Ethik zum nuklearen Frieden* (Frankfurt am Main: Suhrkamp, 1990).

40. Both perspectives are connected in an exemplary manner by W. Huber and H. R. Reuter, *Friedensethik* (Stuttgart: Kohlhammer, 1990), esp. 209ff.

41. Cf. L. R. Brown et al., *State of the World 1990: A Worldwatch Institute Report on Progress toward a Sustainable Society* (New York: W. W. Norton, 1990), 3, 60ff.

greater extent and cutting down their forests in greater quantity
than is ecologically responsible. The international division of labor
and the worsening terms of trade that are its consequence force
Third World countries in this manner into an environmental
catastrophe. Under such conditions the rate at which the terms of
trade have worsened during the 1980s must appear as an additional
cause for anxiety. In the years between 1980 and 1986, the prices of
raw materials sank in real terms by 30 percent. The consequence
for Third World countries was a trade deficit of nearly $100 billion.

During the same time the debt burden of Third World countries
grew at an unimaginable rate. For 1980 the figure is still given at $456
billion; for 1988 the World Bank estimates an overall debt burden of
$1245 billion. The necessary servicing of this debt has in the mean-
time come to be more than double the financial influx from the industrialized countries. The transfer of money from the "developing"
countries to the "developed" countries has in the meantime come to
be disproportionately higher than in the other direction.[42]

The underlying causes are not autonomous and automatic processes that we have no choice but to accept. They are massive exploitative interests, politically and economically governed and made to look
better by the use of morality and the mass media. This is clear from the
following observations.

China, for instance, has only half as much cropped land per person
as India, yet Indians suffer widespread and severe hunger while the
Chinese do not. Sri Lanka has only half the farmland per person
of Bangladesh, yet when effective government policies kept food
affordable, Sri Lankans were considerably better fed than Bang-
ladeshis. Costa Rica, with less than half of Honduras' cropped acres
per person, boasts a life expectancy—one indicator of nutrition—
fourteen years longer than that of Honduras, and close to that of
the industrial countries. And Cuba, which leads the third world in
life expectancy, low infant mortality rates, and good nutrition, has
a population density similar to Mexico's, where hunger is rampant.
[The problem of whether human beings have enough to eat can
thus not simply be traced back to the direct relation of the number
of people to the amount of resources.]

---

42. Huber and Reuter, *Friedensethik*, 347–48.

The same simplistic formulation must be rejected when it comes to environmental destruction. An obvious example is the ecological havoc now being wrought in the Brazilian Amazon. The slash-and-burn agriculture of Brazilian peasants often gets the blame. But if land in Brazil were not the monopoly of the few—with 2 percent of the landowners controlling 60 percent of the arable land—poor Brazilians would not be forced to settle in the Amazon, destroying the irreplaceable rain forest. And surely the logging and cattle ranching, also destroying rain forests, reflect not population pressure but market demand for meat and wood by better-off consumers, largely in the industrial countries.[43]

The direct, massive, and brutal strangulation of the poor majority of the world's population and the endangerment of the life interests and life possibilities of all people, even of the rich minorities—a danger that is still repressed by many people—are accelerated by a multiplicity of powerful developments that likewise made their appearance only a few decades ago. Among them are the worldwide chemicalization of agriculture; the systematic covering of the world with electricity, automobile transportation, and roadways; routinized air travel and mass tourism; the various sorts of "experiments" and "accidents" in the area of nuclear technology; the rapid growth of the garbage piles of the industrialized nations; and the systematic, large-scale pollution of the air and water. Although these developments have been around for only a few decades, they have already combined to form a kind of avalanche, an extremely dangerous, irreversible intervention in the most basic conditions of the life of all: climate, atmosphere, air, and water. In view of this diagnosis, ecological skepticism is indicated.[44] The world seems destined to die by poisoning and suffocation through the fault of human beings.

The most that now seems conceivable is that the self-imposed global ecological danger—without of course being banished—will

---

43. F.M. Lappé and R. Schurman, "The Missing Piece in the Population Puzzle," Food First Development Report 4 (San Francisco: Institute for Food and Development Policy, 1988), 11, 13. Cf. F. M. Lappé and J. Collins, World Hunger: Twelve Myths (New York: Grove, 1986), esp. 137.

44. Cf. N. Luhmann, Ecological Communication, trans. J. Bednarz, Jr. (Chicago: Univ. of Chicago Press, 1989); in addition, §1.5.

surrender its number one spot among humanity's self-imposed dangers to another threat caused by human beings themselves: namely,
worldwide struggles for the remaining resources between those who
are rich, those who are poor, and those who are becoming poor.
Moreover, these struggles occur in the context of movements of emi-
gration and immigration that are becoming increasingly aggressive,
and in the context of new, nationalistic segmentation of the political
world.

The spirit of the Western world has made possible and solidified
the development leading to self-imposed global danger. It has done so
by producing the types of individuality and sociality corresponding to
this development. Clear individual incarnations are the newspaper
readers and television viewers who are in fact cynical in the way they
carry out their lives. These "observers," particularly in the so-called industrialized nations, are paralyzed and thrown back on themselves by
the apparently "comprehensive" information about the state and
course of the world, and about the complexity of their own societal situation. With only intermittent "pleasure," to be sure, alternating between terror and the relief of having escaped one more time, this
incarnate spirit hovers over reality, as it is presented in the media, in a
posture of apparently pure observation.

The most striking collective incarnation of this is what Germans
call "the enterprise" (*das Unternehmen*), which in every operation for
"the general public," the market of the greatest possible extension,
must pursue its own self-preservation. Specifically, it must do so by
being attuned to "the market's" resonance to its operations of self-
preservation. Whether the automobile industry, air travel, the tourism
industry, deep-sea fishing, the chemical industry, or the power plant
industry—powerful enterprises, in their every operation intent on
their self-preservation and expansion, chew their way from many different directions into the ecological substance of the earth. In accord
with the Western spirit, they must guard against all sensibilities and
operations that endanger their *self-continuation*, that do not immediately or mediately affect their self-preservation, self-reproduction, and
self-extension. They must—at least selectively—close themselves off
from other domains and keep the horizons of ignorance closed if they
do not want to endanger their "success" and thus their own continued
existence. Even the societal subsystems responsible for the "common

good," even the "nonprofit enterprises" must first gear their operations to their own self-preservation and to the "political mood" in the land if they want to operate steadily and efficiently.

The apparently comprehensively informed individual who—simply by virtue of being a consumer—is involved in many enterprises, seems to be condemned to one of two things. Either this individual is condemned to letting her striving for moral and ecological sensitivity and for a responsible conduct of life sometimes issue in a well-intentioned but powerless "symbolic action." Or this individual is condemned to blunting this striving and to using busyness, compulsive consumption, and drugs to cover her anxieties, her self-hatred, and contempt on the part of those who surround her who are more strongly affected and sensitive.

This situation is accepted with objectively cynical exhaustion by the part of the world's population living in relative or great prosperity. This exhaustion serves the stabilization of a life that, in spite of all endangerment of self and of others, is still comfortable. This situation drives the majority of the poor part of the world's population, suffering diverse needs, either to despair or to voiceless, inarticulate suffering. This imprisoning situation and the spirit that maintains this prison are without question a crushing reality and a violent power in this perishing world. But they are not "the" reality and the "all"-ruling spirit, even when they gladly assume that air and present themselves as such. They must be recognized and made recognizable as such, but they need not and must not be accepted as "the" reality, as a destiny without alternative.

Just as it is important to recognize the spirit of the Western world with sobriety and clarity, it is equally important to recognize the Spirit of God in the Spirit's nearness and world-overcoming power. The Spirit of God is not an ideal, a product of wishful thinking, a dream of a different future, or a general moral alternative to be uncovered or conjured up. Instead the Spirit is a reality that, to be sure, becomes recognizable and attested in various times and various surroundings and world situations with different degrees of determinacy and clarity, but one that is no less surely effective "in this world" than is the Western spirit. The world that endangers and destroys itself need not and must not be accepted, because human beings in the Spirit of Christ, in the Spirit of love, of righteousness and of peace in the communion of the sanctified belong—consciously or unconsciously, whether they expressly attest to this or not—to a reality that is present in this world, one that works against the power of the spirit of the Western world.

Inasmuch as human beings are taken into this communion, their isolation as weak, consumeristically corrupted individualities, intoxicated by the mass media and without public resonance, is dissolved both for them and through them. Before, they were bound into economic, political, ethnic, and other systems and subsystems that in all external operations gave constant priority to their immediate self-preservation and their assertion of self before others. Now that condition of being bound is relativized. Before, they were bound into a world order and a real constitution of the social world that was constructed according to the standard of dominant monocultures, one that in relation to past and future conditions of the world seeks to exercise imperialistic control over the resources of creation. Now that condition of being bound is also relativized. This relativizing of the spirit of the Western world by the power of God's Spirit and by the communion of the sanctified is a fact. The Spirit of righteousness, of mercy, of free self-withdrawal in love, the Spirit of liberation from self-destroying compulsions, the Spirit of valid life is by no means at work and detectable only in visible churches. The Spirit becomes more or less clearly and unambiguously recognizable in many religious and secular environments.[45] The Spirit also becomes more or less clearly recognizable in the churches' surroundings and in the midst of the real and perceivable churches, although they are also busy with their "fleshly" self-preservation, are corrupted by the Western spirit, and are trapped in many forms of faintheartedness.

The true and real church, the ecumenical and transcontinental church, the church that extends beyond particular epochs, and thus also the visible body of Christ, concretely present here and now, was and is built up by the Holy Spirit (cf. Acts 9:31; 11:24; and passim).

---

45. The difficulties in identifying this action of the Spirit must not be suppressed by means of abstract oppositions between the "Spirit-filled church" and the "Spirit-less world," or with the help of perfectionist models in which the action of the Spirit occurs only on the sanctified—however they might be "sanctified." An early negative paradigm of this use of perfectionist models is found in Origen, *On First Principles*, trans. G. W. Butterworth (Gloucester, Mass.: Peter Smith, 1973), above all bk. 1, chap. 3, pt. 5ff., pp. 33ff., esp. 36ff.

This church defined by the power of the Spirit may come across from time to time and from place to place as paltry, out of touch with the world, uninteresting and insignificant, or may appear as suppressed, almost extinguished (cf. 1 Pet. 4:14). It is always in need of the discernment of spirits: that is, it is always corrupted by other spirits, powers, and morals, by cultural, political, economic, national, and other interests and ideologies.[46] Yet in the midst of seeming insignificance and de facto corruption, the Spirit of God joins together people called to communion with Christ from among "Jews and Greeks, slaves and free" (1 Cor. 12:13; Gal. 3:28: Col. 3:11), men and women, old and young, out of many times and many countries of the world. Here a powerful communion is being formed. A communion is being formed for which the exclusion of God's Chosen One, the expulsion of the suffering righteous person from the world has become a basic experience, just as has contemporaneity with all times and all states of the world. The Spirit constitutes a communion with the Crucified and Risen One that not only has gone through the experience of anxiety in the world, but that extends beyond particular conditions and states of the world, and thus can be characterized as "heavenly" communion with Christ (cf. Eph. 1:3). Yet this powerful communion, not tied to specific earthly conditions and states of the world and not dependent on them, is realized under the conditions of the finite, perishable world, and on, through and for fleshly, mortal creatures.

Through human beings and in their midst, God *inscribes* Godself in this world by the Spirit; through human beings Christ addresses the world (cf. 2 Cor. 3:3 as well as 1 John 4:1ff.). In this transcontinental communion that extends beyond particular epochs yet is also realistically present in this world, the persons joined together by God's Spirit participate in the power of the resurrected Christ (cf. Rom. 1:4). This power consists not in a quantitative superiority over other groups of people, interest groups, religions, national or economic unions, or political powers. The great power of the "communion of the Holy Spirit" (2 Cor. 13:13), a power that in this world overcomes the world, consists in the fact that the persons whose services are enlisted by the

---

46. See also chap. 3 as well as J. D. G. Dunn, "Discernment of Spirits—A Neglected Gift," in W. Harrington, ed., *Witness to the Spirit: Essays on Revelation, Spirit, Redemption* (Dublin: Koinonia, 1979), 79ff.

Spirit become "one Spirit with Christ." This means that they become one Spirit with the Risen and *Crucified* One.

The mystery of self-giving, of free self-withdrawal for the benefit of the world, is revealed to these persons defined by the Spirit. Specifically, it is the mystery of free self-withdrawal for the benefit of a world that in ever-new ways closes itself off to God's presence with religious, judicial, and moral, as well as with nationalistic, sexist, and other forms. In place of God's presence, this world clings to itself, to its own model of the world, to its own shaping of the world—or it attempts to cling to these. The mystery of self-giving, of free self-withdrawal, is revealed to these persons defined by the Spirit. Specifically, it is the mystery of free self-withdrawal for the benefit of a fleshly-perishable life, for a life that in diverse ways makes itself immune to God's action, in order to hold tight to itself, to its own—veiled—frailty.

The persons who arrive in the communion of the Holy Spirit and who are filled with the Spirit of Christ (cf. 1 Cor. 2:16) not only perceive the revealed mystery of sacrifice and free self-withdrawal and the revitalization released by this free self-withdrawal. They become witnesses of this "life-giving Spirit" (1 Cor. 15:45); they become sisters and brothers of Christ; they become members of Christ's body; they stand in intimate communion with Christ; through word and deed they pass on Christ's message, the expression of Christ's will.[47] The people who participate in this power of free self-withdrawal and of sacrifice for the benefit of others in order likewise to help others to know their lostness, their deliverance, and their vocation as witnesses to this power of the Crucified One—these people are addressed as those who are "called to holiness." They are assured: "you were washed, you were sanctified, you were justified in the name of the Lord Jesus Christ and in the Spirit of our God" (1 Cor. 6:11). Or: God has chosen you "for

---

47. Cf. 2 Cor. 3:3; 1 Pet. 1:2. The fact that only the Holy Spirit makes possible the "knowledge" of Christ and the transmission of this knowledge was emphasized in diverse ways by Luther. Cf., e.g., *The Large Catechism*, in T. G. Tappert, ed. and trans., *The Book of Concord: The Confessions of the Evangelical Lutheran Church* (Philadelphia: Fortress, 1959), 415–20; *The Small Catechism*, in Tappert, ed., *Book of Concord*, 345; "Predigt am Pfingstag nachmittag, 16. Mai 1529," WA 29, 355–56. Cf. also R. Slenczka, "Die Erkenntnis des Geistes, die Lehre vom Geist und die Unterscheidung der Geister," in J. Heubach, *Der Heilige Geist im Verständnis Luthers und der lutherischen Theologie*, Veröffentlichungen der Luther-Akademie Ratzeburg 17 (Erlangen: Martin-Luther, 1990), esp. 79ff.

salvation through sanctification by the Spirit and through belief in the truth" (2 Thess. 2:13).

This communion of the sanctified points in constantly new ways to the selfless person of the Crucified One. This communion has the vocation of being this person's domain of influence and resonance. It has the vocation of making this person present in diverse ways under the conditions of earthly, finite life.[48] Inasmuch as this communion has a share in the "Spirit of Christ" and thus "is one with Christ," the *public person of God's Spirit* is concretized and realized in this communion.[49] This is not to say that this communion is all there is to the

---

48. Cf. esp. §§4.5 and 5.1. This vocation to be a community of testimony must not be obscured by fixing on a cognitive "belief" confined to an inner sphere, or by defining "union with Christ" as *"mystica unio."* Calvin marks the problem in the *Inst.*, vol. 1, 3/1, 1ff. and 3/11, 10. See also his emphasis on the *"extra nos"* (3/11, 23); W. Krusche, *Das Wirken des Heiligen Geistes nach Calvin*, Forschungen zur Kirchen- und Dogmengeschichte 7 (Göttingen: Vandenhoeck, 1957), 265ff., esp. 269 and 273ff.; H. J. J. Quistorp, "Calvins Lehre vom Heiligen Geist," in *De Spiritu Sancto* (Utrecht: Kemink, 1964), 132ff. Luther's insistence that the Holy Spirit places human beings outside themselves and draws them into the "external being of Jesus Christ" is less open to misunderstanding, but is likewise in need of development (*The Large Catechism*, in Tappert, ed., *Book of Concord*, 419; *Lectures on Romans*, ed. H. C. Oswald, trans. W. G. Tillmans and J. A. O. Preus, *LW* 25, 143–44). See W. Mostert, "Hinweise zu Luthers Lehre vom Heiligen Geist," in Heubach, *Der Heilige Geist*, esp. 31ff.; R. Prenter, *Spiritus Creator*, trans. J. M. Jensen (Philadelphia: Muhlenberg, 1953), 27ff.

On the basis of the differentiation of God's Spirit from Aristotelian conceptions of spirit, it becomes clear that this process of being placed outside of oneself cannot be understood as mere self-transcendence. See as well B. Lonergan, "Mission and the Spirit," in P. Huizing and W. Bassett, eds., *Experience of the Spirit* (New York: Seabury, 1974), 69ff. and 77; W. Pannenberg, "Ekstatische Selbstüberschreitung als Teilhabe am göttlichen Geist," in Heitmann and Mühlen, eds., *Erfahrung und Theologie des Heiligen Geistes*, 176ff.

49. With regard to the following discussion, see M. Welker, "The Holy Spirit," trans. J. Hoffmeyer, *Theology Today* 46 (1989): 17ff.; as well as I. Hermann, *Kyrios und Pneuma: Studien zur Christologie der paulinischen Hauptbriefe*, SANT 2 (Munich: Kösel, 1961), esp. 140ff.; P. W. Newman, *A Spirit Christology: Recovering the Biblical Faith* (Lanham, Md.: University Press of America, 1987), 171ff. I am grateful to B. O. Brown for pointing out that the idea of the Spirit as a "public person" is found not explicitly, but de facto in the work of J. Haroutunian (see Haroutunian, *God with Us: A Theology of Transpersonal Life* [Philadelphia: Westminster, 1965], esp. 70ff). On Haroutunian's unpublished papers, see O. Otterness, "The Holy Spirit and the People of God in the Theology of Joseph Haroutunian," *Princeton Seminary Bulletin* 1, n.s. (1977): 68ff.

Spirit. The Spirit of God, not the communion of the sanctified itself, is the power that recognizes, enlivens, and maintains the body of Christ in constantly new ways. Yet in this communion that is concentrated on the Crucified and Resurrected One, that acquires a share in Christ's self-withdrawal and presence, the Spirit takes on definite contours, becomes knowable.

The Holy Spirit is thus certainly to be understood as a person, but as a *public person*. Where a person is thought and conceived only as an individual-human center of action, the personhood of the Holy Spirit remains obscure. Admittedly, the Holy Spirit is concentrated on the individual person of Jesus Christ. The Holy Spirit points in complete selflessness to Jesus Christ. This is picked up by the New Testament statements that characterize the Holy Spirit as the Spirit of Christ (e.g., Romans 8). If we are seeking for a clearly definable *individual* center of action of the Holy Spirit, if we are searching for personhood in *this* sense, we are referred to Jesus Christ in response to the question about the personhood of the Spirit. Jesus Christ is the primary individual-human center of action of the Spirit.[50] To be sure, it is not a mistake to characterize the Holy Spirit in this way, but it is a reductionist presentation of the Spirit. The reason for this widespread reductionist presentation lies in an orientation that is typical of the Western spirit. Specifically, it is the orientation to a one-sided and foreshortened concept of the person that does not do justice to the personhood of the resurrected and ascended Christ.

Nor does the concentration on an active, centering, individual agent guarantee an adequate understanding of the person in extra-theological contexts of experience. An individual center of action, even when it self-referentially governs itself and develops a self-consciousness, does not yet constitute a person. It is only in exchange with an organized social environment that an individual center of action becomes a person. A self-referentially centering agent becomes a

---

50. In particular the Johannine texts define the *selflessness* of the Spirit along these lines, since the Holy Spirit does nothing other than bear witness to Jesus Christ and point to him. Cf. John 14:26 and 16:13-14: "The Holy Spirit . . . will teach you everything, and remind you of all that I have said to you." The Spirit of truth "will not speak on the Spirit's own, but will speak whatever the Spirit hears, and will declare to you the things that are to come. The Spirit of truth will glorify me, because the Spirit will take what is mine and declare it to you" (cf. John 15:26).

person only in union with this organized social sphere, in the latter's relation to the former. To characterize this sphere, we shall follow a proposal advanced by Niklas Luhmann and employ the concept of *resonance*.[51] It is only by means of a *domain of resonance* that a center of action becomes a person.

A self-referentially governed center of action can be a totally unpredictable or a robot-like phenomenon that does not deserve the designation "person." Human beings or social agents acquire the features of personhood only by being formed in diverse webs of relationships. Here the human beings or social agents may center the webs of relationships on themselves, or vice versa. As a rule "the person" exercises a formative influence on these webs of relationships. But they are not fruits of the person's own activity. We are persons inasmuch as we are children of our parents, relatives of our relatives, friends of our friends, colleagues of our colleagues, contemporaries of our contemporaries. We are persons because we thus stand in webs of resonance that we help to shape as much as we are marked by them. These webs of resonance are *only partially* dependent on our activity.[52] We can only partially govern the domain of resonance that constitutes our person, even though it is centered on us. This domain of resonance is only partially clear and transparent to us, even though *we* are its central focus. We never fully attain the unity of the perspectives on us that constitutes our "public person" as it exists—objective and objectified in diverse ways—for our environment. Conversely, we also have the feeling again and again that

---

51. Luhmann, *Ecological Communication*, 15–21. A *"domain* of resonance" refers to a centered multiplicity of relations of resonance that, once one moves beyond their shared centering, can be independent of each other. These relations are not necessarily coordinated with respect to each other. Nor are they necessarily coordinated with respect to their "center of resonance." One and the same person can at the same time be loved and hated. One and the same person can be understood, misunderstood, and consciously misunderstood—all in the same affair. The same person can even be perceived and understood in ways that are coordinated and objectified, but that are different than the ways in which she understands herself, or would like herself to be understood. The readily imaginable but naive concept of the person as a "point of reference" does not articulate these important features.

52. We remain the child of our parents, whatever changes our attitude toward our family might undergo. By our development we can disappoint our friends, and they may even be completely agreed in their evaluation of our disappointing person—even if we see this and "our person" in a totally different manner.

our person has been treated without any "justice" in this or that utterance or expectation. Or we have the feeling that we cannot unify our
public person, and thus cannot connect it with what we (at any rate
those of us marked by the Western spirit) envisage as our "innermost
self."[53]

A self-conscious center of action is one thing. That unity of person that we are in the external perspectives on us, that unity of person
that we are in the domain of resonance centered on us, is something
else. We must take note of the difference between the two if we want
to understand the personhood of the Holy Spirit and the otherwise inexplicable biblical statements about the Spirit.[54]

The Holy Spirit is initially to be understood as the pluriform unity
of perspectives on Jesus Christ, of relations to Christ, and of the spoken and lived testimonies to Christ. In this respect the Spirit is a unity
in which we participate, a unity that we help to constitute.[55] The
Spirit is Christ's domain of resonance. The Spirit is the public person
corresponding to the individual Jesus Christ.[56] Nevertheless we cannot

---

53. Cf. C. Keller's inspired initiative toward developing a challenging, non-
androcentric concept of the person (From a Broken Web: Separation, Sexism, and Self
(Boston: Beacon, 1988), esp. 216ff. Cf. as well the differentiation of the concept of
existence already undertaken by J. Cobb, The Structure of Christian Existence (New
York: Seabury, 1979), esp. 107ff.

54. Cf. A. I. C. Heron's discussion of the use of the conventional concept of
the person in pneumatology (The Holy Spirit [Philadelphia: Westminster, 1983], esp.
167ff.). Cf. as well Heron's reflections on the necessary development of a challenging concept of the person in the doctrines of God and of the Trinity (ibid., 173ff.).

55. Cf. the astounding directness of the relation to the Holy Spirit, indeed of
the act of laying claim to the Spirit, that is brought to expression above all in the
Acts of the Apostles: e.g., Acts 15:28; 20:28; as well as 8:29; 10:19; 11:12; 13:2, 52;
16:6-7; 20:22-23; 21:4, 11. Cf. also H. Mühlen's accurate description of "participation" through the Spirit in "Jesus' fullness of grace." This fullness of grace is
to be understood in a differentiated, determinate, and "concretional" manner
(H. Mühlen, "Das Christusereignis als Tat des Heiligen Geistes," in MySal 3/2,
540ff. Cf. in addition G. Ebeling, Dogmatik des christlichen Glaubens, vol. 3, Der
Glaube an Gott den Vollender der Welt (Tübingen: Mohr, 1979), 117ff.

56. See the comparative listing of New Testament expressions by Y. Congar,
I Believe in the Holy Spirit, vol. 2, The Holy Spirit in the "Economy": Revelation and
Experience of the Spirit, trans. D. Smith (New York: Seabury, 1983), 37–38; also the
reflections on the "ecclesiological 'we'" by Mühlen, Der Heilige Geist als Person,
190ff.

regard the person of Christ and the person of the Spirit as an indissoluble unity. In view of the Crucified One, abandoned by all the world and divesting himself of all resonance, we are compelled to insist on the *difference* between the person of Christ and the person of the Spirit. In view of the Crucified, it becomes clear that there is no access to God that we can produce and put in place on our own initiative.[57]

In view of the Crucified, the extremely dangerous confusion between God's Spirit and the spirits of more or less complex relative worlds meets its match at a fundamental level.[58] To a world conspiring against God, God gives God's Spirit. God builds up the church without preconditions, where the preconditions are beyond our control (cf. Rom. 8:27), indeed into the human destruction and obstruction of all preconditions. It is the forgiveness of sins that creates the unity of human beings with God. The forgiveness of sins awakens the world-overcoming power of sacrifice and free self-withdrawal—a power that proceeds from the communion of the sanctified in a self-endangering world. By the act of liberation from the power of sin, the presence of the Holy Spirit as a saving public person comes to be felt in worldwide influence and effectiveness.

6.3: The forgiveness of sins and life reborn on the basis of God's righteousness

The "forgiveness of sins" has nothing to do with a lenient "letting it ride" or with a mild "It's okay." Nor does the idea of an admonition or a reprimand in view of some sort of misdeeds give articulation to the power at work in the forgiveness of sins, a power that changes human beings and worlds. "Forgiveness" is not an act in which a God who normally reacts to bad thoughts and deeds with claims for compensation forgoes pushing through these claims. And "sin" is not some sort

---

57. Cf. Philem. 1:29 and indirectly Rom. 8:9. See Slenczka's thoughts concerning the practice of speaking of the "person" of the Spirit ("Die Erkenntnis des Geistes," 89ff.); see in addition G. T. Montague, S.M., *The Holy Spirit: Growth of a Biblical Tradition* (New York: Paulist Press, 1976), 367–68 and passim.

58. K. Barth, "Die Not der evangelischen Kirche," *Zwischen den Zeiten* 9 (1931): 89ff.; D. Bonhoeffer, *The Cost of Discipleship*, rev. ed., trans. R. Fuller and I. Booth (New York: Macmillan, 1963), 337ff.

of misbehavior. It is certainly not a form of misbehavior that human beings could avoid as easily as traffic offenses or the vices of consumption[59] that it would be more rational, or more in keeping with medical counsel, to leave off.[60]

According to the understanding of the biblical traditions, "sin" is that action, that behavior, or that posture and exercise of influence by which—over and above every concrete delinquency and misdeed—the foundations of life-promoting behavior and the possibilities of repentance are destroyed. Sin annihilates the prospects for a change of behavior. For the agents and for their surroundings, sin obstructs and destroys the powers that make possible a renewal of orientation, a change of direction in life gone awry.

It is inadequate to try to pin down and define "sin" concretely by means of the rules of judgment of a moral market or of a judicial system. Instead, moral markets or judicial systems can themselves come under the power of sin. They can be used by sin in order to strengthen and spread sin itself. Human communities can establish and fine-tune forms of behavior and practices that are to a high degree detrimental to life. They can even do this with full knowledge and the best of

---

59. The common German expressions used here are *Verkehrssünden* and *Konsumsünden*: literally, "traffic sins" and "sins of consumption"—TRANS.

60. In recent years a number of pathbreaking works have made clear that the widespread attempt to base religious ideas of compensation in the theology of atonement is incorrect. See H. Gese, "The Atonement," in *Essays on Biblical Theology*, trans. K. Crim (Minneapolis: Augsburg, 1981), 93–116; B. Janowski, *Sühne als Heilsgeschehen: Studien zur Sühnetheologie der Priesterschrift und zur Wurzel KPR im Alten Orient und im Alten Testament*, WMANT 55 (Neukirchen-Vluyn: Neukirchener, 1982); P. Stuhlmacher, "Recent Exegesis on Romans 3:24-26," in *Reconciliation, Law, and Righteousness: Essays in Biblical Theology*, trans. E. Kalin (Philadelphia: Fortress, 1986), 94ff.; P. Stuhlmacher, "Sühne oder Versöhnung," in U. Luz and H. Weder, eds., *Die Mitte des Neuen Testaments: Einheit und Vielfalt neutestamentlicher Theologie: Festschrift für Eduard Schweizer zum siebzigsten Geburtstag* (Göttingen: Vandenhoeck, 1983), 291ff.; O. Hofius, "Sühne und Versöhnung: Zum paulinischen Verständnis des Kreuzestodes Jesu," in *Paulusstudien*, Wissenschaftliche Untersuchungen zum Neuen Testament 51 (Tübingen: Mohr, 1989), 33ff. For a critique of ideas of compensation in connection with sin and forgiveness, see the illuminating discussion by C. Gestrich, *Die Wiederkehr des Glanzes in der Welt: Die christliche Lehre von der Sünde und ihrer Vergebung in gegenwärtiger Verantwortung* (Tübingen: Mohr, 1989), 244ff. and 366ff. In the following pages I will take up and further develop the approach that I began to articulate in "The Holy Spirit," 12–14.

consciences because they are blind to the danger, or only to the alterna-tives, or because they render themselves immune to better insight. Communication capable of arriving at consensus and orders structured around "values" can also come under the power that destroys the *foun-dations for the regeneration and renewal* of human persons.

Christof Gestrich has provided an accurate clarification of this, in which it is obvious that he has in mind the systematic devastation of natural environments by societies of the late twentieth century.

> The robbery of possibilities of being and the destruction of creation by sinners generate factual results that either cannot be undone at all, or cannot be undone without God's help. The ugliness and the lackluster quality of the remains left by the sinner can be compared only with the sight of objects on a garbage heap. The objects that arrive there cannot be restored. In the best of cases, in time they become overgrown with grass and cease to be an eyesore. The re-mains of sinners, though, are similar in their ongoing effect to toxic waste, which burdens future life as well.[61]

Whether intended or not by the person acting, sin unleashes com-plex chain reactions with both direct and indirect effects as well as extended repercussions. Sin generates entanglements from which hu-man beings cannot free themselves simply with moral appeals and sanctions. It is essential to see that the human person possessed by sin is in a situation that he admittedly helped to cause, but one that has gone beyond his control. The human person in the grasp of sin is in a situation of distress. This is not to say that he is consciously suffering under this distress or that he recognizes the distress. The human per-son under sin is a helpless creature who not only disempowers himself, but who has come under a power that disempowers him.[62] In this situ-ation of distress "forgiveness is the—only—possibility for preventing the consequences of sin from continuing to devour its victims. Forgive-ness breaks off the pro-cess (advance) of sin."[63]

---

61. Gestrich, *Wiederkehr*, 366.
62. See G. Schneider-Flume, *Die Identität des Sünders: Eine Auseinandersetzung theologischer Anthropologie mit dem Konzept der psychosozialen Identität Erik H. Erik-sons* (Göttingen: Vandenhoeck, 1985), 125ff.
63. Gestrich, *Wiederkehr*, 366.

The action of God's Spirit in forgiving sins thus begins at a more basic level than that of individual and societal possibilities for renewal, despite the fact that this action of the Spirit takes place in earthly life, in this world. The forgiveness of sins acts at a more basic level than that of our "goodwill," at a more basic level than that of our morally or otherwise conditioned capacity to improve. The forgiveness of sins enables not only a "new beginning," but the production of new structural patterns of life. Disintegrated persons and communities are stabilized and regrouped. They are given a new capacity to act. Hard-pressed persons and communities with no firm foothold experience the power of preservation. Old forms of power and domination are replaced; bearers of hope appear unexpectedly and unforeseeably on the scene. Evil spirits and lying spirits, mechanisms of disintegration and of destruction, factors that unleash distress, and the vicious circles that form such a tenacious part of that distress are prophetically recognized and are made accessible to public knowledge by the forgiveness of sins.

All these events *can* be first indications that the Spirit of the forgiveness of sins is at work. As we have seen, though, they are in themselves unclear and ambiguous.[64] Prophetic knowledge can remain without effect. People may lack the power to escape the demonic mechanisms that have been recognized. The supposed bearers of hope can prove to be people who make the situation worse. The replacement of one system can lead out of the frying pan and into the fire. "Preservation" can degenerate into a diet of "pie in the sky" and into maintenance of the status quo. The "gathering" of a disintegrated society can become the first step in unleashing new demonic powers. Both for individual persons and for whole societies, sin can unquestionably generate the illusion of deliverance and can hide its operation behind that illusion. But how is clear knowledge of sin possible? How does such knowledge go beyond the mere terrified recognition: "But daily deeper still I fell; / My life became a living hell, / So firmly sin possessed me"?[65]

---

64. Cf. §§2.1–2.4.

65. M. Luther, "Dear Christians, One and All," trans. R. Massie, *Lutheran Book of Worship* (Minneapolis: Augsburg; Philadelphia: Board of Publication, Lutheran Church in America, 1978), hymn 299, 2d stanza. K. Scharzwäller has shown that Luther sees "all the offices of the church in their relation to the forgiveness of sins effected by the Holy Spirit" ("Delectari assertionibus: Zur Struktur von

The search for clear knowledge of the Spirit's action, constant prayer for this knowledge, and persistent questioning concerning the criteria of the Spirit's action—over and above superficial displays of power—are indispensable to the knowledge of sin in the light of the power that liberates from sin.

According to the testimonies of the prophetic texts and promises, the creation of righteousness and of peace were the criteria for the action of the Spirit who delivers out of distress, preserves, renews, mediates knowledge, and forgives sins. On the one hand, the Spirit's action brings help to concrete human beings and enlists the services of actual human beings. On the other hand, the Spirit's action is a process that human beings cannot "make happen," cannot manage, cannot bring under their control. It is a process that accrues to them, that comes upon them, and into which they are drawn. The people who are a part of the Spirit's action of forgiving sins and who are affected by this action are not only bearers, but also are borne. They are not only mediators, but also receivers. They not only exercise an influence on their surroundings, but also are affected, strengthened, challenged, and changed by the actions and reactions of others. In this experience of being surrounded and borne up, the persons who are renewed by the action of the Spirit and are borne up by the process are indeed themselves changed. They themselves are a part of this process, and they themselves collaborate in it. This experience of being surrounded and borne up, this uncontrollability of the new beginning established by the forgiveness of sins, this resistance to all attempts to assert the power of "making it happen"—this uncontrollability of the concrete process and experience is accurately described by the expression "rebirth":[66]

Luthers Pneumatologie," *Luther Jahrbuch* 38, ed. F. Lau (Hamburg: F. Wittig, 1971), esp. 39ff. See also E. Herms, *Luthers Auslegung des Dritten Artikels* (Tübingen: Mohr, 1987), 96–97.

66. Cf. O. Weber, *Foundations of Dogmatics* 2, trans. D. L. Guder (Grand Rapids, Mich.: Eerdmans, 1983), 356ff. On the one hand, Weber—accurately—critically engages A. Ritschl and the understanding of rebirth as a mere "awakening of a new self-understanding and of a changed world view and ethic." On the other hand—in a problematic way—Weber attempts by means of a *pure* futurization to conceive the interconnection of rebirth's world-changing power and of rebirth's uncontrollability (cf. ibid., 357). Cf. H. Berkhof, *The Doctrine of the Holy Spirit* (Richmond: John Knox, 1964), 79ff.; R. Bohren, *Vom Heiligen Geist: Fünf Betrachtungen*, Kaiser-Traktate 57 (Munich: Kaiser, 1981), 40ff.

> God saved us, not because of any works of righteousness that we
> had done, but according to God's mercy, through the washing of
> rebirth and renewal by the Holy Spirit. This Spirit God poured out
> on us richly through Jesus Christ our Savior, so that, having been
> justified by God's grace, we might become heirs according to the
> hope of eternal life. (Titus 3:5-7)

Rebirth establishes a new beginning to life, gives a new identity, creates new surroundings. It leads to a discontinuity with the life lived up to the rebirth, but at the same time—as *re*birth on the basis of the *forgiveness* of sins—it restores the life and the identity that had previously existed. The Spirit who creates righteousness enlists the services of the "old" life with its fulfilled and its disappointed expectations of righteousness, and with its actions aimed at righteousness, whether successful, unsuccessful, or left undone. The "old" life is transformed and renewed. God's Spirit who forgives sins and creates new life effects a righteousness that, on the one hand, transcends human beings' specific expectations of righteousness and specific efforts to bring about righteousness. On the other hand, it leads human beings out of their unsuccessful and corrupted efforts for righteousness, as well as out of the efforts that they neglected ever to make. It leads them into a new life reality. On the basis of God's turning to the weak, people are incorporated into a new life. Life that had hitherto been defined by unrighteousness is changed for both the strong and the weak by this new life. The Spirit of God effects a righteousness in which, on the basis of the divine mercy, on the basis of God's turning to human beings, Godself opens new actualities and possibilities of life to those who have fallen into distress, those who are lost, those who lack orientation, and those who are helplessly oppressed, as well as those who are oppressors.

On the one hand, this action of the Spirit that makes possible a new beginning for life is characterized by the *pouring out* of the Spirit. That is, it is characterized by the Spirit simultaneously descending on people in various contexts of life and experience. As a result of the pouring out of the Spirit, from this variety arises a process of mutual challenge and empowerment on the part of persons upon whom the Spirit comes. On the other hand, the Spirit's action of forgiving sins, which leads to a new beginning for life, is defined by the fact that here a public person and power is acting who in complete selflessness and self-withdrawal acts for the benefit of others. The one who is publicly powerless, the one who publicly suffers, enables sinners to be horrified at themselves and at their hopeless situation, and to strive for renewal of themselves, their life, and the structural patterns of their life. This renewal enlists their services. They can entrust themselves to it as persons who have been incorporated into it, although it goes beyond what they can do on their own and transcends their own power.

The universal spread of the interconnection of justice, mercy, and knowledge of God opens the prospect of fulfilling the messianic promises of the Spirit-bearer and of the Spirit-bearer's action. In the power of the forgiveness of sins, this spread of justice, mercy, and knowledge of God actually takes place. It cannot be brought about by merely moral or merely political means. It cannot be brought about by only one time, one nation, one culture, one race, or one class of people. The forgiveness of sins is a process that aims at the rebirth and renewal of the whole creation, and that therefore affects and includes the whole creation even in the most concrete realizations of this process.[67]

The Holy Spirit's action of forgiving sins and of renewing life is broad, universal, and uncontrollable. It is not something that we can make happen. This is not to say, though, that this process takes place in abstraction from individual, fleshly-finite creatures. The Christ is installed in publics that extend far beyond specific publics that are moral, political, or confined to a certain time period. Yet Christ acts in these publics on concretely suffering, powerless individuals. In these publics Christ brings the renewal and restoration of finite, earthly life. People are rescued from demonic forces that have limited and perverted their possibilities for life. Demonic powers are driven out of the actual, earthly, individual, and communal life that they hold "possessed," that they torment, hinder, and turn into a torment and hindrance for others.[68]

---

67. Cf. §§3.1–3.5 and the reflections of H.-J. Kraus, *Heiliger Geist: Gottes befreiende Gegenwart* (Munich: Kosel, 1986), 108ff.; as well as E. Schweizer's presentation of the Spirit's action in creation and new creation (*The Holy Spirit*, trans. R. H. Fuller and I. Fuller [Philadelphia: Fortress, 1980], 67–73).

68. It is not moral denunciation, admonition, and instruction, but the pure promise of liberated, unhindered life that lies in the apparently offensive words with which Jesus addresses the paralyzed man: "Son, your sins are forgiven." See Mark 2:5, 9; Matt. 9:2, 5; Luke 5:20, 23.

This renewed life rescues people from suffering and from causing suffering to others, including that which involved no subjective fault on their part. This renewed life serves as a testimony to God's deliverance and God's glory. It is this life that is the "renewed life on the basis of God's righteousness." It is this life that is wrought through liberation from the power of sin.

This liberation from the power of sin is not a process that takes place only in isolated cases and in a way that cannot be understood by others. The power that effects this liberation wills to surround and to "come upon" human beings from every direction. The testimony that all this is the case is entrusted to the "communion of the sanctified." In a self-endangering world, this communion of the sanctified is to make clear in diverse and continually renewed ways that the promise of the presence of the Paraclete and the promise of the pouring out of God's Spirit are *fulfilled.* Through the Paraclete, through the poured out Spirit, the action of the Spirit to forgive sins and to renew life in Jesus' name is present in diverse forms of authenticity and concreteness.

The Spirit forgives sins and not only makes new life possible, but makes it actual. From various life contexts, the Spirit releases forces that exercise a strengthening influence on each other. It is this Spirit who stands in constant confrontation with the demonic powers that attempt to seize control of finite life and the perishable world, and indeed are successful in doing so (cf. Eph. 2:2 and passim). Their power breaks people apart and scatters them, making them hostile or indifferent to each other. It is in opposition to this power that the Spirit acts.

Through human beings, God's Spirit testifies to "our spirit" concerning God's deeds of power. The Spirit who does this wills to lead the world out of the process of diverse forms of self-isolation detrimental to life.[69] The Spirit of the forgiveness of sins, the Spirit of rebirth

---

69. W. Krötke has rightly pointed out that on the basis of this action of the Spirit, the community of Christ, "in the midst of the world of sin," is given the capacity to act freely, including in institutional forms, "toward the goal of the worldliness and humanity desired by God" ("Weltlichkeit und Sünde: Zur Auseinandersetzung mit Denkformen Martin Luthers in der Theologie D. Bonhoeffers," in *Die Universalität des offenbaren Gottes: Gesammelte Aufsätze,* BEvT 94 [Munich: Kaiser, 1985], 163). In this context it is crucial to distinguish this "free

rescues from the diverse forms of distress, powerlessness, hostility, and indifference that are bound up with self-isolation. The Spirit rescues from the conscious and unconscious violence and brutality that are bound up with the attempt to put oneself first at the expense of others. The Spirit rescues from omnipotent mistrust, from contempt and hatred.

This Spirit acts "not only on me," but on persons of all times and of all relative worlds. Nor does this Spirit act everywhere in one and the same manner, according to one "global formula." Instead this Spirit acts in diverse concrete contexts, including those that conflict with each other and those that are supposedly incompatible with each other. By acting in these diverse ways and contexts, the Spirit seems to be numinous, incomprehensible, and inconceivable.[70]

This action is experienced in the force fields of faith and hope. The experience is mediated in such a way that particular forms of experience are not posited as universal and absolute. In faith and in hope, experiences of the Spirit and of the Spirit's action are mediated in such a way that the most determinate attestation remains open to further illumination, and the most profound disappointments do not lead to resignation. In faith and in hope, the relativity of the setting of one's own world becomes manifest. The same is true of the relativity of the long-range perspective and the circumspection both of one's

---

action" in pneumatological determinacy from conceptions of freedom that pick up on Aristotelian traditions. Cf. as well W. Dantine, *Der Heilige und der unheilige Geist: Über die Erneuerung der Urteilsfähigkeit* (Stuttgart: Radius, 1973), 201ff.; H. Kägi, *Der Heilige Geist in charismatischer Erfahrung und theologischer Reflexion* (Zurich: Theologischer Verlag Zurich, 1989), 152ff.

70. Thus it is true that "there can be no final word that closes the subject of the life and proclamation of reconciled human beings in a world of sin" (Krötke, "Weltlichkeit und Sünde," 163). Cf. W. Krötke, *Sünde und Nichtiges bei Karl Barth*, 2d ed., rev. and enl., Neukirchener Beiträge zur Systematischen Theologie 3 (Neukirchen-Vluyn: Neukirchener, 1983), 105ff. Picking up on Luther (cf. M. Luther, *Against the Heavenly Prophets in the Matter of Images and Sacraments*, pt. 2, trans. C. Bergendoff, *LW* 40, 147), L. Grönvik has shown that precisely the "external sign" of baptism brings to expression the fundamental dependency of human beings on the constantly renewed liberating action of the Spirit ("Taufe und Heiliger Geist in der Sicht der Theologie Luthers," in P. Mäki, *Taufe und Heiliger Geist: Vorträge auf der 14. Baltischen Theologenkonferenz 1975*, Schriften der Luther-Agricola-Gesellschaft, ser. A, 18 (Helsinki: 1979), 106ff.

own experience in any particular case and of the experiences of others in any particular case. These relativities become manifest despite the fact that the real world and real experiences are taken with the utmost seriousness as domains of the Spirit's action, since this action aims at *their* renewal. Fleshly, earthly life, its limited powers of cognition and volition, and the earthly world—the "totality" that is always only relative[71]—can be taken seriously because of the very fact that they need not answer for "all reality" and for "all possible knowledge," but instead are open in all respects to free development and free self-withdrawal, to completion and self-correction.

The Spirit places fleshly, earthly creatures into this substantial liberation and freedom (2 Cor. 3:17)—a liberation and a freedom that can be experienced and demonstrated in diverse ways. This is a freedom that can constantly connect authentic experience and clear testimony with the act of striving for greater truth and for greater knowledge of the truth. This is a freedom that can constantly connect free self-development with a love that: (1) places the greatest worth on the self-development of other persons and on the cultivation of life contexts that serve their self-development; and (2) collaborates with other persons in the preservation and retrieval of such life contexts. This is a freedom that does not sail off into an indeterminate abundance of possibilities and into a vague, "relational," universal reciprocity. This freedom enables us to recognize in these merely obfuscatory formulas for salvation the comfortless, abstract "beyond" of two-world theories that are always postponing salvation until a "pie in the sky in the sweet by-and-by."

The freedom wrought by the Spirit leads into God's presence in the midst of creaturely life. In the midst of creaturely life, the presence of God makes itself accessible to experience.[72] In this way what is fleshly and perishable, what is fixed on the relative earthly world particular to it, what is defined by and dependent on its relative earthly

---

71. See M. Welker, *Universalität Gottes und Relativität der Welt: Theologische Kosmologie im Dialog mit dem amerikanischen Prozessdenken nach Whitehead*, 2d ed. (Neukirchen-Vluyn: Neukirchener, 1988), 35ff.

72. In the—justified—interest of distinguishing between Spirit and creature, Athanasius fell into a false abstraction (see *Ad Serapion*, PG 26, 577ff.). This influential abstraction has had major consequences.

world, is initiated into a more comprehensive reality.[73] A more comprehensive creaturely reality, the "heavenly" reality, is intended for human beings as their form of existence, their domain of life and of
experience. Inasmuch as the Spirit's action of forgiving sins and creating life places earthly, fleshly creatures into this reality, the Spirit does
not lead people into an empty, indeterminate "world above," into a
mere "beyond," and certainly not into wretched worlds of empty fantasy and pie in the sky.[74] Instead the Spirit leads people liberated from
the power of sin—exalting and illumining them—into the *valid reality*
of the communion of the living and the dead.

6.4: Exaltation and illumination in the communion of the living and the dead

Liberation through the Holy Spirit from the power of sin does not lead
to an empty new beginning, to an indeterminate null point, but to a
renewal of life that is in bondage, loveless or unloved, and existing in
diverse forms of distress. This renewal distances frail, perishable, and
finite life from its attempts to go on and on clinging to itself, and from
its attempts to procure validity and glory for itself by oppressing and
destroying other life. Insofar as life regards its fleshliness and frailty as
the sole criterion and as the only agent of its deliverance, it experiences this process of being distanced only as annihilation and death. It
battles against this "becoming-distanced-from-itself" and attempts to
preserve itself in its "being-toward-death." It goes so far as to fight
to preserve itself in a life that affirms its invalidity, indeed that is
about the business of invalidating itself. It fights to remain surrendered, or to be surrendered, to what the biblical traditions call God's
"judgment."

---

73. Cf. Heb. 12:23 as well as §§5.4 and 6.4. See H. U. v. Balthasar's reflections
on the interconnection between Spirit, creation, and new creation in *Spiritus Creator: Skizzen zur Theologie III* (Einsiedeln: Johannes, 1967), esp. 153ff.; as well
as C. Schütz, *Einführung in die Pneumatologie* (Darmstadt: Wissenschaftliche Buchgesellschaft, 1985), 227ff.

74. See the critique of K. Blaser, *Vorstoss zur Pneumatologie*, ThSt[B] 121
(Zurich: Theologischer Verlag Zurich, 1977), 19–20.

By contrast, that life that lets itself be defined and renewed by the Spirit is claimed for life that has validity, for eternal life. That definition and renewal happen through free self-withdrawal for the benefit of other life. The life that freely withdraws itself is precisely not annihilated, but becomes the good seed that bears diverse fruit and allows diverse fruit to be produced. It is not easy to grasp this process of life becoming present and effective in other life by free self-withdrawal. To the "spirit of modernity," this process can appear to be simply "ghostly" and insubstantial. This is a process of self-withdrawal that acts beyond the limits that one has experienced to one's own action, and beyond one's own death. It is a life-promoting entrance into other structural patterns of life. The biblical traditions comprehend it as "resurrection of the flesh."[75]

The expression "resurrection of the *flesh*" retains—above and beyond the perspective of rebirth—the continuity of life that by self-withdrawal has entered in a constitutive way into other structural patterns of life. Life that experiences resurrection is led out of the discontinuity signified by its own death. It is led through this discontinuity. In the process its vitality and fleshliness are changed, but they are not lost.

> Some of the ancient Christian creeds which have been passed down to us heighten the statement still more and talk expressly about the resurrection of *this*—i.e., this present, mortal—flesh. That corresponded to the Pauline saying that "*this* perishable nature must put on immortality" (1 Cor. 15:53). The stress on the identity of the flesh in spite of its transformation is directed against the Platonic idea of the rebirth of the soul in a different body. It means that a man's identity depends on the uniqueness and nonrecurrence of his physical existence.[76]

---

75. In this context "withdrawal of self" must not be understood only as a process that is initiated and carried out by one's own action. As in all action of the Spirit, here also we are to think of an emergent reciprocal interconnection with other life. This emergent reciprocal interconnection cannot be calculated and dominated from any one "side." Along this line lies the double perspective provided by speaking of both "resurrection" and "raising from the dead." The double perspective of these two ways of talking is a matter for Christology to treat in more detail.

76. W. Pannenberg, *The Apostles' Creed in the Light of Today's Questions*, trans. M. Kohl (London: SCM Press, 1972), 171, translation altered. (The usual English

In the resurrection, fleshly life is not only placed beyond the reach of the power of sin, whose goal is self-endangerment, the endangerment of others, and destruction—and not simply destruction, but destruction of the foundations of possible renewal and of the possible avoidance of doom. In the resurrection fleshly life is placed beyond the reach of death, of sin's triumphant success, of successful destruction, of the path back into chaos.[77] Death has no destructive power over life in the Spirit, which is always more precisely *fleshly* life *in the Spirit.*[78]

The resurrection of the flesh is not to be confused with an explicit or implicit condition of merely being remembered. Still less is it to be confused with the "renown of the deeds of those now dead," that according to some cultures "remains forever." The "resurrection" is not only an automatically effective "vital presence" in which the remembrance and imagination of absent persons and life actively exercise an influence on the life processes of those doing the remembering and imagining.[79] Resurrection life is life that is *no longer at the mercy* of the capacity of finite, frail, sinful human beings to remember and to imagine. Resurrection life is life that human beings can no longer distort

---

version of the Apostles' Creed speaks of the "resurrection of the *body*," although "of the *flesh*" is the obvious translation of both the Latin *carnis* and the Greek *sarkos.* The German *Auferstehung des Fleisches* follows the Latin and Greek.—TRANS.)

77. Cf. above all §3.5. In a christological perspective, see also J. H. Yoder's excellent presentation of the critical engagement of the "work of Christ" with the "fallen powers" in *The Politics of Jesus: Vicit Agnus Noster* (Grand Rapids, Mich.: Eerdmans, 1972), 135–62.

78. See Irenaeus of Lyons' struggle for a valid interpretation of 1 Cor. 15:50 in *Irénée de Lyons, Contre les hérésies* 5/2, ed. A. Rousseau, L. Doutreleau, and C. Mercier, Sources Chrétiennes (Paris: Cerf, 1969), 5, 9, 106ff. Picking up on Luther, Prenter (*Spiritus Creator,* 191ff.) shows that the creator Spirit makes the reality of God present in fleshly life that has fallen victim to death. He rightly highlights the "bibilical realism" that is confirmed precisely in this recognition. See also K. Froelich, "Charismatic Manifestations and the Lutheran Incarnational Stance," in P. D. Opsahl, ed., *The Holy Spirit in the Life of the Church: From Biblical Times to the Present* (Minneapolis: Augsburg, 1978), 136ff.

79. On the "spiritual presence" that in "bodily absence" goes beyond remembrance and imagination, cf. 1 Cor. 5:3-4; Col. 2:5. I. U. Dalferth has offered illuminating reflections on this vital co-presence as an interactive agent that helps to define structural patterns of social life and social processes of decision (*Kombinatorische Theologie: Probleme theologischer Rationalität,* QD 130 (Freiburg: Herder, 1991), 99ff., esp. 144ff.

and can no longer destroy.[80] It is difficult to grasp and to render plausible how life can both be placed beyond the reach of death and nevertheless be resurrected *flesh*. It is difficult to grasp and to render plausible how life can both be placed beyond the reach of historical relativizing and nevertheless, through the Spirit, not only be contemporary to all times and all worlds, but also have repercussions for all times and all worlds. As a result, thought and imagination have often given up when confronted with this life and have banished it into an entirely removed "beyond" or into naked unbelievability.

Resurrection life is life that is enabled to fulfill its calling of *perceiving and reflecting God's presence in an unobstructed manner*. As such, it is life that can no longer be made dependent on situations and conditions of the world that are not contemporary with it.

People have attempted over and over to comprehend this definitive communion of the sanctified, the definitive forgiveness of sins, definitive eternal life, by imagining a condition of reality *after* all possibly conceivable situations and conditions of the world. On this view, the entirety of earthly life—what is living and what is dead—would enter into this imagined condition either in stages or all at once.[81]

This approach makes use of a heuristic device that attempts to express the *validity* appropriate to this life by means of a *post*-temporally conceived "supratemporality." On the basis of the pneumatological insights that we have acquired, this heuristic device can be superseded. The resurrection of the flesh to eternal life signifies more than deliverance of fleshly life in the sense that fleshly life would be removed from the earthly world. The resurrection of the flesh has a positive significance: namely, that this determinate life—a fleshly life marked by

---

80. See A. M. Aagaards' well-placed critique of the tendency "constantly to degrade the Holy Spirit to an irrelevant, unknown entity of the metaphysical beyond" ("Der Heilige Geist in der Welt," in *Wiederentdeckung des Heiligen Geistes: Der Heilige Geist in der charismatischen Erfahrung und theologischen Reflexion*, Ökumenische Perspektiven 6 [Frankfurt am Main: Lambeck, 1974], 103, cf. 103ff.). Her justified effort to bring to bear the "specific historical dimension" (109) of the Spirit's action must be protected against the false consequence of also permitting historical relativizing of eternal life.

81. Cf. 1 Cor. 15:51-52; 1 Thess. 4:16-17; Matt. 24:31; as well as the language of dying daily in 1 Cor. 15:31 and 2 Cor. 4:10-11.

transitoriness that has been delivered—achieves enduring validity and decisive significance in all relative times and worlds.

Through the resurrection of the flesh, life in its concrete reality becomes contemporaneous to what is dead and what is living on earth in each particular case. Through the Spirit, the resurrection of the flesh sets the standard for life that in earthly terms is relatively past or relatively future—the standard toward which it makes its way *and* from which it comes. Life that has been raised from the dead sets the standard and establishes what counts as valid with respect to both judgment and deliverance. Through the Spirit, it provides orientation in faith, in love, in hope, in growth in righteousness, and in the act of striving after clearer knowledge of God. It is deemed worthy of having a part in the resurrection life of Christ, of being exalted not only "for itself" as Christ's body but, as Christ's surroundings that can be made palpably present through the Spirit, of acting on other life.

The Spirit of God thus not only effects "real life" in the communion of the sanctified present in each particular earthly case. Nor does the Spirit only, by the power of the forgiveness of sin, remove real life from the reach of the powers of the world that are hostile to God and to creation. The Spirit certainly does all that as well. The Spirit delivers and preserves real life. This preserved and delivered life is not placed in a numinous "communion" at an obscure end point beyond all times. Instead life that has been preserved and delivered is exalted and illumined by the Spirit.[82] What does this mean?

---

82. With regard to the following discussion, cf. the "classic" text of Basil of Caesarea (St. Basil the Great, *On the Holy Spirit*, trans. D. Anderson [Crestwood, N.Y.: St. Vladimir's Seminary Press, 1980], esp. chap. 19, 42–44); cf. W.-D. Hauschild, *Gottes Geist und der Mensch: Studien zur frühchristlichen Pneumatologie*, BEvT 63 (Munich: Kaiser, 1972), 285ff. In the familiar dichotomies of the bipolar relation between consciousness and the object of perception—dichotomies that have come to obscure more than they make clear—one can certainly speak of "subjective and objective" exaltation and illumination. Life delivered and preserved by the Spirit is ("objectively") enabled to fulfill its vocation of reflecting God's glory, and ("subjectively") it receives a part in revelation and is infused with this glory. The detailed exposition of this process is a theme for eschatology. First steps toward a connection of the two thematic domains in terms of a "theology of hope" were already taken by E. Brunner, *Vom Werk des Heiligen Geistes* (Tübingen: Mohr, 1935), 52ff., esp. 72ff.

Exaltation and illumination by the Spirit means nothing less than that real fleshly life is enabled by the Spirit and in the Spirit to be the place where God's glory is made present. Regardless of its "sublated" creatureliness, indeed *in* its sublated creatureliness, exalted and illumined life serves to make present the glory of God. Although the glory of God is reflected in and through it, exalted and illumined life serves the experience and knowledge of God. In spite of being infused with God's presence, it mediates knowledge of God. In spite of remaining fleshly, it is infused with God's glory.[83]

The biblical traditions clarify this process by talking about people being called to be "children of God." They clarify it by talking about people being "built together in the Spirit into a dwelling place for God" (Eph. 2:22), about their bodies being called to be "a temple of the Holy Spirit" (1 Cor. 6:19), about their being a temple in which God dwells (1 Cor. 3:16), and about the fact that they should let themselves "be built into a spiritual house" (1 Pet. 2:5).

The Spirit-wrought raising of the flesh from the dead, the resurrection of the flesh, means that life upon which the Spirit has come, life that has been preserved, delivered, and exalted by the Spirit, receives "wisdom and revelation" not only for itself (cf. Eph. 1:17), that it does not merely *itself* "taste the heavenly gift" (cf. Heb. 6:4). Again and again the futile attempt has been made to conceive this kind of "resurrection" that remains within the limits of the "western Spirit." Although resurrected flesh is "illumined," although resurrected flesh is infused with God's revelation and God's presence, the resurrection of the flesh is not an event "to be experienced only for one's own private consumption." Regardless of the delivered, exalted, and illumined fleshliness, the resurrection wrought by the Spirit is a process that, through its "exaltation," is of equal benefit before God to the universal communion of the living and the dead. From the living and from the dead, for the living and for the dead, the Spirit sets eternal life, life that has validity, in relief, thereby revealing, making present, and spreading God's glory.

---

83. Picking up on Novatian, J. P. Burns and G. M. Fagin put it this way: "The Spirit shares his own eternity with the flesh and thereby brings the body into eternal life" (*The Holy Spirit,* Message of the Fathers of the Church 3 [Wilmington: M. Glazier, 1984], 215).

Through the Spirit and from the Spirit, earthly, frail, and perishable life is treated as life in accord with God. It is rescued from death and is removed from under the sway of transitoriness. As heavenly life—as life that stands in contrast to all relative, perishable times and worlds, and at the same time is present to them—it becomes the domain where God is made present. As newly formed, valid, orientation-giving life—as "eternal life"—it does not hover over times and worlds, but lets God assume God's rightful place in them. Through the Spirit and the Spirit's action on creaturely life to sanctify, to forgive sins, and to raise from the dead, all times and worlds acquire the living standard from which and toward which they have lived, do live, and will live.[84] Through the Spirit, life in all times and worlds is illumined and exalted inasmuch as it serves to illumine other life.

6.5: Intimacy with God, free self-withdrawal, participation in God's glory, and enjoyment of eternal life

The Holy Spirit brings about intimacy with God. Indeed the Spirit of God is this intimacy.[85] This intimacy draws us into the overwhelming fullness of the presence of God. Yet this intimacy is not to be confused with an ineffable, obscure mystical relationship whose intensity condemns us to saying nothing, or whose hypercomplexity leads to diffusion and dissolution of determinate experience. Inasmuch as the Spirit effects intimacy with God, the Spirit makes possible an intimate relationship with God that allows us to recognize the diversity of God's action of kindness and righteousness, of judgment and deliverance, and that makes it possible for human beings to recognize and to locate themselves and their relative worlds in this action.

---

84. See the exposition of the Spirit's action in Oration 16 (for Pentecost) of Gregory of Nazianzus, PG 36, 444; as well as Pannenberg, *Apostles' Creed*, 172–74; H. Küng, *Eternal Life: Life after Death as a Medical, Philosophical and Theological Problem*, trans. E. Quinn (Garden City, N.Y.: Doubleday, 1984), esp. 220ff., 231ff.

85. "These things God has revealed to us through the Spirit; for the Spirit searches everything, even the depths of God. For what human being knows what is truly human except the human spirit that is within? So also no one comprehends what is truly God's except the Spirit of God" (1 Cor. 2:10-11; cf. John 4:23-24).

Several biblical traditions bring this to expression with the assurance that in God's Spirit human beings are enabled to call upon God as "Abba," as "dear Father."[86] In other words, in and through human beings, the Spirit of God calls upon God as a person who combines the highest degree of intimacy, affection, and kindness toward human beings with the power to act effectively on the basis of this loving interest in them. The same state of affairs is brought to expression from another perspective by means of the assurance that human beings led by God are "children of God," and that this is made clear to them by the Spirit (cf. Rom. 8:14, 16).

The Spirit brings about an intimate, trusting relation to the person of God, who is the epitome of kindness and affection and of love that has the power to carry out its purposes. This relation, though, has been corrupted and obscured by traditions that have made of this a relation of mere dependency and have glorified what is no more than a relation defined by a sheer drop-off in relative power.[87] The Spirit effects an intimate, trusting relation that grounds the dignity and honor of human beings, their security, and their capacity to be responsible. This relation has been corrupted and obscured by traditions that gave religious legitimation to patriarchal relations of domination and violence, and that projected their ideologies of domination back onto the relation between God and human beings.

These traditions have masked the dignity and honor of human beings in their vocation as "children of God." They have likewise obstructed the experience and the expectation of the interconnection between tender affection and forceful love, between intimacy and power that is expressed by calling upon God as "Abba."[88] They have

---

86. Cf. Gal. 4:6; Rom. 8:15.

87. A. N. Whitehead criticized both the "idolatry" of fashioning "God in the image of the Egyptian, Persian, and Roman imperial rulers," and those tendencies of thought that present "God in the image of a personification of moral energy" and "in the image of an ultimate philosophical principle" (*Process and Reality: An Essay in Cosmology*, ed. D. R. Griffin and D. W. Sherburne [New York: Free Press, 1978], 342–43).

88. See esp. the following articles in J.-B. Metz, E. Schillebeeckx, and M. Lefébure, eds., *God as Father* (New York: Seabury, 1981): J. Cone, "The Meaning of God in the Black Spirituals," 57–60; C. Halkes, "The Themes of Protest in Feminist Theology against God the Father," trans. D. Smith, 103–110; J. Moltmann, "The

placed the Christian church in a position where it must face the question of whether concepts like "rule"[89] and "father" need to be reconceived and retranslated in order to mediate the meanings that faith originally intended for them to express. Just as God's Spirit does not will to generate numinous feelings and diffuse moods, so the Spirit who bears witness to free self-withdrawal for the benefit of others does not will to exemplify, legitimate, and spread patriarchal relations of power and violence,[90] or primitive, oppressive, neurosis-inducing experiences of dependency.[91]

The Spirit brings about a familiar, intimate, clear relation that grounds and reveals God's affection for human beings and the dignity of human beings who have received a share of this affection. But this does not mean that human beings can always appropriately experience, grasp, and express this relation at will. On the one hand, the intimacy with God wrought by the Spirit and the vocation of human beings to be God's children have in themselves great richness and an abundance of consequences. On the other hand, earthly, perishable life relations are in themselves closed and resistant to this action of the Spirit. As a result, individual persons, groups of people, and historical periods have great difficulty in giving expression to this intimacy and to their vocation. In the midst of God's presence in the Spirit, human beings suffer under the overwhelming difference between what is earthly and perishable, on the one hand, and what is divine, on the other. They are paralyzed by the power of sin as it obstructs and distorts God's presence and God's saving power. They simply do not know, they simply do

---

Motherly Father: Is Trinitarian Patripassianism Replacing Theological Patriarchalism?," trans. G. W. S. Knowles, 51–56; R. R. Ruether, "The Female Nature of God: A Problem in Contemporary Religious Life," 61–66. See also J. Jeremias, "Abba," in *The Prayers of Jesus*, Studies in Biblical Theology 6, 2d ser. (Napierville, Ill.: Alec R. Allenson, 1967), 11–65.

89. The German noun *Herrschaft* can have the broader sense of "rule." For instance, the central gospel notion of the *basileia tou theou* is often rendered in German as "*die Gottesherrschaft*," corresponding to "the rule of God" in English. Or *Herrschaft* can have the narrower sense of "domination"—TRANS.

90. Cf. §§3.4, 5.1, and passim.

91. Cf. §§3.1, 3.2, 3.5, 4.3, and passim, as well as I. de la Potterie, "Le chrétien conduit par l'Esprit dans son cheminement eschatologique (Rom. 8:14)," in L. de Lorenzi, ed., *The Law of the Spirit in Rom. 7 and 8* (Rome: N.p., 1976), 209ff.

not see how they and others ought to call upon God and glorify God. They do not see how they and others could become recognizable and manifest, in the earthly-perishable world, in their vocation to be God's children (cf. Rom. 8:23, 26).

God's Spirit helps people precisely in these great tensions and uncertainties. The Spirit strengthens, comforts, and illumines them. The Spirit of God helps human beings to perceive *God in the midst of creation*, to experience God under the conditions of earthly life relations, and to live in a secure, strengthened, and dignified manner in God's community. The Spirit of God makes it possible to live lovingly, responsibly, and honorably precisely under the conditions of fleshly-perishable existence. As has been clearly shown from many perspectives, this does not occur by the Spirit initiating people into an obscure mystical experience, into a chronic feeling of dependency, or into the consciousness of a divine "ubiquity" that can be arbitrarily expected and summoned up. Instead the Spirit brings people's uncertainties before God. The Spirit brings before God the human expectations that do not attain the divine kindness and glory. The Spirit brings before God the human expectations that are not adequate to and not in accord with the powers of divine deliverance. With "sighs too deep for words," the Spirit represents human beings before God—human beings who do not know how they ought to call upon the divinity who is near; human beings who do not know for what they ought rightly to pray for the sake of their deliverance (Rom. 8:26).

Why does the Spirit *help* human beings with this? The Spirit is not ignorant of the concrete situations of distress and the concrete complaints of human beings. The Spirit does not allow their complaints and their search for God to be dissipated in a haze of indeterminacy or to be caught in the deceit of a merely formal, invariant recognition that God is, in some undefined way, "everywhere." The Spirit enables human beings to experience their intimacy with God in the tension between their recognition of their lostness and their vocation to have a part in God's glory. This occurs inasmuch as the "children of God" identify and recognize themselves in their communion with the crucified and risen Christ—a communion that leads out of the God-forsaken abyss into the fullness of God's presence.

Communion with Christ is not limited to earthly life, but is universal and eternal. Through this communion human beings are blessed "with every blessing of the Spirit of God" (cf. Eph. 1:3). By the power of the Spirit and in this power, this eternal, valid communion is concretized and *realized* under the conditions of fleshly life and in the midst of the earthly-perishable world. By the Spirit, intimacy with God and participation in the divine glory become possible for and manifest to human beings, even under the conditions of the earthly-perishable world and of their earthly-finite life.[92] This means that a response is given to the profound doubt concerning a *bodily, palpable* presence and experience of salvation, a doubt that unleashes so many pressing and tormenting questions. An indissoluble connection with the Christ,[93] a process of being conformed to Christ's humanity that not only lives, but also enlivens and gives life (cf. 1 Cor. 15:45), is intended for human beings through the Spirit.[94] This Spirit's identity as the "Spirit of Christ" becomes clear in temptation and affliction; the Spirit becomes recognizable in temptation on account of Christ (cf. 1 Thess. 1:6; 1 Pet. 4:14). This Spirit is experienced as God's delivering, liberating righteousness and as God's power that brings peace. Certainty of the Spirit is acquired in loving, free self-withdrawal for the benefit of others.

---

92. Ephesians 1:14: "The Spirit is the pledge of our inheritance toward redemption as God's own people, to the praise of God's glory." See K. Stendahl, *Energy for Life: Reflections on the Theme "Come, Holy Spirit—Renew the Whole Creation,"* Risk Book 45 (Geneva: World Council of Churches, 1990), esp. 44ff.; Chung H. K., "Come, Holy Spirit—Renew the Whole Creation," in M. Kinnamon, ed., *Signs of the Spirit: Official Report of the Seventh Assembly of the World Council of Churches* (Grand Rapids, Mich.: Eerdmans, 1991), 37–47.

93. Cf. 1 Cor. 6:17. See also the interconnection in Luther's thought, delineated by R. Otto, between, on the one hand, becoming "of one mind" with God and Christ through the Spirit and through faith and, on the other hand, the realism of the appropriation of the "heavenly things" (*Die Anschauung vom heiligen Geiste bei Luther: Eine historisch-dogmatische Untersuchung* [Göttingen: Vandenhoeck, 1898], esp. 31ff.); as well as Calvin's emphasis on the restoration of the *imago Dei* by the Holy Spirit (*Inst.,* vol. 1, 3/3, 9).

94. "The Christian moves in this light, in order to be a light himself. . . . Christians are messengers in Christ's stead" (K. Barth, *Dogmatics in Outline,* trans. G. T. Thomson, Harper Torchbooks, The Cloister Library [New York: Harper & Row, 1959], 149, translation altered). On the weaker language of the CD concerning the "symbolic" being and action of Christians as they are defined by the Spirit, see P. J. Rosato, *The Spirit as Lord: The Pneumatology of Karl Barth* (Edinburgh: T. and T. Clark, 1981), 87ff.

In constantly new ways, the Spirit leads people into communion with the resurrected *Crucified* One. In doing so the Spirit makes manifest on, for, and through human beings the lostness of the world in its self-isolation from God. The Spirit makes manifest the suffering caused by this distance, the desperate attempts bound up with this suffering to release the power of redemption by using what is perishable and mortal as the starting point, and the great distress that results from these attempts. In judgment and in disclosure, the Spirit definitively reveals the sinful lostness of the world in its powerlessness and dangerousness. The Spirit thus reveals life that is heading for perdition, that is wretched and lacks validity, and that has no secure foothold. This life seeks to secure its position by clinging to itself. It seeks to glorify, illumine, and exalt itself, to make itself eternal by its own means and powers. The Spirit leads people to this knowledge, though, by awakening and enlivening the community of the crucified *Resurrected* One, enabling it to become a force that promotes and strengthens other life in the midst of this perishing world.

This community awakened by the Spirit attests to God's love and God's peace in the power of free self-withdrawal for the benefit of others. The community of the children of God that in this way is constantly surpassing its previous limits and pointing beyond itself reflects God's glory (cf. 2 Cor. 3:18). In free self-withdrawal these persons make room for a life in which they acquire a part, even beyond their death. They participate in and impart valid, enduring, eternal life. This life through the Spirit and in the Spirit expresses itself in experiences that are determinate in each particular case and not uniform, but diverse.

The Spirit of God is a power that delivers and liberates human beings. This power delivers human beings out of individual and communal distress and oppression, whether acute or chronic. Wherever the Spirit of God acts, there is liberation and freedom (2 Cor. 3:17). But not *every* human *experience* of *liberation and freedom* is necessarily an experience of God's Spirit. Forces that are spiritless, disintegrative, and are detrimental to life, indeed even forces that are demonic powers, can also generate the illusion of freedom and can elicit misleading experiences, experiences of supposed freedom. By no means need these experiences be merely subjective and short-lived. They can be supported by a broad consensus and can outlast a series of generations.

In diverse ways, the early experiences of the power of the Spirit have directed our attention to this lack of clarity, to this ambivalence of experiences of liberation mediated by violence. It likewise has become clear that the *preservation* of people and of communities in and beyond long-term affliction remains in itself problematic and ambiguous. Although the Spirit of God is a power that preserves in affliction and that grants comfort and steadfastness, not every experience of preservation and maintenance in individual and collective distress is as such an experience of God's Spirit. Experiences of liberation and of preservation that are experiences of the Spirit press toward clearer revelation and knowledge of God's Spirit and power. They press toward discerning the spirits. The case is similar with regard to the public transformation of people, of those who hold power and of political, religious, and other structures of power. To be sure, the delivering and preserving Spirit of God can become recognizable in such transformations, in such breaks in the customary flow of experience. But not every discontinuity, not every completely unexpected, dazzling, and spectacular discontinuity in lived life relations is a result of the action of God's Spirit.

This does not amount to a confirmation of the relativistic view that "everything" is ambiguous, including the Spirit of God and this Spirit's action. Nor does it amount to a glorification of a naive, indifferent, or cynical attitude of "You never know." Even the early and still unclear experiences of the Spirit's power delineate a clear and sharp difference: the goal of God's Spirit is the liberation of human beings, not their oppression; the goal of God's Spirit is the preservation and encouragement of human beings, not their destruction and despair. The Spirit of God becomes recognizable by "charismatic" actions of transformation and renewal;[95] the Spirit is not a force that remains hidden in a numinous "beyond."

It was in view of the prophetic promises that it became possible for the first time to distinguish this Spirit more clearly from all sorts of

95. See G. Theissen's differentiated exposition of "the experience of faith in an evolutionary perspective" (*Biblical Faith: An Evolutionary Approach* [Philadelphia: Fortress, 1985], 140–74. With regard to the following discussion see esp., on the one hand, ibid., 163ff., and on the other hand, L. Boff's exposition of "Charism as the Organizing Principle" in *Church: Charism and Power: Liberation Theology and the Institutional Church*, trans. J. W. Diercksmeier (New York: Crossroad, 1985), 154–64.

powers and forces of this world, and from the efforts of human beings to gain force and to achieve power (although the services of human beings are enlisted in the midst of the powers of the world and with their capacities and powers). It became possible to distinguish the Spirit of God in principle from some sort of force acting in a spectacular manner, orchestrating some kind of preservation, and carrying out supposed or actual actions of deliverance. The Spirit of God became recognizable as the *Spirit of righteousness and of peace,* who—resting on the powerless bearer of the Spirit—wills to bring the Spirit's presence to bear in acts of deliverance, preservation, transformation, renewal, and instruction in the discernment of powers and spirits.

As the bearer of this Spirit, the promised Messiah, and the action of the Spirit that extends beyond the powers of the world have emerged more clearly, it has become recognizable that this Spirit extends beyond particular pluriform, relative worlds, and in so doing seeks out and includes life that is weak, powerless, and unprotected. It has become possible to recognize that it is precisely in this manner that this Spirit creatively acts and gives life.

The delivering and preserving action of the Spirit aims at the establishment of righteousness. This righteousness is inseparably bound up with the establishment of mercy, the ongoing inclusion of those who are weaker, and the constant renewal of justice for the benefit of the weak. The universal extension of the knowledge of God was bound up with this extension of the righteousness that grows out of the interconnection of justice and mercy. The extension of the knowledge of God did not occur by means of only one time, one culture, one nation, one history, one institution, one race, one class, or one form of life. The fact that being "poured out," that coming "from on high" is essential to the Spirit meant that this power of God neither wills to benefit, nor does in fact benefit, only specific persons or groups of people, however large they might be. The Spirit also benefits their spatial and temporal, proximate and distant environments. It has become recognizable that the Spirit of God is a power that can enlist the services of all creatures for their deliverance, preservation, renewal, and enlivenment.

In contrast to all so-called natural pneumatologies, which impose themselves on the basis of this recognition, it has become clear that the Spirit does not "somehow or other" enlist the services of "everything." Instead, the Spirit who acts in the fullness of time "rests" decisively on the selfless, suffering, and despised Messiah, who claims nothing for himself and who does not desire to acquire any power *for himself*. The Spirit does not rest on the striving of that which is creaturely for preserving self, putting self first at the expense of others, and extending self. The Spirit does not rest on the struggle for these things, whatever the coalitions of mutual interests involved in this struggle might be, and whatever limited, calculated regard for others might be displayed.

The Spirit of God of course does not sanctify fleshly life's interests in putting itself first at the expense of others, and of course does not seek any accommodation to the powers and laws of nature and of each particular political world. But in contrast to all "pneumatologies of the 'beyond,'" it has become clear that God's Spirit acts in, on, and through fleshly, perishable, earthly life, and precisely in this way wills to attest to God's glory and to reveal the forces of eternal life.

The action of the Spirit became unambiguous in its connection with the Messiah who has come, in its connection with the action of Jesus Christ. The selfless liberation of human beings from obvious suffering and obvious powerlessness—a process not oriented toward achieving success and finding resonance—made recognizable the concrete presence of the Spirit with all its improbability and seeming insignificance. In Jesus' action the power of free self-withdrawal for the benefit of others became clear. Jesus carries out his action in a multiplicity of concrete and palpable experiences of liberation that cannot be avoided, but are simply to be accepted with joy and gratitude. Jesus carries out his action in the proclamation of the reign of God that "comes" unpretentiously and hidden in earthly powerlessness.

Faced with the evidence of this selfless liberation and of the free, totally unforced emergence of God's reign, "blasphemy of the Spirit," the claim that God's Spirit is a demonic superpower that spreads bondage and distress, has become invalid and unbelievable in itself. It has become an "impossible possibility" that at the most would be an option for transparent and brutal purposes and practices of persecution.

In the Spirit and through the Spirit, God is present in the midst of creation, establishing liberation. God is present in and through the Spirit not as a numinous entity, not as some sort of "beyond" in the "here and now," nor as a factor that is superficially present "everywhere," and certainly not as a mere intellectual construct. This presence and effectiveness of God in the Spirit is highlighted by the

Apostles' Creed from four different points of view. Human beings live in this power and acquire a share in it in the communion of the sanctified, in the forgiveness of sins, in the resurrection of the flesh, and in eternal life. Through the communion of the sanctified, through the forgiveness of sins, through the resurrection of the flesh, and through the imparting of eternal life, God rescues the good creation from corruption. God preserves, enlivens, and renews creation. Creation is enabled to be a bearer of God's righteousness and glory. Creation is given an unending joy over the revelation of God's affection and kindness.

In the power of the Spirit, enjoyment of valid, liberated, and liberating life is awakened in creatures. Through the communion of the sanctified and through the forgiveness of sins, valid, liberating, and free life is present in the midst of a world marked by suffering and death. In the midst of massive self-endangerment, destruction and hopelessness, God's reality is present: the power of God that works renewal and that persistently changes the process of decay. In diverse, often seemingly insignificant concreteness, in concreteness that sometimes comes across as miraculous, the power of God acts against the powers of sin, despair, cynicism, and death.

In the Spirit and through the Spirit, the creation is also present and effective in God's life.[96] Through the resurrection of the flesh and through participation in eternal life, creation that has been rescued from corruption receives an importance of the highest order. In the Spirit, creation receives an unimpeachable dignity and validity. This importance, this dignity and validity are not subject to further states and conditions of the world, so that they could be destroyed by them. It is this importance, this dignity and validity that are determinative. Every further growth in faith, in the knowledge of God, and in love is shaped by the reality and the knowledge effected and preserved by the Spirit. Resurrected flesh, eternal life is not formless. Through the Spirit this life orients our faith, our love, and our hope. It enlivens our act of striving after justice, mercy, and knowledge of God. The Spirit of God works enjoyment of the heightening of justice, mercy, and

---

96. K. Barth, *Credo* (New York: Scribner's, 1962), 171: "We can spare ourselves many unnecessary pains . . . if we hold fast to what is the decisive feature of eternal life: that it is eternal in its being lived in the unveiled light of God and in so far participating in God's own life." See also E. Schlink, *Ökumenische Dogmatik: Grundzüge* (Göttingen: Vandenhoeck, 1983), 713ff.

knowledge of God, enjoyment of the spread of righteousness and of clearer knowledge of God. The Spirit of God awakens enjoyment of the replacement of imperialistic structures by the rich world of the Joel promise. The Spirit of God awakens enjoyment of the restoration of structural patterns of life and of understanding where people and cultures had written each other off. The Spirit works enjoyment of the fact that polarized divisions into "friends" and "enemies," accustomed forms of indifference as well as disempowerment and hatred are replaced by reconciliation, mutual understanding, mutual love, and restoration and respect of dignity.

The Spirit of God awakens enjoyment of concrete liberation from individual powerlessness and hopelessness, enjoyment of every seed of the reign of God, however veiled, suppressed, and impaired its growth might be. The Spirit awakens enjoyment of improbable, universal understanding concerning God's powerful action on human beings in the midst of the rich diversity of human languages, cultures, traditions, and visions of the future. The Spirit awakens enjoyment of the force fields of faith, hope, and love, which, in the midst of a fleshliness and a world assailed and marked by sin and death, make it possible to recognize and to attest to God's presence and God's will in constantly new ways.[97] The Spirit of God awakens enjoyment of the Spirit's action. The Spirit of God awakens inspiration.[98]

This action of the Spirit reveals the unbreakable interconnection between free self-withdrawal for the benefit of other creatures and the reflection of God's glory. The Spirit mediates that enjoyment of God that the world can grasp: an enjoyment of God's presence and of the valid life distinguished by this presence.

---

97. Cf. P. Tillich, *Systematic Theology* 3 (Chicago: Univ. of Chicago Press, 1963), 129–38, 401–3. Picking up on John 15:11-12; 16:22; 17:13; Phil. 1:25; 3:1; 4:4; Rom. 15:13; and other passages, M. Kähler emphasized that through the Spirit a "new, true life" is imparted to human beings "which carries in itself the guarantee of indestructibility, even in the face of death's doom . . . and which finds its expression in *joy*, in the consciousness that life is being fostered" (*Die Wissenschaft der christlichen Lehre von dem evangelischen Grundartikel aus im Abrisse dargestellt*, 3d ed. [Leipzig: 1911; reprint, Neukirchen-Vluyn: Neukirchener, 1966], 433; cf. 529, 667, and passim).

98. See R. Bohren, *Predigtlehre*, 4th. ed., Einführung in die Evangelische Theologie 4 (Munich: Kaiser, 1980), 86ff., 278–79.

Scripture Index

Author Index

Subject Index